The Lion of Tashkent

Cherniaev as governor general of Turkestan in 1882

THE LION OF TASHKENT
The Career of General M. G. Cherniaev
by
David MacKenzie

University of Georgia Press

Library of Congress Catalog Card Number: 73–81625
International Standard Book Number: 0–8203–0322–4

The University of Georgia Press, Athens 30602

Printed in the United States of America

To My Father and Mother

Contents

viii

List of Illustrations

x

List of Maps

List of Source Abbreviations

Archival Sources

AII, Ristić	Arhiv Istoriskog Instituta (Belgrade), Zbirka Jovana Ristića
ASANU	Arhiv Srpske Akademije Nauke i Umetnosti (Belgrade)
DAS PO	Državni Arhiv Srbije (Belgrade). Fond Poklon i Otkupa
FO	Public Record Office (London), Foreign Office
GIM	Gosudarstvennyi Istoricheskii Muzei (Moscow), Otdel Pismennykh Istochnikov, Fond M. G. Cherniaeva
HHSA	Haus-, Hof-, und Staatsarchiv (Vienna), Politisches Archiv
IISG	Internationaal Instituut voor sociale Geschiedenis (Amsterdam), Arkhiv Cherniaeva
ORBL	Otdel rukopisei biblioteki imeni V. I. Lenina (Moscow)
ORSS	Otdel rukopisei publichnoi biblioteki imeni M. E. Saltykov-Shchedrina (Leningrad)
TSGADA	Tsentralnyi gosudarstvennyi arkhiv drevnykh aktov (Moscow)
TSGALI	Tsentralnyi gosudarstvennyi arkhiv literatury i iskusstva (Moscow)
TSGIAL	Tsentralnyi gosudarstvennyi istoricheskii arkhiv v Lenin-

grade (Leningrad)

TSGVIA   Tsentralnyi gosudarstvennyi voenno-istoricheskii arkhiv (Moscow)

TSGAOR   Tsentralnyi gosudarstvennyi arkhiv oktiabrskoi revoliutsii (Moscow)

Published Sources

BV   *Birzhevye Vedomosti* (St. Petersburg)

IV   *Istoricheskii Vestnik*

JMH   *Journal of Modern History*

KA   *Krasnyi Arkhiv*

MV   *Moskovskie Vedomosti* (Moscow

NFP   *Neue Freie Presse* (Vienna)

OSOB PRIB   *Osobye pribavleniia k opisaniiu russko-turetskoi voiny, 1877–1878 gg. na Balkanskom poluostrove* (St. Petersburg, 1899–1903)

OSVOB   Akademiia Nauk SSSR, Institut Slavianovedeniia. *Osvobozhdenie Bolgarii ot turetskogo iga* (Moscow, 1961–1967, 3 vols.)

RA   *Russkii Arkhiv*

RS   *Russkaia Starina*

RT   *Russkii Turkestan*, Vypusk III (Moscow, 1872)

RV   *Russkii Vestnik*

SR   *Slavic Review*

TURK KRAI   *Turkestanskii krai. Sbornik dokumentov* (Tashkent, 1908–1915)

VE   *Vestnik Evropy*

VISB   *Voenno-istoricheskii Sbornik*

VS   *Voennyi Sbornik*

Russian Bibliographical Terms

d.   delo (file)

ed. khr.   edinitsa khranenii (folder, catalog unit)

f.   fond (archival collection)

k.   karton (box)

l.   liniia (sheet, page)

op.   opis (inventory)

xiii

Preface

MANY PERSONS and institutions assisted me during the research and writing of this book. Grants were provided by the American Council of Learned Societies, the Inter-University Committee on Travel Grants and the American Philosophical Society. Wells College in Aurora, New York, gave me a sabbatical leave and a supplementary grant which enabled me to write the first draft of the manuscript. The Research Council of the University of North Carolina at Greensboro supplied a grant for the typing of the manuscript. Professor P. A. Zaionchkovskii of Moscow State University provided guidance and helpful advice on sources. I am indebted to Professor Alfred Rieber of the University of Pennsylvania for reading and commenting upon the entire manuscript and for permitting me to utilize the "Dela Serbskie" from the Miliutin Papers of the Manuscript Division of Lenin Library, Moscow. Professors E. Willis Brooks and John Beeler of the University of North Carolina read portions of the manuscript and made valuable suggestions. The staffs of the Helsinki University Library, Institut für osteuropäische Geschichte (Vienna), the manuscript divisions of the State Historical Museum and Lenin Library (Moscow), the Institute for Social History (Amsterdam), and the Serbian Academy of Sciences (Belgrade) were most helpful and cooperative. Without my wife's sacrifices, encouragement and constructive criticism the book could not have been completed.

In transliterating Russian names the Library of Congress system has been used except for well-known persons such as Nicholas I, Tolstoy, etc. The English translations from foreign language originals are by the author unless otherwise indicated. Russian diacritical marks in place of soft and hard signs have been omitted.

Introduction

IN THE SUMMER of 1876 the name Mikhail Grigorevich Cherniaev was well-known throughout Russia and the Slav world. As
commander of the main Serbian army fighting the Turks, he summoned the Christian peoples of the Balkans to rise against the decaying Ottoman Empire. Millions of Slav Christians hailed Cherniaev
as their champion and deliverer, as his forces advanced into Bulgaria. In mid-August in the trenches before the key Serbian fortress of
Šumatovac, he personally inspired the Serbs to repel several Turkish
assaults. The success of this battle brought him congratulatory telegrams from all over Russia. Even the ultimate defeat of his Serbo-
Russian army failed to dispel a romantic aura around his name,
identified with Russian efforts to emancipate the South Slavs. Like
his contemporary, General Custer, he gained more fame from disaster than others had from victory.

Eleven years earlier with less than two thousand Russians Cherniaev had assaulted Tashkent, Central Asia's greatest city. At dawn
on June 15, 1865, disregarding a cautionary telegram from the war
minister, he moved against a fortified town manned by thirty thousand Kokanese defenders. Failure would have meant death for the
attackers and grave danger to Russia's position on a distant frontier.

After two days of fighting, Tashkent lay conquered. Russian power was permanently established in Turkestan, and to Central Asians Cherniaev became a byword for audacity. They called this Russian gambler "the lion of Tashkent."

Cherniaev's campaigns in the Balkans and Central Asia were important milestones in Russia's imperial expansion. In 1864 he helped to link scattered outposts east of the Aral Sea into a continuous fortified line guarding Russian territory from neighboring nomadic tribes. In 1865 his sudden advance beyond the Chimkent line, where his government had assured the world that Russia would halt, led to the annexation of the thickly settled oases of Central Asia. Tashkent became the heart of a vast imperial domain, now the last major European holding in Asia. Subsequently he involved Russia prematurely in a conflict with the Khanate of Bukhara, the spiritual and military leader of Central Asian Moslems.

In the Balkan crisis of the 1870s Cherniaev sought to liberate the South Slavs and unite them under Russia's aegis. He alone attempted to implement the vague doctrines of Russian Panslavism proclaimed by his more literary contemporaries, N. Ia. Danilevskii and R. A. Fadeev. Providence, he believed, had selected him to fulfill Russia's manifest destiny: to free the Slavs, link them indissolubly with Russia, and restore the Christian faith to Constantinople. Mikhail Grigorevich envisioned a resurrected Orthodox Russia ruling the Turkish Straits and the Balkan peninsula; he did not reckon with the odds. His crusade helped to drag his reluctant government into a war with Turkey which it could ill afford.

For a generation Cherniaev played a curious role in Russian domestic politics. In 1865, as military governor, he sought to free Turkestan from bureaucratic control by distant Orenburg province; later he helped persuade the emperor to create a separate Turkestan governor generalship. As a spokesman for conservatives opposing military officialdom, Cherniaev, in his newspaper *The Russian World*, sharply criticized the war ministry and the Turkestan regime of his successor, General K. P. fon-Kaufman. In 1882, on his return to Turkestan as governor general, he attempted to make it a boon instead of a burden to Russia only to be removed once more for disregarding government directives and urging Russia's involvement in war. The epilogue to his career was a typical polemic against the construction of the Central Asian Railroad, a pet project of the war ministry.

Although at different periods during his career Cherniaev enjoyed the favor of four Romanov emperors, he was twice recalled for insubordination, twice called a traitor by the war minister, and for three years he was under police surveillance for suspected antidynastic activity. His victories in Central Asia won the support of Alexander II but Cherniaev dissipated it by quarreling with his superiors. In 1866 and again in 1876 he obtained that emperor's forgiveness by a personal magnetism and simplicity which appealed to Alexander's emotional nature. For twenty years he enjoyed the patronage of Alexander III, first as heir to the throne and later as emperor. But during the Russo-Turkish War of 1877 he joined a dissident group which aimed to remove the Romanov dynasty and return Russia's capital to Moscow or Kiev. The incredible leniency of both emperors toward him baffled and amazed his contemporaries.

Cherniaev's complex character reflects the attitudes and conflicts of a certain type of Russian officer during the age of imperialism. At first glance he seemed a hero. Boldness, charm, and energy won him the devotion of his men. His deep religious faith, apparent idealism, and love of country exemplified the best Russian qualities. However, other characteristics made him a tragic, even pathetic figure. Stubbornness and hypersensitivity to criticism produced frequent conflicts with his superiors. Though schooled from childhood in military discipline, he defied the government and war office repeatedly to pursue his own course. When thwarted, Cherniaev launched intrigues against rivals and ministers of state who he believed were denying him deserved glory. Egomania, nervous tension, and delusions of grandeur drove him to the brink of madness, as his imagination conjured up conspiracies threatening him and Russia with ruin.

Cherniaev's life reveals how a paranoid personality in a position of power can deflect a great nation from its normal course. Deriving satisfaction from engaging in hopeless struggles and lost causes, he defied ultimately the Russian dynasty, bureaucracy, military establishment, and secret police. His reckless campaigns, prompted by a restless search for prominence, glory, and applause, drew Russia into unwanted confrontations with the Ottoman Empire and the Khanate of Bukhara.

Cherniaev's inner conflicts mirrored some currents of his age. A nobleman in an era of rising capitalism, his failures in the commercial world epitomized the impracticality and ineffectiveness of his class. A romantic who idealized the outdated institutions of Nicholas I, he found the values he defended most strongly—Orthodoxy, duty, discipline and aristocratic predominance—being undermined. The 1860s were years of change when the unfettered autocracy and serfdom of Nicholas's time yielded to reform. The emancipation of the serfs in particular threatened the landed gentry's influence and traditional way of life.

The career of Cherniaev is closely linked with several major issues of Russian nineteenth-century history. Why did an already vast Russia seek to dominate the Balkans and expand in Central Asia? Which elements in Russian society favored imperial expansion? How can the vogue of Panslavism in Russia after the mid-sixties be explained? Why were military heroes so popular in a country preoccupied with domestic problems? What motivated conservative opponents of the reforms of Alexander II? I hope that this study will help to answer these questions.

During his lifetime Cherniaev was a controversial figure in Russia and abroad. To Russian conservatives he was a patriot and hero unfairly vilified and persecuted by the military establishment, bureaucrats, foreigners, and radicals. To liberals he was a reactionary intriguing against overdue reform, a soldier-adventurer threatening to involve Russia in needless conflicts. His eldest daughter Antonina described episodes from his career for conservative Russian historical journals, and in 1906, under a pseudonym, she published a laudatory biographical sketch. Three years later the liberals retorted with G. K. Gradovskii's "Archstrategist of the Slav War," a devastating though faulty summary of his career. In emigration Antonina drafted a full-length biography exclusively from her father's viewpoint omitting all derogatory information. Its numerous factual errors, naiveté and religious emphasis make it unsuitable today. Despite pleas by another daughter, Nadia, Soviet historians generally have relegated the General to obscurity. However, Professor S. A. Nikitin's *The Slav Committees in Russia* (1960) summarizes Cherniaev's role in the Slav movement of the 1870s.

Utilizing the extensive archival, newspaper, and published materials now available, the author has surveyed the career and probed the character of a neglected Russian imperialist and Panslav. Though never the great man he sought so eagerly to become, Cherniaev was associated with the leading figures and events of his epoch. He reflected the frustrations of his class and the desire of his countrymen for recognition from more advanced western Europe. Cherniaev's strivings, successes and failures will be significant as long as men seek fame and military glory.

David MacKenzie

Russian and Central Asian Terms

Bek	A native governor in Central Asia
Desiatina	A Russian land measure (about 2.7 acres)
Duma	A Russian assembly
Khalat	A native gown in Central Asia
Kopek	1/100 of a ruble
Oblast	A Russian province
Pud	A Russian measure of weight (36.1 pounds)
Ruble	Russian monetary unit ($0.51 in 1914)
Saklia	A native dwelling in Central Asia and the Caucasus
Shariat	Moslem religious law
Sotnia	A squadron of Cossack cavalry (about 130 men)
Verst	Russian measure of distance (about 3,500 feet or 2/3 of a mile)
Zemstvo	District and provincial assemblies set up in Russia beginning in 1864

CHAPTER I

Education and First Battles

FOR CENTURIES Cherniaev's family had performed military and state service for the tsars. Almost automatically his father decided that he should pursue a military career. Young Cherniaev's education in civil and military schools under Nicholas I (1825–1855) imbued the future conqueror of Russian Central Asia with a profound conservatism, a love of order and tradition. Worshipping the august emperor, he strove to become an exemplary Nicholaevian officer: obedient, patriotic, and God-fearing. But the chief personal influence upon this intelligent, sensitive boy was a restless and ambitious father, chronically dissatisfied with his duties and superiors. This dual legacy would always perplex and trouble Cherniaev.

In 1478 when Ivan III of Moscow conquered Novgorod, the Cherniaevs, a family of lesser nobility, were exiled to remote parts of Russia. One branch settled near Belgorod on the turbulent Ukrainian border where service to Muscovy brought it landed estates. In 1783 Catherine the Great awarded hereditary nobility to Nikita Isaevich Cherniaev, the general's grandfather; later, he moved to Mogilev province, acquired in the first partition of Poland.

Grigorii Nikitich Cherniaev, the general's father, the youngest of five sons, graduated from the Shklov cadet corps near Mogilev. He served as an officer in the Austro-Russian army which was defeated by Napoleon at Austerlitz in 1805. During Napoleon's invasion of Russia in 1812, Cherniaev was wounded and decorated. In 1818, while serving as a major in the occupation army in France, he married the young daughter of the former mayor of Le Quesnoy. Their marriage of mutual love and understanding lasted over fifty years.

Grigorii Nikitich resigned his commission and took his French bride to Tubyshki village in Mogilev province. There on a four thousand acre estate he built his "nobleman's nest." Thirty miles by rutted roads from Mogilev and seventeen from Tolochin, it lay virtually isolated from Moscow and St. Petersburg. Wolves, bear, and elk roamed through towering pine forests extending for miles on every side, and vast swamps populated with wild birds covered large sections of the province. Grigorii Nikitich, a zealous proprietor of modest means, had an orchard planted, a pond dug, and a watermill constructed. Between the orchard and the courtyard lined with farm buildings rose two frame houses with shingled roofs. When his older brother died, Grigorii Nikitich became sole owner of the estate and two hundred serfs.

Madame Cherniaev bore him eighteen children, nine surviving to adulthood. Sophie Delmas, her energetic and devoted French companion, ran the household and handled the children expertly. As French was often used in the household, the children became almost bilingual.

In 1824 Grigorii Nikitich returned to state service. Restlessness, his wife's boredom with country life, and the expense of a growing family, led him to turn to Count M. S. Vorontsov, governor general of Bessarabia, who obtained a post for him at Bendery on the Dniester River. Mikhail Grigorevich, their second son, was born there October 22, 1828. Frail and sickly in infancy, little Misha almost died of a respiratory infection during a long trip to France with his parents, but Sophie nursed him back to health. While they visited Madame Cherniaev's relatives, Elizaveta (Liza) was born. She became Misha's favorite playmate and confidante.

Soon dissatisfied at Bendery, Grigorii Nikitich again resigned and returned to Tubyshki with his family. His wide travels and varied experiences made him a popular local figure. Misha's years at Tubyshki in the peaceful Belorussian countryside left him many happy memories. While his older brother, Filip, prepared for a military career in a Moscow cadet corps, Misha played with peasant children from the village. With his three sisters he romped in the woods, rode horseback, and swam in the pond on the estate.

Again his father grew restive. Made commandant of Ismail on the Danube, within a year he transferred to Kiev as chief of police. Less than twelve months later he resigned and returned to Tubyshki. His frequent shifts in and out of state service revealed a congenital restlessness and inability to get along with superiors. Misha was doubtless affected by his father's attitude and the frequent moves. Identifying closely with a father who took him hunting and encouraged his lifelong interest in books, especially on Russian history, he too became nomadic, independent, and often quarrelsome with his superiors. The bases were laid for personality problems which caused Misha anguish in adulthood. The size of the family, his position as second of three sons, and his father's ceaseless quest for a meaningful post apparently overstimulated his ambition. He always sought consciously to excel, to attract attention, and to escape mediocrity and routine.

After home tutoring Misha's first formal schooling was in gymnasia, which stressed harsh discipline and memorization of classical texts. After a year in Kiev he attended the Mogilev gymnasium, boarding with the school inspector and spending weekends at Tubyshki. So thoroughly did Misha learn Cicero that in his old age he could still recite long passages. In later life he advocated classical learning as the soundest basis for intellectual development. The pupils were mostly Polish Catholics who mixed little with the Russian minority. A Polish boy, he recalled, once made fun of the religion instructor behind his back. The Russian pupils informed the school inspector, a retired sailor, who later boasted loudly, "I gave him 100 lashes as an example to the others not to scoff at our [Orthodox] clergy." The Russian boys were thunderstruck. When the unfortunate Pole staggered in, they sought his forgiveness. Under Nicholas I school discipline was severe.

Grigorii Nikitich's decision that Misha should become an officer forced the frail, intense boy to compete with his father and older brother. At eleven his father took him to a reunion of Borodino veterans. The next year he and Liza were entered in boarding schools in St. Petersburg; the others accompanied Grigorii Nikitich to his new post in Berdiansk on the Black Sea. At twelve, Misha left his family and beloved Tubyshki, to enter a harsh military world.[1]

Soon he was accepted into the Noble Regiment, an elite secondary school for future officers. In an effort to make Russia impregnable, Nicholas I lavished money and attention on his army. Top officers were trained in the Corps of Pages, Noble Regiment, and the Engineer and Artillery schools. The Noble Regiment, founded in 1807, had been noted formerly for boisterous pupils who terrorized St. Petersburg residents. The year before Misha entered, discipline was tightened and the school now provided an excellent education, mainly for sons of the gentry. Although he missed the comfort and security of Tubyshki, Misha adjusted to the Spartan life and developed the rugged health and endurance demanded by war. His excellent showing in the entrance examinations reflected good preliminary schooling, wide home reading, and high aptitudes. A conscientious student, he remained near the top of his class but was no teacher's pet. "I was flogged for smoking," he recalled, "but was not downhearted and continued to be in excellent standing."[2] His vivacity, charm, and generosity won the dark-haired lad many friends and companions.

Cherniaev later defended Nicholas's cadet corps against charges of obscurantism, mania for drill, and brutal punishments. All schools, he argued, had harsh discipline during this time, but corporal punishment at the Noble Regiment was rare. Intellectual achievement was prized as well as obedience, religion, and moral training. He defended the austere Regulation of 1830: "Their [the cadets'] conduct must be based upon love of God, reverence for the decrees of the Holy Church, filial devotion to the Throne, unselfish love of the fatherland, conscientious recognition of duty to family and society, and the present condition of knowledge in the educated world." Knowledge, one notes, came last. Cherniaev praised these traditional principles throughout his life though they conflicted with his yearning for independence and self-expression.

Life in the Regiment was regulated meticulously. The cadets, ages twelve to eighteen, rose at 5:30, attended prayers, and had classes until 11:00 A.M. Following inspection came ninety minutes of drill. After dinner came more classes, physical training, and more drill.

---

1. IISG, ed. khr. 2 and 20; A. Cherniaeva, "Letopis semi Cherniaevykh," RA, 1909, I: 175–208.

2. IISG, "Biografiia," p. 35; "Avtobiografiia," p. 3.

The curriculum included the Russian language, literature, history, and some mathematics and natural science. In the upper forms military subjects were added. Drill time, affirmed Cherniaev, ordinarily consumed only three hours a week, but before the big May parade came two weeks of intensive drilling and long rehearsals by the St. Petersburg cadet corps.[3]

Although he favored strict discipline, Cherniaev condemned the paradomania which prevailed under Nicholas. Like his military model, Marshal A. V. Suvorov (Catherine the Great's talented and victorious commander), he believed that soldiers should learn only what was useful in war. That some cadets could present arms without spilling water from a pitcher on their heads left him unimpressed. He deplored the ferocious punishments in the Nicholaevian army. The public lashing of a soldier in Semenovsk Square affected him deeply. It was carried out at dawn before an eager crowd including society ladies in their finest furs. Misha found this spectacle extremely replusive.

The cadets dreaded the semiannual examinations in which all the Petersburg corps tested and compared their knowledge. Parents, guests, and members of the imperial family attended. The solemn atmosphere gave the impressionable Cherniaev nightmares for years afterwards. In the library stood huge blackboards listing vacant posts in various regiments, and the immediate future of the students depended upon their examination performances and school recommendations. A commission of cadet company commanders chaired by the school inspector called in the graduating cadets in order of academic rank. Artillery and Guards regiments were the most coveted; less able graduates went to line regiments or garrisons. Though eligible by his marks for the artillery, Cherniaev selected the Pavlovsk Guards Regiment, an elite unit in the capital. The government uniform allowance for new officers was most inadequate for service in the capital, so Grigorii Nikitich sent additional funds. On August 14, 1847, Misha Cherniaev entered the imperial service as a junior lieutenant.

Soon the devoted son visited his parents in Berdiansk. His sisters found their slender, intense brother happy and optimistic, but frequent uncontrollable outbursts of laughter revealed his nervousness. The family occupied a large sprawling building in the main square. On the outskirts of town Grigorii Nikitich had built a small summer

3. M. G. Cherniaev, "Nashe voennoe vospitanie," RV (Jan. 1891), pp. 37–47.

retreat. Misha's younger sisters attended boarding school in Odessa; his younger brother Nikolai was enrolled in a St. Petersburg cadet corps.

Cherniaev soon grew bored with garrison duty in his regiment. His lively intelligence and determination to outdo his brothers made him dissatisfied with the routine. In peacetime, without wealth or court connections, an officer had little prospect of adventure or distinction. Poor and unknown, but very ambitious, he applied to the Military Academy of the General Staff and was readily accepted.[4]

The Academy had been founded in 1832 as a military university to train staff officers in strategy, tactics, and military history. Tsar Nicholas, favoring practicality and drill, appointed as director General I. O. Sukhozanet whose slogans were: "Without knowledge victory is possible, without discipline never," and "Knowledge in warfare is no more than a button on your cap." A legless veteran of the Polish campaign of 1831, he was despotic and irritable, stressing discipline and proper uniform to the point of mania.[5] Scolding subordinates for not enforcing every regulation, he once exploded: "This is not a university where one can complain to some worthless little professor. . . . Here you can place an officer under arrest any time. . . . That is the true meaning of military discipline. Only inspired by such principles will you be able to lead people to death."[6] Under Sukhozanet the position of Academy students was unenviable. Learned officers were suspect and until 1851 the General Staff remained a closed corps. Transfer to other branches was difficult, prospects were slim of promotion beyond corps quartermaster, and staff officers rarely obtained independent commands. Academy enrollments dipped sharply: in 1849 Cherniaev was one of only thirteen incoming students.[7]

Surprisingly it still attracted able students and professors. In 1845 D. A. Miliutin, an outstanding Academy graduate, had returned as professor of military geography and statistics. During eleven years there he wrote important theoretical works and broadened the curriculum.[8] Later Cherniaev denounced the Academy as too theoreti-

4. IISG, "Biografiia," pp. 40–53.

5. N. G. Zalesov, "Zapiski," RS, CXIV (June 1903), 530–531.

6. "Iz dalekogo proshlago," RA, XIII, 1875, I: 219–220.

7. "Piatidesiatiletnyi iubelei Nikolaevskoi Akademii generalnogo shtaba," VS (Jan. 1883), pp. 13 ff.; N. P. Glinoetskii, *Istoricheskii ocherk Nikolaevskoi akademii generalnogo shtaba* (St. Petersburg, 1882), pp. 104 ff.

8. G. Khristiani, "Graf Miliutin i voennaia statistika," *Izvestiia Imperatorskoi Nikolaevskoi*

cal because Miliutin, who became war minister and Cherniaev's principal opponent, had been its outstanding professor. "Military geography," recalled Cherniaev, "was taught in the dullest fashion by Miliutin, who possessed no creative ability but merely the capacity to imitate."[9] But he admitted that the Academy had developed his capacities and broadened his intellectual horizon, enhancing his career prospects.

In 1851, following an investigation of falling enrollments, conditions at the Academy began to improve. Most formal drill was abolished. Staff officers could transfer freely, and the new post of divisional chief of staff offered better prospects for graduates. But these improvements came too late to provide Russia with educated staff officers in the Crimean War.

Mikhail Grigorevich attended the Academy before these reforms were implemented but benefited from them after graduation. Sharing a small apartment with several other officers, he obtained money from his father to supplement his meager pay. A classmate and friend, N. P. Ignatiev, later became ambassador to Constantinople, and collaborated with Mikhail Grigorevich to promote Russian expansion in Central Asia and the Balkans.

Upon graduation Cherniaev could have served with the General Staff, but since the Guards' pay had been raised and he desired financial independence, he returned to his regiment. By the next year he had outgrown it. To enter the General Staff he had to take a new examination and familiarize himself with the cavalry and artillery. At the beginning of the Crimean War, he was assigned to active service as a junior captain (*shtabs-kapitan*) of the General Staff.[10]

His first battlefield experience came in a war ending in Russia's defeat. In the Danubian campaign of 1854 he achieved some prominence commanding the Cossack vanguard in the disastrous Karamzin affair. Then he fought at Inkerman and in defense of Sevastopol.

The Crimean War resulted from miscalculations by Russia and the western powers, Britain and France. The "Iron Tsar," guardian

---

Voennoi Akademii, xxviii (April 1912), 543–546. After his first year of teaching, Miliutin's superiors commented: "His abilities and knowledge, and his exceptional zeal in his job, . . . unquestionably bring much benefit to the Academy."

9. But Zalesov ("Zapiski," June 1903, p. 531), entering the Academy a year after Cherniaev, referred to Miliutin's excellent lectures.

10. IISG, "Avtobiografiia," pp. 3–4; "Biografiia," pp. 53–61.

of conservatism and legitimacy at home and abroad, sought to combat French influence at Constantinople which threatened Russian predominance. Confident of Russia's might, he counted upon British neutrality, Austrian friendship, and Prussian support. In July 1853, when the Turks rejected the ultimatum of Prince A. S. Menshikov, Nicholas ordered an invasion of the Danubian principalities of Turkey.

The army of elderly Prince M. D. Gorchakov met no resistance, but Britain, France, and the German powers protested sharply. On September 22 the Turks declared war on Russia.[11] When the Russians destroyed part of the Turkish fleet at Sinope, the western powers demanded that Russia leave the principalities. Ignoring this ultimatum, Nicholas faced war with Turkey, England, France, and later Sardinia.[12] The war plan of old Fieldmarshal I. F. Paskevich had foreseen a quick Russian strike into the Balkans to rouse their Christian inhabitants to revolt. Immediate and determined action might have succeeded, but Paskevich feared an Austrian flank attack. Russian commanders in the Danubian campaign refused to take the risks required for victory. Scattering their forces they acted defensively and were weak everywhere. "In the first months of the war," recalled one officer, "we sat with folded arms awaiting a favorable result from negotiations."[13]

In August 1853, Junior Captain Cherniaev was assigned as a staff officer to the Little Wallachian detachment of some seven thousand men. Hastening to overtake his unit, he accompanied it to Kalafat, under siege by the Russians. Under enemy fire he inspected Cossack outposts while his superiors let the Turks reinforce the city. "By nature I was personally inclined toward war," he affirmed, "but the mood in the army and the population was not enthusiastic. An animated national feeling and concern was only manifested later at Sevastopol."[14] In late October the detachment suffered a galling setback: it had almost

11. All dates are given by the Julian calendar used in Russia and other Orthodox lands ("old style") which is twelve days behind the "new style" dates of western Europe in the nineteenth century. For events of unusual European significance, both dates are cited, e.g., May 10/22.

12. M. Florinsky, *Russia: A History and an Interpretation*, 2 vols. (New York, 1953), ii: 865–869; E. Tarlé, *Krymskaia voina*, 2 vols. (Moscow, 1950), i: 478.

13. V. I. Vasilchikov, "Sevastopol," RA, 1891, vi: 167–173.

14. IISG, "Biografiia," p. 61.

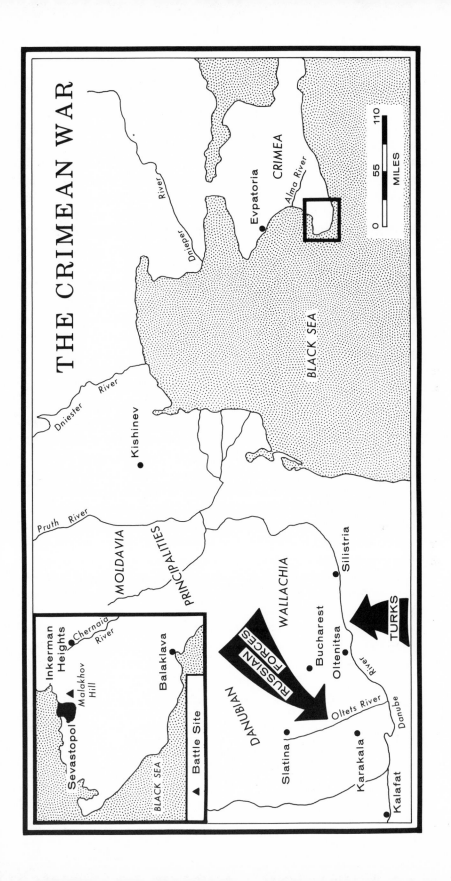

THE CRIMEAN WAR

MILES
0   55   110

Dnieper River

CRIMEA

Evpatoria

Alma River

BLACK SEA

Dniester River

Kishinev

Pruth River

MOLDAVIA

PRINCIPALITIES

WALLACHIA

Silistria

Bucharest

Oltenitsa

RUSSIAN FORCES

TURKS

DANUBIAN

Oltets River

River

Danube

Slatina

Karakala

Kalafat

Inkerman
Heights

Chernaia River

Balaklava

Malakhov
Hill

Sevastopol

BLACK SEA

▲ Battle Site

captured Oltenitsa when General P. A. Dannenberg suddenly ordered retreat. His troops retired in disgust.[15]

A Russian withdrawal from the Danubian provinces soon became unavoidable. Nicholas I authorized it with extreme reluctance.[16] During the retirement to the Russian frontier the Karamzin affair, Cherniaev's first important engagement, took place. Typical of the dismal Danubian campaign, it revealed the numerous shortcomings in Nicholas's army. Andrei N. Karamzin, son of the famous historian,[17] and a prominent figure in Petersburg society, had recently joined the Little Wallachian detachment. Leaving his wife's palace for the rigors of war earned him applause, but he was a dilettante in search of glory. While he was personally brave, he lacked a sound military education or battle experience; nevertheless he was put in command of the "Warsaw" Hussar Regiment over officers who had served in it for many years.

Early in May 1854, the detachment halted briefly at Slatina. Reconnaissance parties were sent out to watch the Turkish cavalry. On May 9 Karamzin accompanied a scouting expedition under General Salkov. Learning from residents that the Turks were plundering nearby villages, Karamzin urged immediate pursuit. Instead, Salkov ordered his men back to camp. Furious, Karamzin accused him of losing his nerve: "I am sure," he boasted, "that with my heroes I would beat that swarthy rabble [the Turks]."

A week later his opportunity came. Karamzin was to conduct a reconnaissance with six squadrons of hussars, a Cossack *sotnia* (a squadron of Cossack cavalry containing about 130 men) under Cherniaev, and four horsedrawn cannon—about one thousand men in all. Even before they left there was dissension. Lieutenant Colonel Dika doubted that a green colonel like Karamzin should direct the operation. Summoning his officers, Karamzin pledged to accept any reasonable advice. "Colonel," responded Dika dourly, "you are now our detachment commander. We must

15. The men blamed Dannenberg, but Gorchakov who had sent inadequate forces to storm Oltenitsa shared the responsibility. M. I. Bogdanovich, *Vostochnaia voina* (St. Petersburg, 1876), I: 135–138.

16. Tarlé, I: 492–503.

17. N. M. Karamzin (1766–1826), author of *Istoriia gosudarstva rossiiskago*, 3 vols. (St. Petersburg, 1842), a patriotic history glorifying the tsars.

execute all your orders and directives unconditionally."[18]   His reply reflected the Nicholaevian tradition of unreasoning obedience.

At dawn on May 16 the battalion set out. Karamzin was to advance to the Oltets River and determine enemy strength. He was ordered to take strict precautions and to avoid large Turkish forces.[19] Karamzin ordered Cherniaev to ride ahead with his Cossacks and report whatever he observed. The weather was extremely hot, and after a few *versts* (a verst is about two-thirds of a mile) Mikhail Grigorevich, concerned for his men and horses, halted them at the first water, galloped back to Karamzin and asked to rest his men. "I don't consider that necessary," retorted Karamzin. Cherniaev rode off and the entire force advanced rapidly thirty-five versts to the Oltets River.

As the main force halted near a narrow bridge spanning the river, Mikhail Grigorevich set up outposts on the far side and sent out scouts. Senior officers urged him to warn Karamzin that a further advance would be unwise. Men and horses were exhausted, and the detachment was isolated. As a junior officer Cherniaev refused to shoulder such a disagreeable task. "I decided not to report this," he recalled, "and suggested that they go to Karamzin themselves, but they did not go." He merely informed the colonel that Turkish cavalry had been sighted about ten versts away.

After lunch Karamzin ordered the advance resumed. Cherniaev, leading his Cossacks over the bridge, was amazed to see the entire detachment following close behind. Soon a Turkish picket spotted them and fled. Further on Karamzin paused before a marshy stream for a council of war. Most of his officers wanted to cross—in a retreat the horses could easily ford the stream. Noting their exposed position, Cherniaev and a few others objected, but the colonel paid them no heed.

Soon Mikhail Grigorevich returned to report that ahead lay another narrow bridge over a swamp. Pondering briefly Karamzin declared: "With a regiment so famous for its bravery I do not believe that we should retreat. . . . With these heroes we must always advance!" Cherniaev, the trained staff officer, objected that it was very

18. P. F. Vistengof, "Andrei Nikolaevich Karamzin," RS, XXII, 1878, II: 197–207. Vistengof was a lieutenant in the Aleksandriisk regiment.

19. Bogdanovich, II: 78–79, order of 15 May.

dangerous to cross such bridges without knowing the enemy's strength, but in war one cannot stand around arguing with the commanding officer. Shrugging his shoulders, Cherniaev rode back to his men.

The detachment crossed a bog onto a broad plain. In the distance loomed the towers of Karakala. A Cossack reported to Cherniaev that four Turkish columns lay before them. He went and pointed them out to Karamzin. When inferior in numbers, he warned, the Turks usually retired; large enemy forces must be concealed nearby. Lowering his field glasses Karamzin declared that he saw two Turkish squadrons and two fences. As Cherniaev stared in disbelief, Karamzin announced: "We shall approach to within cannon range of the Turks, open fire and compel them to reveal their strength." To avoid Salkov's "cowardice," he disregarded Cherniaev's advice.

The Russians advanced, their four cannon opened fire, and the Turks wavered. Then the guns fell silent. In the haste to break camp, sufficient shells had not been packed! Turkish irregulars were turning the Russian flanks. Mikhail Grigorevich implored Karamzin to sound the retreat. Instead he ordered a general assault. On exhausted horses the hussars attacked a far stronger enemy and were repelled. Confusion spread in the Russian ranks while the Turks rushed to cut off their escape.

Cherniaev was with the artillery. The horses dragging the cannon were killed, the guns were abandoned. A mass of Turks surrounded Karamzin at the bridge. Noticing that Cherniaev was an officer, several Turks rushed at him. Galloping along the bank, Cherniaev was saved when a Cossack just ahead of him became mired. While the Turks captured him, Cherniaev crossed further upstream ignoring his men's safety and charged ahead to report the defeat. He learned later that Dika had extracted most of the battalion. Karamzin, captured at the bridge, had seized a sabre and fought furiously until cut down. The Turks later returned a hacked body with seventeen wounds.

In his report Cherniaev listed over one hundred officers and men put out of action and blamed the defeat on Karamzin's impetuousness, poor intelligence work, and Turkish numerical superiority. Karamzin's heroic death, he felt, had expiated his grievous errors. Nicholas I commented: "Take note of this young officer." Mikhail Grigorevich would always recall with pride the emperor's praise.[20] His battle reports had proved highly success-ful.

The Battle of Karakala caused comment abroad and recrimi-nations in St. Petersburg but it had little effect upon the outcome of the campaign, since Nicholas had already decided to retreat. In the army, indignation against Karamzin because of needless loss of men remained strong. The first phase of the war ended with Russian morale severely impaired.

The Russian command wondered where the Allies would strike and whether Austria or Prussia would join them. Late in August 1854 a seventy-thousand-man Franco-British expeditionary force landed in the western Crimea. Prince Menshikov, commander in chief in the Crimea, moved northward from Sevastopol, head-quarters of the Black Sea fleet. He was defeated at the Alma River, and only the Allies' dilatory pursuit and the Sevastopol garrison's frantic efforts prevented a quick end to the campaign.[21]

These events brought Cherniaev to the Crimea. Perceiving the danger to Sevastopol, Prince M. D. Gorchakov ordered the Fourth Corps to the Crimea. Mikhail Grigorevich's regiment was ordered to move out quickly: "We departed on October 7 [actually October 15]. The roads were dry and we were borne along by cart day and night. They fed us well and there was no shortage of provisions. In the Crimea we ran into cold weather and dug holes to protect ourselves from the wind."[22] On October 21 they entered the Cher-naia River valley. Far to the right rose Inkerman heights where a major battle would be fought.[23] The campaign depended on how the high command would utilize these reinforcements.

Prince Menshikov placed General Dannenberg in command, in spite of his failure at Oltenitsa. He planned to throw the British from Inkerman heights, then drive the Allies into the sea. This required precise coordination of several Russian detachments, but Dannen-berg failed to explain clearly to his commanders his changes in Menshikov's original dispositions or where they would proceed after

---

20. Tarlé, I: 515–516; GIM, ed. khr. 3, Cherniaev to Brigade Commander; ed. khr. 31, "Kavaleriiskii boi . . . ,"; A. M. Cherniaeva, "M. G. Cherniaev vo vremia russko-turetskoi voiny, 1853–1856 gg.," RA (1906), I: 449–455; IISG, "Biografiia," pp. 62–69; Vistengof, pp. 193 ff.; Alabin, *Pokhodnye zapiski* (Viatka, 1861), I: 195–197.

21. For a general account of the Crimean campaign see W. B. Pemberton, *Battles of the Crimean War* (New York, 1962).

22. IISG, "Avtobiografiia," p. 9.

23. L. G. Dukhonin, "Pod Sevastopolem v 1853–56 gg.," RS (July 1885), pp. 263–264.

seizing initial objectives.[24] His ignorance of the terrain exacerbated these problems. War Minister Chernyshev finally sent him the only available detailed map, but it arrived *after* the Battle of Inkerman.[25]

Captain Cherniaev drew up battle plans for General Pavlov's detachment. P. B. Alabin, acting as his secretary, recalled that several of them gathered in his tiny shelter of boughs: "Cherniaev had no map on which the battle area was described in detail with even the approximate location of enemy forces. . . . His plan consisted mainly of indications as to which units of the detachment should follow which, when the advance would begin and who should go where after crossing Inkerman bridge. The subsequent order of march and the goal each unit should seek to reach could not be determined." Pavlov's staff made minor changes, then sent the plan to headquarters.

Later that evening came Dannenberg's marching orders. At 2:00 A.M. the Tenth Division would move out, then Cherniaev leading the artillery, and finally the Eleventh Infantry. Pavlov's men were to cross Inkerman bridge as soon as it was repaired and storm the heights. Dannenberg's changes astounded Cherniaev. Unless General Soimonov, coming from the other side, received the altered plans in time, terrible confusion would result.

Boggy ground and bridge repairs delayed Pavlov. Struggling painfully to the summit of Sapun-gore under English fire, his men discovered that Soimonov's force was in their positions. Uncertain where to go, Pavlov's regiments were decimated by English artillery. Confusion spread in the ranks of General Soimonov who lay mortally wounded. P. D. Gorchakov's powerful force remained passive permitting the French to reinforce the battered English and drive the Russians from Inkerman heights into a ravine.[26]

Cherniaev recalled his own modest role. In a heavy rain his men assaulted Inkerman heights clutching at bushes to avoid falling back into the ravine. At the top "our battalion's formation became confused forming a disorderly mass," but it captured some English

24. N. K. Shilder, *Graf Eduard Ivanovich Totleben*, 2 vols. (St. Petersburg, 1885–1886), ɪ: 360; E. I. Totleben, *Opisanie oborony Sevastopolia* (St. Petersburg, 1863), Part l, pp. 425–426. Generals Pavlov (16,000 men) and Soimonov (19,000) were to attack Inkerman heights from two sides while P. D. Gorchakov (22,000) engaged the French and the Sevastopol garrison made a sortie. Pemberton, pp. 117 ff.

25. Vasilchikov, pp. 203–207.

26. Alabin, *Pokhodnye zapiski*, ɪɪ: 66–69, 83–87.

positions. As Cherniaev approached an enemy battery, an English soldier tried to bayonet him, but Cherniaev struck him with his sabre and rushed on. Suddenly French reinforcements joined the fight. "Crying hurrah! we rushed to meet them and drove them back, . . . but our forces fell into a sack and were barely able to escape. . . ." In his Okhotsk regiment only six hundred men survived out of three thousand.[27] Mikhail Grigorevich's first battles were inglorious Russian defeats.

Two weeks later Admiral V. I. Istomin summoned Cherniaev to Sevastopol. Taking two regiments of his reinforced division to posts in the defense perimeter, Mikhail Grigorevich was heartened by the sailors' high morale.[28] During the siege of Sevastopol Cherniaev served eight months at Malakhov Hill, a key fortress dominating the harbor. He survived almost continual Allied bombardment and several French assaults. "I came out of it safely," he recalled. "During the entire period one horse was killed under me and I was slightly injured by an exploding bomb." Malakhov, he noted, was an almost closed, egg-shaped fortress divided by traverses and containing several powder cellars. In the rounded portion closest to the enemy stood a stone tower which was gradually destroyed by bombardment.[29] If Malakhov fell, the Allies could compel the Russians to evacuate Sevastopol.

Cherniaev, jealous of his rivals' fame, refused to credit Colonel E. I. Totleben and his military engineers with a major share in Sevastopol's defense. Before the French besieged Malakhov, Cherniaev and Istomin inspected a nearby height and agreed that the construction of a redoubt there would guard Malakhov. Totleben, claimed Cherniaev, refused to authorize this. Later, realizing his error, he ordered one built at a terrible cost in lives. Totleben, he asserted, buried his glory beneath Malakhov Hill; his acquaintance with the heir to the throne, however, brought him subsequent prominence.[30]

27. IISG, "Avtobiografiia," p. 9; "Biografiia," pp. 70–72; A. Cherniaeva, "Cherniaev vo vremia . . . ," pp. 455–456.

28. Alabin, II: 116.

29. IISG, "Avtobiografiia," p. 10; N. A. Kryzhanovskii, "Sevastopol i ego zashchitniki v 1855 g.," RS, L (1886), 406.

30. Gorchakov declared that the Selenginsk outpost and Totleben's other advanced positions should have been built three months sooner. But Shilder (*Totleben*, I: 415) noted that Prince Menshikov had refused to allow their construction. Prince Vasilchikov, the able chief of staff, considered Totleben's reputation inflated but praised his determination and resource-

16   *Chapter I*

Sevastopol's supreme commanders deserved no praise. Prince Menshikov hampered the defense until removed early in 1855. His successor, Prince M. D. Gorchakov, virtually deaf and blind, epitomized Nicholas's rotten system. Incompetent in Russian, he gave orders in French, the language of the enemy. Sevastopol's defenders complained: "We have no commander in chief."[31]

The Black Sea admirals were different. Cherniaev served at Malakhov under Istomin and Nakhimov whose tireless activity and personal courage inspired their men. Istomin labored night and day supervising construction of trenches and traverses. "Everywhere is seen the determination to fight and die. The hill is Istomin's ship and he runs it as such."[32] After Istomin was killed, Admiral P. S. Nakhimov took command and courted death almost daily. He would mount the ramparts, his white uniform with its admiral's epaulettes clearly visible, and calmly observe the French positions through his field glasses. For Cherniaev he set an example of dauntless courage.

By Easter Malakhov's garrison could reply only occasionally to severe Allied bombardment. Wrote Cherniaev: "Gorchakov came to us during Holy Week. We had scarcely any powder when the enemy began to bombard us. The French would fire, jump up on their ramparts to see if they had scored a hit and grew very skilled. To celebrate Holy Week we merely asked Gorchakov for 150 rounds. No sooner had he left than the English exploded our powder cellar."[33]

On April 4, recounts Alabin, while Cherniaev and other officers were at lunch, a bomb penetrated the wall and exploded inside the tower. As the horrified officers watched, blood of the dead and wounded mixing with water from a ruptured tank poured into the room, then clouds of fire and smoke followed by sand and stones. Mikhail Grigorevich believed that his last moment had come. Then there was silence soon broken by cries of the wounded. Within minutes the survivors were handling the dead and wounded and repairing the tower. Cherniaev's bravery and calm attention to duty won his comrades' respect.[34]

---

fulness. Vasilchikov, pp. 184–186. For Cherniaev's critique see IISG, "Biografiia," pp. 73–74.
  31. "Kniaz M. D. Gorchakov v 1855–1861 gg.," RS (Sept. 1880), pp. 120–121; Tarlé, II: 275.
  32. Alabin, II: 184–185.
  33. IISG, "Avtobiografiia," p. 10; A. Cherniaeva, p. 457.
  34. Alabin, II: 218, entry of April 4, 1855.

Although a massive Allied attack (June 6) was repelled, the French tunneled closer to Malakhov. An intense Allied bombardment of Sevastopol (August 24–26) killed seventy-five hundred Russians and largely destroyed their fortifications. On the twenty-seventh there came a lull in the shelling. Cherniaev recorded cryptically: "Malakhov Hill was taken at 11:00 A.M. while the troops were eating. When I rushed there from the right bastion with the order to withdraw [General] Khrulev had been wounded. . . . The French placed two guns on Malakhov Hill and accompanied us with canister shot. . . . It fell to me to withdraw the troops from the bastions and trenches."[35]

G. K. Gradovskii, Cherniaev's bitterest critic, asserted that after the initial French assault Khrulev had sent Cherniaev to ascertain Malakhov's situation: "Without going as far as the most dangerous point of the battle, Cherniaev learned by questioning retreating wounded that all attempts to regain the bastion had been repelled. Cherniaev then turned back and reported this to his commander silent about the fact that his information had been obtained at second hand." Cherniaev, suggested Gradovskii, had acted in a cowardly, dishonorable manner.[36] Cherniaev's own reticence lends credence to this accusation. Already he had concealed unfavorable information and taken the easier path.

His friend, Alabin, also remains curiously silent about Cherniaev's role. At precisely 11:30 A.M., with Malakhov's guns silent, the French had attacked from trenches a stone's throw away. The few Russians on the ramparts were quickly subdued; only the tower still resisted. In the attempt to recapture Malakhov before the French could mount artillery, General Khrulev was severely wounded and the relief attempt foundered.[37] Elsewhere the Allies were repelled, but Malakhov's fall necessitated withdrawal since enemy guns commanded Sevastopol. After the garrison was evacuated, Cherniaev and two other officers crossed the bay in a small boat, reaching the northern shore unscathed.[38]

The war, so costly to Russia, brought Cherniaev decorations and promotion. For Malakhov he received a Saint Vladimir Fourth Class

35. iisg, "Avtobiografiia," pp. 10–11; A. Cherniaeva, p. 457.

36. Gradovskii ("Arkhistratig," p. 120) obtained this information from N. F. Kozlianinov, General Osten-Saken's chief of staff in Sevastopol.

37. Alabin, ii: 367–372; Shilder, i: 478–479.

38. iisg, "Avtobiografiia," pp. 10–11.

and a golden sabre. Since a month's duty at Sevastopol was counted
as a year of peacetime duty, he was promoted to lieutenant colonel.
At Karakala he had first led troops and learned the exorbitant price
of recklessness; at Malakhov he had served under the chief Russian
heroes of the war and faced death constantly. Cherniaev had displayed coolness and courage under fire, but he had refused to assume
extra responsibility to save men entrusted to his command. He
lacked the unusual dedication and sense of responsibility of the
greatest commanders.

CHAPTER II

Central Asia and the Caucasus
(1857–1863)

AFTER brief service in Russian Poland, Cherniaev spent two years in the Central Asian areas he would later conquer. A quarrel with his commanding officer hastened his transfer to the Caucasus. When that theater became inactive, he obtained a post in Orenburg and led an important reconnaissance expedition to Suzak in 1863. During these years Mikhail Grigorevich acquired a practical knowledge of steppe warfare which he later used effectively in his campaigns in Turkestan.

After Sevastopol Cherniaev enjoyed a deserved rest in Berdiansk. He found his parents dismayed over Grigorii Nikitich's sudden dismissal from the service for allegedly falsifying reports to his superiors. In a letter to General Vasilchikov, deputy war minister, whom he knew from the Danubian campaign, Mikhail Grigorevich revealed a deep loyalty to his family. "I merely request justice for my father," he wrote, "and legitimate reward for his half century of unselfish service." His intercession succeeded. His father was promoted to major general and pensioned in uniform. This mollified the old man without erasing the ignominy of abrupt dismissal. "People find that I have become very much like my father," noted Cherniaev later, "and the circumstances of our service have much in common. Both he and I ended our lives insulted and deprived."

Mikhail Grigorevich visited Berdiansk whenever possible. Grigorii Nikitich yielded to his wife's pleas to remain there close to their married daughters. The elder Cherniaevs sold their large home, and with their two younger daughters and Sophie Delmas moved to their summer house, where Grigorii Nikitich fished and read until his death in 1868. Sophie followed him to the grave in 1872. Nadezhda and Anna, the younger daughters, cared for Madame Cherniaev until she died in 1880.

Cherniaev, dissatisfied as chief of staff of the Third Infantry Division in Poland, arranged through Vasilchikov a transfer to the staff of Governor General A. A. Katenin of Orenburg at the edge of the steppe.[1] In March 1858 Katenin sent him to Fort Perovskii as chief of staff under Major General A. L. Danzas commanding the Syr-Daria Line.[2]

For over a century Russia had extended its control over the vast, arid steppe south and east of Orenburg. By 1850, having overcome sporadic resistance by Kazakh nomads, Russia firmly established her presence along the northern shores of the Aral Sea and began to move up the Syr-Daria River. From western Siberia, detachments moving south and west founded Vernyi in 1854 as their chief base. Between Vernyi and the Syr-Daria lay a thousand miles of steppe and desert with no defined frontier. To the south in the rich Syr-Daria and Amu-Daria oases lay the Moslem khanates of Bukhara, Kokand, and Khiva—semi-feudal states which often fought each other. Their inhabitants, mainly farmers, traders, and artisans, were disunited and lacked the means to halt the Russian advance.

In the early 1850s the Orenburg command set up the Syr-Daria Line as the western arm of Russian pincers. In 1852 Governor General V. A. Perovskii captured Ak-mechet, a Kokanese fortress well up-river. As Fort Perovskii it became the region's chief bastion. By 1855 three more forts had been built on the Syr-Daria's right bank. In the steppe to the east, there were nomadic tribes who owed only a shadowy allegiance to Russia or the khanates. Garrisons were

1. IISG, "Biografiia," pp. 81–89; "Avtobiografiia," p. 11. Cherniaev's recollection is most inaccurate: Vasilchikov is described as war minister (he was Sukhozanet's deputy), and the period, 1858–1863, is omitted probably because Cherniaev was not proud of his obscure role.

2. Danzas was a strong-willed, well-educated officer who became Orenburg's chief of staff (Autumn 1859). Zalesov, "Zapiski," RS, CXV (July 1903), 27–28.

kept small since most supplies had to come from Orenburg. Communications between the Russian forts were complicated by drifting
sand and spring floods.[3]

St. Petersburg remained unwilling to commit much money or
military force in Central Asia. Until 1860 pacification of the Caucasus tied down its best troops. Concerned with the imminent emancipation of the serfs and appalled by Russia's war debts, the emperor
opposed advances which might bring complications. But alarmed by
Prince A. I. Bariatinskii's reports about British designs on the Caspian Sea area, he approved preparatory moves. Special missions were
sent to the khanates to gather commerical and military data. In
October 1857 Colonel N. P. Ignatiev, Cherniaev's Academy classmate, journeyed to Bukhara and Khiva to assess Russian political
and trade opportunities. Ignatiev, an ardent expansionist, sought
vainly to persuade Petersburg to ally with Bukhara, dismember
Kokand, and advance to Tashkent.[4]

A tangled web of personal, economic, and patriotic factors motivated Russian imperialists in Central Asia. Seeking prominence and
fortune, they rationalized their personal ambition as Russia's great
mission to conquer and civilize backward Asiatics. The lure of riches
in the fabled khanates drew them onward. To hesitant merchants
and an impoverished government they explained the manifold advantages of new Asian markets if the trade routes could be secured
from nomadic raids. Later, the Panslavs would argue with equal
eloquence for intervention in the Balkans to free the Slavs.

For military men like Cherniaev, expansion in Central Asia presented obvious advantages. Officers and men eagerly awaited action
to break the dull routine of garrison duty. Unknown territory attracted the venturesome, and the enemy was neither formidable nor
dangerous. The armies of the khanates were undisciplined, inadequately armed, and poorly led. Resolute attacks by small, mobile
Russian units could provoke disorderly flight and bring cheap victories. Even princely titles beckoned to successful generals. Could the
government fail to reward new conquests? Expansion might readily
be justified by "legitimate" aims of security and self-defense.

Ignatiev's trip, revealing the khanates' weaknesses, encouraged
Cherniaev and like-minded expansionists to urge military action.

3. F. Lobysevich, "Syr-Darinskaia liniia," vs, xxxviii (Aug. 1864), 396 ff.

4. N. A. Khalfin, *Politika Rossii v Srednei Azii v 1857–1868 gg.* (Moscow, 1960), pp. 62–95;
N. P. Ignatiev, *Missiia v Khivu i Bukharu v 1858 g.* (St. Petersburg, 1897).

Diplomacy, they claimed, was ineffective with small, disorderly Asian states; Asians understood only force. In the khanates Russian merchants were exposed to violence, even death. "We definitely cannot remain in our present position," General Katenin warned the foreign ministry in July 1858. "We must occupy Turkestan [city] and Tashkent in order to consolidate our position in Central Asia and protect the Syr-Daria Line." Among his officers who favored action the most outspoken was Cherniaev who advocated immediate seizure of Dzhulek and a broad offensive against Kokand: "We have the resources for this, but they are being kept under wraps. Have we really come here to live comfortably and set up housekeeping? For that we have plenty of land in Russia and better for that purpose too. We need this region to extend our influence over Central Asia."[5] He would not rest until this had been achieved.

While exploring the steppe around Kazalinsk he attempted to remove the wraps. He encouraged Kazakh nomads to seek Russian protection and demanded reinforcements to attack Dzhulek. But Katenin ordered him back to Kazalinsk. Cherniaev complied but advocated sending detachments from Fort Perovskii and Vernyi to join near Suzak.[6] Later the government would adopt this proposal to close the lines in the steppe.

Then the Doschan affair exploded wrecking his relations with his superior, General Danzas. A Kipchak nomad Doschan Demantuganov, responding to Katenin's circular which promised to pardon convicts who turned themselves in, surrendered to O. Ia. Osmolovskii, administrator of native affairs on the Syr-Daria Line. Doschan recounted his entire story with naive sincerity. He had been convicted of assaulting a liquor dealer near Troitsk and condemned to be flogged twice through a line of a thousand men armed with birch whips. He escaped from Siberian exile, stole a Russian officer's horse and some sheep, and with his family crossed into Kokand. Serving the *bek* (governor) of Turkestan, Doschan raided tribes under Bukharan and Russian rule and robbed caravans. He became homesick, however, and when he learned of the Katenin circular he returned to Russia.

General Danzas, denying that the circular applied to Doschan, imprisoned him, and to the Kazakhs' dismay a Russian military

5. Khalfin, pp. 120, 105.

6. GIM, ed. khr. 4, 1. 2; A. Cherniaeva, "M. G. Cherniaev v Srednei Azii," IV, CXL (June 1915), 841–842, 861–863.

court condemned him to death. Osmolovskii pleaded his case, but Danzas refused to see him or have it submitted to Katenin.[7] Admiring Doschan's boldness, Cherniaev wrote Danzas privately: "Not sympathy alone compels me to speak for a criminal who with his whole family voluntarily put himself at the Russian authorities' mercy, but also the conviction that his execution would be incompatible with our government's dignity and would lead to loss of faith in our appeals just as all faith in our threats has been lost already." The military court, argued Cherniaev, had not taken all the circumstances into consideration.[8]

Danzas ordered Doschan executed. Angered by the intercession of his chief of staff, he called Cherniaev's arguments baseless and threatened to forward their correspondence to Katenin.[9] Unwisely Cherniaev persisted: anyone confirming a death sentence, he wrote Danzas, should have all the facts: "I would lose my self-respect if purely from fear of attracting my superior's disapprobation I had renounced a legitimate attempt to save a condemned man's life. After eight months at Sevastopol face to face with death, I understand the value of human life and place only duty and honor higher." He reminded Danzas that "between a commander and his subordinates, besides official correspondence, there may exist also another kind based on mutual trust."[10] He could not resist the devastating rejoinder.

Danzas retorted angrily to Cherniaev's renewed intervention. "Inasmuch as you have neither definite duties nor responsibilities in this case . . . , you should not have interfered when you were not asked to and still less review the line commander's directives." Noting that Cherniaev had returned his recent letter unopened, Danzas concluded: "Finding this strange series of actions out of keeping with a staff officer's behavior, besides which you have violated military order and discipline setting the most deplorable example for men of the line entrusted to me, I am compelled to order Your Excellency to leave for Orenburg as soon as possible."[11]

Avoiding open insubordination, Mikhail Grigorevich complied

7. Ibid., pp. 869–872.
8. GIM, ed. khr. 5, ll. 16–17, Cherniaev to [Danzas], 27 December 1858.
9. Ibid., l. 13, Danzas to Petr (sic) Grigorevich [Cherniaev], 28 December 1858.
10. Ibid., ll. 18–20, [Cherniaev] to Aleksandr Loginovich [Danzas], n.d.
11. Ibid., l. 21, Danzas to Cherniaev, 30 December 1858.

but did not let the matter rest. In Orenburg he explained that he had interceded privately. That would have ended it "had not General Danzas expressed his indignation to me in insulting terms. . . ." He had returned Danzas's second letter unopened "fearing to find in it even greater insults compelling me to demand an explanation from him contrary to discipline." Katenin upheld Danzas fully. Refusing to ask Danzas's forgiveness, Cherniaev wrote self-righteously: "Believing that I am right, I reject any decision in the form of generous condescension to avoid my colleagues' reproaches that I could not preserve the dignity of my uniform. . . . I turn to Your Excellency requesting another assignment outside of Orenburg region where I, with my convictions, can no longer be useful."[12]

Both men had displayed poor judgment. Danzas possessed the authority to execute Doschan and dismiss Cherniaev, but his heartless inflexibility antagonized many Kazakhs. Cherniaev's stubborn independence and tactless criticism of his superior were intolerable for the army; impetuous and easily aroused, he would often usurp his superiors' authority. Without studying the case, he had affirmed his position with utter certainty. Extreme sensitivity to any rebuke and a tendency to transform minor disputes into questions of personal honor suggested a mental imbalance which would eventually wreck his career.

Before leaving the Orenburg command Cherniaev went on the Kungrad expedition of 1859, a modest attempt to forward Russia's interests in Central Asia. Far short of Katenin's expansionist program submitted the previous December, it was all that the government, worried about the Piedmontese-Austrian crisis, would authorize. While escorting home a Bukharan envoy, Captain A. I. Butakov was to sail up the Amu-Daria to Kungrad and Bukhara and give support to Mahomet Fany, a Kungrad chieftain defying Khiva. If the Khivans resisted, Cherniaev's 125 infantrymen were to break through. The Bukharan envoy refused to sail on a Russian ship, but Butakov was ordered to "investigate the Amu and determine a point convenient for our future commercial relations inside Bukhara."[13]

The Kungrad expedition, asserted Cherniaev later, was poorly conceived and needlessly risky. With one flatbottomed steamship, a sloop, three barges and only two hundred men Butakov entered

12. Ibid., ll. 49–50, Cherniaev to "Your Excellency," 9 April 1859.
13. Khalfin, *Prisoedinenie Srednei Azii k Rossii v 60–90–kh godakh XIX veka* (Moscow, 1965), pp. 108–114; GIM, ed. khr. 11, ll. 41–42, Katenin to Butakov, 21 April 1859.

uncharted territory ignorant of potential foes. Crossing the stormy Aral Sea, the flotilla entered a branch of the Amu and sailed laboriously toward Kungrad. One of nine officers under Butakov, Cherniaev kept a diary throughout the campaign despite intense heat, crowded quarters, and clouds of mosquitoes.[14]

As they approached Kungrad, the Kichkina River became shallow and narrow, its shores rocky and inhospitable. From some Karakalpaks, an agricultural and fishing tribe, the Russians learned that the Khivan army blocked their path. A horseman descended from a high sand dune and demanded: "Halt in the khan's name!" Butakov disdained any reply, but then his ship ran aground in front of the six-thousand-man Khivan army. Some of the Russians jumped into the river to free it. The Khivans withdrew after a cautious display of force. Butakov assured their emissary that he would not harm them and would sail on to Bukhara. After the Khivans left, the ship floated free, but shallow water soon stopped the Russians again.

Early on June 22 Mahomet Fany's emissary, Shah Niaz, came to conduct them to Kungrad. Butakov sent Cherniaev and two other officers (one knew the native tongue) to congratulate Mahomet for surviving the Khivan siege, and to select an anchorage and obtain small boats. They passed wild Turkoman tribesmen who fired in the air and performed daring feats of horsemanship. In small boats they crossed an estuary to the walled city where they were greeted warmly by its people. At the landing Cherniaev gave each boatman a silver ruble. Such acts of largesse would win him many supporters in Central Asia.

Kungrad's interior was dismal. The Khivan bombardment had destroyed most houses and the inhabitants huddled in tents next to their hired Turkoman allies. The filth was indescribable. A crowd swarmed around the Russians near Mahomet's palace, where Kungrad's blackbearded ruler sat on a throne surrounded by his entourage. How could this unimpressive man, wondered Cherniaev, declare Kungrad's independence and withstand a nine-month Khivan siege? Now fierce Turkomans virtually controlled him and Kungrad.

To Cherniaev's congratulations Mahomet replied: "I have long awaited your coming. You are our deliverers, and all my goods, my

14. M. G. Cherniaev, "O pisme Admirala Butakova k Kniaziu Bariatinskomu," RA (1889), III: 272; "Dnevnik M. G. Cherniaeva. Pokhod v Kungrad," RA (1906), I: 464–482.

wives and daughters are yours." He readily offered boats when Cherniaev explained that the Russian ships could not reach Kungrad. Next day Captain Butakov and his officers went to announce Katenin's wishes. The audience chamber was lighted by a campfire. A carpeted elevation had been prepared for Butakov and stools covered with ancient rugs for his officers. The Russians were served cookies, sugar, and apricots. Mahomet had sought to delay the audience, but when Butakov insisted, he appeared preceded by two men with tallow candles. All present salaamed.

Butakov disappointed Mahomet: wishing to rid himself of the Turkomans, Mahomet urged Butakov to leave men and guns in Kungrad, but the captain refused. Instead he ordered Mahomet to remain at peace with Russian tribesmen and to protect caravans entering Russia from the khanates.

Cherniaev recalled vividly their final meeting with Mahomet. The Russian officers and a single Cossack went to bid farewell. The khan entered the hall with his suite and a crowd of excited and fully armed Kungraders. Smoking torches cast an eerie light over the audience chamber. Asked again about his plans, Butakov explained that the Russians would have to leave. The assemblage buzzed ominously. Cherniaev looked uneasily at their lone Cossack guard. One word from Mahomet and the Russians could be massacred. For the moment they were allowed to depart and hastened back to camp, but later that evening they learned that Mahomet had decided to seize them and their weapons. Piling everything into their ships the Russians quickly weighed anchor, and Mikhail Grigorevich led his infantry company along the Amu covering the retreat. He expected to be surrounded, but the Russians returned unscathed to Kazalinsk.

It was three years before Cherniaev returned to Central Asia. When he left Orenburg, he was assigned briefly to the General Staff in St. Petersburg. In November 1859 he was sent as quartermaster to Terek province in the west Caucasus and gained valuable experience in guerrilla warfare.

For half a century Russia had been fighting the hardy Caucasian highlanders. After lowland Georgia and Armenia had been incorporated, the Russian advance provoked an Islamic resistance movement known as Muridism. It was led by Shamil and Hadji Murat, romantic figures immortalized by Leo Tolstoy in his short novel, *Hadji Murat*. Under Nicholas I Moslem tribesmen from virtually inaccessible valleys and mountain slopes inflicted shocking defeats upon the army of the Caucasus. However, Shamil's failure to make gains during the Crimean War presaged the ultimate defeat of his movement.

Alexander II's appointment of his boyhood friend, Prince Bariatinskii, as Viceroy of the Caucasus (1856), changed matters dramatically. The energetic prince and his chief of staff, Colonel D. A. Miliutin, overhauled the Caucasus command. In fast-moving campaigns (1857–1859) they captured Shamil and subdued the eastern Caucasus. The army of the Caucasus became Russia's best. Far from the parade ground, led by tough, resourceful commanders, it displayed courage and endurance against a tireless, elusive foe. Warfare involving deadly skirmishes where every log and bush threatened death demanded mobility, keenness, and patience.[15]

Bariatinskii envisioned the Caucasus as a secure base for expansion into Central Asia, but some west Caucasus tribes remained unconquered. In May 1860, when disorders erupted in remote Ichkeria, security in the entire region was imperiled. Cherniaev described for Prince Tumanov, his superior, the revolt of the warlike Benoevtsy. Resenting Russian efforts to resettle them, they had escaped into the forests and mountains, where they launched raids and killed Russian stragglers. Naib Uma of Shamil's entourage led a rebellion which spread to the Argun gorge. Emboldened by early successes, they attacked Russian transports and forts and carried on intermittent guerrilla warfare.[16]

Summoning his commanders to Vladikavkaz, Prince Bariatinskii placed M. I. Evdokimov, a bold general, in command of the west. Late in 1860 he launched a powerful and effective offensive. Bariatinskii's draconian policies included trying captured mountaineers by field court-martial. Many others fled into Asiatic Turkey and Russian Kuban Cossacks resettled the region. By 1862 the west Caucasus also was largely pacified.[17]

Admiring Bariatinskii's boldness, decisiveness, and independence, Cherniaev adopted many of his views and methods. Later, they would collaborate in opposing the war ministry.[18] Bariatinskii also

---

15. I. Drozdov, "Posledniaia borba s gortsami na zapadnom Kavkaze," *Kavkazskii sbornik* (Tiflis), II: 388–391. See A. L. Zisserman, "Feldmarshal Kniaz A. I. Bariatinskii," RA (1889), I and II, and Alfred Rieber, *The Politics of Autocracy* (The Hague, 1966), pp. 62 ff.

16. GIM, ed. khr. 13, ll. 1–3, 15–22.

17. Zisserman, RA (1889), III: 425–429.

18. See Chap. 7, pp. 103–104.

advocated Slav emancipation: serfdom and brutal repression of the Poles had long hampered Russia's leadership of the Slav cause. After the emancipation of February 1861, the prince urged the tsar to free Poland and to champion the Slavs still under foreign rule, but he was ignored.[19] Discouraged at this and crippled by gout, Bariatinskii went abroad to seek a cure.

Prince Bariatinskii and his subordinate, R. A. Fadeev, had helped awaken Cherniaev's Slavophile sympathies. Mikhail Grigorevich first expressed Panslav views in response to the first issue of *Den* (*The Day*), newspaper of Ivan S. Aksakov, a prominent Moscow Slavophile. Reading the lead article about the interests linking Slav peoples, he urged his fellow officers to contribute to the Moscow Benevolent Society, a philanthropic organization founded in 1858 to aid the Balkan Slavs. Bringing more Slavs to Russia on scholarships and supporting their studies, argued Cherniaev, would counter generous Catholic grants to those in Western Europe. If South Slav intellectuals were beholden to the west, they would be alienated from Russia and from their own people. If Russia did not challenge such western influences vigorously, the South Slavs would go Catholic and be lost to Russia. Could not Russian officers find a few kopecks to aid their brother Slavs? Contributions from the distant Caucasus would arouse Russian public sympathy for the Slavs. Cherniaev planned to found a Slav committee in Vladikavkaz but then abandoned the idea.[20] This was his first political foray on the Slav question. His Panslav ideology would be much influenced by Fadeev and Aksakov.

Early in 1862, as fighting waned in the Caucasus, Cherniaev sought transfer to an active post. A letter suggesting personal friction with his superiors, referred vaguely to his "indeterminate status." "I do not satisfy the conditions required of a staff officer here," he complained.[21]

That spring A. P. Bezak, governor general of Orenburg, visited the capital in his search for a new chief of staff. Bezak, a short man with an elaborately curled wig, created a poor impression with his severe exterior and abrupt speech, but he knew his job well. Hearing favorable comments about Cherniaev,[22] Bezak ar-

19. Bariatinskii to Alexander ii, cited in Rieber, pp. 90–91.
20. GIM, ed. khr. 30, ll. 1–2, "Po poluchenii pervogo No. 'Dnia' vo Vladikavkaze v 1861 g."
21. Ibid., ed. khr. 13, l. 34, [Cherniaev] to Prince Dmitrii Ivanovich [Mirskii?], n.d.
22. Zalesov, RS (July 1903), pp. 34–35. Probably Ignatiev and V. A. Poltoratskii, his

ranged his appointment. N. G. Zalesov, knowing both men, feared they would quarrel.

In midsummer Cherniaev reached Orenburg. Zalesov, who knew him from the Academy, warned that Bezak was abrupt and autocratic. The governor arrived from his *dacha* and greeted Cherniaev warmly: "I am entrusting you as my closest colleague with the entire military side. Do what you wish, but please report it to me. For me personally civil affairs will be plenty." Cherniaev had wide latitude, but his impatience and hypersensitivity ruined matters. Within a month the first crisis arose over inadequate food supplies in the steppe forts. Cherniaev, reproached by Bezak, blamed Levkovich, the chief of commissariat. Zalesov considered this unfair, but Bezak backed Cherniaev and Levkovich resigned in disgrace.

That fall their relations worsened during Bezak's feud with V. V. Grigoriev, who was in charge of native affairs. Distrusting influential subordinates, Bezak investigated the independent Grigoriev's department and complained to Petersburg. Bezak demanded that Grigoriev and Cherniaev, who had been friends since the latter's previous service in Orenburg, sever relations, but Cherniaev refused. Bezak went to Petersburg, saw the emperor, and had Grigoriev removed. Afterward Cherniaev and Bezak patched up their differences and Cherniaev remained chief of staff, but Bezak, still suspicious of him, arranged for him to command a reconnaissance expedition the following spring.[23]

Local commanders and governors, dissatisfied at the slow Russian advance, were flooding Petersburg with proposals on Central Asian policy. In November 1861 Bezak had recommended a campaign from Orenburg and western Siberia to "join the lines" and conquer Tashkent.[24] General E. P. Kovalevskii urged bringing the nomads of western Siberia and Orenburg under a steppe governor generalship at Tashkent. In St. Petersburg a special committee discussed these suggestions with the emperor.[25]

---

comrades from the Academy, had praised Cherniaev.

23. Ibid., pp. 30–36.

24. Bezak argued that expanding to Tashkent would: (1) give Russia an excellent frontier; (2) facilitate local support of Russian forces; (3) acquire fuel supplies for the Aral Flotilla; (4) end Kokanese raids; (5) give Russia vital lead ore; (6) give Russia decisive influence over the khanates; and (7) meet all expenses of the Syr-Daria Line from Tashkent's tax revenues.

25. L. Kostenko, *Sredniaia Aziia i vodvorenie v nei russkoi grazhdanstvennosti* (St. Petersburg, 1871), pp. 149–154.

There were now convincing reasons for the government to respond to impatient diplomats and generals. The prospect of sizable, inexpensive gains in Central Asia tempted a regime anxious to restore its shaken prestige and prove Russia's equality with the western powers. The burdensome Caucasus war was over. Though less susceptible than his father to the blandishments of military glory, Alexander II found expansion pleasurable so long as it was successful and cheap.

Expansion appealed to merchants and textile manufacturers from the central industrial provinces who found it difficult to compete with advanced European countries in western markets. Unwilling to risk precious capital in the khanates without government protection, they pressed the authorities to provide security and promote trade with the east. The disruption of American exports during the Civil War produced a world shortage of raw cotton. Prospects of abundant cotton from Turkestan and Bukhara attracted Russian manufacturers hard pressed to meet burgeoning domestic demand. Only direct Russian control over Central Asia, some believed, would insure access to these supplies and provide security for their commerce.[26]

In 1862 preparatory moves were initiated. The Syr-Daria corps occupied a small fort beyond Ian-Kurgan, and Colonel N. A. Verevkin, an energetic young officer, assumed command of the line. From Siberia, Colonel Kolpakovskii captured the Kokanese fortress of Pishpek.[27] In February 1863 a special committee of ministers advocated closing the remaining gap. The finance minister advised delay. The governor generals disagreed: Bezak of Orenburg favored action, Diugamel of western Siberia opposed it. Finally St. Petersburg authorized reconnaissance operations between the Syr-Daria and west Siberian lines.[28] This decision was implemented swiftly. On March 5 Bezak ordered Cherniaev to take a Cossack detachment to assist Admiral Butakov's flotilla in the exploration of the upper Syr. "We were both instructed to display the greatest peaceableness," recalled Butakov, "and use arms only in case of extreme necessity." But Cherniaev was unleashed.

Leading his Cossacks through late winter snow, then under the

26. M. K. Rozhkova, *Ekonomicheskie sviazi Rossii so Srednei Azii 40–60–e gody XIX veka* (Moscow, 1963), pp. 143 ff.; Khalfin, *Prisoedinenie*, pp. 139–146; A. L. Popov, "Iz istorii zavoevanii Srednei Azii," *Istoricheskie zapiski*, ix (1940), 209.

27. ORBL, Miliutin, "Moi starcheskie vospominaniia" (1862), ll. 96–97.

28. Kostenko, p. 154; Khalfin, *Prisoedinenie*, pp. 147–148.

broiling desert sun, Cherniaev advanced right to Turkestan city
without meeting Kokanese resistance. He charted the region from
Dzhulek to Turkestan, then crossed the Karatau Mountains. On
May 30, as he approached the Kokanese fortress of Suzak his vanguard was fired upon. When the youthful Russian commander ordered Suzak bombarded in retaliation, the terrified garrison surrendered. Entering the town in triumph, Cherniaev promised the city
elders Russian protection. He captured Chulak-kurgan on June 8,
and part of the Bishtamgalingan tribe requested Russian rule. Back
in Orenburg he asserted that the rich lands around Suzak could
support the entire Syr-Daria Line and Aral Flotilla. Sixty thousand
native households were clamoring for Russian rule.[29]

Cherniaev's aggressive expedition alarmed his immediate superiors. Bezak pointedly dissociated himself from his unauthorized exploits and Colonel Verevkin objected: "Suzak's conquest . . . would
be wonderful, but I fear it might lead to unpleasant queries from St.
Petersburg and cause a furor in the political world. At present,
because of our tense relations with England, they [Russian leaders]
fear to provide the English with pretexts for dissatisfaction."[30]

They had misread the signs. Colonel V. A. Poltoratskii,
Cherniaev's friend who headed the General Staff's Asian section,
rejoiced: "Generally your stock stands very high here. We expect
that you and the others will get rewards."[31] Russia's position had
changed: its brutal suppression of the Polish Insurrection brought
western protests and ended a Franco-Russian entente. Worsening
relations with England caused the war minister to welcome
Cherniaev's bold action. Summoning Zalesov to Petersburg, Miliutin sketched the situation: "In case of war we cannot harm England
in Europe; there remains only Asia. You know that area and can
assist us should it become necessary to arrange an expedition . . . ,
if not for an invasion of India, then at least to draw off English
strength from Europe and cause their commercial interests as much
harm as possible." If war came with England, confided Ignatiev,
director of the Asiatic Department, a detachment from Orenburg
under Cherniaev would advance up the Amu to Kabul and meet

29. "Iz arkhiva Bariatinskogo," RA (1889), no. 3, pp. 136–137, A. I. Butakov to Bariatinskii, September 1864; M. A. Terentiev, *Istoriia zavoevaniia Srednei Azii*, 3 vols. (St. Petersburg,
1906), I: 274.

30. Khalfin, *Prisoedinenie*, pp. 148–150.

31. GIM, ed. khr. 49, ll. 8–11, Poltoratskii to Cherniaev, 14 August 1863.

another from the Caucasus. However, the western powers confined their intervention in Poland to oral protests, and the plan was dropped.[32]

Cherniaev's Suzak venture by a small, hand-picked force requiring little expenditure became the model for further expansion in Central Asia. On August 1, 1863, the war and foreign ministries agreed to join the steppe lines to simplify frontier administration and increase "commercial and political benefits to the Russian empire." Dismissing Diugamel's objections, Ignatiev noted that had the west Siberian detachment advanced like Cherniaev's, the lines would be joined already. Disorder in Kokand, argued Ignatiev, justified Russian occupation of the Suzak-Aulie-Ata line. Unless prompt action were taken, the task would have to be achieved later under worse circumstances.

Cherniaev supported Ignatiev enthusiastically. From Orenburg he sent the war ministry a memorandum which emphasized the vital national significance of uniting the steppe lines and deplored obstacles thrown up by local governor generals. The government must act promptly and resolutely and end "negotiations and meetings which have been continuing uselessly for fifteen years."[33] A quarrel with Governor Bezak almost prevented his directing the line-closing operation. Bezak's instructions during the Suzak expedition, he complained, had hamstrung him. "I promised the foreign minister," retorted Bezak, "not to start hostilities in Central Asia during tension with the western powers." Cherniaev's disregard for instructions had discredited Bezak with the tsar. Zalesov sought to calm the two strong-willed men.

When Cherniaev came to see the governor, Zalesov was also in the waiting room. As the two men entered his office, Bezak came to Cherniaev, seized his hands, and burst into tears. (Zalesov: "I had not expected that sort of comedy.") "Don't be angry, my dear Mikhail Grigorevich," pleaded Bezak. "I could act no differently in that [Suzak] affair." He continued pompously, "I am a statesman and must act in the interest of all Russia." Cherniaev replied coldly and they parted enemies. Cherniaev tarried awhile vainly awaiting Poltoratskii's assistance, then went to St. Petersburg without requesting permission.[34]

32. Zalesov, RS, CXV (Aug. 1903), 322–326.
33. Khalfin, *Prisoedinenie*, pp. 150–151, "O soedinenii granits Orenburga i Sibiri."
34. Zalesov (pp. 326–328), a sober, responsible officer, witnessed the interview and there

Cherniaev sensed that the government favored his aspirations. The influential Ignatiev considered him the perfect instrument for expansion. Temporarily though, noted Antonina, Cherniaev "found himself in a very difficult position." He threatened to go to remote Vologda province as an arbiter of the peace, but this was probably a ruse. Behind the scenes Ignatiev and Poltoratskii worked for him. In February 1864 the war minister appointed him commander of the west Siberian detachment to join the lines.[35] His pressure tactics had succeeded.

Cherniaev's reconnaissance of Suzak triggered a rapid Russian advance in Central Asia. His bold methods appealed to Ignatiev and did not yet alarm the war or foreign ministries. Later, Mikhail Grigorevich recalled proudly that as a mere colonel he had helped to shape a government decision bringing a major increase in Russia's imperial domain.

---

is no reason to question his account. Antonina attributed the quarrel to Bezak's unfair treatment of the Bashkirs, concealed Cherniaev's responsibility for it and his tactics to obtain his own way: iisg, "Biografiia," p. 122.

35. Miliutin requested Governor Diugamel, 12 January 1864, to entrust this command to Cherniaev, "a very capable and experienced staff officer." Diugamel was happy to comply. turk krai, xvii: 7.

Military operations in the conquest of Turkestan com-
prise many glorious pages in the records of our fighting
past . . . demonstrating brilliantly how one can achieve
tremendous results with insignificant resources. . . .
(*Turkestanskii krai*, xvii, iii)

CHAPTER III

The Campaign of 1864

MILIUTIN had decided to utilize Cherniaev to join the steppe lines.
The war minister and Ignatiev dispelled Foreign Office fears that the
British might object. Unruly Russian governors and commanders
often promoted conflict, admitted Miliutin, but advances against
semiwild Asian tribes were inevitable.[1] Russia would win prestige
without having to fight a major power.

Russian leaders disagreed about policy toward the Central Asian
khanates. Ignatiev's faction, fearing delay might create a new Caucasus problem, urged their speedy conquest. Gorchakov's group,
including P. N. Stremoukhov, who succeeded Ignatiev late in 1864,
favored normal diplomacy.[2] They reached a compromise. When the
Syr-Daria and west Siberian lines had been linked, a temporary
frontier would run along the northern slopes of the Karatau Mountains. Later, but not in 1864, it might be advanced to the Arys River
from Aulie-Ata through Chimkent.[3]

On February 9, 1864, Miliutin ordered Cherniaev to Omsk to
command the west Siberian detachment. "Relying fully upon your
ability and zeal, I am confident that you will do your utmost to

1. ORBL, Miliutin, k. 15, no. 1, ll. 119 reverse-121.
2. D. I. Romanovskii, *Zametki po sredne-aziatskomu voprosu* (St. Petersburg, 1868), p. 29.
3. TURK KRAI, XVII: 4, Miliutin to Gorchakov, 9 January 1864.

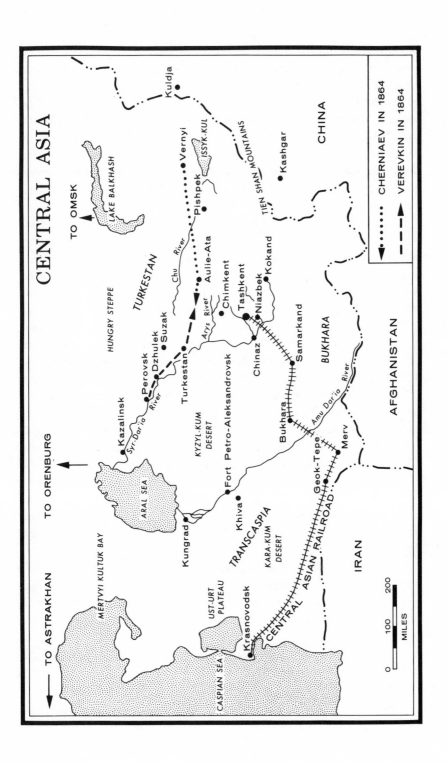

CENTRAL ASIA

TO OMSK

TO ORENBURG

TO ASTRAKHAN

LAKE BALKHASH

Kuldja

Vernyi
Pishpek
ISSYK-KUL

TIEN SHAN MOUNTAINS

CHINA

Kashgar

TURKESTAN

HUNGRY STEPPE

Chu River

Aulie-Ata

Chimkent

Arys River

Tashkent
Niazbek
Kokand

Suzak
Dzhulek
Perovsk

Chinaz

Samarkand

BUKHARA

Turkestan

Kazalinsk

Syr-Daria River

KYZYL-KUM
DESERT

Fort Petro-Aleksandrovsk

Amu Daria River

Bukhara

Merv

AFGHANISTAN

ARAL SEA

Khiva

Geok-Tepe

MERTVYI KULTUK BAY

Kungrad

TRANSCASPIA

KARA-KUM
DESERT

CENTRAL ASIAN RAILROAD

IRAN

UST-URT
PLATEAU

Krasnovodsk

CASPIAN SEA

0   100   200
MILES

CHERNIAEV IN 1864
VEREVKIN IN 1864

execute the important task assigned to you. . . ."[4] Unexpended west Siberian funds were to finance the campaign. To the war minister's dismay only one hundred fifty thousand rubles could be gathered. Cherniaev declared that this would be enough if he could allocate money at will; Miliutin consented.[5] In Omsk, the west Siberian capital, Cherniaev received instructions to occupy Aulie-Ata and refortify it. "With your experience in equipping troops for campaigns and investigating the steppe," wrote Governor Diugamel hopefully, "you should be able to make considerable savings."[6]

Led by the bellicose Kipchak tribe, the Kokanese prepared for war. Alimkul, an able commander, served as regent for the twelve-year-old khan. He inspected vulnerable cities, appointed new governors, and extorted tribute from the nomads. Alimkul promised rewards to tribesmen who would fight,[7] mobilized the Kokanese troops, and tried to create cohesion out of chaos.

In Vernyi Cherniaev assumed his first major command. Colonel Kolpakovskii, Vernyi's commander, proved cooperative, but Mikhail Grigorevich found his men uncertain in discipline, low in morale, and equipped with obsolescent rifles. The horsedrawn artillery, consigned to Siberia in 1815, could operate only against an inferior foe. The Siberian infantry's fighting qualities were high, but Cherniaev recalled, "Before we left Colonel Kolpakovskii warned me that they were all drunk, but that I should not worry . . . and truly on the first march only a tenth of the detachment reached camp, and the other nine-tenths lay along the road. Afterwards I soon brought them around." At first the Siberian Cossack cavalry "took refuge behind the infantry," but the Ural and Orenburg Cossacks who joined him later were most dependable.[8]

Late in April Cherniaev's detachment of some 2,500 men, 447 horses and 4,000 camels left Vernyi. Somewhat later Colonel Verevkin's smaller force moved eastward from the Syr-Daria Line.[9] There was no unified command: the two forces were

4. Ibid., p. 50, Miliutin to Cherniaev, 9 February 1864.

5. Ibid., pp. 5, 45–48, 50, 55, Miliutin to Diugamel, 11 January 1864; 9, 13 February 1864.

6. Ibid., pp. 81–86, Diugamel to Cherniaev, 12 March 1864.

7. Terentiev, *Istoriia*, I: 274–275; Khalfin, *Prisoedinenie*, p. 154.

8. "Dvadtsatipiatiletie," pp. 217–219.

9. Romanovskii, *Zametki*, appendix, pp. 135–136. A. I. Maksheev's *Istoricheskii obzor Turkestana* (St. Petersburg, 1890), p. 219, listed 2,571 men, 789 horses, and 3,981 camels. Verevkin

subordinated respectively to Omsk and Orenburg separated by one thousand miles of steppe. Coordination would prove difficult.

On June 2 Cherniaev approached Aulie-Ata on the Talas River. When his vanguard moved against strategic heights overlooking the town, the Kokanese abandoned them.[10] Wishing to spare the city, Mikhail Grigorevich wrote its *bek*, Niaz Ali: "At the Great Emperor's will I have come with my detachment to occupy Aulie-Ata. Surrender the fortress or suffer Pishpek's fate . . . [bombarded and captured by the Russians in 1862]. In the name of my sovereign, I pledge to spare the lives and property of all Kokanese subjects in the fortress and give them their freedom if the fortress is yielded without firing. My troops' temporary occupation of Suzak and Chulak last year proves my word can be trusted."[11] Niaz requested two weeks' time, but Cherniaev demanded immediate surrender.

Disdaining Central Asian forts as "clay flowerpots," he believed they should be stormed after a brief bombardment. A reconnaissance revealed that Aulie-Ata's artillery was poor and its walls on the west were low. Orchards and gardens would screen a Russian approach.

On June 4, concealing his intent to assault Aulie-Ata, Cherniaev crossed the Talas and bombarded the walls at close range. The Kokanese replied ineffectively. Cherniaev calculated that the driving rain would hamper the enemy infantry's fire. Driving the Kokanese from positions before the walls, his men pursued them into the town through breaches in the walls. The demoralized enemy fell in droves. In two hours the city, fortress, and citadel were captured. Over three hundred enemy dead lay in the streets; only three Russians had been slightly wounded. "Such an easy success," reported Cherniaev, "can be attributed to the unusually successful action of our artillery and the infantry's precipitous attack."[12] Actually, the primitive Kokanese were no match in armament or discipline for Russian regulars.

Aulie-Ata, noted Cherniaev, "comprised the final goal set this year for the detachment." At the intersection of trade routes from

---

had five infantry companies, 200 Cossacks, 44 officers and 1,593 men.

10. Romanovskii, appendix, pp. 137–138, Cherniaev to [Diugamel], 6 June 1864.

11. TURK KRAI, XVIII: 293, June 1864.

12. Romanovskii, appendix, pp. 138–139; Maksheev, pp. 219–220. A highly inaccurate account of this operation, probably from Kokanese sources, is in M. A. Khan, *England, Russia and Central Asia, 1857–1878* (Peshawar, 1963), p. 41, asserting that 1600 Kokanese and 500 Russians died at Aulie-Ata.

Tashkent, and Kokand, it was important commercially and militarily. The region's wealth, he predicted, would more than cover the expedition's cost and caravans would now be secure.[13]

Meanwhile Verevkin was advancing from the west. St. Petersburg authorized him to seize Turkestan city as an administrative center for the steppe lines.[14] Requesting Cherniaev's aid to capture it, he noted, "Your resources are considerably greater than mine."[15] But Cherniaev replied that he could do nothing until his camels returned with provisions. Immediate action on his part "could only help if you suffered a severe setback. I certainly do not anticipate this knowing you personally and convinced that you will undertake nothing incommensurate with your resources." Later they could meet at Chulak. Indeed, Verevkin, aided by popular dissatisfaction with an oppressive local ruler, captured Turkestan on June 12,[16] but Cherniaev's refusal of aid ignited a bitter feud between the two men.

By late June they had joined the lines and achieved the campaign's stated purpose. St. Petersburg rejoiced at an inexpensive victory and promoted both commanders to major general. But much good campaigning weather remained. Cherniaev now embarked upon a reckless, independent course which brought him fame but led ultimately to disaster. His appetite for conquest had merely been whetted. Russia possessed an unbroken Central Asian defense line, but while Kokand retained the fortress of Chimkent, communications between Aulie-Ata and Turkestan remained precarious. Why not achieve the government's maximum plan immediately by moving the frontier to the Arys River? Poor communications with Omsk and Orenburg encouraged him to pursue his own policy.

His deteriorating relations with Verevkin revealed the danger of a divided frontier command. Verevkin complained that Cherniaev's failure to meet him at Chulak required him to make long, superfluous marches. Cherniaev claimed that Kokanese activity and the dispersal of his forces had prevented his meeting Verevkin's subordinate Captain Meier there. Mikhail Grigorevich announced that he would advance to Chimkent and establish an Arys frontier. According to his scouts' reports, eight thousand Kokanese troops were

---

13. IISG, ed. khr. 17, Cherniaev to his parents in Berdiansk, 29 June 1864.
14. TURK KRAI, XVII: 97–98, Bezak to Miliutin, 4 April 1864.
15. Ibid., pp. 127–128, Verevkin to Cherniaev, 25 May 1864.
16. Ibid., pp. 156–157, Cherniaev to Verevkin, 11 June 1864; Khalfin, p. 156.

around Chimkent. He requested Verevkin to send men to join his offensive.[17]

Verevkin's reply was rude and negative: only six hundred Kokanese were at Chimkent; there were no enemy concentrations to disperse. If Cherniaev wished to occupy Chimkent, he could do it alone. Without orders from Orenburg Verevkin refused to garrison a city outside the Syr-Daria region. He added facetiously that his men must build winter quarters and cut hay for the horses.[18] Cherniaev was repaid in kind.

Despite Verevkin's refusal to help, Cherniaev advanced with fourteen hundred men and informed his superior, General Diugamel, that Kokand was preparing a holy war against Russia. Kokanese religious leaders were exploiting the Russian capture of Turkestan city to arouse Moslem fanaticism. With some exaggeration he reported, "Because Kokanese concentrations grow daily our [native] population is losing confidence in us and has begun to adopt an ambiguous position, so I have decided to protect Aulie-Ata and nearby nomads by advancing toward Chimkent and operating there according to circumstances."[19] To await authorization, he argued, would risk disaster. He received Verevkin's refusal to cooperate at his camp on the upper Arys about sixty versts from Chimkent. Native scouts reported that there were ten thousand Kokanese troops in and around Chimkent.[20]

Mikhail Grigorevich's prediction of a holy war was coming true. A Kokanese source boasted with typical hyperbole that Regent Alimkul had raised fifty thousand men. Before leaving to fight, Alimkul prayed to Allah: "All powerful God, do not let your slave be downhearted. Many infidel troops have come. If there is no help from you, what shall I do? Infidels have seized my city and brought dishonor upon us. How shall we efface this insult? Your name be merciful . . . , give us help!"[21]

While Cherniaev tarried, Verevkin tried to forestall him by sending Captain Meier with three hundred men to seize Chimkent and

17. TURK KRAI, XVII: 203–204, Cherniaev to Verevkin, 2 July 1864; pp. 211–212, 4 July 1864.

18. Ibid., pp. 143–144, Verevkin to Cherniaev, misdated 2 June 1864; Terentiev, *Istoriia*, I: 283–284.

19. TURK KRAI, XVII: 213–214, Cherniaev to Diugamel, 6 July 1864.

20. M. G. Cherniaev, "Sultan Kenesary i Sadyk," RV, CCIII (Aug. 1889), p. 35; TURK KRAI, XVII: 225, Cherniaev to Verevkin, 10 July 1864.

21. N. I. Veselovskii, *Kirgizskii rasskaz o russkikh zavoevaniiakh v turkestanskom krae* (St. Petersburg, 1894), pp. 11–12.

garner laurels for Orenburg. Informing Cherniaev that he would meet him on the Arys, Meier instead rushed headlong toward Chimkent. On July 13, while camped in an exposed hollow at Akbulak, he was surrounded by Alimkul who mounted artillery on the heights and bombarded his force.[22] Two days later Cherniaev learned of this and managed to rescue Meier.

Alimkul sent peace overtures, but Cherniaev replied that hostilities could be halted only on Russia's terms. Alimkul told Cherniaev's delegate that Meier had been released from encirclement after promising that Russia would return captured cities to Kokand. Cherniaev rejected this interpretation and when Alimkul again demanded that the cities be returned, he ordered the Kokanese envoy out of camp immediately, and negotiations were broken off.[23]

Meanwhile Petersburg had strengthened Cherniaev's authority. On July 9 Poltoratskii proposed creating an advance line under Orenburg to deal with the khanates. To achieve frontier unity, the war minister placed Cherniaev in charge of this "New Kokand Line" and subordinated Verevkin to his command.[24]

Cherniaev conducted his "reconnaissance" of Chimkent July 19–22 without knowing this. To withdraw without giving battle would encourage Kokanese attacks. "Therefore I resolved to advance to Chimkent's walls, draw them [Kokanese] into the field and defeat them." As Cherniaev approached the city, masses of Kokanese cavalry appeared. When they stayed out of range, the Russians drew closer and exchanged fire with the enemy artillery. Kokanese cavalry, uttering terrible screeches, charged the square Russian formation. Whoever has not been attacked by an Asian horde, related Cherniaev, cannot imagine the effect of these inhuman cries on the nerves. Russian artillery, grenades, and rifle fire repelled the assault. Hundreds of Kokanese dead lay scattered about while the Russians had three men slightly wounded. This revealed again the vast disparity in the firepower and discipline of the two armies.[25]

At Chimkent, affirmed a Kokanese account, hordes of Russians

---

22. Terentiev, *Istoriia*, i: 286–287.

23. RT, appendix, pp. 66–68, Cherniaev to [Diugamel], no. 577; Terentiev, i: 288–290; Cherniaev, "Sultany," pp. 36–38.

24. TURK KRAI, XVII: 218–220, 228, Poltoratskii's memorandum and Miliutin to Diugamel, 12 July 1864; XVIII: 239–240, 18 July 1864, tgr.; ORBL, Miliutin, k. 15, no. 1, l. 122.

25. Cherniaev, "Sultany," pp. 28 ff.; Cherniaev reported on 8 August that the Kokanese lost 400 men in this battle and almost 3,000 during his Chimkent operations. RT, appendix, pp. 68–69.

attacked them from Aulie-Ata. The valiant Alimkul exhorted his troops: "Moslems be not afraid! You are firm in your faith. Do not grieve, true believers. God will mourn for us. . . . If you died or are killed, you will die only once and you cannot escape it. Be courageous. . . . Do not fear death and rely on God."[26] Accompanied by shouts and martial music, the Kokanese advanced but could not defeat the infidels.

Cherniaev, after three days at Chimkent, realized that an assault would be foolhardy and retired to Aulie-Ata. Lack of food and fodder would soon force the huge enemy concentrations to disperse.[27] But the Chimkent venture was not the unqualified success Cherniaev claimed. Central Asians considered all reconnaissances to be repelled assaults and celebrated victory afterward. Thus some Russian officers preferred examining enemy defenses quietly with a few men.[28]

The Kokanese then slaughtered pro-Russian residents of Chimkent. Baizak, an old man, whose relatives had joined the Russian army, was labeled a spy and shot from a cannon. Such barbarity boomeranged: many Uzbeks sought Russian protection and clamored to aid Cherniaev. He permitted those with arms to join him. The others protested that they could help by shouting at the enemy.[29]

Soon Alimkul left Chimkent to repel a Bukharan invasion of Kokand. A sizable garrison remained, but Cherniaev grasped his opportunity. "I consider it a vital necessity to seize Chimkent," he wrote Verevkin, "to deliver a decisive blow to the remaining Kokanese troops so they cannot serve as a nucleus for new concentrations." Cherniaev ordered him to send infantry and Cossacks toward Chimkent.[30]

Cherniaev asked Colonel Poltoratskii to forward his letters to the war minister. For capturing Aulie-Ata, he complained, he and his men had not been adequately rewarded. More generous recompense was needed to attract able officers "in case it is proposed to keep me [in command] here." He demanded full authority over troops in Turkestan city. With Kokand in turmoil, "now is the most conveni-

26. Veselovskii, pp. 12 ff.
27. Cherniaev, "Sultany," pp. 38–39.
28. Terentiev, I: 291.
29. TURK KRAI, XVIII: 114–115, Cherniaev to Poltoratskii, 20 August 1864.
30. Ibid., pp. 28–30, Cherniaev to Verevkin, 11 August 1864.

ent time to deal them the final blow, then we will become masters of the occupied region." The Arys line must be secured: "Taking into account that Chimkent's seizure before winter is not only beneficial but essential for the region's peace and considering it awkward to reject overtures by natives regarding us as their defenders against the Kokanese, I have decided to conquer Chimkent on my own responsibility." Invariably he found good reasons to do precisely what he wished.

With customary impatience Cherniaev refused to await instructions from Omsk. Abandoning any pretense of defensive action, he advocated a decisive blow against Kokand khanate to put Tashkent at Russia's mercy. Foreign reactions need not be feared, he declared, since few Europeans even knew Chimkent's location. With Uzbek support, he wrote cynically, "we can dress ourselves in the clothing of defenders of an exploited people." That should be sufficient to justify Russia's actions to England. Delay would be dangerous. Kokanese artillery improved yearly. The khanate must be crushed before it received European technology. Once Chimkent had been taken, he could hold on until spring with existing forces; later he would require four more infantry companies and some Cossacks.[31]

The letters to Poltoratskii revealed increasing assertiveness and confidence in his imperial mission. He questioned Petersburg's past decisions and struck out on his own. Cherniaev's actions, scarcely affected by economic considerations, were dictated mainly by ambition and desire for conquest.

He hastened to Turkestan, collected most of Verevkin's troops, then departed for Chimkent on September 12 with about seventeen hundred men. Lieutenant Colonel Lerkhe, his subordinate, joined him with a smaller force from Aulie-Ata. Probing the defenses of Chimkent, a small walled city, Cherniaev moved up artillery, but hard ground and an enemy sortie delayed the emplacement of Russian batteries until the next day. After the Kokanese moved artillery into a long trench opposite the Russian trenches, Lerkhe requested permission to attack. Cherniaev consented and approached the citadel at one corner of the city wall with his own force. Lerkhe's precipitate assault caused the enemy to panic, and his men followed them into the town and swiftly captured it.

The citadel, built on a lofty height, seemed inaccessible from

31. Ibid., pp. 111–116, Cherniaev to Poltoratskii, 18, 20 August 1864.

without. The only external access was through a waterpipe a yard wide and sixty feet long. Cherniaev plunged into the pipe, bending double to get through the arched passage in the wall, and his men rushed after him. His act of reckless courage succeeded. The citadel's defenders, dumbfounded by the sudden appearance of the Russians, leaped to their deaths, were cut down, or fled along the Tashkent road. Reporting this victory Cherniaev boasted that his small force had overcome a fortress city manned by ten thousand Kokanese regulars. To assure maximum rewards for himself and his men he exaggerated the region's population and resources.[32]

The Kokanese, rationalizing a shattering defeat, vastly inflated the Russians' numbers and glorified Cherniaev. "Look at the numerous infidels! They come like a thundercloud . . . and Cherniaev is clearly a hero," affirmed one account. "Even lions grow rigid with fear unable to withstand his terrible mien and truly heroic onslaught. Seducing men with his strength, he was called Shirnaib [representative of lions]. . . . The Russians gathered infidel warriors from the entire world. The Russian troops are countless, never tire, and come in masses and masses."[33]

Cherniaev's complaints about insufficient rewards for the capture of Aulie-Ata irritated the war minister and presaged trouble between them: "He [Cherniaev] has neither the right nor cause to complain about inadequate rewards which I consider wholly adequate since they were assigned by the emperor. . . . In any case it was unseemly and inappropriate for General Cherniaev to express his dissatisfaction even in a private letter since it was for transmission to the war minister." Poor communications made it difficult to control the general, but Miliutin telegraphed Governor Diugamel: "Hasten to instruct him in no case . . . to go further than was proposed."[34]

However, St. Petersburg and Omsk responded enthusiastically to Chimkent's capture. Calling it "a glorious affair," the emperor awarded Cherniaev the Saint George's Cross third class and promoted his chief subordinates.[35] Rejoiced General Diugamel: "Indeed it pleases me exceedingly that in higher governmental circles they

32. RT, appendix, p. 73, Cherniaev to Diugamel, 25 September 1864.
33. Veselovskii, pp. 35–36.
34. TURK KRAI, XVIII: 116–117, Miliutin comment of 29 September 1864; p. 117, Miliutin to Diugamel, 30 September 1864. Later, Miliutin agreed that Chimkent's occupation safeguarded Russian communications. ORBL, Miliutin, k. 15, no. 1, ll. 124–125.
35. TURK KRAI, XVIII: 139, 159.

appreciate the glorious exploit achieved by our troops and that the labors borne by your brave associates has not gone without deserved compensation."[36] Congratulating his friend, Poltoratskii wrote that his feat had "brilliantly dispelled all doubts and fears here. . . ." But Miliutin had misgivings: "Fine, but who will guarantee that after Chimkent Cherniaev won't consider it necessary to take Tashkent, then Kokand, and there will be no end to it."[37] His words were prophetic.

The government debated where to set the boundary and whether to advance into the heavily populated Central Asian oases. Some leaders wished to halt at Chimkent although that small oasis, surrounded by steppe, could not satisfy Russian administrative or military needs. Only sixty miles southeast lay rich Chirchik oasis with the great commercial entrepot of Tashkent which could supply essential food and tax revenues. As Cherniaev and the emir of Bukhara both coveted Tashkent, a collision there was likely.

Why did Cherniaev advance beyond Chimkent? Controlling trade routes and securing markets were secondary for him. By seizing Chimkent he had gained renown in Central Asia and support at home. Insatiable ambition spurred him now to take excessive risks with his small forces. From Chimkent, in a new *fait accompli*, he informed Diugamel on September 25 that he was advancing on Tashkent "not to occupy it, but if circumstances prove favorable, to forestall the plans of the emir of Bukhara" and enable St. Petersburg to "deal with this populous, commercial city at its discretion." The operation would take two weeks.[38]

Later Cherniaev sought to justify his sudden move. When Chimkent fell, vague and contradictory rumors had circulated of Tashkent's secret dealings with the emir. A reconnaissance was essential "to clarify matters and the enemy's remaining resources." Many Tashkent residents desired Russian protection, but since his troops were few, he had not intended to capture the city. "I thought it possible to exploit the Chimkent defeat . . . , drive the Kokanese garrison from Tashkent," then leave the administration to its inhabitants.[39] Tashkent was a target of opportunity which might bring him a princely title.

---

36. Ibid., 123–124, Diugamel to Miliutin, 5 October 1864; GIM, ed. khr. 6, ll. 25–26, Diugamel to Cherniaev, 2 November 1864.

37. Ibid., ed. khr. 49, Poltoratskii to Cherniaev, 22 October 1864.

38. TURK KRAI, XVIII: 142–143, Cherniaev to Diugamel, 25 September 1864.

39. RT, appendix, p. 73, Cherniaev to Diugamel, 14 October 1864.

Despite his colleagues' clear warnings, Cherniaev sought to impose new obligations on his government. Poltoratskii, knowing that Miliutin opposed further advances in 1864, had urged him to remain on the Arys. But since August Cherniaev had wished to restore Tashkent as a vassal khanate. When General Kachalov, his chief of artillery, warned that Tashkent could not be assaulted with a thousand men, Cherniaev denied he intended to do so.[40]

On September 27 his fifteen-hundred-man detachment left for Tashkent. En route Cherniaev learned that a Kokanese garrison was in firm control of the town and had barred his envoys. On October 1 the Russians halted at the city's southeast corner. After a bombardment the next day, Lieutenant Colonel Obukh investigated the results. Deceived by a hillock, he reported that the wall had been breached and proposed an assault. Relying upon Obukh's experience and judgment, Cherniaev sent him reinforcements and the reply: "If it is possible, then God be with you," and advanced to support him. When Obukh and Lerkhe reached the moat, they found that the Kokanese had removed the drawbridge and repaired the wall. Obukh was mortally wounded and Lerkhe suffered serious injuries. Deprived of their top officers and unable to scale the wall, the troops took cover and began to fire back. "Approaching with my two companies . . . and looking over the situation," reported Cherniaev, "I had to renounce an assault in view of its evident impossibility without siege works." The assault troops were withdrawn, but sixteen men were dead and sixty-two wounded. The troops longed for another assault, but Cherniaev realized that "to risk the only reserve of the entire region in a new attack would mean placing at stake the very security of the New Kokand Line."[41] During the retreat officers and men were gloomy. The glory of Russian arms had been dimmed. Cherniaev expected to be removed.[42]

Neither Omsk nor St. Petersburg learned officially of this reverse until later. Did Cherniaev conceal it deliberately? His com-

40. Khalfin, *Prisoedinenie*, p. 160. Terentiev (I: 295), defending Cherniaev's expedition, argued that the pro-Russian faction in Tashkent appeared to constitute the vast majority of the population.

41. RT, appendix, pp. 74–76, Cherniaev to Diugamel, 14 October 1864.

42. K. Abaza, *Zavoevanie Turkestana*, p. 85; "Dvadtsatipiatiletie," p. 225.

plete report dated October 14 finally arrived in Omsk on November 22; his summary which reached Diugamel October 23 merely stated Russian losses and confirmed the detachment's safe return.[43] Only on December 1 could Miliutin send Cherniaev's full report to the emperor who commented, "I greatly regret that he decided upon a useless assault costing us so many men."[44]

General Diugamel deplored this delay since the war minister might believe that he wished to conceal the true situation. The Tashkent operation, he asserted, had been foolish. How could a reconnaissance become an assault on a fortified city whose conquest had not been authorized? "The latest unfortunate incident has ruined everything and produced a very unfavorable impression in St. Petersburg." He ordered Cherniaev to report everything occurring on the forward line.

Cherniaev replied defensively that his full report had been sent promptly. The expedition had been launched "not to reap new laurels but to consolidate finally and introduce complete calm in the Trans-Chu region whose acquisition is indissolubly linked with my name." He had sought to prevent the enemy from maintaining fifteen thousand cavalry only sixty miles from Chimkent. Then Cherniaev's bravado deserted him: "Continual worry, uninterrupted work with very few assistants and the difficult climate have undermined my health and compel me to request Your Excellency to nominate a successor."[45] Actually, the brief march to Tashkent had not wrecked his health nor were his administrative responsibilities heavy. It had not been necessary to attack Tashkent. He worried because he had deliberately disobeyed orders and concealed a defeat endangering the region's security. This suggested how brittle his courage and self-confidence were.

Cherniaev had overestimated his danger. The Tashkent affair, wrote Poltoratskii, had not made such a bad impression in the capital. But Miliutin was not deceived. When Poltoratskii remarked that Cherniaev had not tried to capture Tashkent, the war minister exclaimed, "Why else would one go there?" He ridiculed Cherniaev's

43. TURK KRAI, XVIII: 155–156, 23 October 1864, tgr.; p. 204, Kroierus to Miliutin, 23 November 1864.

44. Ibid., pp. 184, 221–222, Miliutin's memoranda and emperor's comment, 2 December 1864.

45. GIM, ed. khr. 6, ll. 27–28, Diugamel to Cherniaev, 12 November 1864; ll. 29–30, Cherniaev to Diugamel, 17 December 1864, draft.

"reconnaissance" camouflage. This setback, he feared, would deflate Russian prestige and embolden the enemy. Cherniaev had acted on his own initiative disregarding the most categorical instructions.[46] Nonetheless, the storm blew over leaving him only slightly damaged. Forgetting his plea to be relieved, Mikhail Grigorevich regained robust health.

Meanwhile St. Petersburg sought to clarify its policies, guide its commanders, and reassure London. Miliutin asked the foreign minister abruptly: now that Chimkent has fallen, what is your policy? Replied Gorchakov: to avoid further expansion, reduce expenditures, and protect Russian commerce. Hitherto, he explained, "despite our consistent reluctance to expand by conquest, our dominions under influence of our commerce's insistent demands and some kind of mysterious but irresistible attraction to the Orient have steadily advanced into the heart of the steppe." Russia had responded to "inexorable necessity." How could a civilized power act wholly peacefully toward neighboring half-wild tribes? Unless they elevated themselves to Russia's level, these tribes must be devoured as the United States had absorbed the Indians.

Where should Russia halt? The war ministry opposed stopping on the frontier achieved by closing the lines since it must then renounce Chimkent and confirm the Asian belief in Russia's weakness. Perhaps the Arys River line? The foreign ministry approved, but Miliutin, considering Chimkent vital to Russian security, preferred a border between it and Tashkent. Cherniaev, he believed, could delineate the precise boundary. Should Russia capture Tashkent and set up a vassal khanate there? Gorchakov objected that such a move would mean unlimited expansion and involve Russia in all Central Asian wars. To administer Tashkent would be difficult and expensive and would fatally antagonize the khanates.[47]

Gorchakov's instructions of October 31 stated that, if captured by Cherniaev, Tashkent must be evacuated after paying an indemnity. Other captured cities would not be returned, but "we have resolved firmly not to occupy additional lands." Russia desired peace: she wished friendship with Kokand, but any Kokanese attack would bring swift reprisal. Present Russian frontiers, insisted Gorchakov, must remain immobile. Unaware of Cherniaev's advance on Tash-

---

46. Khalfin, *Prisoedinenie*, p. 162; ORBL, Miliutin, k. 15, no. 1, ll. 125 ff.

47. TURK KRAI, XVIII: 159, Miliutin's memorandum, 27 October 1864; pp. 165–172, Gorchakov's report, 31 October 1864; pp. 182–183, memorandum of 9 November 1864.

kent, Miliutin reluctantly accepted this concept but warned that only Cherniaev could supply the information needed to establish stable frontiers. He would instruct him not to go beyond Chimkent in 1864.[48]

The war and foreign ministries' joint memorandum of November 20 declared that Russia had acquired territory "under the influence of temporary circumstances and the personal, sometimes one-sided views of local commanders." Eventually she must occupy Kokand and reach the Tien Shan Mountains and the Kyzyl-Kum Desert. But Khiva and Bukhara did not now threaten Russian security whereas marauding bands made Kokand a troublesome neighbor. Instead of seeking to incorporate Central Asia's settled population, Russia should halt at Chimkent, consolidate control of the steppe, and civilize its nomads. The emperor ordered these policies implemented.[49]

However, the two ministries did not agree fully. Reproached for condoning arbitrary actions by unruly subordinates, Miliutin recalled: "Demanding that local commanders observe instructions as far as possible, I felt it harmful to deprive them completely of independent initiative. Fear of punishment for every departure from instructions can destroy energy and enterprise. There are cases when a commander must act on his own responsibility, not as forseen in a plan drawn up earlier." From his own experience Miliutin realized that field commanders could not be effective if bound by rigid, detailed instructions.[50]

After the Tashkent venture, Cherniaev and N. A. Severtsov recommended a merger of the Syr-Daria Line and Trans-Chu region into a frontier province with its own administration and the creation of a separate Tashkent khanate. Turkestan region's great distance from Omsk and Orenburg and its proximity to hostile khanates required an independent authority responsible to the central government alone; otherwise, frontier authorities could not act promptly toward Asians who needed a decisive local power. Cherniaev warned prophetically: "If the local administration is not given sufficient power by law, it must, to

48. Ibid., pp. 246–250, "Proposals of the Foreign Ministry."

49. Ibid., pp. 196–201, report of war and foreign ministers to emperor, 20 November 1864.

50. ORBL, k. 15, no. 1, ll. 125–128. Khalfin (*Prisoedinenie*, pp. 160–167) suggests that cheap expansion satisfied the tsarist regime and helped it maintain firm control at home.

maintain itself, appropriate it in practice outside the law."[51] His appeal for independent authority contained an implied threat to seize it.

Reports from Tashkent convinced Cherniaev that the Kokanese would remain quiet. Alimkul had reinforced Tashkent to resist a possible second Russian attack. Overburdened by the large garrison, its inhabitants sought to turn the city over to Bukhara, but Alimkul crushed their insurrection ruthlessly.[52] Cherniaev, confident his area was now secure, assured Omsk that he needed no reinforcements until spring: "Alimkul's army because of insufficient food . . . has been almost completely dispersed. . . . The general condition of the region is wholly calm; not even small bands of Kokanese have shown themselves."[53] His intelligence service was faulty. Only a few miles away a small Cossack detachment was fighting Alimkul's entire army. On December 3, Turkestan's commander Colonel Zhemchuzhnikov, learning that a large Kokanese raiding party had been spotted on the Chimkent road some forty miles away, had sent a Ural Cossack *sotnia* under Captain Serov to discover the enemy's strength and intentions.

Approaching the village of Ikan toward dusk next day the Cossacks were surrounded by masses of Kokanese cavalry. Serov's well-disciplined men, reacting swiftly, repelled the enemy's assaults, and a courier managed to reach Turkestan with the news. Zhemchuzhnikov sent out a relief force under Lieutenant Sukorko which was instructed to return without relieving Serov if it met large enemy forces. When they encountered the Kokanese army, Sukorko, to his troops' disgust, insisted upon retreat. Serov's men, though discouraged by this, resisted as long as possible, then charged the enemy and broke through. Not daring approach closely, the Kokanese harried the Cossacks' painful retreat toward Turkestan. Famished and thirsty after two days of battle, the Russians finally reached Sukorko who had been dispatched again from Turkestan. The surviving Cossacks were borne on stretchers to the city. The Kokanese wreaked terrible vengeance on the dead and heavily wounded: Alimkul later pre-

51. GIM, ed. khr. 7, ll. 1–40, "Poiasnitelnaia zapiska."
52. TURK KRAI, XVIII: 160–161, Cherniaev to Miliutin, 27 October 1864.
53. Ibid., pp. 209, 224–225, Cherniaev to Diugamel, 30 November 1864, 6 December 1864.

sented forty Cossack heads to Iakub-beg, ruler of Kashgar. Fifty-six Russians had died; Saint George's crosses were awarded to the survivors.[54]

Cherniaev learned of this struggle too late to affect its outcome. After the Kokanese had retreated, he reported: "The battle at Ikan should in all justice rank among the most brilliant encounters ever fought in Central Asia. . . . But a handful of men, however brave and fearless, could not perform the impossible. . . . Almost all of them fell defending their position. . . . But if this handful succeeded not merely in holding back the 10,000 man horde but to inflict huge damage upon it, then had reinforcements arrived in time, there would have been a complete victory saving the sotnia from major loss."[55] Mikhail Grigorevich accused Sukorko of cowardice and turned him over to a military court, but higher authorities promoted him and decorated him for bravery! Cherniaev wrote the Orenburg governor: "I feel that legal vindication of Lieutenant Sukorko will never wash out the spot he acquired by his shameful conduct at Ikan. . . . I do not consider that I have the right to retain in the forces entrusted to me . . . an officer who impassively sacrifices his comrades while having full responsibility to save them. I humbly request Lieutenant Sukorko's transfer from Turkestan region *which would not exist if everyone acted as he did.*"[56]

Alimkul had caught Cherniaev napping. Only Serov's Cossacks had prevented a major disaster. But now the time of Russian reverses was over: Mikhail Grigorevich could plan new and greater advances.

54. On Ikan see "K," "Delo Uraltsev pod Turkestanom v dekabre 1864 g.," vs, xliii (May 1865), 115–124; Romanovskii, appendix, pp. 151–154; turk krai, xviii: 229–234; Ia. Polferov, "Pozornoe delo," iv, xcvii (Dec. 1904), 1011–1016.

55. Romanovskii, appendix, pp. 151–154.

56. Polferov, p. 1016, citing Cherniaev to Kryzhanovskii, 31 August 1865.

Cherniaev as a young officer (1850s)

Cherniaev's wife, Antonina A. Vulfert

During the night of June 14-15 the city and citadel of
Tashkent were taken by our assault on ladders. . . .
With Tashkent's occupation we have acquired in Central Asia a position corresponding to the interests of the
empire and the power of the Russian people. (Cherniaev
to Kryzhanovskii, June 17, 1865)

CHAPTER IV

Victory at Tashkent

CHERNIAEV was determined to restore his prestige and to cement
Russia's shaky hold over the Uzbeks—to erase recent setbacks with
one bold stroke. Tashkent, the coveted prize, lay but sixty miles
away. Restive under Kokanese rule, that great city dominated a rich
oasis and controlled much of Central Asia's trade.

Winter in Chimkent was frustrating for Cherniaev and his men.
"Boredom from inaction in that incredible hole was terrible," recalled an eyewitness. Mail arrived only once a month. The
detachment's silver currency was exhausted; the Uzbeks honored
Cherniaev's signature but not paper rubles. For the entire winter,
noted General Kachalov, "Cherniaev raved about Tashkent," and
of the triumph which had eluded him there.[1]

The war minister's encouraging letter, reported Cherniaev in
January, "gave me new strength to continue my activity in this
distant region which I have already requested permission to
leave. . . ." The forward line, he felt, would become fully secure
only when Kokand had been defeated. Meanwhile mobile forces
provided the best protection against marauders. Turkestan, he reiterated, should be subordinated directly to the war ministry; its com-

1. Khalfin, *Prisoedinenie*, p. 192; "Dvadtsatipiatiletie," pp. 225–227.

mander required sweeping powers.[2] His plea to eliminate cumbersome links with Orenburg was convincing but it was a thinly veiled demand for carte blanche.

Cherniaev requested the war ministry to assign him Colonel Poltoratskii to help with administration; meanwhile Cherniaev wrote to Poltoratskii:

> I shall await your arrival with impatience. You cannot imagine what I have endured this past year and when you see me you will probably find me aged ten years. If it had not been for Dmitrii Alekseevich's [Miliutin] letter, no power on earth would have kept me here. When you get here you will be convinced that the attack on Tashkent was not as pointless as my friends in St. Petersburg claimed. Had it not been for instructions, by now I would have driven the Kokanese from that little town of 200,000 people in response to Alimkul's raid upon Turkestan's environs. To us here it appears unwise to leave a Kokanese garrison in Tashkent and everyone feels it would be calmer for us in Chimkent if [Tashkent] were either independent or belonged to us, but in St. Petersburg, of course, they know better.[3]

His braggadocio and sarcasm were now unrestrained.

A special committee of ministers and generals had already decided to combine the frontier lines into a new Turkestan region under Orenburg. Miliutin's order of February 12, 1865, created it and named Cherniaev military governor and commander of troops.[4] This gave him broader scope, but he remained subordinate to Orenburg.

Cherniaev's draft statutes and staff proposals went to a special committee headed by Count F. L. Geiden, the chief of staff. Although Poltoratskii and Severtsov were members, the committee rejected Cherniaev's suggestion for a separate Turkestan military district. However, Turkestan's governor would obtain special military and administrative powers. Approving the general's ideas on native administration, Miliutin cautioned him to reduce gradually the Moslem clergy's influence and the *shariat* (Islamic law). Abrupt

2. TURK KRAI, XIX: 26–30, Cherniaev to Miliutin, 21 January 1865. By the time this reached St. Petersburg, Turkestan oblast had already been established.

3. Ibid., pp. 33–34, Cherniaev to Poltoratskii, 22 January 1865.

4. Ibid., pp. 37–40, Journal, 25 January 1865; Romanovskii, appendix, p. 154. Turkestan's frontiers would be: Kara-Kum desert, the Hungry Steppe, Chu River, the lower Syr-Daria and Kokand khanate. VS, XLIII (March 1865), 57–59.

interference with native ways, he warned, might arouse fanatical opposition.[5]

In a telegram of December 28, 1864, Cherniaev inquired how he should act if the Tashkenters revolted and requested his aid. Because your troops are few, replied Quartermaster Verigin, let Tashkent run its own affairs. Later, if the emperor so wishes, it can be occupied after reinforcements arrive: "Knowing the bold and venturesome character of [Cherniaev] . . . , I consider it the more necessary to be cautious in giving him permission. Thus I feel he should only be allowed to observe closely everything that occurs in Tashkent."[6] The war minister ordered Orenburg to instruct Cherniaev to undertake nothing until reinforcements came except to "maintain ties with the inhabitants and not deprive them of hope of eventual aid."[7]

The foreign ministry also outlined its position. To prevent Cherniaev from making his own policy, P. N. Stremoukhov, Gorchakov's cautious new assistant, warned him to follow instructions and request new ones for unforseen situations. Let Tashkent win its independence and serve Russia as a market rather than a possession.[8] Gorchakov opposed intervening in Kokand unless Russian territory or commerce were threatened. He favored creation of a separate Tashkent principality leaving the city's ultimate fate "to the course of events" but opposed a Bukharan occupation as harmful for Russian trade.[9]

N. A. Kryzhanovskii, the new governor general of Orenburg, forwarded these instructions and urged Cherniaev to consolidate previous gains and improve Turkestan's administration. A strong force should remain at Chimkent, able if necessary to invade Kokand. Cherniaev should set boundaries insuring Russian control of the main routes to the khanates and to Kashgar. Announcing plans for an August visit to Turkestan, Kryzhanovskii asked Cherniaev to arrange meetings for him with the rulers of Kokand and Bukhara. Meanwhile Cherniaev was to encourage

5. TURK KRAI, XIX: 89–90, Verigin to Cherniaev, 26 February 1865.

6. Ibid., pp. 47–49, Levengof to Miliutin, 31 January 1865.

7. Ibid., pp. 49–50, Miliutin to Levengof, 2 February 1865, tgr.

8. Khalfin, *Prisoedinenie*, pp. 186–187.

9. TURK KRAI, XIX: 81–85, Gorchakov to Orenburg governor, 23 February 1865. Miliutin, claimed Antonina, was planning a large expedition with siege guns to take Tashkent. IISG, "Biografiia," p. 161.

Tashkent to become "a domain independent of Bukhara and Kokand but a vassal of Russia."[10]

These somewhat contradictory instructions left Cherniaev considerable latitude. Gorchakov opposed further expansion, but he had neither specified a frontier nor forbidden an advance upon Tashkent. Would not Kryzhanovskii later lead such an expedition? Should he wait for his supreme commander and entourage to arrive "dreaming of a pleasant fall trip in the steppe . . . and the calculation of obtaining a Saint George's cross?" Only inadequate forces limited Cherniaev's movements.[11]

He had broken relations with his old rival, General Verevkin. Cherniaev urged him to remain as commander of the Syr-Daria Line, but Verevkin refused to serve under him. "I would be exposed to much unpleasantness from a man who has always entertained irreconcilable hatred toward me." He had lost respect for Cherniaev who had blamed his reverses on Verevkin's lack of support. "This was slander of the most unfortunate type which I can prove any time with incontestable documentary evidence," asserted Verevkin. Cherniaev had then deluged him with "impudent, confused and arrogant papers." Verevkin had replied properly "since both right and common sense were on my side."[12] Personal rivalry and competition for authority had completely estranged the two men.

Cherniaev resented dictation by Orenburg bureaucrats. On one officious directive he commented: "It is clear that none of us is doing things as we ought. . . . Correspond over a distance of 2000 versts as much as you want and nothing will come of it." Underneath he added: "The commanders of artillery and engineers have already begun to instruct on their own commanders of corresponding bureaus in Turkestan region: chaos is developing worse than before. One throws up one's hands."[13]

He resolved to seize Tashkent before Kryzhanovskii came. Egomania fortified his audacity. Cherniaev feared, Kachalov wrote, that his superior "would take it into his head to lead the army to Tashkent himself, capture it, obtain a count's title, and we workingmen

10. TURK KRAI, XIX: 85–87, Orenburg commander to Cherniaev, 25 February 1865.
11. Terentiev, I: 307.
12. TURK KRAI, XIX: 115, Cherniaev to Orenburg commander, 2 April 1865; pp. 152–155, 11 May 1865; pp. 186–187, Verevkin to Kryzhanovskii, 2 June 1865. Verevkin became ataman of the Ural Cossacks.
13. Ibid., pp. 144–145, Orenburg district commissary to Cherniaev, 31 April 1865 (sic).

would be made fools of."[14] Refusing to share the glory, Cherniaev and his aides decided to advance immediately.[15]

Bukharan troops, he wrote to Kryzhanovskii en route, had invaded Kokand and were threatening Tashkent: "Since in Tashkent itself the general mood is unfavorable to Kokand and its inhabitants have long been oppressed by Regent Alimkul's despotism, I could not remain indifferent to the emir's attempts and was compelled, without awaiting arrival of reinforcements on the line, to advance now along the road to Tashkent . . . to make it dependent directly upon us."[16] These arguments were specious. The Bukharans posed no direct threat to Tashkent. Some wealthier Tashkenters did favor Russian control because the severing of normal commercial ties and nearby warfare had ruined their trade. The populace, impoverished by war taxes and food requisitions, resented Kokanese rule,[17] but the Russians could not expect wide support.

Leaving Chimkent with thirteen hundred men and twelve guns,[18] Cherniaev turned off the Tashkent road and compelled the surrender of Niazbek, controlling Tashkent's water and grain supplies.[19] By diverting the Chirchik River Cherniaev hoped to make Tashkent submit. But the garrison carefully watched the pro-Russian commercial element in the western and central districts. In the southeast lived the khan's former entourage of aristocrats and soldiers: some favoring a Tashkent khanate, others desiring Bukharan control.[20]

On May 8 Cherniaev conducted a reconnaissance of the city's northeast corner. Pro-Russian elements were to open the gates, but Alimkul's arrival with six thousand men and forty guns foiled them. Though his army was inferior in training to Cherniaev's smaller force, Alimkul resolved to fight. On May 9 he

14. TSGVIA, f. 67, "A. L. Danzas," d. 270, l. 16, Kachalov to Danzas, 5 August 1865.

15. Terentiev, *Istoriia*, I: 307–308; IISG, "Biografiia," p. 161.

16. TURK KRAI, XIX: 146–148, Cherniaev to Kryzhanovskii, 2 May 1865.

17. Khalfin, *Prisoedinenie*, pp. 184–185.

18. Ibid., p. 192. Khan. citing Eugene Schuyler, *Turkistan* (New York, 1876), I: 113, claims wrongly that Cherniaev had 10,000 Russians and 5,000 Cossacks! Presumably he was reinforced prior to the attack on Tashkent when he had 1,951 men.

19. TURK KRAI, XIX: 146–148, Cherniaev to Kryzhanovskii, 2 May 1865. The emperor awarded Cherniaev a Saint Anne first class. Ibid., p. 191.

20. TSGVIA, f. 400, d. 55, l. 100, Cherniaev to General Staff, 4 October 1866, cited by Khalfin, *Prisoedinenie*, p. 185; K., P. M., "Russkoe znamia v Srednei Azii," IV, LXXVI (1899), 116; TURK KRAI, XIX: 177–182, "Zapiska o mestnykh usloviakh russkoi politiki v Srednei Azii," June 1865.

assaulted Cherniaev's camp but was mortally wounded and died that afternoon. Morale fell since only he could inspire his men and hold Kokand together.[21]   A Russian counterattack supported by artillery caused the Kokanese to flee toward the city walls. Cherniaev reported: "Although at that moment, perhaps, it would have been possible to occupy the city, I could not risk my last reserves and returned to camp deciding to remain there observing events in the city and utilize the first opportunity to occupy it."[22]

Was this truly why he retired? In June he would risk his last reserves in an equally perilous situation. At Chimkent success had come from pursuing a disorganized foe into the city. The same tactic might have worked at Tashkent. Nonetheless, defeat and Alimkul's death shook the Kokanese. Disdaining modesty, Cherniaev asserted that the battle of May 9 had "resolved the fate of Central Asia."[23]

Meanwhile Petersburg was reaffirming its previous policies. Cherniaev was to assist Kokand and Tashkent in maintaining themselves as semi-independent states. "Their governments should be our vassals and offer guarantees for our trade . . . and therefore our frontiers should not be advanced."[24] These instructions reached Cherniaev too late to affect his actions. Expecting war ministry backing and rewards from the emperor, he played a bold hand. He still hoped an assault on Tashkent would be unnecessary. To prevent reinforcements from reaching the city, he cut the Bukhara-Tashkent highway, occupied the main crossing over the Syr-Daria, and invested Tashkent from three sides. Prisoners confirmed that the city was hungry, but the garrison still resisted. A second armed reconnaissance on June 6 failed because pro-Russian elements could not open the gates.[25]

This was Cherniaev's final bid to expel the Kokanese with the Tashkenters' aid. Precisely when he decided on an assault

21. Ibid., pp. 152–153, Cherniaev to Kryzhanovskii, 11 May 1865; Smirnov, *Sultany*, appendices, pp. 80–82; Veselovskii, *Kirgizskii*, pp. 50–53.

22. TURK KRAI, XIX: 153–155, Cherniaev to Kryzhanovskii, 11 May 1865.

23. For a time Cherniaev even wished to be buried at Shor-tiube. IISG, "Biografiia," p. 161. If this settled Central Asia's fate, then Tashkent's capture, of which he was so proud, was a mere footnote!

24. TURK KRAI, XIX: 192, Kryzhanovskii to Levengof, 5 June 1865; pp. 192–193, Gorchakov to Kryzhanovskii, 5 June 1865.

25. Ibid., pp. 201–204, Cherniaev to Kryzhanovskii, 11 June 1865. Native reports alleged that it was an abortive assault: "Thus these Moslems drove the infidel army from the fortress." Veselovskii, *Kirgizskii*, p. 59. Kozlianinov also refers to a repelled assault which was probably this same "reconnaissance." Gradovskii, "Arkhistratig," pp. 120–121.

remains unclear. An eyewitness reported that some officers opposed an assault at a war council after the second reconnaissance. Cherniaev delayed it ten days to complete preparations.[26] After the reconnaissance failed, claimed N. F. Kozlianinov, Cherniaev ordered a retreat and sat in his tent completely dejected. "We should all perish in a retreat, an Asian horde would descend on us like locusts," objected Captain A. K. Abramov. "What shall we do then?" queried Cherniaev desperately. "Repeat the assault this very evening when it will not be expected! If we perish, then better with glory, but we shall take Tashkent!" Abramov declared.[27] For his part, Cherniaev boasted, "Deciding everything myself, I never resorted to military meetings, but here I made an exception, not to learn my officers' views but just their attitudes. Their mood was excellent and I decided on the assault."[28] Similarities between his and Kozlianinov's account lend some weight to the latter's version.

While the Russians prepared, the young Kokanese khan and his entourage secretly left Tashkent on June 9 to become hostages of the emir. A small Bukharan force slipped in and took control of Tashkent's defense. The emir's main forces moved into Kokanese frontier forts. The emir, argued Cherniaev, must be prevented from seizing Tashkent: "To oppose 1951 men and twelve guns . . . to a city which could concentrate against us at any point we attacked up to 30,000 men and 50 guns in the shortest time, and to await demonstrations simultaneously by the emir of Bukhara was clearly impossible. To withdraw from the city would mean giving the emir immense prestige in Central Asia and strengthen him with all the sinews of war in Tashkent. Consequently, I decided to seize the city by open force."[29]

It required reckless courage (whether Cherniaev's or Abramov's) to attack with so few men. Extending in an irregular oval almost bisected by the Boz-su Canal, Tashkent was a labyrinth of narrow, winding streets lined with low buildings of clay and stone. The city wall, with twelve fortified gates, was eighteen

26. "Dvadtsatipiatiletie," p. 229.

27. Gradovskii, pp. 120–121. This account may be partly true, but the chronology is confused. There was no assault the day before Tashkent fell. No other reference could be found to a decision to withdraw. Kozlianinov, however, assured Gradovskii that Abramov had documentary evidence confirming his version.

28. IISG, "Biografiia," pp. 161–162.

29. TURK KRAI, XIX: 244–254, Cherniaev to Kryzhanovskii, 7 July 1865.

miles long and guarded by a deep moat and sixty-three cannon.[30] But Cherniaev expected success if he could mount a surprise
attack and capture the wall before the enemy could concentrate his
superior might.

The assault began the night of June 14–15. Before dawn
Cherniaev's main force approached Kamelan Gate while Colonel
Kraevskii feinted against Kokand Gate on the opposite side. Near
the walls Captain Abramov's men in Cherniaev's vanguard placed
scaling ladders on their backs and, utilizing darkness and dense
cover, reached the outer wall undetected. Prodded awake by Russian
bayonets, sentries at Kamelan Gate revealed a secret entry. Russian
volunteers moved through it and took the gate without loss.[31] Captain G. A. Vulfert then led a few men along the walls and chased
the enemy at bayonet point from the parapets.

Russian reserves poured through the gate and fanned out
overcoming Kokanese infantry and guns protected by barricades.
Near the bazaar similar barricades had been erected and riflemen
occupied some squat native houses (*sakli*). Charging with bared bayonets, the Russians took these obstacles and reached the citadel,
already occupied by other Russians. On the other side Kraevskii's
cannonade had drawn off Kokanese strength. When the main force
reached him, his infantry entered the city. Kraevskii's Cossacks pursued some five thousand Kokanese cavalry which, discarding banners and weapons, dashed to the Chirchik River where they drowned
by the hundreds.

Clearing most of Tashkent, Cherniaev's main force was then post-
ed at Kamelan Gate. Toward evening enemy riflemen occupied
nearby sakli and severed communications with Kraevskii. Barricades mushroomed on street corners. As night approached, Cherniaev learned that Kokanese at the bazaar had sworn to fight to the
death, and he acted to protect his exhausted men. Ordering sakli
ignited in a semicircle around Kamelan Gate, he separated his men
from the enemy with a ring of fire. Protected by their riflemen, the
Russians slept while artillery pounded enemy positions in the city.
The Kokanese could neither extinguish the flames nor break
through the Russian lines.[32]

The next day the Russians encountered more barricades and rifle

30. "Vziatie Tashkenta," vs, xlv (Sept. 1865), 68–70; "Russkoe znamia," p. 116.
31. Terentiev, *Istoriia*, i: 314–315.
32. "Dvadtsatipiatiletie," p. 231; ii, "Avtobiografiia," p. 12.

fire. Again the barriers were overrun and the citadel destroyed, but before sundown the streets were clear. Tashkent's elders requested a formal meeting, and on June 17 they submitted unconditionally.

The task of burying the dead and rewarding the victors remained. The garrison had contained some thirty thousand men; sixteen banners and all the cannon were captured. Russian losses numbered three officers wounded, twenty-five soldiers killed and eighty-five wounded. Singling out some for special praise,[33] Cherniaev concluded his report: "This exploit could only have been achieved by troops already fully hardened and used to victory. . . . Please call the emperor's attention to this handful of tireless, fearless warriors who have established the prestige of the Russian name in Central Asia in a manner commensurate with the dignity of the empire and the power of the Russian people."

Tashkent's stubborn resistance, unusual in Russia's conquest of Central Asia, resulted from the large pro-Bukharan party and the city's tradition of independence. Only briefly a Kokanese dependency, it had never been wholly subjugated. By size, material wealth, and commercial significance, Tashkent had more prerequisites for independence than Kokand itself.

Cherniaev left a sizable Russian garrison in the city to prevent factional quarrels and protect it from the khanates. He proposed garrisoning Niazbek and Chinaz also and requested immediate reinforcements. "The country occupied this year and last," he added, "possesses all the resources for independent existence, and nothing is required from Russia except shells and powder."[34] By taking Tashkent Russia had acquired great prestige, a firm frontier, grain supplies for her troops, and a vital commercial center, "knocking a window into closed barbaric Asia."[35] Here Russia was Europe's vanguard.

Cherniaev's feat committed Russia, contrary to official intent, to conquer and civilize all Central Asia. Tsarist leaders, reading Cherniaev's dramatic reports, began to consider Tashkent the key to the oasis region. Had his assault been repelled, Russian control of

33. Kraevskii, Vulfert, Abramov, Makarov, Ivanov, and Priest Malov were cited for conspicuous bravery. Of Abramov Cherniaev wrote: "Leading the storming column, he mastered the fortified [Kamelan] gate which was the reason for the seizure of Tashkent." TURK KRAI, XIX: 244 ff.

34. RT, documents, pp. 91–98, Cherniaev to Kryzhanovskii, 7 July 1865; "Vziatie Tashkenta," pp. 76–77.

35. S. N. Iuzhakov, *Shestnadtsataia godovshchina* (St. Petersburg, 1882), p. 3.

southern Central Asia would have been delayed or prevented.[36] Tashkent's occupation, while a terrible humiliation for Kokand, compelled Russia to pacify and administer a heavily settled area. Once committed there, reasoned Cherniaev, St. Petersburg could not withdraw. His personal compulsion to achieve prominence and glory had accelerated Russian expansion.

The months following Tashkent's capture marked the zenith of Cherniaev's prestige in Central Asia. Seizing this prize without authorization or support, he represented—until General Kryzhanovskii appeared—unchallengeable authority to Tashkenters accustomed to autocracy. He gloried in this role, but his impetuousness and disregard for instructions brought down the government's wrath upon him.

St. Petersburg rejoiced at Tashkent's fall.[37] The emperor responded to Cherniaev's initial report with an order to "present rewards to those who distinguished themselves." Alexander commented on Cherniaev's July 7 dispatch, "A glorious affair." He praised the responsible officers and awarded two rubles to every soldier.[38] The future Alexander III rejoiced at Cherniaev's success and thanked him for some captured trophies: "These items will always remind me of the glorious battles fought by our valiant troops under Your Excellency's command."[39] Henceforth he was Cherniaev's loyal patron. Thus did the Court reward successful disobedience.

London reacted calmly and accepted Russian assurances. On June 19 Gorchakov told Ambassador Andrew Buchanan that Tashkent probably would not be occupied. Russia, warned Buchanan, must not reward officers "who heedlessly and for selfish ends undertook military operations on the frontier which were inconsistent with the declared policy of the government." All Russia could do, retorted Gorchakov, was to employ intelligent officers and acquaint them fully with its views. Later London was told that Cherniaev had occupied Tashkent to assure its independence.[40]

36. Edward Allworth, ed., *Central Asia: A Century of Russian Rule* (New York, 1967), p. 59.

37. Claimed Khalfin (*Prisoedinenie*, p. 191), Tashkent's capture "corresponded to the plans of the government, the military-feudal aristocracy and commercial-industrial circles."

38. TURK KRAI, XIX: 270, Kryzhanovskii to Miliutin, 14 July 1865, enclosing Cherniaev's report of 17 June; VISB (1915), no. 2, Kryzhanovskii to Miliutin, 30 July 1865, and the emperor's comment of 9 August.

39. GIM, ed. khr. 2, l. 3, Aleksandr Aleksandrovich to Cherniaev, 13 November 1865.

40. FO, 65/867, Buchanan to Russell, 15 June 1865, tgr.; 19 June 1865; Lumley to Russell,

The first days after the fall of Tashkent were tense. While the populace was stunned, Cherniaev exiled potentially dangerous Uzbek leaders. Some Tashkenters feared he would ban Islam, but he respected their faith and customs and forbade arbitrary billeting and recruitment. Ending unfair ancient levies, he freed Tashkent for a year from all taxes. Such measures, undermining hostile activity by clerical and pro-Bukharan elements, promoted stability.

Cherniaev's display of personal courage created a local legend. On the fourth day of the occupation, with his staff and five Cossacks, he rode through obscure side streets, visited the bazaar, the main mosque, and Moslem schools. Some Uzbeks, wrote N. P. Ostroumov, had believed that Russians were ogres, "and suddenly they see that along their streets comes quietly and joyfully an almost legendary conqueror. They see that neither he nor his entourage are one-eyed monsters but real and even reasonable people. They see that General Cherniaev, holding Tashkent and its environs in terror, politely bows to the conquered, peacefully enters the house of the *kazi-kalian* [chief justice and head of the Moslem clergy]." Then Cherniaev proceeded calmly to the public baths. To many Uzbeks he became the dauntless lion of Tashkent.[41]

At first Cherniaev ruled from a two-room hut outside Kamelan Gate. On its porch he heard petitions and satisfied them as best he could. Later, it bore the inscription: "the first house of military governor, Major General Cherniaev," and the street running past it was named after him. Wrote Evgenii Markov, a Cherniaev admirer: "This Spartan dwelling is very characteristic of all Cherniaev's activity. He remained a soldier even when others easily became satraps and was able to accomplish the greatest deeds with the smallest resources."[42] Soon tiring of simplicity, Cherniaev wrote Poltoratskii: "Today [August 31] I moved into the khan's palace. I did not do so earlier because there was no glass. Having settled in a fine room after a year and a half of semi-barrack life, I am peacefully enjoying myself."[43] Creators of the Cherniaev legend somehow overlooked such passages.

2 August 1865, enclosing an article from the semiofficial *Journal de St. Pétersbourg.*

41. He was called "Shirnaib," which could be translated as "lion commander" or "unconquerable commander." N. P. Ostroumov, *Sarty* (Tashkent, 1896), pp. 281–282; *Istoriia uzbekskoi SSR* (Tashkent, 1968), ii: 23–24.

42. iisg, "Biografiia," p. 171; E. Markov, *Rossiia v Srednei Azii* (St. Petersburg, 1901), p. 477.

43. turk krai, xx: 38, Cherniaev to Poltoratskii, 21 August 1865.

By training and inclination Cherniaev was a warrior, not an administrator. He expressed utter contempt for bureaucrats. The scanty references to governmental matters in his reports and letters suggest he was little interested in building a sound Turkestan administration. Nonetheless he became known as a masterly and humane governor. To Antonina he was a benevolent, farseeing statesman who preserved all native customs compatible with Russian law. He ran Turkestan, she affirmed, with only six officials and two translators, collecting taxes, establishing postal communications with Orenburg, and achieving security on the roads.[44] Eugene Schuyler, an American diplomat, affirmed that Cherniaev "with great good sense administered the newly acquired territory with as little change as possible from native usage and native law and by means of native officials." This exemplary administrator with unfailing instincts, concluded Schuyler, permitted a maximum of self-government, enhanced Russia's moral authority and spared the treasury.[45]

Cherniaev's laissez-faire policy toward the Uzbeks, though creditable, resulted more from preoccupation with conquest than from wisdom.[46] Tashkent's administration continued as before except that Cherniaev made final decisions and Serov supervised the police.[47] Recent crushing Kokanese defeats simplified the problem of keeping order.

Despite Cherniaev's boast that everything was so well in hand that with reinforcements "any fool can hold on here," the financial picture grew bleak. He toured the frontier to inform nomads they must pay an annual tax of one sheep per hut, which he estimated would raise one hundred fifty thousand rubles. But to win urban support he instituted a tax moratorium for 1865, compelling him to seek forced loans and to borrow gold objects from his officers.[48] Cherniaev had been unable to handle money in public or private life, and later accounts blamed Turkestan's financial plight on his poor accounting and his largesse to natives. His superiors' deafness to his requests for funds contributed to this indebtedness.[49]

44. IISG, "Biografiia," pp. 171–172.
45. Schuyler, II: 203, 210.
46. R. A. Pierce, *Russian Central Asia, 1867–1917* (Berkeley, 1960), p. 22. A pro-Cherniaev account ascribed this to the Russians' ignorance of Turkestan: Iuzhakov, *Itogi dvadtsatisemiletnago upravleniia Turkestanskim kraem* (St. Petersburg, 1895), p. 12.
47. A. I. Dobrosmyslov, *Tashkent v proshlom i nastoiashchem* (Tashkent, 1911–1912), p. 60.
48. TURK KRAI, XX: 39–40, Cherniaev to Poltoratskii, 31 August 1865.
49. Zalesov, "Zapiski," RS, CXV (Aug. 1903), 332–334, emphasizes Kryzhanovskii's refusal

Cherniaev's achievements were more notable as commander than as administrator. Winter quarters for troops, Antonina emphasized, were built speedily despite shortages of funds and materials. He conserved his troops' strength and health. On hot marches heavy items were sent by camel, and a sunshield was designed to protect the necks of marching soldiers. Sick men were few on his campaigns, and his solicitude for the men earned him the nickname "Dedushka" (grandfather). His relations with his officers were open and direct; orders were executed unconditionally. Cherniaev's forte was caring for an army, not governing a province.

The general worried increasingly about the war threat posed by Bukhara. The Russians' position was precarious: with only eleven hundred infantry, a newly conquered Moslem city at his back and large Bukharan armies nearby, Cherniaev concentrated his men near the Kamelan Gate to prevent surprises. The emir wrote haughtily that Tashkent and Russia itself had belonged to his forbears. Unless the Russians withdrew from Tashkent, he would annihilate them. Summoning the city elders, Cherniaev had the emir's letter read aloud and watched their horrified expressions. They knew the fate of a city conquered by the emir. Cherniaev recalled the tense situation:

> Thus the city's destiny balanced between two fires. . . . Whom should they support? I removed them from their quandary by stating that I would go forth to meet the Bukharans and if I were victorious, everything would remain as it was. If I were beaten, then my advice was to attack me in the rear to win favor from the emir. Until the struggle had been decided, I asked them to block up all the gates and let no one enter or leave the city. For a moment they stood stroking their beards, then they promised to do everything they had been told.[50]

The emir, surmised Cherniaev, might try to conquer all of Kokand and Tashkent or even restore Tamerlane's mighty fourteenth-century Central Asian empire.[51] Standing at Khodzhent with eighty

to provide adequate funds as does Terentiev, I: 320–321.

50. IISG, "Biografiia," pp. 167–175.

51. Tamerlane (correctly Timur), 1333?–1405, conquered all of Central Asia, Persia, and parts of Russia.

thousand men and one hundred cannon, he gazed toward Russia itself. "If the emir decided to attack us with those forces," warned Cherniaev, "it would be most difficult with our small resources to keep the whole region calm."[52]

Refusing to humor the truculent emir, Mikhail Grigorevich replied untruthfully: "I occupied Tashkent at the emperor's instruction . . . and without orders I shall not retreat one step." In another *fait accompli*, he ordered all Bukharans in Turkestan region detained and their goods confiscated, then urged that this be done throughout the empire. Kryzhanovskii's position was awkward: to repudiate this action would ruin Cherniaev's and Russia's prestige in Asian eyes. Instead, he had Bukharan merchants in Orenburg region arrested.[53] Cherniaev's move would have fateful consequences.

Events in Kokand temporarily averted the Bukharan threat to Tashkent. From Khodzhent the emir moved against Kokand, captured it, restored Khudoiar as khan, and forced the Kipchaks to flee to the mountains, where he defeated and dispersed them. Brutal executions accompanied his advance. Cherniaev breathed easier when an uprising in Bukhara induced the emir to return home.[54]

The emir now became conciliatory: he sent Cherniaev a friendly personal letter, accompanied by gifts, in which he dropped demands for Tashkent's evacuation and agreed that the Chirchik River should separate Russian and Bukharan forces in Kokand. Cherniaev concluded that the emir needed time but might attack Tashkent later, and advised a waiting game. Let the brainless Khudoiar, the emir's father-in-law, retain the Kokanese throne. That would increase the emir's dependence on Russia's friendship. But a curious postscript seemed to contradict this: "Perhaps circumstances will make it possible now to side with the Kipchaks and assist to raise to the khanly title not Khudoiar but some other member of the Chingiz family. In any case the person selected as khan will comply with the aims of the Russian government."[55] Did this mean that besides making his own policy toward Bukhara that he would intervene in Kokanese internal politics?

52. TURK KRAI, XIX: 238–240, Cherniaev to Kryzhanovskii, 29 June 1865.

53. Ibid., pp. 254–255; 270–273, Verevkin to Kryzhanovskii, 2 July 1865, citing Cherniaev's reports of 26 June; Cherniaev to Kryzhanovskii, 8 July 1865; Kryzhanovskii to Miliutin, 15 July 1865.

54. "Izvestiia iz Turkestanskoi oblasti," VS, XLVI (Dec. 1865), 205–206.

55. TURK KRAI, XIX: 263, Cherniaev to Kryzhanovskii, 12 July 1865; XX: 3–12, 6 August 1865.

The emir's growing deference encouraged Cherniaev to advocate a policy toward Tashkent contrary to official assurances to England. Earlier he had urged a separate Tashkent khanate, but "I have grown convinced that such a proposal is inapplicable in practice." Tashkenters would regard a vassal khanate as concealed Russian rule. In Tashkent peace had been restored easily, and now, with a small Russian garrison in the citadel and some supervision, it could govern itself. A Syr-Daria frontier, incorporating the fertile Chirchik valley in the empire, would permit the Russians to navigate the entire river and watch Kokand only forty versts away.

Cherniaev displayed a growing truculence. False reports in the capital, he wrote Poltoratskii, "compel me to speak wholly frankly abandoning for once my system of speaking with deeds alone." He virtually advocated the annexation of Tashkent, explaining that it "has been so firmly joined to Russia that to abandon it now is impossible." Under his benevolent rule, its inhabitants were happy and secure. "My directives are executed with a precision unusual with us," he added. Tashkenters would not join Kokand or Bukhara and feared civil strife if the city were allowed full independence. They had even requested him to confirm their religious officials in office. The emir's recent humble letter had amazed them and revealed Cherniaev's vast prestige. Why should General Kryzhanovskii visit Tashkent when Cherniaev was called "the White Tsar's envoy in place of his own eyes?" Little remained to be done to consolidate the governor's dignity in Turkestan. Cherniaev complained:

> I cannot remain silent about the dishonorable intention to attribute all I have done to the new governor general [Kryzhanovskii], supplying him with all the means to seize Tashkent. If that had happened, what would have remained for me? They should be reminded that I was given no instructions except to take Aulie-Ata, that I took everything on my own responsibility and accomplished nine-tenths of the affair with a handful of men and without a kopeck. Have they taken into account that besides the enemy, I have met only opposition on every side? . . . I must be less trusting than before and consider the quickest possible departure from here.

Poltoratskii commented disgustedly in the margin: "If ambition is beginning to torture you, spit it out quickly. By God, it isn't worth it."[56]

56. Ibid., pp. 22–25, Cherniaev to Poltoratskii, 15 August 1865.

Cherniaev's unpleasant attributes and disturbed personality were beginning to emerge. Repudiating government policy, he intimated that his superiors were conspiring to steal his deserved glory. Turkestan had been acquired, he claimed, solely by his initiative and ability. In an effort to prevent legitimate supervision by his superior, Cherniaev hinted that unless his demands for a free hand were met, he would depart and let Turkestan collapse. He was posing as a misunderstood hero persecuted by an ungrateful government, the innocent victim of an evil bureaucratic conspiracy. His letter to Poltoratskii revealed Cherniaev as an ambitious, egotistical adventurer who believed he had become indispensable.

Major General Cherniaev merely communicates accomplished facts to me involving the necessity either to confirm measures wholly incompatible with our general aims or revoke these measures and injure the prestige of our authority. (Kryzhanovskii to Miliutin, November 14, 1865)

CHAPTER V

The Commanders Quarrel

LATE IN 1865 Cherniaev's dispute with his superiors over Central Asian policy widened rapidly. His personal and political rivalry with Kryzhanovskii of Orenburg and his policy differences with the government provoked a crisis which St. Petersburg could resolve only by removing Cherniaev. Before it could do so, he embarked on another unauthorized campaign. His advance to Dzhizak involved Russia prematurely in a war with Bukhara and compelled the government to sanction further Russian advances.

Official policy remained based on Kryzhanovskii's June 5 instructions to Cherniaev: Tashkent must become independent and Russia would occupy the upper Syr-Daria forts only temporarily. The war minister reaffirmed this instructing the Orenburg governor not to hamper Cherniaev's actions unless they clearly contradicted government policy.[1]

Mikhail Grigorevich's sudden arrest of the Bukharan merchants aroused censure from St. Petersburg. Kryzhanovskii extended the ban to Orenburg, but he refused to apply it elsewhere. Meanwhile resentment was growing in Russia: Orenburg merchants pleaded with the governor to rescind the order before it ruined them. Kryzha-

1. TURK KRAI, XIX: 241, Kryzhanovskii to Cherniaev, 3 July 1865; pp. 291–292, Miliutin to Kryzhanovskii, 29 July 1865.

novskii warned Miliutin: "For my part I am convinced that if this measure remains in effect long, the sequestered goods will be damaged, depreciate in value and not reach the Nizhnii-Novgorod trade fair, their only market. . . . This measure's harmful consequences would fall with full weight not upon Bukharan citizens against whom it was adopted but primarily on Russian commercial houses."[2] Cherniaev's "extremely ill-considered, precipitate measure," declared a private letter reaching Miliutin from Orenburg, "giving the Bukharans a light tap, gave us a body blow."[3] In St. Petersburg the Committee of Ministers rescinded the ban: local commanders were to foster Russian trade with Central Asia and adopt no extraordinary measures without permission.[4] Cherniaev's action had been repudiated.

Russia, however, would not yield to the emir. Peace with Bukhara would only be maintained if compatible with Russian honor. The emir's demands for Tashkent's evacuation provoked Gorchakov to defiance: "We cannot retreat now. It is unthinkable to bow before the emir." Miliutin's instructions to Kryzhanovskii made it clear that Russian interests and dignity would permit no such concessions. Russia should avoid conflict unless the emir proved bent on conquest; operations should be launched only if success were certain since even a minor failure could wreck Russian prestige. Turkestan would be reinforced to sober the emir.[5] Cherniaev retained much leeway to deal with Bukhara.

On Tashkent Russian leaders seemed in substantial agreement. The war minister, to be sure, favored holding the upper Syr-Daria forts until Tashkent and Kokand became Russian vassals whereas Gorchakov urged abandoning the forts unless they were needed to protect commercial navigation. The foreign ministry wished Tashkent and its environs to be an independent khanate protected by Russia. Kryzhanovskii agreed but argued that to protect Tashkent,

2. Ibid., p. 265, Kryzhanovskii to Miliutin, 13 July 1865, telegram and war minister's comments; pp. 278–279, 19 July 1865.

3. Ibid., p. 283, Gorchakov to Miliutin, 23 July 1865; pp. 292–293, Miliutin to Kryzhanovskii, 29 July 1865; ORBL, k. 15, no. 2, l. 75; TURK KRAI, xx: 20–22, Acting Finance Minister to Miliutin, 14 August 1865; pp. 37–38, no. 212.

4. Ibid., pp. 152–153, Journal of the Committee of Ministers, 19 and 23 October 1865. Both Romanovskii (*Zametki*, p. 33) and Terentiev (i: 324–325) believed that Cherniaev's trade ban against Bukhara had been necessary.

5. TURK KRAI, xix: 283, Gorchakov to Miliutin, 23 July 1865; pp. 292–293, Miliutin to Kryzhanovskii, 29 July 1865.

Russia needed the forts and a strongpoint nearby. Cherniaev, rejecting a khanate as impractical, desired a government he could
manipulate. Even he advocated self-rule for Tashkent, so Miliutin
concluded that they could agree on Tashkent's government and the
Syr-Daria forts.[6]

Thus Cherniaev's August 6 report on relations with the khanates
appalled his superiors. It failed to say where the emir and his army
were located, and the postscript, suggesting support for the Kipchaks, contradicted the rest of the report. Deeply perplexed, Miliutin
wrote Kryzhanovskii that field commanders must report promptly
everything that happened and "explain carefully why they feel that
principles already approved should be changed."[7]

Believing that the Kokanese imbroglio would enhance his and
Russia's prestige, Cherniaev pursued his own course. The Kipchaks
and Bukharans, he wrote Poltoratskii, having weakened each other,
both required Russian support. The emir had sent envoys to Tashkent and presents to his errand-runners: "Thus the idea . . . about
the need to raise the Russian governor's prestige above that of local
khans has virtually been realized. When the Bukharan delegation
arrives to see me, I hope also to achieve another of my cherished
ideas: to gain free access to Bukhara for our merchants with the emir
taking responsibility for securing their lives and property." "From
this you can see in part," boasted Cherniaev, "what has been accomplished in Central Asia in the past year and a half."[8]

Before Kryzhanovskii reached Tashkent, Cherniaev abruptly
broke a de facto truce with Bukhara. Rustem-bek, the emir's subordinate, had raided Russian territory and curtailed food deliveries to
Tashkent, causing prices to rise in that tense city. The situation was
intolerable, asserted Cherniaev, so "I . . . decided to take appropriate measures." On September 12 Lieutenant Colonel Pistolkors
crossed the Chirchik River, forced Rustem to flee, erected barracks,
and established communications with Tashkent.[9] This unauthorized
move secured a rich agricultural area containing Tashkent's grain
supply and tightened Russia's grip on that city.

6. Ibid., xx: 61–63, Miliutin to Gorchakov, 9 September 1865; pp. 63–65, Gorchakov to
Miliutin, 11 September 1865; pp. 36–37, Kryzhanovskii to Miliutin, 26 August 1865; p. 63,
Miliutin to Gorchakov, 10 September 1865.

7. Ibid., pp. 36–37, Kryzhanovskii to Miliutin, 26 August 1865; pp. 72–73, Miliutin to
Kryzhanovskii, 20 September 1865.

8. Ibid., pp. 38–39, Cherniaev to Poltoratskii, 31 August 1865.

9. Ibid., pp. 86–91, Cherniaev to Kryzhanovskii, 28 September 1865.

A clash between Kryzhanovskii and Cherniaev became inevitable. Kryzhanovskii, well-educated, capable and ambitious, envied Cherniaev his victory at Tashkent. Soon after Kryzhanovskii became Orenburg's commander the first misunderstandings occurred. The arrest of the Bukharan merchants and Orenburg's parsimony deepened the rift. Kryzhanovskii wanted Cherniaev to remain quiet until he had set up a vassal Tashkent khanate and gained the plaudits of its populace.[10]

Mikhail Grigorevich dreaded his arrival. "After Tashkent's fall," he wrote Poltoratskii, "Kryzhanovskii ceased being pleasant. He began writing unceremonious orders and making appointments without consulting me." He was coming as "the terrible judge to show all Petersburg that two and two make four, that I conquered the region only because I didn't encounter a real enemy, but that I couldn't pacify it, whereas he, the great maestro, can do so."[11] Cherniaev feared that his superior would emasculate his authority.

Ostensibly Kryzhanovskii came to restrain Cherniaev. En route he announced that Russia already had too much territory. Conquests were easier and more satisfying than consolidation. He would "pull in the reins" and direct Cherniaev's "warlike ardor" to peaceful construction.[12] Inspecting some Turkestan troops on the way, asserted Cherniaev, he cursed them and shouted: "You should be given brooms instead of rifles." In mid-September he swept into Tashkent. Fearing a scene Cherniaev feigned illness and sent his assistant to meet him. "When he took up quarters in the same house with me, I sent someone to inform him that though very unwell, I could present myself to him there. He received me very coldly."[13] Though angered by Cherniaev's behavior, Kryzhanovskii did not desire an open breach. He informed Cherniaev that the government opposed new expansion. He should build barracks, hospitals, and roads, improve native conditions and his troops' financial position.

Without consulting Cherniaev he summoned Tashkent's chief citizens and urged them to select a ruler. To his amazement, fear of arbitrary khans and Cherniaev's pressure caused them to prefer direct Russian rule. Seid Azim, a wealthy merchant, exhorted his

10. Ibid., xix: 294–295, Kryzhanovskii to Miliutin, 30 July 1865; xx: 36–37, 26 August 1865; Zalesov, "Zapiski," rs, cxv (Aug. 1903), 332–334.

11. turk krai, xx: 38–40, 31 August 1865.

12. Ibid., pp. 47–49, Kryzhanovskii to Stremoukhov, 3 September 1865.

13. iisg, "Avtobiografiia," p. 13.

fellows to affix their seals to a petition to Kryzhanovskii dated September 18.[14] "For us to name a ruler from ourselves," it stated, "would be presumptuous and inappropriate." Cherniaev should name their civil and religious officials: "He has been in this region for two years and after taking control of Tashkent was so indulgent toward its inhabitants that instead of evil he did good for them and none of Tashkent's inhabitants was offended. Besides, General Cherniaev knows everyone here very well, great and small, good and bad."[15]

This unexpected opposition, fostered by Cherniaev's largesse, foiled Kryzhanovskii. Mikhail Grigorevich wrote Poltoratskii triumphantly: "I had feared that the governor general's arrival would weaken my prestige in the eyes of a populace used to obeying me unconditionally, but my fears proved groundless. Kryzhanovskii did not have much of an effect here and alarmed the city by his inappropriate proclamation about a khan. Fortunately he stopped in time and renounced his intention to celebrate his arrival by naming a khan and forming a Tashkent state." Why must Petersburg issue impractical instructions and send Kryzhanovskii to implement them? The war minister should not decide the Tashkent question until experts had examined it.[16] Clearly Cherniaev intended to remain in charge.

But the government repudiated his approach toward Tashkent and the khanates. The foreign ministry argued that to inform the emir that Tashkent had accepted Russian rule would contradict official policy. Arbitrary departures from that program, warned Miliutin, might "create immense future difficulties for us and even damage Russia's general political position."[17]

Kryzhanovskii had written the emir suggesting a meeting at a neutral point. He would parley, warned Cherniaev, only if humiliated and convinced of Russian power. When the emir failed to reply, Kryzhanovskii reluctantly empowered Cherniaev to secure protection for Russian caravans and have a consulate opened in Bukhara. "If you encounter anything going beyond your instructions, request

14. Terentiev, I: 326–327; Khalfin, *Prisoedinenie*, pp. 204–205.

15. Romanovskii, pp. 177–179. Miliutin suggested that Cherniaev may have instigated the Tashkenters' negative response which "coincided completely with Cherniaev's aims." ORBL, Miliutin, k. 15, no. 2, ll. 75–76.

16. TURK KRAI, XX: 79–80, Cherniaev to Poltoratskii, 25 September 1865; pp. 81–82, Cherniaev to Miliutin, 28 September 1865.

17. Ibid., pp. 72–74, Miliutin to Kryzhanovskii, 20 September 1865.

orders before deciding on a course of action,"[18] he cautioned. Cherniaev would scarcely heed such a caveat.

Nor did he like Kryzhanovskii's other orders. He should assist the Orenburg commissariat to draw up estimates of supplies for Turkestan in 1866. He must spend money properly and keep careful account. Angered at such officiousness, Cherniaev appealed to Poltoratskii: "For God's sake obtain some money if you want me to act like Evdokimov.[19] The region is truly rich, but inattention to my limited resources has proceeded to the point of cynicism. Remember that two years ago I received 1,350 silver rubles, but nothing since."[20]

In Tashkent, Kryzhanovskii warned against risky military operations. Reinforcements could not arrive before spring and "any advance not required by extreme circumstances would be dangerous." These admonitions were merely *pro forma*. Kryzhanovskii, seeking glory during his visit, suggested that they advance to Kokand. Protesting that his troops were tired, Cherniaev retorted: "As you like, but in that case I shall request permission to leave the region because you would gain the victory and depart, and how would I hold on here then until summer without reinforcements?"[21] Kryzhanovskii, now claiming that Cherniaev had plenty of free troops, suggested cynically: "In case of an advance, leave three companies in Tashkent and let the inhabitants cut themselves to pieces if that pleases them." All in vain. Kryzhanovskii left Tashkent frustrated.[22]

Mikhail Grigorevich had personal reasons to return to St. Petersburg. On September 27 he announced his engagement to Antonina Aleksandrovna Vulfert, sister of the Major Vulfert he had met in Orenburg. In 1863, when Cherniaev went to the capital, Vulfert had given him a shawl for his sister. Taking it from Cherniaev, Antonina donned the snow-white garment before a large mirror. Then and there he fell in love with her. Visiting the wounded Vulfert after Tashkent's capture, Cherniaev begged him to spare himself for his

18. Ibid., p. 102, Kryzhanovskii to Cherniaev, 29 September 1865; pp. 82–85, 28 September 1865.

19. A general, renowned for his boldness and efficiency, who pacified the western Caucasus (1861–1864). See p. 27.

20. TURK KRAI, XX: 79–80, Cherniaev to Poltoratskii, 25 September 1865.

21. Ibid., pp. 98–101, Kryzhanovskii's instructions to Cherniaev, 29 September 1865; IISG, "Avtobiografiia," p. 13.

22. Terentiev, I: 328, citing Kryzhanovskii to Cherniaev, 30 September 1865.

sister's sake; he permitted Vulfert to write her this. A courtship began by letter. In December Cherniaev's parents joyfully gave their blessing.[23] There is no evidence that Cherniaev had had any previous lasting heterosexual relationship. He had suppressed his homosexual tendencies, engaging in dramatic but inconclusive "conquests" of women.[24] Perhaps his decision to marry made him even less willing to accept unwanted orders.

Before receiving Kryzhanovskii's report on his visit, Petersburg disavowed Cherniaev's independent course. His August 6 report, noted Stremoukhov, deviated drastically from official plans. The government, commented Miliutin, could only allow its agents to decide secondary questions retaining the exclusive right to set basic policies. Otherwise either the central government must cancel local authorities' directives and undermine its agents, or subordinate itself to them and sacrifice its general policy. Here was the basic issue which led to Cherniaev's recall.

Stremoukhov sharply questioned Cherniaev's recent actions. Why should Russia support the Kipchaks against the emir? Why had a commercial ban been instituted against Bukhara without authorization? Why had he advanced the frontier beyond Chimkent? Cherniaev had destroyed from beginning to end the official plan sent to guide him. Stremoukhov objected to his efforts to annex Tashkent: if Russia incorporated every city and warlike tribe, she must expand indefinitely.[25] Cherniaev's differences with the government had become a vast gulf.

Asserting that Kryzhanovskii had given him full authority to negotiate, Cherniaev resumed his dealings with Bukhara. (Kryzhanovskii: "This is untrue. I transferred it conditionally.") Good relations with Bukhara would be assured, continued Cherniaev, if the Russo-Kokanese frontier ran along the Syr-Daria and Naryn rivers. (Kryzhanovskii: "This is incompatible with our government's views and declarations.") Hearing that English officers were negotiating with the emir and hoping to prevent his falling under English influence, Cherniaev sent the Struve mission to Bukhara and suggested

23. IISG, "Biografiia," p. 196. Cherniaev's letter to his parents of 27 September 1865 was not preserved.

24. See below p. 106. Curious omissions and excisions—parts of letters snipped out—in Cherniaev's personal papers suggest this conclusion. The exclusively male environment during Cherniaev's adolescence reinforced his marked homosexual tendencies.

25. TURK KRAI, XX: 66–70, "Zamechaniia" (apparently by Stremoukhov).

partitioning Kokand between Russia and Bukhara. The mission to Bukhara, he boasted, would undercut English influence and secure the emir's friendship.[26]

Back in Orenburg Kryzhanovskii quickly patched up his differences with St. Petersburg and reiterated the official line. Now he blamed Cherniaev for an expansionism he himself had advocated in Tashkent. Conditions in Turkestan favored expansion, he noted, but there was no hurry. Tashkent did desire a Cherniaev administration, he admitted, but he preferred a khan.[27] The government approved Kryzhanovskii's views.

Cherniaev's report of October 23 angered Kryzhanovskii. Why had Cherniaev withheld his proclamation of Tashkent's independence and letter to the emir? The general's tale of English officers in Bukhara was fabricated. "Even stranger" were Cherniaev's comments to the emir about the Syr-Naryn frontier. Strangest of all was his sending an unauthorized delegation to Bukhara "with instructions which remain a mystery to me and composed of persons not even at your disposition." Kryzhanovskii demanded an explanation and forwarded Cherniaev's reports to St. Petersburg.

The Orenburg governor urged Miliutin to remove Cherniaev for exceeding his authority and violating orders. He had frustrated the government's plans for Tashkent and undermined Kryzhanovskii's negotiations with Bukhara. Cherniaev failed to inform Kryzhanovskii of important developments in Turkestan: he presented him with *faits accomplis* which contradicted Russia's general aims. He adhered stubbornly to his own ideas and usurped vast authority. Kryzhanovskii's efforts to reason with him had failed: "I have no right to tolerate longer even more blatant disobedience and exceeding of his authority."[28] Cherniaev must go.

The government backed Kryzhanovskii fully, Miliutin wanted Russian troops to remain in Tashkent while it elected an administration, but not necessarily a khan. Cherniaev must explain his actions to Orenburg, then he and Kryzhanovskii were to proceed to the capital to discuss new policies. Turkestan needed a proper adminis-

26. Ibid., pp. 105–106, Cherniaev to emir, October; pp. 119–121, Cherniaev to Kryzhanovskii, 22 October 1865.

27. Ibid., pp. 103–104, Stremoukhov to Kryzhanovskii, 30 September 1865; pp. 111–112, Miliutin to Kryzhanovskii, 5 October 1865; pp. 123–129, Kryzhanovskii to Gorchakov, 23 October 1865; pp. 134–140, Kryzhanovskii to Miliutin, 23 October 1865.

28. Ibid., pp. 187–188, Kryzhanovskii to Cherniaev, 14 November 1865; pp. 184–186, Kryzhanovskii to Miliutin, 14 November 1865, no. 22.

tration and a well-supplied, reinforced army to improve Russia's precarious position in Central Asia.[29]

On November 26 Miliutin telegraphed Kryzhanovskii that the emperor wished Cherniaev recalled. Summon him to Orenburg, he added, and inform him of his removal there. Kryzhanovskii ordered Cherniaev to yield his post to Colonel Kraevskii,[30] but circumstances would delay this several months. In self-justification Cherniaev emphasized that a local commander must act, not await detailed instructions. Kryzhanovskii, he asserted, had granted him carte blanche to negotiate with Bukhara. His instructions to Struve and his letter to the emir merely "clarified Bukhara's relationship with Russia." He had withheld Kryzhanovskii's proclamation and letter to the emir because Tashkent truly desired Russian rule: "Having in view only our country's good without ulterior motives or selfish aims, I am in nowise departing from government plans . . . , but in order to implement these instructions successfully, I must take local conditions and circumstances into account rather than lose opportunities by awaiting permission for each action."[31]

Could a dedicated soldier be passive while Russia's prestige suffered? Mikhail Grigorevich's reply presented superficially convincing reasons for disobedience. But clearly Kryzhanovskii had granted him only limited authority to negotiate. Regardless of circumstances, no government can permit a commander to flout its instructions or upset its stated policies. Cherniaev's rebuttal failed to allude to that issue.

Orenburg's dictation, affirmed Severtsov, was one cause of the dispute. Unless Tashkent were removed from its control, one or the other must lose authority. If Tashkent did, Russian commerce and prestige in Central Asia would be gravely damaged. But could the able Orenburg governor renounce participation in the only vital affair in his region? The emir's conduct had proved that Turkestan's subordination to Orenburg was futile: he sent compliments to St. Petersburg but negotiated with Cherniaev as an equal. Thus he had

29. Ibid., pp. 183–184, Gorchakov to emperor, 14 November 1865; p. 190, Gorchakov to Kryzhanovskii, 15 November 1865, telegram; pp. 193–196, Miliutin to Kryzhanovskii, 17 November 1865; pp. 196–197, Miliutin to Diugamel, 17 November 1865; ORBL, Miliutin, k. 15, no. 2, ll. 75–77.

30. TURK KRAI, xx: 242–243, Kryzhanovskii to Cherniaev, 29 December 1865. According to Zalesov ("Zapiski," Aug. 1903, p. 334), Kryzhanovskii's telegram to Gorchakov urging Cherniaev's removal unless he wanted a general war in Central Asia had proved decisive.

31. TURK KRAI, xx: 211–215, Cherniaev to Kryzhanovskii, December 1865.

recognized Russia to be superior to Bukhara. If the emir learned of this quarrel, Cherniaev's prestige, raised high before Asian khans, would fall because they would cease to believe him. Cherniaev did not object to Orenburg's control out of ambition, argued Severtsov, nor did he demand Turkestan's complete separation, merely that Tashkent be able to decide current military and diplomatic issues. Were Kryzhanovskii to move to Tashkent, the Turkestan governorship could be abolished. But if Cherniaev were removed summarily, his work and perhaps Turkestan would be lost.[32] Because of friendship, Severtsov underestimated Cherniaev's jealousy and ambition.

The general explained his dispute with Kryzhanovskii in a letter to Poltoratskii. Turkestan's inferior status, he claimed, made "the direct road" impossible: "I have no right to write officially to Petersburg; to write via Orenburg is useless; to execute Orenburg's orders contradicting local conditions is harmful for the peace of the region I am responsible for; not to carry them out is harmful for me—there is just no way out." Cherniaev blamed their quarrel on Bukhara: "Under other circumstances I probably would have gotten on with Kryzhanovskii despite his roughness. Under present conditions we have become enemies, though on parting we swore eternal friendship. Involuntarily I recalled Manilov's dreams when the government learned of his tender friendship with Chichikov[33]—it promptly makes them both generals. All these Manilovesque dreams were dispelled by the Bukharan emir—in him has lain the root of the evil from the start." St. Petersburg underestimated Turkestan's problems and dangers: "We cannot relax here yet. Wait until four more battalions come, then you can issue orders from Orenburg. . . . My good name is dear to me, and I will execute only what I can." Then Cherniaev struck a hero's pose: "I will not do what is impossible though you may try me and shoot me at any time." Good personal relations between the Tashkent and Orenburg commanders would not bring harmony "when people are 2,000 versts apart, one having authority and the other the responsibility." His prediction had come true that unless given sufficient legal authority he would have to usurp it.

Cherniaev explained his policy toward Tashkent. To proclaim its

32. Ibid., pp. 223–226, Severtsov to Poltoratskii, 15 December 1865.
33. Two characters in Nikolai Gogol's *Dead Souls*, a famous satire on Russian provincial officialdom.

independence would have meant repudiating his pledges to its inhabitants. "At one stroke I would have sunk to a bek's level in the view of the emir and the populace." His tender ego was uppermost. Even Kryzhanovskii knew that Russian troops could never leave an occupied region. Then how could Russia evade Gorchakov's November 1864 circular? Protests could be sent to Kryzhanovskii against creating a separate khanate followed by a Tashkent delegation "with whatever petition the government considers necessary to dictate." No one could prove that such a declaration had been forced. To demonstrate Tashkent's support Cherniaev enclosed a letter signed by its leaders which praised him as a deliverer.[34]

Refusing to admit errors in judgment, Cherniaev affirmed that his relations with Kryzhanovskii were direct and frank; actually he had been evasive and devious. His disobedience resulted partly from fear that executing the government's program would damage his personal prestige. He justified his actions by alleging an external threat from Bukhara. He defied the government to do its worst, believing that his victories would protect him; however, by November 1865 Petersburg had decided to remove him though to do so would prove more difficult than it imagined.

That fall, when the emir sent an envoy, Ishan-hodzha, to Tashkent, he had appeared to be resuming his traditional pro-Russian policy. To mislead Cherniaev, Ishan had spread rumors about British agents in Bukhara and requested a Russian delegation. Cherniaev should have realized that the emir sought Russian hostages.[35]

Muzaffar-ad-Din, emir of Bukhara (1860–1885), exemplified the feudal Islamic order ruling the khanates. He was resistant to any domestic reforms in Bukhara, and he failed to grasp the importance of Russia's advance. Muzaffar, who had never journeyed further than neighboring Kokand, ignored the superiority of Russian firepower over his ramshackle army. He claimed to lead Central Asian Moslems and shifted allies as readily as he added wives to his harem. The emir's principal concern was power and prestige; his friendship for Russia stemmed from expediency not sympathy. Until convinced of his impotence against Russia, he would be an unreliable ally. Nor was he truly master at home where a xenophobic clergy dominated

34. TURK KRAI, xx: 230–238, Cherniaev to Poltoratskii, 20 December 1865, enclosing the letter from the Tashkenters containing a panegyric of Cherniaev as administrator.
35. Terentiev, I: 328–329.

Bukhara and decided everything according to the Koran. He exercised imperfect control over a corrupt, inept administration which despoiled his subjects and kept them in darkness. Muzaffar and his advisers counted upon Islam and vastly superior numbers to defeat the infidel Russians.[36]

First the emir had tried threats and blackmail. Cherniaev had hoped that his response to Muzaffar's repeated requests for a Russian mission would cement peace; instead it led to war. Cherniaev sent K. V. Struve of the Asiatic Department and thirty-one other officials to the emir with a letter and presents. Among them was A. I. Glukhovskii instructed to gather data about Bukhara's army and topography.[37] Unwittingly Cherniaev let the emir display his wiles before millions of fellow Moslems.

On October 19, 1865, the Struve mission left Tashkent with the Bukharan envoy, Ishan-hodzha. They traveled via Chinaz and the Hungry Steppe—the same route Cherniaev would take in his attempt to rescue them. Once in Bukhara, Ishan requested the Russians to avoid prying questions. In Samarkand they were given no food and denied permission to buy any or send a report to Tashkent. The emir had apparently already decided to detain them. In Bukhara city Ishan warned them to expect a long stay and confined them in a courtyard. The audience with the emir was described by their chronicler, Tatarinov. Muzaffar appeared in a red *khalat* (native gown), his black beard wrapped in a white turban. He fairly exuded hauteur and ignorance, and his arrogant airs gave the envoys little cause for optimism. Weary weeks of imprisonment followed. Nonetheless, recalled Tatarinov, "we were confident that the letter of our general [Cherniaev], whose name resounded throughout Central Asia, would effect our release."[38]

With growing anxiety Cherniaev awaited news of his envoys. Initial Bukharan reports claimed that they were being well received. Then came a rumor (false) that one envoy had died, and that the Russians' letters to him had been confiscated (true). Cherniaev made inquiries. His courier learned that the mission was being held incommunicado in Bukhara. Mikhail Grigorevich demanded an explanation. The emir, confident that he held the stronger hand, replied

36. P. P. Shubinskii, *Ocherki Bukhary* (St. Petersburg, 1892), pp. 8–9; Becker, pp. 113–114.
37. TURK KRAI, XX: 118–119, Cherniaev to Struve and Glukhovskii, 18 October 1865. A. I. Glukhovskii, a staff officer, went to gather secret data about the Bukharan army for Cherniaev.
38. A. Tatarinov, *Semimesiachnyi plen v Bukhare* (St. Petersburg, 1867), pp. 1 ff.

impudently that the Russians would be held until the tsar received
a Bukharan delegation. His caravans' safe return from Russia contributed to the emir's recalcitrance.

The powerful White Tsar, replied Cherniaev, desiring commerce
not conquest, had authorized the Orenburg governor to negotiate,
and the latter transferred this authority to him. The emir had requested a Russian mission and promised to return it within five
weeks. Thus Cherniaev had permitted the Bukharan envoys at Fort
No. 1 to proceed toward St. Petersburg. Their admission to the tsar
would depend on Struve's safe return. "Consequently, fulfillment of
your wishes depends wholly upon you. As for me, in my subsequent
actions, I shall execute the will of my all-powerful sovereign."[39]
Bukharan stubbornness, emphasized Cherniaev, would bring military retribution.

Cherniaev, who blamed Orenburg's handling of the Bukharans
for the emir's defiance, feared that he would be the scapegoat for its
mistakes. He refused to wait. Tashkent went on a war footing: Cherniaev sent a rifle battalion across the Syr-Daria at Chinaz, and
requested Kryzhanovskii's cooperation "to maintain Russia's honor
and dignity in Central Asia." His chief of staff, Colonel Nikolai
Rizenkampf, explained that the emir's tone and Struve's detention
were intolerable. The envoys must be recovered by threats or by
force.[40]

When his Chinaz demonstration elicited no response, Cherniaev
resolved impetuously on a massive punitive expedition into Bukhara.
Ten more infantry companies and six sotnias were brought to Chinaz. "With such a detachment and such men," boasted Abramov,
"one can teach all Central Asia." As the emir mobilized and sought
aid from Khiva and the Turkomans, Cherniaev warned the emir:
"I come not with the aim of conquest, but because Russian officers
have been detained in Bukhara and thereby the White Tsar and all
his 75,000,000 subjects have been insulted. I must advance until I
meet my envoys and then I shall return."[41] The war ministry accounts of the Dzhizak expedition, declining to wash Russia's dirty

39. Romanovskii, appendix, pp. 179–183, Cherniaev to Kryzhanovskii, 12 January 1866,
and enclosures of the emir's undated letters.

40. TURK KRAI, xx: 226, Severtsov to Poltoratskii, 20 December 1865; xxi: 7–9, Cherniaev
to Kryzhanovskii, 12 January 1866; pp. 20–21, Rizenkampf to Kryzhanovskii, 14 January
1866.

41. Ibid., p. 22, Abramov to Makarov, 15 January 1866; pp. 25–27, Cherniaev to Kryzhanovskii, 20 January 1866, enclosing Cherniaev to emir.

linen before the Bukharans, blamed the emir for the conflict. "We did everything possible to avoid hostilities with Bukhara. Friendship with that country and fostering our Central Asian trade were our direct interests."[42] Actually, Cherniaev's naive reliance on the emir's promises, his impatience and arbitrary acts had helped to provoke war.

On January 21, 1866, Cherniaev's formidable force began crossing the Syr-Daria. A week later fourteen infantry companies, six sotnias, sixteen guns, and a month's supplies loaded on twelve hundred camels stood on the far side. An envoy arrived from the bek of Dzhizak, but no message came from the emir: threats had failed, now force would be employed.

On February 1 Cherniaev's detachment moved into the Hungry Steppe, a desert expanse which the Bukharans considered impassable by an army. Learning of this advance, the emir informed Cherniaev on his second day's march that he would send the Russian envoys via Samarkand to rejoin him. Calculating that this response stemmed from fear, Cherniaev replied that he must advance to the first water source to await the envoys before returning to his base.[43] The winter advance to Dzhizak was extraordinarily difficult. Cherniaev's own report was silent about this, but Lieutenant Bukharin, commanding a Cossack artillery platoon, recalled that they had struggled through a level, barren desert covered with one to two feet of snow. The trackless route was torture for the artillery. Even harnessed to four horses, ammunition wagons would barely move. Over the entire dreary stretch there was no fuel, fodder, or water. Men and animals slaked their thirst with snow. On the last two marches before Dzhizak the snow disappeared, but the mud was as hard to traverse as the snow had been.[44] Cherniaev was oblivious to such problems.

On February 4 the detachment halted at the first fresh water five miles from Dzhizak. The next day a note came from the emir asking that the Russians please avoid hostilities, and promising that Struve's party would reach Samarkand the same day. When the emir kept his promise, replied Cherniaev, he would return to base. Now that

42. "Bukharskie dela," vs, xlix (June 1866), 167–168; l (July), 48–49.

43. turk krai, xxi: 40–41, Cherniaev to Kryzhanovskii, 31 January 1866; pp. 75–76, 19 February 1866.

44. rt, documents, pp. 106–107, Bukharin's report of 10 March 1866; F. I. Lobysevich, *Postupatelnoe dvizhenie v Sredniuiu Aziiu* (St. Petersburg, 1900), p. 165.

he had clarified his relations with the emir, he asked the bek of Dzhizak to sell him wood and hay. The bek agreed, then added that he needed the approval of the emir. The need for supplies was so urgent that Cherniaev threatened force if they were not provided. When no response came, Cherniaev sent Pistolkors to Dzhizak. If supplies were refused, he was to seize them but not resort to arms unless the Bukharans did.

Masses of armed Bukharans met Pistolkors at Dzhizak. They parleyed, then withdrew. When Pistolkors followed, they erected a barricade across a street and fired at his men, but the Russians assaulted the barricade, pursued the Bukharans and entered the bazaar. Foraging parties gathered wood and hay from houses and courtyards. The heavily fortified citadel fired on the Russians but did no damage. The Cossacks covering Pistolkors' withdrawal were surrounded, but Cherniaev sent reinforcements to free them. In these skirmishes with some six thousand Bukharans, eight Russians were killed and nine wounded.

Cherniaev warned the emir that these hostile acts might compel him to assault the citadel. The next morning Cherniaev had to disperse fresh Bukharan troops near his camp with cannonfire. The bek deplored these incidents as "misunderstandings." If permitted, he would gladly sell supplies to the Russians. But when a foraging party reached the designated spot, the residents refused to come forth.

Realizing his perilous position, Cherniaev resolved to return to his base: "Seeing from the Bukharan actions that they sought to win time, and keeping my movements punitive, I decided, having two letters from the emir renouncing his former pretensions, to return to my base since lack of fodder for the horses barred a longer stay." On the ninth another foraging expedition was conducted. Next day came a third letter from the emir pledging to return the envoys and supply Cherniaev with hay and wood. The general reported: "Adhering to my earlier intention to withdraw to the Syr-Daria, since the Bukharans could engage in new delays, I began retiring February 11 and informed the emir that to prove that my only aim had been to recover the envoys, I would return to the Syr-Daria and await them as promised by his three letters."[45]

Cherniaev's battle report, composed at leisure in camp, distorted

---

45. TURK KRAI, XXI: 78–79, Cherniaev to Kryzhanovskii, 19 February 1866.

these events to conceal failure. Surely he had not believed promises which he had dismissed earlier as worthless, but he could not admit his blunders. Cherniaev should have known that food and fodder would be short at Dzhizak, and that his men would suffer in the Hungry Steppe. The emir's delaying tactics should have been anticipated. Was not his hasty retreat before Struve's arrival still another error?

Without denying these mistakes, General Terentiev justified the retreat. Dzhizak's citadel with a double wall manned by thousands of Bukharans seemed so formidable that Cherniaev doubted it could be taken without scaling ladders and siege equipment. A repulse could demoralize the only Russian offensive force, cut off by desert from supplies and reinforcements. Even success might doom Struve and his men to horrible deaths. Yet to withdraw without defeating the enemy was inglorious for a bold commander. Terentiev continued:

> The feelings contending within Cherniaev were understandable. In his place many would have risked an assault rather than lose glory. But not Cherniaev. He preferred to sacrifice his name, bear his subordinates' complaints and angry glances, and endure the government's dissatisfaction rather than risk the lives of men whom he had placed in a desperate position. Only a few appreciated his honorable choice, but never did Cherniaev reach loftier moral heights. True heroism is found not only on fortress walls but in such difficult situations. It required more courage to decide upon retreat than to order an assault.

An evil fate pursued Cherniaev, concluded Terentiev. He had failed in initial attempts against Chimkent and Tashkent. Given a second chance, he would have captured Dzhizak too.[46]

This charitable explanation rings only partly true. During the retreat, Cherniaev issued no commands about the order of march suggesting loss of nerve. He virtually abandoned active command. His officers and men were downhearted and angry. Fortunately Pistolkors took charge, ably covering the retreat and fending off masses of Bukharans. The retreat, confirmed Bukharin, was even more arduous than the advance. Bukharan cavalry attacked the exhausted troops; the horses suffered severely from lack of

46. Terentiev, i: 332–333.

fodder.[47] Could his men appreciate Cherniaev's "loftier moral heights"?

Cherniaev knew that the Moslems considered any Russian withdrawal a defeat for the infidel. The emir boasted that he had defeated the invincible general, attributing his retreat to Bukharan heroism. The Dzhizak reverse encouraged the emir to reject conciliation for holy war.[48] Cherniaev's retreat dimmed the hopes of the Struve mission. Only on February 6 did the delegates leave Bukhara, reaching Samarkand on the 13th, two days after Cherniaev's withdrawal. There Ishan-hodzha told them that the emir had driven Cherniaev away. The Russians languished in detention until freed four months later by General Romanovskii's victory at Irdzhar.[49]

The dispirited Russians reached camp February 14 and spent a month recuperating. During this time the Bukharans kept the region in turmoil, sending out raiding parties to attack isolated groups of Russians. On March 10 Cherniaev shifted camp to the mouth of the Chirchik. When Bukharan raiders threatened Russian communications, Abramov forced them to evacuate their base at Chardar.[50] These were the only significant operations, but Russia's hold on Turkestan grew precarious. Its prestige slipped dangerously while the Tashkent lion licked his wounds. The ill-conceived Dzhizak venture ended his military career in Central Asia ingloriously aiding the government to justify his removal from the region he had conquered.

47. Ibid., p. 333; Lobysevich, pp. 166–167.

48. Romanovskii, appendix, p. 193; Maksheev, p. 240. A pro-Cherniaev account ("Sh-skii," "Cherniaev," VISB (1915), no 3, pp. 111–113) blamed Kryzhanovskii for the Dzhizak reverse for not providing sufficient resources. However, he had never authorized the Dzhizak operation.

49. Tatarinov, pp. 47 ff. Struve defended the Dzhizak venture as having shown all Central Asians "our troops' superiority and heroism, and Cherniaev's name became still more terrible . . . ," TURK KRAI, XXI: 281–285, Struve to Stremoukhov, 7 July 1866.

50. Romanovskii, appendix, pp. 188–189, "Zhurnal voennykh deistvii."

84

CHAPTER VI

Removal and Intrigues (1866–1867)

To REMOVE a hitherto successful general without provoking indignation from his supporters and the public is a delicate operation for any government. Cherniaev's superiors, while anxious to camouflage his departure from Turkestan with his request for a transfer, had resolved to act promptly in any case. The war minister explained the government's dilemma to Kryzhanovskii. To remove Cherniaev outright would greatly damage his self-esteem: "Besides, the sudden removal of one who has revealed such brilliant abilities and acquired such popularity among the troops and in all Central Asia after achieving numerous resounding exploits would cause an unfavorable impression among the public and produce contradictory rumors, since the public would not know the need for such a measure." Cherniaev's impending marriage, surmised Miliutin, would soon bring him to Petersburg; as a married man he would not wish to return to Turkestan.[1]

Dismissing him, agreed Kryzhanovskii, would be difficult. In Tashkent Cherniaev had mentioned his desire to go to Petersburg. Kryzhanovskii had tried to lure him to Orenburg by asking him to bring various drafts and reports; when this failed he ordered him to

---

1. TURK KRAI, XXI: 32–33, Miliutin to Kryzhanovskii, 24 January 1866, no. 3.

come. His successor, stressed the governor, must reach Tashkent by late February in order to master local problems before the emir's anticipated spring offensive.[2] Instead Cherniaev had gone to Dzhizak.

Who would succeed him? Kryzhanovskii suggested Zalesov, but poor health and "the chaos on the Syr" made him hesitate. Miliutin first favored Cherniaev's old rival, Verevkin. Though loath to move his family to Turkestan, he consented like a good soldier. Then Miliutin telegraphed Orenburg that he had appointed Major General D. I. Romanovskii, former editor of the ministry's official organ *Russkii Invalid.* This trusted Miliutin subordinate had gone to Tashkent with Kryzhanovskii in 1865 and knew the situation. Miliutin arranged for Colonel Count I. I. Vorontsov-Dashkov to accompany him. Officially this imperial aide would reward the Turkestan troops for unusual exertions; privately he would assess their condition and morale.[3]

Cherniaev disrupted this timetable. On January 14 his chief of staff wrote Kryzhanovskii that he had withheld the letter ordering Cherniaev to Orenburg. Turkestan required an energetic commander personally interested in repairing previous mistakes, noted Rizenkampf. Replacing him now would prevent punishment of Bukhara, Russia's only worthy response. He had withheld the letter "knowing that upon receiving it, he [Cherniaev] would have left immediately, and it is hard to imagine the difficulties and disorders this would produce." Should the emir release Struve, he would give Cherniaev the letter immediately. If Muzaffar proved obdurate, he would hold it and await orders. Probably Cherniaev, to delay his departure, had ordered Rizenkampf to flout Orenburg's intentions. A week later Rizenkampf informed Miliutin that Cherniaev was leaving for Chinaz.[4] Evidently the Dzhizak campaign was partly Cherniaev's desperate attempt to recoup his fortunes.

2. Ibid., pp. 34–35, Kryzhanovskii to Miliutin, 25 January 1866. "I would very much wish to avoid ruining his [Cherniaev's] prestige in a region which he has conquered especially since for many of his qualities he deserves full indulgence, but unfortunately it will apparently be necessary to summon him without awaiting news of Struve's return." xx: 257, 31 December 1865.

3. Zalesov, "Zapiski," rs, cxv (Aug. 1903), 336; turk krai, xxi: 45–49, war minister to Alexander ii, 4 February 1866; pp. 54–55, Miliutin to Kryzhanovskii, 8 February 1866; orbl, Miliutin, k. 15, no. 3, ll. 123 ff.

4. turk krai, xxi: 20–22, Rizenkampf to Kryzhanovskii, 14 January 1866; pp. 27–28, Rizenkampf to Miliutin, 21 January 1866. The colonel was a loyal, admiring member of Cherniaev's entourage.

Even victory at Dzhizak could not have averted Cherniaev's dismissal. On one report the director of the Asiatic Department commented: "I find so many sophisms and false interpretations in Cherniaev's report that I want to discuss his comments in detail in order to demonstrate their utter absurdity and incompatibility. More than ever I fear that we shall have to pay dearly for his escapades and arbitrary acts."[5] And Kryzhanovskii complained that Cherniaev had not even informed him of Struve's arrest and had frustrated his diplomatic efforts. "Knowing from experience how the Turkestan military governor acts, I am virtually certain that at this very moment he is on the road to Bukhara . . . with his troops." How could he (Kryzhanovskii) negotiate with the emir while Cherniaev invaded his territory? "This time too, as has always been true before, Cherniaev has limited himself to reporting accomplished facts."

Puzzled by Cherniaev's financial reports, Kryzhanovskii sent officials to audit Turkestan's finances, then set up a commission to assess its findings. The four hundred thousand rubles Cherniaev demanded for current operations, concluded the governor, must be supplied though "no one can expect an account in proper form from him." Cherniaev, commented Miliutin, "disposes of money in Asiatic rather than European fashion." Later, Miliutin wrote: "His wilfulness, disobedience and petty tyranny amounted to clear violations of the basic rules of the military service. Drawn on by inexorable thirst for military glory, Cherniaev did not measure his operations with his resources, and acting contrary to instructions, found himself with a handful of troops facing two enemies: Bukhara and Kokand."[6]

Kryzhanovskii firmly controlled Central Asian policy from Orenburg. He knew little about Asia, asserted P. I. Pashino of the Asiatic department, but his subordinates invariably agreed with him in order to win favors for their relatives. "The servility here is terrible though Kryzhanovskii apparently does not seek or notice it." The Dzhizak campaign caused great excitement in Orenburg. "All yearn to be there," wrote Pashino, "all want to distinguish themselves. Even I dreamed of a Saint George's cross."[7] Kryzhanovskii had strong personal motives to remove Cherniaev.

5. Ibid., p. 39, Stremoukhov to Miliutin, 28 January 1866.
6. Ibid., pp. 60–64, Kryzhanovskii to Miliutin, 14 February 1866; ORBL, Miliutin, k. 15, no. 3, ll. 123 ff.
7. TURK KRAI, XXI: 81–84, Pashino to Stremoukhov, 24 February 1866, no. 1.

On February 10 Romanovskii and Vorontsov left Petersburg, stopped briefly to confer with Kryzhanovskii, then proceeded to Tashkent. Cherniaev's recent moves, wrote Romanovskii, had antagonized the khanates. Henceforth local commanders must obey foreign office circulars and avoid contrary public statements. No one now favored an independent Tashkent, so Cherniaev's view had prevailed in part, but the government should delay any final decision. Romanovskii, a moderate who preferred moral suasion to force in handling the khanates, viewed Cherniaev's irresponsible acts as the chief obstacle to peace.[8]

Romanovskii's November 1866 memorandum condemned Cherniaev's advance beyond Chimkent and assaults on Tashkent. Struve's detention revealed Bukharan defiance, and the retreat from Dzhizak had made matters worse. Most Uzbeks believed that the emir would drive Russia from Turkestan. "Talk such as this could be heard at any bazaar."[9] Cherniaev's dismissal, intimated Romanovskii, was caused by rash moves endangering Russia's control of the region. But he shared Cherniaev's sense of urgency about reinforcing Turkestan. The emir was gathering forty thousand men at Dzhizak. Romanovskii's first move on becoming acting military governor March 11 was to plead for immediate reinforcements from Orenburg.[10]

Meanwhile "Tashkent's inhabitants" hailed Cherniaev's rule and lamented rumors that he would soon depart. Treating all citizens equally regardless of wealth and position, he had established unprecedented tranquility. They wrote the tsar: "Placed right in the enemy's path, we are greatly upset and dismayed at this report because a general like Cherniaev, humiliating the enemy with powerful blows and acquiring glory in the region as the bravest of warriors, as stubborn as a falcon, striking the enemy in battle and firmly barring his way is recalled to Russia. . . . What will become of us unfortunate ones? Repeating these words day and night, tearfully we beg the Creator on high not to remove our General Cherniaev."[11] How strange that news of his removal, rumored in Tashkent, was

8. Ibid., pp. 50–52, Romanovskii memorandum, 8 February 1866; Romanovskii, pp. 37–40.

9. TURK KRAI, XXII: 176–178, Romanovskii memorandum, Nov. 1866.

10. Ibid., XXI: 99, Kryzhanovskii to Miliutin, 10 March 1866; p. 97, Cherniaev to Kryzhanovskii, 7 March 1866; p. 122, Romanovskii to Kryzhanovskii, 18 March 1866.

11. Ibid., XXII, 4 March 1866. Original is in Persian with a seal at the end.

unknown to the general himself! Having boasted that he could manipulate Uzbek opinion, Cherniaev doubtless inspired this letter to demonstrate his indispensability.

At Chinaz late in March, Romanovskii formally received authority over Turkestan. Reluctantly yielding his command, Cherniaev commented peevishly: "When they [Romanovskii and Vorontsov] arrived in Tashkent, I was in camp facing the Bukharans. Romanovskii came to me, but in my troops' presence I dispatched an aide to tell him that I would not receive him, but I did receive Vorontsov and soon afterwards left for Petersburg. Actually, I was very much outraged."[12]

Miliutin described differently the changeover at Chinaz. Cherniaev had instructed his chief of staff to ignore Romanovskii and write only to Vorontsov. In Fort No. 1, Romanovskii proclaimed himself acting Turkestan commander, but Cherniaev wrote Vorontsov: "Judging from the tone he has adopted in Turkestan region, I can conclude that I have been removed from my post and that he has been sent to replace me. In any case for the sake of *the region created by me* under present circumstances General Romanovskii should not announce this to the populace until he has received the post from me." At Chinaz Cherniaev obstinately refused to receive Romanovskii until Vorontsov induced him to yield. Then he was transformed: haughty impertinence gave way to utter desperation and he burst into tears. After handing over command to Romanovskii, he penned this curious little note:

> Respected Dmitrii Ilich [Romanovskii]:
>
> In view of the danger threatening the region *created by me*, I request permission to remain in the detachment as your orderly.
>
> > Your faithful servant,
> > M. G. Cherniaev

"Such self-disparagement resembled irony," remarked Miliutin, but the good natured Romanovskii, overlooking Cherniaev's impudence, supported his plea.[13]

Soon Cherniaev renounced this humility. As the Bukharans re-

12. IISG, "Avtobiografiia," p. 14; "Biografiia," pp. 181–182.
13. ORBL, Miliutin, k. 15, no. 3, ll. 124–126.

mained quiet and Romanovskii refused to budge, he left for Tashkent on March 31 with Vorontsov having promised to proceed immediately to Petersburg.[14] "Immediately" took an entire week. In Tashkent, Cherniaev received a letter from Petersburg which lifted his despondency. Had it come earlier, he declared, he would not have relinquished his command. He tarried hoping that a sudden Bukharan move would repair his fortunes. He issued orders as if he were still in command, inspected troops and lavishly distributed presents to Tashkenters. There were extravagant farewell celebrations where his former subordinates gave speeches which Miliutin felt violated decency and military discipline. Cherniaev wrote insultingly to Romanovskii: "When you left Petersburg, they [the government] did not know the situation in the [Turkestan] region or they would not have sent you. But now the deed has been done and having removed the head, one should not cry over the hairs."[15] In this undignified manner he departed from Tashkent.

He alluded sarcastically to Romanovskii's dispersal of "Bukharan cavalry" on April 5. Colonel Pistolkors, realizing that an approaching mass was sheep, reported this to Romanovskii. The latter, claimed Cherniaev, found this at odds with his desire for glory. He ordered a charge. Accurate artillery fire and an infantry assault caused "the enemy" to flee in panic. Taken prisoner were fifteen thousand sheep and one shepherd. Official reports stated that three thousand enemy cavalry had been dispersed. Known in Turkestan as "the sheep battle," this episode caused guffaws there long afterward.[16]

However, Romanovskii soon achieved genuine exploits. Cherniaev's retreat from Dzhizak had made the emir overconfident and aggressive. A month after the general's departure Romanovskii smashed the Bukharan army at Irdzhar. One bold stroke restored Russian prestige and security. "Our success at Irdzhar and Khodzhent's occupation," wrote Romanovskii later, "transformed the situation." Russia could halt for awhile. Romanovskii refused to plunge into Bukhara despite Kryzhanovskii's efforts to provoke further war.[17]

14. Terentiev, ɪ: 335.

15. ORBL, Miliutin, k. 15, no. 3, ll. 124–126.

16. Terentiev, ɪ: 342. Maksheev's account (p. 241) recorded this incident as a cavalry encounter!

17. TURK KRAI, XXII: 178, Romanovskii memorandum of November 1866; ORBL, Miliutin,

Irdzhar confirmed Miliutin's confidence in Romanovskii, dubbed by the Uzbeks, "the new Cherniaev." His task, noted Miliutin, was to build, not conquer, to repair what Cherniaev had spoiled and achieve peace. Since he had not gone to Turkestan to perform exploits "or write brilliant military reports," he could restore order and develop trade. Cherniaev's behavior, confided Miliutin, had been unpardonable. "His petulance and false pride took him beyond the bounds of reason."[18]

The war ministry's official journal, aimed at Russian officers, assessed Cherniaev's work in Turkestan more positively. His victories had promoted Russia's prestige in Central Asia. He had created order, destroyed slavery, and acquired the natives' trust. His troops had revered him and faced any danger at his command.[19] Cherniaev's legend was promoted in the army.

Cherniaev's rule found other defenders. He left Tashkent, wrote Zalesov, amidst fond farewells from Uzbeks and subordinates who appreciated his directness and generosity. With slight resources he had conquered a broad region. "Arrogantly and boldly he threw himself upon the enemy with tiny forces getting money wherever he could find it."[20] Antonina lamented, with some exaggeration, overlooking Romanovskii's services: "No one could replace Cherniaev in Tashkent where he had performed lengthy, absorbing and productive work for the good of Russia and the conquered region."[21]

The English were understandably relieved by his departure. Crealock, the military attaché, reported to the ambassador: "It seems that General Tchernaieff . . . is a man of a very excitable and impetuous temperament. He has for some time caused alarm to the Orenburg governor and others lest by rashly attacking the enemy on the frontier he should commit the Government to military operations." Ambassador Buchanan reported, "The independent and insubordinate proceedings of General Tchernaieff have induced the emperor to recall him to St. Petersburg." Now one could hope that Russia would repudiate rash policies and avoid annexing regions

---

k. 15, no. 3, 11. 126–130 reverse.

18. Ibid., 36/21, Miliutin to Romanovskii, 16 May 1866.

19. vs, LXIII (Sept. 1868), 126.

20. Zalesov, "Zapiski," (Aug. 1903), p. 337. But earlier he commented (p. 334): "A brave man of irreproachable honor, but . . . a bad administrator, a commander touchy to the point of pettiness and constantly acting on first impulses."

21. IISG, "Biografiia," p. 188.

which would be expensive and difficult to administer.[22] Cherniaev's swift removal reassured London.

Kryzhanovskii accused Cherniaev of undermining Russian credit in Turkestan by extravagance and indiscriminate borrowing. His unauthorized expenditures had included both Tashkent campaigns, the Struve mission, and the Dzhizak affair. He had concealed these by illegal borrowing, withholding pay from his men, and confiscating private monies sent to Turkestan: "Under such circumstances the natives, seeing Russian soldiers without pay, meat, and partly without uniforms and their commander always without money and borrowing from the defeated, probably concluded that Russia was a poor country, unable to pay its soldiers. No wonder that our credit was undermined."[23] Russian paper money, retorted Cherniaev, had not been used in Turkestan since the Uzbeks would not accept it. He had asked for hard currency to purchase supplies from the inhabitants. In almost every letter he had pleaded for money. Beyond his appropriation for 1864 he had spent eighty-five thousand rubles by September 1, 1865. "No one can cite a military operation cheaper than the conquest of Turkestan region," affirmed Cherniaev. When no orders came, he had built barracks and begun postal service. Because his superiors withheld money, he had borrowed from Tashkent merchants and used the wage fund to buy provisions. "I personally reported this to Kryzhanovskii and that the troops were not being paid. . . ." His soldiers had been well-fed, healthy and in proper uniform. Where had Kryzhanovskii obtained contrary information? Kryzhanovskii's extraordinary expenses during two visits to Tashkent, countered Cherniaev, almost equalled the cost of conquering Turkestan.[24]

His defense was superficially persuasive, and some of Kryzhanovskii's charges were inaccurate, but Cherniaev's superiors had ample cause to recall him. The foreign minister had urged removal of commanders who disregarded Russia's stated policy in Central Asia, but as affairs in Germany neared the crisis, which culminated in the Austro-Prussian War (June–July 1866), he dared not antagonize England. The war minister could no longer tolerate

22. FO, 65/868, Crealock to Buchanan, (11)/23 February 1866; Buchanan to Clarendon, (16)/28 February 1866, no. 71.

23. Terentiev, III, appendix, pp. 3–7, Kryzhanovskii to Miliutin, 17 March 1866.

24. Agreeing, Terentiev estimated the cost of these trips and replacing Cherniaev—which he felt was unnecessary—at 60,000 rubles (p. 21). For Cherniaev's reply to Kryzhanovskii's charges see ibid., pp. 7–20.

Cherniaev's blatant disregard for instructions. But the controversy over his role did not end there. Cherniaev would discover means to plague his successors and complicate their rule in Turkestan.

On April 4, just before Cherniaev left Tashkent, D. V. Karakozov, a nihilist student, fired at Alexander II. He missed his target but frightened the emperor and stimulated conservatives to resist further reform. The removal of liberal ministers and the official outcry against radicalism created a political climate conducive to Cherniaev's intrigues against the war ministry and Turkestan administration.

During the previous five years Alexander had emancipated the serfs and introduced local self-government (*zemstvo*) and a western type court system. The press was partially freed from oppressive censorship. War Minister Miliutin modernized and liberalized the army. Now, exploiting the Karakozov incident, a powerful group of conservative noblemen fearing loss of power and prerogatives, redoubled their "defense of autocracy" against terrorism and revolution. Karakozov's action reinforced the emperor's basic caution and shattered liberal dreams of a constitution. The conservative Count D. A. Tolstoi became minister of education and Count Petr A. Shuvalov, spokesman for the former serfowners, was made chief of gendarmes. They were harbingers of a rising tide of reaction.[25]

These ministerial changes weakened the position of War Minister Miliutin, Cherniaev's chief opponent. Until 1866 the military reforms had progressed rapidly. Now the new ministers opposed Miliutin and his relations with other ministers grew strained. The finance minister, accusing the war office of extravagance, urged that its appropriations be cut. Count Shuvalov's clique acquired vast power over domestic affairs, nominating new ministers and controlling most provincial governors. For the next five years few appointments to high posts occurred without his consent. He consolidated his authority by playing on the emperor's fear of revolution. Shuvalov was universally feared; the public pronounced his name in whispers. He strengthened the police, and emphasized order and aristocratic prerogatives. Disgruntled conservatives like Cherniaev turned to him to redress their grievances.[26]

25. B. B. Glinskii, *Revoliutsionnyi period russkoi istorii* (St. Petersburg, 1913), I: 272 ff.; Florinsky, II: 1033 ff.; P. Alston, *Education and the State in Tsarist Russia* (Stanford, 1969), pp. 78–80. Reactionary trends within Alexander II's regime began long before Karakozov's shot. See P. A. Kropotkin, *Zapiski revoliutsionera* (Moscow, 1966), pp. 170–175.

26. ORBL, Miliutin, k. 15, no. 3, ll. 134–141; Zalesov, pp. 537–539; P. A. Valuev, *Dnevnik*

The government's far-reaching constructive measures of the early 1860s yielded to aimless repression. The emperor convened the Committee of Ministers only *pro forma*. At one session Foreign Minister Gorchakov, already slipping mentally, forgot what he was reading while the emperor dozed.[27] How could one rejoice, asked A. V. Nikitenko, when the Shuvalovs headed the bureaucracy, and the ministers "travel to and from Moscow to ask [M. N.] Katkov and [K. N.] Leontiev[28] what to do and how to do it?"[29] Reactionaries exulted.

Dazed by his sudden fall and unaware of these events, Cherniaev dallied on the Volga feigning illness. He was reluctant to face his angry superiors in St. Petersburg. His devoted friend V. V. Grigoriev remonstrated: "You belong to Russia. . . . In this capacity as a public figure you cannot, or at least should not, act precisely as you wish. You should behave so that your conduct does no damage to your country. . . . Operating in the depths of Asia you perhaps do not know how popular you have become in the heart of Russia. Let those who envy you intrigue as long as they fail to destroy the legend which you have become already." Cherniaev could not be useful in Samara, pleaded Grigoriev, and no one would believe he was ill. He must hasten to the capital: "Chagrin is the fate of all who rise above the ordinary level. You have experienced [reverses] and will suffer more, but you must not heed them. I am confident that you need go only as far as Moscow to find public sympathy . . . [which] will give you strength to come to St. Petersburg not as a victim but triumphant over all your enemies. . . . But above all you must execute the emperor's will. Otherwise all is lost."[30]

Perhaps Grigoriev's letter persuaded Cherniaev to return to Petersburg. His plea to obey the emperor foreshadowed Ivan Aksakov's advice a decade later. His deafness to such counsel would bring him grief and misfortune. But the letter contained a dangerous message: you are popular, a living legend. This fed his overweening pride and penchant for intrigue.

Late in April, Mikhail Grigorevich met with the emperor, the

P. A. Valueva, ministra vnutrennykh del (Moscow, 1961), ii: 121, 123, 143.

27. Ibid., ii: 104, meeting of 17 February 1866.

28. Katkov was editor of the conservative daily, *Moskovskie Vedomosti*. Leontiev was professor of Roman literature at Moscow University and Katkov's close collaborator.

29. A. V. Nikitenko, *Zapiski i dnevnik* (St. Petersburg, 1893), iii: 170–171.

30. GIM, ed. khr. 45, ll. 5–6, V. V. Grigoriev to Cherniaev, 26 April 1866.

foreign minister, and the war minister. Foreign Minister Gorchakov received him at the Winter Palace. To Cherniaev's amazement he asked Count Ignatiev: "What is that hole of an Aulie-Ata which Cherniaev mentioned?" The foreign minister was ignorant of a major Central Asian city captured by Russian troops. The war minister, recalled Cherniaev, "was obviously set against me." Had he not upset Miliutin's plans for an elaborate expedition to Tashkent? "Why didn't you get along with Kryzhanovskii?" inquired Miliutin. "You know the reason!" retorted the general. "That he is jealous of your capture of Tashkent," mused Miliutin, "is no wonder." Declared Cherniaev: "I hope such an event happens again during your ministry." Miliutin lectured him for not welcoming Kryzhanovskii to Tashkent.[31] "I told him frankly my opinion of his behavior and concealed nothing from the emperor." Alexander refused to receive Cherniaev until Kryzhanovskii interceded, then the emperor treated him "more graciously than he deserved."[32]

Their interview was dramatic, claimed Cherniaev. Entering the audience chamber, he bowed low but did not embrace the emperor as was customary. "Kiss me," ordered Alexander kindly. Cherniaev obeyed and both burst into tears. Though dissatisfied at his relations with Kryzhanovskii, Alexander added, "Just remain here for two years or so and I shall give you an assignment that will make you forget your Tashkent." Cherniaev believed that his career was made. His personal magnetism had won the emperor's forgiveness.

Cherniaev became absorbed in domestic matters. In May he married Antonina Vulfert in a St. Petersburg church, and they rented a cottage near Gatchina, a fashionable suburb. To his amazement he learned that during summer maneuvers the emperor and his suite would stop in for breakfast. In St. Petersburg he left orders for food and waiters to be sent to his dacha when he telegraphed. Gatchina's commandant, General Baggovut, assured him: "Don't worry about that, Mikhail Grigorevich. I'll let you know the day before."

A few days later the Cherniaevs were awakened by two officers of the imperial suite preceding Grand Duke Nikolai Nikolaevich, the emperor's brother. Hastily donning his uniform Cherniaev tried to explain. "You should have checked personally every day for orders," declared the grand duke sternly and rode off. Cherniaev was deeply dismayed. General Baggovut, chagrined that he could

31. IISG, "Biografiia," pp. 187–188; "Avtobiografiia," pp. 14–15.
32. ORBL, Miliutin, 36/21, Miliutin to Romanovskii, 16 May 1866.

not entertain the emperor, had purposely deceived Cherniaev. His mother-in-law, Lady Vulfert, was certain that his career was ruined.[33]

Nonetheless, Cherniaev sought to restore himself to prominence and participated in discussions on the future of Turkestan. That region still lacked statutes and proper administration. Even under the easygoing Romanovskii the disadvantages of ruling Turkestan from Orenburg were evident. At meetings held at Miliutin's home in St. Petersburg that winter,[34] all but Kryzhanovskii, who was protecting his vested interest, agreed that a separate Turkestan governor generalship and military district should be created. The emperor approved and the Committee of Ministers drew up a draft statute.[35] Coveting the post of governor general, Cherniaev intrigued with his supporters to block Romanovskii's nomination. Count Vorontsov-Dashkov, having succumbed to Cherniaev's charm, became his patron and advocate before the heir. The plotters utilized an Uzbek delegation which presented to the emperor a vaguely worded petition denouncing Romanovskii's administration. A clever translator, probably paid by Cherniaev's backers, assured Alexander that conditions in Turkestan had been far better under Cherniaev. Tendentious articles against Romanovskii appeared in *Birzhevye Vedomosti*, a leading St. Petersburg daily.

Their target was an honorable, intelligent officer who had displayed uncommon humanity and restraint toward the enemy. Romanovskii, who respected Moslem customs scrupulously, was esteemed by both his troops and the Uzbeks. Compared to the time of the Khans, the Uzbeks paid insignificant taxes. Governor for only a few months and absorbed by the war with Bukhara, he had made few innovations. Would people recently conquered and ruled kindly complain so soon of Russian oppression?

Cherniaev's intrigue succeeded only in part. Shocked at the calumnies showered upon him, Romanovskii denied them vigorously in *Russkii Invalid*. Then he resigned and requested a formal inquiry into his governorship. Since there were no direct accusations, Miliutin demurred. However, a shadow fell over Romanovskii preventing his nomination as governor general.[36] The British ambassador com-

33. IISG, "Biografiia," pp. 188, 196–203; "Avtobiografiia," p. 14.
34. Terentiev, I: 400–401.
35. ORBL, Miliutin, k. 16, no. 1, ll. 28–31.
36. Ibid., ll. 31 and reverse; G. Arandarenko, "Pamiati D. I. Romanovskogo," RS (May

mented: "I am told that these complaints [by the Uzbek delegation] originated in the intrigues of the friends of General Tchernayeff who had hoped to bring about the reappointment of that officer to the command of which he was deprived last year. General Tchernayeff's former proceedings and aggressive policy have, however, I am assured, rendered his reemployment impossible."[37] Instead, in July 1867 the emperor appointed Konstantin Petrovich fon-Kaufman, a trusted Miliutin understudy, as governor general. Cherniaev's dreams of a triumphant return to Tashkent would take fifteen years to realize.

He explored other avenues. On March 3, 1867, without resigning his commission or informing the tsar, Cherniaev offered his sword to Prince Mihajlo Obrenović of Serbia "to devote myself to the great cause which Your Highness represents and defends." He was ready "to come to Serbia immediately in peace or war. Since enthusiasm is the only reason for my step, Your Highness can rest assured that you will find me a zealous and faithful servant."[38] Cherniaev expected that Serbia would lead the South Slavs against Turkey, and he developed a sudden enthusiasm for its cause, mainly out of personal ambition. His action was inconsiderate of the tsar and illegal.

Since 1860 Prince Mihajlo had aimed to liberate Serbs under Turkish rule and unite them around his semi-independent principality. Inspired by Piedmont-Sardinia's leadership of Italian unification, he sought aid from Russian Panslavs and St. Petersburg. By 1867 Serbia had military alliances with Montenegro and Greece and a friendship pact with Rumania. Cherniaev prepared the way through Sava Grujić, a Serbian artillery lieutenant studying in Russia. According to Grujić, General Cherniaev planned to visit Serbia incognito. Premier Ilija Garašanin of Serbia asked Miliutin for verification and if Cherniaev were a sound military man. Unfortunately, his reply is not known.

Miliutin had provided Serbia with military aid so it could resist Turkey. In April 1867, responding to an official Serbian request, he sent three Russian officers to advise Prince Mihajlo and assess his war preparations. Later, Miliutin explained to one of them that Russia had not urged Serbia to prepare for war and had pointed out

---

1905), pp. 465–468.
37. FO, 65/869, Buchanan to Stanley, 8 May 1867, no. 162.
38. A. Cherniaeva, "Pisma vlastitelei," RA, LII (1914), I: 34–35.

the dangers of such a course. In no case, he warned, should Serbia count upon Russia's participation in such a war. Serbia, reported his officers, was woefully unprepared to fight.[39] Russian diplomatic pressure induced the Turks to evacuate their fortresses in Serbia peacefully.

Still hoping to enter Serbian service, Mikhail Grigorevich wrote to his friend, Ivan Aksakov, leader of the Moscow Panslavs: "My trip to Serbia has been somewhat delayed, but I still have not abandoned hope that it may take place without the [Russian] government's knowledge since it has already renounced any intention to send me there. When I was told this, I immediately sent a Serb [Grujić] to . . . Prince Michael with a letter which he promises to answer from Constantinople."[40]

Cherniaev hoped to foster a Balkan uprising to deliver the Christians from Turkish rule and to become the insurgents' commander in chief. His friend, N. N. Raevskii, a Russian officer who resigned to go to Serbia, planned to foment partisan activity against the Turks in Bulgaria and equip the rebels with ammunition and money sent from Serbia and Moldavia. Revolts were to erupt all over Bulgaria. An experienced officer would be needed to coordinate operations.[41]

Prince Mihajlo sent his reply, requesting Cherniaev to come to Serbia, to the Russian foreign ministry via the Constantinople embassy. In the ministry the letter was opened and shown to Stremoukhov and Miliutin, who informed the emperor. Alexander II ordered, "Rebuke him." The war minister summoned Cherniaev and asked, "Did you write the letter [to Prince Mihajlo]?" "I wrote it," responded Cherniaev. "You are a traitor!" exploded Miliutin. Then there occurred such a scene, recalled Cherniaev inaccurately, "that I never met Miliutin again."[42]

The Serbian affair ended badly for Cherniaev and poisoned his relations with Miliutin. Unfounded rumors circulated that he was in Serbia in disguise. Captain Snegirev, a Russian officer in Belgrade,

39. ORBL, Miliutin, k. 11, d. 8, "Dela Serbskie." This material was obtained courtesy of Professor Alfred Rieber.

40. IISG, ed. khr. 10, Cherniaev to Aksakov, 3 April 1866.

41. GIM, ed. khr. 17, "Proekt Raevskogo organizatsii vosstaniia na Balkanskom poluostrove," 20 April 1866, copy. In this same ed. khr. were letters from Constantinople and Bucharest about a possible Balkan insurrection.

42. IISG, "Avtobiografiia," p. 15; A. Cherniaeva, "Pisma vlastitelei," p. 29. Cherniaev's memory was faulty: only a year later he talked with Miliutin. See p. 102.

was watched constantly by Austrian and Turkish agents who suspected that he was Cherniaev. In Serbia the pro-Austrian party gained strength. Garašanin resigned and Russia suspended war credits.[43] The murder of Prince Mihajlo in May 1868 dissolved the Balkan league and ended close Serbo-Russian collaboration. Cherniaev would have to wait eight years to lead the Serbs in war.

---

43. ORBL, Miliutin, k. 11, d. 8, "Dela Serbskie."

CHAPTER VII

In Opposition (1867–1875)

CHERNIAEV spent the next eight years in semiretirement vainly awaiting a glorious command. Indulging a worsening habit of self-pity, he blamed political enemies for mounting personal and financial woes. He demonstrated and postured counting on the heir and powerful conservatives for support. In his newspaper, *Russkii Mir* (*The Russian World*), he campaigned against the Turkestan administration and war ministry. Dramatizing his own past achievements, he sought to discredit his foes with intrigue and slander.

In May 1867, after a year on military leave, Mikhail Grigorevich resigned his commission "for domestic reasons" and received a small annual pension. On their savings he and his wife visited Helgoland in the North Sea. They attended the Paris world's fair on his winnings at roulette, then returned to Russia in the fall.[1]

Regarding the war minister as a personal enemy blocking his path, Cherniaev sought a prestigious command through Count Shuvalov. He was a very junior major general, but the tsar, probably urged on by Shuvalov, asked Miliutin to make him a divisional commander. To Miliutin's amazement Cherniaev rejected this contemptuously as beneath his dignity. The war minister insisted that

1. IISG, "Biografiia," pp. 203–204; GIM, ed. khr. 1, l. 13.

the tsar *wished* him to command a division, but "I encountered such impudent presumption from him that I regarded him as virtually mad."[2] Cherniaev proceeded to Moscow to become a notary public despite Miliutin's warning that this would offend the emperor. "My position had become desperate," explained Cherniaev later. "At that time I had only recently become a family man and was left without a source of livelihood. I even lacked enough for my daily bread . . . and to save myself and my wife who was then preparing to become a mother, I could not delay." Angrily he rejected Miliutin's assertion that he was demonstrating against the war ministry. "Was it conceivable for me, under the circumstances, to undertake a demonstration?" he asked Vorontsov-Dashkov. "Was it easy on my pride . . . to expose myself to a public examination and compete with youths to obtain a post?" Instead, this was a heavy sacrifice for the sake of his family![3]

Miliutin questioned this. Leaving Turkestan, Cherniaev had received full salary for over a year. Now he was posing as a misunderstood hero in exile. "The man's ambition and conceit," noted the war minister, "approached the point of insanity."[4] Indeed, the notary affair resembled his behavior in 1863 when he had considered going off to Vologda.[5] Surely in neither case did he desire an obscurity which would deny his thirst for prominence and acclaim.

Moscow was surprised by the news that the conqueror of Tashkent had taken a notary's examination. Katkov's conservative organ, *Moskovskie Vedomosti*, accepting his plea of poverty, noted that a Moscow capitalist had paid the required ten thousand ruble deposit.[6] Hostile intrigue, concluded a contemporary, must have forced him to become a notary: "In various quarters I hear him praised and hear indignation expressed against the war ministry. Around town [Moscow] there is much gossip on this score. In any case it will be

2. ORBL, Miliutin, k. 16, no. 1, l. 30 reverse.

3. Ibid., Vorontsov-Dashkov, 82/23, Cherniaev to Vorontsov-Dashkov, 10 November 1873.

4. Ibid., Miliutin, k. 16, no. 1, ll. 31 and reverse. "All these tricks of Cherniaev and company deserve no mention in themselves," wrote Miliutin, "unless Cherniaev succeeds some day, thanks to his intrigues and his admirers' simplicity, to once again swim to the surface of career and play the role of a great man." Sharing his view of the notary affair was the article of the unknown "W. G.," "Feuilleton: M. G. Tschernajeff," NFP, no. 4268, 14 July 1876.

5. See p. 33.

6. MV, mid-November 1867; GIM, ed. khr. 45, l. 7, Grigoriev to Cherniaev, 26 November 1867.

strange to see General Cherniaev, decorated with a Saint George's cross, sitting in a notary's office."[7]

The authorities blocked this maneuver. He had rented an office and Moscow firms had agreements to be notarized. Suddenly Count Shuvalov wrote him that the emperor, doubtful that financial worry had prompted his move, found his new post "not in accordance with your rank or former service."[8] Cherniaev was furious. "Wait and bargain with them from here," advised Katkov. But the enraged general hastened to St. Petersburg. After listening to his tirade, Shuvalov promised to speak to the emperor. "Wait a bit," said Gorchakov. "Today in the State Council I shall ask what this means." Shuvalov sought him a post in the interior ministry, but Alexander II insisted: "If he wants to work, let him enter military service." Cherniaev asserted that if allowed to be a notary, he would have become wealthy.[9] But he gained something he coveted more: sympathetic publicity. Surely he realized that the emperor could not permit a decorated general to draw up contracts.

Reluctantly donning his uniform, he was assigned to Fieldmarshal F. F. Berg's Warsaw command as special military attaché. There in 1868 Mrs. Cherniaev delivered their firstborn, Antonina, who was destined to continue his struggle with authority. In Warsaw the emperor, still irked at his refusal to command a division, told him, "With your junior status there is nothing else to be done." Cherniaev remonstrated with the heir, but to no avail. "Now I cannot count on anything," he informed his brother, Nikolai. "In any case I asked them to leave me in peace until spring and then let God's will be done."

He hoped for personnel changes in the war ministry. Prince Bariatinskii's agitation had badly shaken Miliutin. Soon Cherniaev would know if the ministry would be purged and whether he could obtain a proper position.[10] He had joined the powerful Shuvalov-Bariatinskii group of conservative politicians and officers which aimed to reverse previous reforms, restore gentry predominance and enhance the role of the field generals. At times they almost won over the basically conservative emperor. Late in 1868, with the Committee of Ministers packed with obedient reactionaries, their campaign against Miliutin reached a crescendo.

7. Nikitenko, III: 170–171, entry of 21 November 1867.
8. GIM, ed. khr. 1, ll. 36–37; A. Cherniaeva, "Pisma vlastitelei," pp. 30–31.
9. IISG, "Avtobiografiia," p. 16.
10. GIM, ed. khr. 39, ll. 3–5, M. G. to N. G. Cherniaev, 26 October and 21 December 1868.

The Shuvalov clique accused *Russkii Invalid*, the war ministry's liberal mouthpiece, of opposing government policies. General A. E. Timashev and Shuvalov denounced it in the Committee of Ministers. Shuvalov's ubiquitous police secretly encouraged ex-general R. A. Fadeev's abusive assaults upon the war ministry. Miliutin forbade *Invalid*'s editor to reply until Fadeev spread false rumors that the Russian army was unprepared; then he merely had him warn the public against such misleading declarations. Lacking imperial support, Miliutin decided to suspend *Invalid*.[11]

Its "death notice" induced Cherniaev among others to propose taking it over. The Russian army, he declared, must rise above politics and seek no prerogatives for itself. "Otherwise it would be a Praetorian guard selling its services to the highest bidder instead of being the obedient servant of imperial authority. Its motto . . . must forever remain: I obey." He attributed *Invalid*'s supposed decline to its high price and broad program. Why should company officers read Disraeli's speeches? *Invalid* should confine itself to military affairs and describe political matters only in their final form without polemics. "If these ideas agree with those of your ministry," concluded Cherniaev, "I request permission to undertake publication of *Invalid* at my own risk beginning next year."

Did he really expect Miliutin to allow a bitter opponent to transform *Invalid* into a narrow military organ? In reply Miliutin expressed doubt that a specialized newspaper could support itself, but he agreed to discuss a specific program with the general.[12] His interview with Miliutin ended Cherniaev's hopes: "He virtually refused me outright, although in his letter he speaks entirely differently." Cherniaev explained to Vorontsov-Dashkov that he had no speculative aim in mind. "I am motivated solely by the desire to make good use of my time which I have no way to employ." The war ministry, he complained, had done nothing for the officers and the army had lost much of its former morale and unity. "A military newspaper could help restore both if it were distributed among the majority of officers," but it must never criticize the government. "There is no place for liberalism in a military organ."[13]

11. ORBL, Miliutin, k. 16, no. 2, ll. 52–55.

12. GIM, ed. khr. 28, ll. 5–6 reverse, Cherniaev to Miliutin, Oct. 1868; ll. 7–8, Miliutin to Cherniaev, 4 November 1868; l. 9, "Dokladnaia zapiska," 11 November 1868; l. 10, "Programma."

13. ORBL, Vorontsov-Dashkov, 82/23, no. 3, Cherniaev to Vorontsov-Dashkov, 10 Novem-

Many officers rallied to *Invalid*'s defense. At the emperor's request Miliutin agreed reluctantly to make it a specialized organ supplementing the ministry's monthly, *Voennyi sbornik*. In *Invalid*'s final number in 1868 the editor deplored the intrigue which had emasculated it. Discouraged, Miliutin contemplated resignation.[14]

Eventually, however, the emperor backed him and his military reforms against the Shuvalov-Bariatinskii opposition. In May 1868, Bariatinskii, aroused against the war ministry by Fadeev, returned to Russia and attacked Miliutin's statute about wartime administration of the field army.[15] Pressed by the emperor for explanations, Russia's leading soldier and Cherniaev's hero proceeded with Fadeev to his estate in Kursk province. Sharing their antipathy for Miliutin, Cherniaev joined them. In a memorandum Bariatinskii and Fadeev argued that Miliutin's statute would undermine the commander in chief's authority, divide the army, and place it under the war minister's bureaucratic control. The whole military apparatus, Fadeev complained, favored the general staff and administration, "that is scholastic theory and office staff." The army would lose its fighting spirit and "direct access to the Sovereign."[16] Miliutin called their memorandum "a shameless selection of paradoxes and strained interpretations" tearing his statements from context. Alexander finally accepted Miliutin's view.[17]

This was only the opening round. Cherniaev participated in Bariatinskii's long campaign to oust Miliutin and make himself chief of staff. Prussia's victory over France in 1870 encouraged them since Miliutin's reforms were modeled on the French pattern. France's defeat, asserted Fadeev, proved that Miliutin's reforms were erroneous. Bariatinskii's accusations that the war ministry was extravagant and bureaucratic won finance ministry support, but Miliutin's rebuttal finally persuaded Alexander.[18]

In the Crimea (June 1871) Miliutin analyzed his opponents'

---

ber 1868.

14. Ibid., Miliutin, k. 16, no. 2, ll. 55–58.

15. Ibid., ll. 18 reverse, 21–22 reverse. Fadeev's articles appeared in RV early in 1868; the book *Vooruzhennye sily Rossii*, came out later that year.

16. TSGIAL, Fadeevykh, ed. khr. 34, Fadeev to Prince D. I. Sviatopolk-Mirskii, draft, n.d.

17. Zisserman, "Bariatinskii," RA (1891), I: 81 ff.; ORBL, Miliutin, k. 16, no. 2, ll. 112–113.

18. Fadeev's articles explaining the opposition's views were in *Birzhevye Vedomosti*, Jan. 1871, nos. 1, 2, 5, 9, 12 and 19; ORBL, Miliutin, k. 16, no. 3, l. 136. By 1871, claimed Miliutin, his ministry's staff had been cut almost in half. During the years of his ministry's peak activity (1863–1873), paperwork declined forty-five per cent. VE (1882), no. 1, p. 18.

motives. Some were distinguished older officers disapproving every innovation. The abolition of corporal punishment in the army in 1863 displeased those favoring "patriarchal" relationships with subordinates, and others whose positions or illegal profits were being eliminated. Should he woo these dissidents? No, he could not restore forms repudiated by experience. The dissatisfied would abandon outworn ways only if convinced there would be no return to them.[19]

The climax of Miliutin's struggle with the conservatives came over his plan for universal military training. Count Valuev, impressed by Prussia's efficient mobilization in 1870, backed him and helped win over the emperor. Henceforth all able-bodied males between twenty-one and forty-six would have to serve a specified term in the armed forces.[20] Shuvalov and Fadeev, rarely confronting Miliutin directly, argued that universal service would undermine gentry influence in Russian life. Fadeev proposed a militia directed by noble officers, but this was not a viable alternative. To Valuev, as to Alexander II, Russia's survival in a Europe of rising armaments took precedence over gentry privilege.[21] Early in 1874 the State Council approved universal military service. Miliutin's chief enemies—Bariatinskii, Fadeev, Shuvalov and Cherniaev—had been defeated and dispersed.

Cherniaev's own military views derived partly from Bariatinskii and Fadeev. As a Slavophile anti-intellectual, he denounced Miliutin's reforms and defended the army of Nicholas I: "Our regular army, without violating bases set by Peter I, . . . expanded Muscovy into an empire covering half the globe, repelled the assaults of all Europe, and ended its career on historical foundations with the matchless defense of Sevastopol." In a frantic effort to copy Europe, Miliutin had repudiated these foundations: "Then came the well-remembered era of denying everything developed by preceding generations, the ruthless destruction, using western models, of what existed . . . in order to apply them to Russian requirements no one knew or understood." Miliutin had undermined army unity and morale with his military gymnasia, new districts, and by eliminating the supreme commander. Universal military training, affirmed

19. ORBL, Miliutin, k. 16, no. 3, ll. 136 and reverse, "Pochemu tak mnogo nedovolnykh nashimi voennymi reformami," 2 July 1871.

20. Ibid., k. 16, no. 2, ll. 112–113.

21. Valuev, II: 284–286; Forrestt Miller, *Dmitrii Miliutin*, pp. 202 ff.

Cherniaev, had been instituted first by the French to destroy the army's devotion to Napoleon. Annual call-ups would be expensive and demoralizing. Every campaign would begin with terrible and needless defeats.

Miliutin's educated soldier, argued Cherniaev, was a dangerous anomaly. The army, instead of being a civilizing force, must defeat Russia's enemies and be the reliable instrument of its commander. Morale and leadership, not education, produced victory: "Morale in war predominates over number of troops. . . . The commander's talent consists of understanding his men and utilizing their qualities. Neither one nor the other can be acquired in any academy. A battle between two armies, no matter how large, is a duel between the two commanders in chief."

Mikhail Grigorevich, writing in 1890, vented his anger on Miliutin, to him the epitome of the armchair soldier. In the 1860s academic liberals such as he "fussed and cried for reforms," but their plans were vague and confused. Miliutin had "never directed a single war nor even a battle, . . . spent his life behind the writing desk and the lectern." His qualities were "caution, never speaking out plainly, generalities. . . ." This was grossly unfair. Miliutin, who had been wounded and decorated in the Caucasus, would direct Russia's victory over Turkey in 1877.

Cherniaev romanticized the active field commander who lived with his troops, but he made few suggestions on how to improve the army. Only long years of service, he asserted, produced good cadres and comradeship. He relied upon morale instilled by tradition, discipline, and autocratic commanders, yet he was inconsistent: "Our defeats during the Crimean and Russo-Turkish War of 1877 should be attributed to our backward military technology which always affects the troop's morale adversely. Therefore . . . we must adopt the latest word in military technology since victory is always a thousand times cheaper than defeat."[22] How incongruous to combine modern technology with traditional, patriarchal relationships!

From 1869 to 1875, though technically assigned to Warsaw, he lived mostly in Petersburg drinking in cafes with cronies who shared his views and frustrations.[23] Occasionally he took his family on trips

22. M. G. Cherniaev, "Nashe voennoe vospitanie," rv (April 1890), pp. 244 ff., and (Jan. 1891), pp. 35–54; iisg, "Biografiia," pp. 191–196.

23. These included General R. A. Fadeev; V. A. Kokorev, founder of the Volga-Kama Bank; M. A. Khludov, merchant; N. N. Raevskii, the hussar officer with whom he had plotted

to the Volga or Crimea to relieve an inactivity incompatible with his temperament. Cherniaev had virtually abandoned hope of a prominent role. He wrote Nikolai: "How many times already they [rumors] have appointed me and will do so again, but I am firmly convinced that all this will come to naught in the present reign, and if I live until the next reign, perhaps I will no longer be useful. If they had any assignment in mind for me, five years is plenty of time to think it over. . . . I honestly do not wish to enter service any more. . . . Everything has its time and mine is already noticeably passing."[24] He would serve only on his own terms. A divisional command would have "placed at stake my entire past."[25] An ordinary post would ruin his legend.

In 1872 a Vienna correspondent described Cherniaev strolling in a Warsaw park. A tall, elastic man, "a gloomy fire blazed from his gray eyes." Kept on a tight leash by Count Berg, "he slinks around like a muzzled hunting dog." Why doesn't he wear his uniform or decorations? asked the correspondent. "He hates the army since War Minister Miliutin began to modernize it," replied his companion. For his Tashkent exploit St. Petersburg had given him only a Saint George's cross instead of a princely title.

As Cherniaev approached the correspondent scrutinized him closely. His face revealed the shackled adventurer. "He was humming a Cossack song, but his gloomy face seemed oblivious of this. His broad forehead was clouded and around his thin lips lay a military beard à la royale. . . . He was the embodiment of discontent . . . , of Slav doggedness which lurks in ambush until it can bring its concealed aims again into the open." Bourgeois women, remarked his companion, impressed by Cherniaev's rank and dramatic *Weltschmerz*, succumbed readily to his charm: "He attracts the pretty ones by playing the wild man of Tashkent, and with an affected contempt for all conventional forms rattles his sabre at their hearts. A witty Polish woman whom he tried to enchant this way interrupted him: what do you think about Ostrolenka? As he looked at her perplexed, she added smiling: it must be harder to

---

a Balkan insurrection; V. A. Poltoratskii of the General Staff; V. V. Komarov, editor of *Svet*; Ilia Pokhitonov, editor of *Russkii Mir*; and Pisarevskii, director of the electro-technical school in St. Petersburg.

24. GIM, ed. khr. 39, l. 13, M. G. to N. G. Cherniaev, 23 May 1871.

25. ORBL, Vorontsov-Dashkov, 82/23, no. 2, Cherniaev to Shuvalov, 17 May 1873.

collect trophies in Warsaw than in Tashkent." His hatred of military bureaucracy and the war ministry attracted the youth. The court, worried by this and by his bellicose Panslavism, had placed him under Berg's iron hand to preserve an able officer for the future. He and Fadeev, concluded the correspondent, shared adventurism and false nationalism, "but Cherniaev is more dangerous than Fadeev because he is more brutal and irresponsible."[26]

Despite slender means, Cherniaev became deeply involved in railway and shipping ventures. In this era of speculative enterprise he revealed a penchant for grandiose projects, a gambling instinct and an incorrigible impracticality. Railroad construction boomed. Under Nicholas I the few Russian rail lines had been built mostly by the state, but now the Committee of Ministers yielded to agitation for private construction. In 1865 the government decided that Russia must have an extensive railway network. Delay would perpetuate economic and military backwardness, hamstring commerce, and endanger national unity. The Committee of Ministers would decide which lines must be built, then the government would provide subsidies and guarantees. The next years were Russia's most intensive era of private railroad construction. Numerous small, undercapitalized firms secured concessions. High officials became involved in railroad scandals. "The existence of many of our railroad companies is fictitious," reported the communications minister in February 1873. "Their firms are a mere front, their managing boards are irregular, their shareholders are straw men and their shares were never actually subscribed."[27] Most of these companies soon revealed their incompetence.

Hoping to make his fortune, Cherniaev plunged headlong into this morass. In 1869 he headed a company which offered to construct the Iaroslavl-Rybinsk line north of Moscow. He secured government consent to survey the route, but the project hung fire in the communications ministry and was finally rejected.[28] When the company folded in 1872, Cherniaev lost heavily.

The government also sought to develop Russian commerce in Central Asia, and Cherniaev participated in the abortive Central Asian Steamship and Trade Society. In March 1870 he, Severtsov,

26. NFP, no. 4268, 14 July 1876, "M. G. Tschernajeff."

27. Komitet ministrov. *Nasha zheleznodorozhnaia politika* . . . (St. Petersburg, 1902), I: 171 ff.; Tatishchev, II: 188 ff.

28. GIM, ed. khr. 21, ll. 1 ff.

and the prominent Moscow merchants, M. A. Khludov and I. A. Pervushin, created a company to navigate the Syr-Daria, but they failed to obtain the concession.[29] The Volga-Tver Steamship Company proved more successful. Cherniaev and a certain Evreinov established it and in January 1869 requested official permission to increase its capitalization to a million rubles. "The affairs of our steamship company are taking their course," Cherniaev wrote Nikolai, "but not as rapidly as would be desirable. . . . Everything will depend upon the premium paid upon our shares."[30]

Already in debt Cherniaev borrowed from Vorontsov-Dashkov to finance his ventures. Extremely wealthy and easily swayed, the count shared Cherniaev's conservative views and became his financial adviser and benefactor. As the heir's adjutant, he provided ready access to the future Alexander III. Late in 1869 Cherniaev wrote Vorontsov that he was renouncing public service for a commercial career. Would the count let him wait until 1871 to begin repaying his ten thousand ruble debt? "If you do this, I shall be deeply obligated to you for aiding my career in a new field."[31] Vorontsov agreed, but Cherniaev did not prosper.

Late in 1873 depression struck Russia engulfing thousands of small firms. Cherniaev's remaining enterprises were destroyed. With unusual self-abnegation he turned to Vorontsov: "The eighth year since my recall from Tashkent is passing. . . . I have naturally had time to calm down completely and consider objectively the reasons for my removal. *I have become reconciled to these reasons and blame no one but myself* (italics mine). Intimating that he was ready to serve actively again, he begged the count to secure the tsar's forgiveness: "Believing firmly in the emperor's generosity, I do not consider myself so blameworthy that I should be doomed to complete inactivity . . . , that I am fated to be buried alive. . . . No matter how great my mistakes, I feel that eight years of mental torture have already redeemed them and sufficiently clarified my convictions."[32] But his persistent opposition and unwillingness to accept a divisional command rendered him useless to the government.

Meanwhile Cherniaev had been denouncing the Turkestan

29. Ibid., ed. khr. 22, ll. 1 ff.

30. Ibid., ed. khr. 39, ll. 7–9, M. G. to N. G. Cherniaev, 21 January and 19 April 1869.

31. ORBL, Vorontsov-Dashkov, 82/23, no. 1, 17 December [1869?].

32. Ibid., 10 November 1873. The underlined passage (my italics) undermines his claim that a conspiracy had engineered his recall in 1866.

administration. Only a year after fon-Kaufman's appointment as the governor general, Cherniaev, without meeting him, expressed "utter contempt for the actions of this individual who perhaps is good, but has again fully revealed his lack of ability."[33] In 1872 he marshalled his arguments against fon-Kaufman in a draft memorandum and a letter to the finance minister.[34] Citing little specific evidence, he accused him of imposing an expensive, bureaucratic regime upon Asians who needed a supreme arbiter, not interference in their domestic affairs: "The idea of giving Turkestan a Russian administration in order to unite it with Russia would lead to wholly opposite results, that is to complete disunity. To demand that the kirgiz and the sart [Tsarist terms for Central Asian nomads and city dwellers] be administered just like inhabitants of the Moscow region means violating the natural order of things to our detriment." Kaufman and company, Cherniaev affirmed, were forcing European civilization upon the Uzbeks and alienating them from Russia. His own approach had been to supervise native administration, not replace it. Fon-Kaufman's expensive administration, he asserted, enjoyed less prestige in Central Asia than had his own poverty-stricken one. The Uzbeks were rejecting Russian ways and creating illegal institutions. The choice lay between financial balance and swelling deficits, strengthening or weakening Russian influence, between two types of imperial rule: his or fon-Kaufman's.

Cherniaev urged abolition of the Turkestan governor generalship. Western Siberia could administer outlying portions and Orenburg the rest. Reducing bureaucracy and eliminating the deficit would "suppress the administration's impotent aspirations to reform native customs forcibly, . . . which merely embitters the people and requires extra troops without ever attaining its goal." Russia in Asia must become self-supporting.

His letter to the finance minister opposed fon-Kaufman's new proposed draft statute. Turkestan's expenses, affirmed Cherniaev, exceeded its revenues by four million rubles annually. "I consider it my duty to utter 'one last word of truth,' especially since this word will be the last I shall utter during my career. . . ." (Time would reveal this to be false!) Only the minister's intervention could stop

33. GIM, ed. khr. 39, ll. 29–30, M. G. to N. G. Cherniaev, (Ostende), 30 July [1868?].

34. Ibid., ed. khr. 8, ll. 86–96, "Turkestanskie pisma—II," 11 October 1872; FO, 539/9, pp. 331–335, Loftus to Granville, Jan. 1873, enclosing Cherniaev to Finance Minister, 15/27 October 1872.

expenditures "increasing in direct proportion to the disaffection of a population which has ever been antagonistic to our rule and now revolts against us." In St. Petersburg the emperor convened a special council to consider these charges. Fon-Kaufman, supported by Stremoukhov of the Asiatic Department, successfully defended his policies.[35]

Mikhail Grigorevich castigated the Khiva expedition of 1873 which Miliutin planned and fon-Kaufman commanded. The war ministry was silent about Russian preparations, but Cherniaev informed the British about the expeditionary force. If one Russian column met disaster, he predicted, a general Moslem uprising might compel Russia to retire to its old frontiers. After Khiva fell, he accused fon-Kaufman of exterminating Turkoman villages and levying an excessive indemnity on the rest. This policy fostered Moslem hatred and would endanger Russia's position in Central Asia.[36] To damage his rivals Cherniaev would divulge secret information and discredit his country's policy. Actually, the Khiva expedition, though extravagantly expensive, strengthened Russia's hold on Turkestan.

In *Russkii Mir*, a conservative newspaper backed initially by Count Shuvalov's gentry party, Cherniaev and his friends resumed their attacks on the Turkestan administration.[37] In 1871 he had written Nikolai that he was helping to draw up its program and was much interested in its success. "I think it will justify the [hostile] exclamations by liberal publicist officials. . . ." Three years later he wrote his brother, "I am busy with my newspaper from morning till night."[38]

Late in 1874 *Russkii Mir* demanded an investigation of alleged abuses of the Kaufman regime. In Turkestan officials "break all the laws, defame a person in the press and ruin his credit. Can such an attitude toward merchants assist our Central Asian commerce? Won't the native population interpret this to mean that we are

35. Ibid., Wellesley to Loftus, 24 December 1872, enclosed in Loftus to Granville, 26 December 1872, in "Correspondence respecting Central Asia, 1869–1873," p. 173 reverse.

36. Ibid., 539/11, Wellesley to Loftus, 15 April 1873, pp. 67–69; 12 November 1872 in Loftus to Granville, same date, p. 152.

37. TSGIAL, f. 776, Glavnoe Upravlenie po delam pechati, d. 52, chast 2, ll. 1–6, file on *Russkii Mir*.

38. GIM, ed. khr. 39, ll. 17 and reverse, M. G. to N. G. Cherniaev, 15 August 1871, 27 February 1874. Cherniaev's deepening involvement in *Russkii Mir* is confirmed by TSGIAL, f. 776, d. 52, ch. 2, ll. 160–164. He became its owner on December 3, 1873.

bringing it not civilization and respect for law, but violation of the law?"[39] It republished a dispatch by Eugene Schuyler, an American diplomat critical of the Turkestan administration.[40] His findings, declared a lead article, revealed fon-Kaufman's extravagance and violation of native customs.[41]

Answering this, *Golos*, the leading liberal daily, urged speedy approval of Kaufman's reform proposals, praised highly by most government agencies. It questioned assertions by Cherniaev and the finance ministry that Turkestan was running a deficit and deplored the public's readiness to believe second-hand foreign judgments. Excluding military expenditures, the *Golos* figures for Turkestan's budget revealed a large surplus.[42] A. K. Geins, a former Turkestan official, also strongly defended the Kaufman regime.[43]

Rejecting their testimony, Cherniaev demanded an investigation of the Turkestan administration. Had not Geins, who allegedly spent half his term as fon-Kaufman's office director living abroad, recommended the appointment of three district commanders guilty of malfeasance? Geins and other Turkestan officials were "on trial before public opinion." His Temporary Statute had "caused general insurrection by the Orenburg nomads and in Turkestan the chaos and official autocracy which Schuyler so correctly noted."[44]

In a letter published by Cherniaev a leading Russian Tashkent merchant affirmed that large sums had been lavished on fon-Kaufman's palace, gardens, and club. His engineers had built an expensive water conduit for Tashkent which carried no water and were supposed to erect a bridge over the Chirchik River. "We

39. *Russkii Mir*, Abramov, "Pismo v redaktsiiu," and "Strannoe rasporiazhenie Syr-Darinskoi oblastnogo pravleniia," 24 December 1874.

40. *Papers Relating to the Foreign Relations of the United States, 1874* (Washington, 1874), Schuyler to Jewell, 7 March 1874, pp. 81 ff.; D. MacKenzie, "Kaufman of Turkestan . . . ," sr, xxvi, no. 2 (June 1967), pp. 278, 282–283.

41. *Russkii Mir*, 30 January 1875.

42. *Golos*, 14 January 1875, "Sudba proekta o Turkestanskom krae," lead; 24 January 1875, "Finansovoe polozhenie Turkestanskogo kraia," lead; 11 February 1875, "Depesha Skailera i Turkestanskii biudzhet," lead.

43. Ibid., p. 4, Geins, "Zametka na depeshu g. Skailera." *Novoe Vremia* of 16 April ("Depesha g. Skailera o nashikh sredne-aziatskikh delakh") questioned Schuyler's sources and verdict. Katkov's *Moskovskie Vedomosti* concluded that Schuyler's indictment of the Turkestan administration lacked real significance.

44. *Russkii Mir*, 27 February 1875, lead, "Po povodu zametki g. Geinsa."

Tashkenters probably won't live to see it completed." Thrice flood waters had swept it away at a cost of 105,000 rubles.[45] *Russkii Mir's* suspension choked off other articles against fon-Kaufman.

Why wouldn't *Russkii Mir* discuss Schuyler's report?, wondered *Golos*. Criticism of authority instead of customary press silence on sensitive public issues was praiseworthy, but not the disguised pursuit of personal aims. *Russkii Mir*, it claimed, "uses a double standard, posing as a free thinker whenever the war ministry or Turkestan are involved while defending all sorts of obsolete institutions in other aspects of Russian life."[46] But Cherniaev refused to debate the Schuyler dispatch.

Russkii Mir's unsigned diatribes against fon-Kaufman, affirmed *Golos*, misled the public. Denouncing Romanovskii and fon-Kaufman, it considered Cherniaev's brief governorship ideal. Since then Turkestan's area and population had quadrupled. Cherniaev's prescription for Turkestan, stated Kraevskii, was "an administration without statutes, instructions or accounts after which the government for several years could not discover what it owes and to whom." After Cherniaev's removal, false and sordid rumors had circulated about Turkestan. No sooner had the press refuted one batch, than another appeared. Eventually, "time and truth will claim their own."[47]

S. Ianchevskii ascribed Cherniaev's attacks to jealousy and personal bitterness. He contrasted his successors' supposed greed and incompetence to the golden age of Cherniaev's governorship. If he inspected Turkestan, what a mass of scandal he could uncover! Cherniaev and his colleagues hid behind incognito. In Tashkent "P.,"[48] who initialled some of *Russkii Mir's* attacks, had attracted disappointed office-seekers and supplied Schuyler with garbled reports from the Moslem clergy and the Tashkent prison.

Should Cherniaev boast of his exploits in Turkestan? Ianchevskii demanded some answers. Why had Cherniaev ordered the abortive assault on Tashkent in 1864? Had he then from irritation ordered the first Uzbeks who came to his army shot as spies? Why had civilians been slaughtered in Aulie-Ata and Tashkent? Had he

45. Ibid., 2 March 1875, p. 3, A. Gromov, "Vesti iz Tashkenta."

46. *Golos*, 2 March 1875, "Proshlaia nedelia v Rossii i zagranitsei," lead; MacKenzie, "Kaufman," p. 283.

47. *Golos*, 19 March 1875, lead, "K voprosu ob upravlenii sredneaziatskoiu okrainoiu."

48. Perhaps Pisarevskii, later director of the St. Petersburg electrotechnical institute, who wrote many articles for *Russkii Mir*, according to Gradovskii.

weighed the risks before moving against Dzhizak? Why had he then retreated from there? Finally, "how [can one] explain the strange circumstance that despite the *sincere support* of the people which Cherniaev supposedly acquired in 1865, one could not go a rifle shot's distance from Tashkent without risking one's life, and officers riding through the native city were exposed to abuse from all sides in the foulest Russian words and not infrequently were met by stones thrown from the roofs of houses? Was such boundless support the result of his humane treatment of the people?"[49] These queries were never answered. Henceforth *Russkii Mir* referred sparingly to Turkestan.

Fon-Kaufman, refusing to dignify Cherniaev's accusations with a formal reply, thanked Kraevskii for presenting his regime and its problems objectively. He referred to "the filthy clique" which sought to destroy public confidence in the Turkestan administration.[50] The Cherniaevs claimed that fon-Kaufman sought revenge by seeking to collect a debit of 3,931 rubles 9¼ kopecks which Cherniaev had supposedly incurred in Turkestan ten years before. Early in 1875 the police came to *Russkii Mir*'s offices to demand the money. The heir finally halted this sinister conspiracy, asserted Antonina, by telling chief of staff Count Geiden: "Stop this nasty business against Cherniaev."[51]

Later, utilizing official documents, fon-Kaufman's son denied that his father had initiated the "Tashkent debit." The Orenburg Control Commission, unconnected with fon-Kaufman's office, had done so. Not only had fon-Kaufman not seen the debit before it went to Cherniaev, but in 1878 he persuaded Miliutin to cancel it using the very words which Antonina ascribed to the heir![52] Indeed, fon-Kaufman apparently did not respond to Cherniaev's diatribes and the debit was unrelated to them. Antonina's distortion of the debit revealed the Cherniaevs' hatred of the successful fon-Kaufman and the cumbrous nature of the imperial bureaucracy. A trivial affair

49. *Golos*, 6 May 1875, pp. 4–5, S. Ianchevskii, "*Russkii Mir* po otnosheniiu k turkestanskomu kraiu," Tashkent, 27 March 1875. He was a Turkestan official.

50. orss, f. 391, Kraevskii, Kaufman to A. A. Kraevskii, 18 April 1875.

51. A. Cherniaeva, "O M. G. Cherniaeve," ra (Dec. 1909), p. 527; ibid., "Iz proshedshikh sudeb Turkestana. Pravda o nachete na M. G. Cherniaeva," (1911), i: 443 ff.; gim, ed. khr. 56, l. 41, 10 October 1896, draft by Cherniaev; ed. khr. 1, ll. 39–40. Terentiev (iii, appendix, pp. 22–23) generally supported the Cherniaevs' position.

52. P. fon-Kaufman, "K. P. fon-Kaufman i M. G. Cherniaev," ra (1910), iii: 468–473. His letter was dated 25 January 1910.

dragged on thirteen years involving two Orenburg agencies, the Warsaw command, the Military Council, the war ministry, and the commandant of St. Petersburg.

The war ministry was Cherniaev's other major target as his *Russkii Mir* sought to discredit Miliutin. "Our entire army," asserted its editors, "is a disorganized mob, and the new military reforms brought it to this." A suspiciously lenient censorship did nothing. However, the next month *Russkii Mir* was gently rebuked for claiming that army discipline was deteriorating. Then it was warned for attacking military courts and the war ministry.[53] The paper published Fadeev's ponderous *What is to become of us?* which denounced universal military service and claimed that soldiers needed little education or scientific preparation. "For military purposes primeval forces are wholly sufficient."[54] After suspension its attacks grew oblique: the war ministry's extravagance caused taxes to rise, but the army was still "the worst equipped in Europe and wholly unprepared for war."[55] Yet the Russo-Turkish War of 1877 vindicated Miliutin's new army and refuted Cherniaev's accusations.[56]

Russkii Mir, though consistent on Turkestan and the war ministry, was torn by dissension. L. Slonimskii, later its editor, recalled its "strange dual character." Fadeev's confused, reactionary polemics were juxtaposed with a courageous campaign against the arbitrary, swollen bureaucracy. Muscovite and Slavophile, it "touched the sensitive spots of our official life." Continued Slonimskii: "From personal conversations with Cherniaev I gained the impression that his attacks on the bureaucracy and German rule went much further and deeper than his allies and supporters realized. Extremely reserved and gentle by nature, he spoke out with true military directness about matters considered forbidden for the press . . . although he understood the internal situation rather poorly."[57]

Gradovskii, with typical exaggeration, found the newspaper completely reactionary and Cherniaev a straw man. He neither heard Cherniaev express definite opinions nor saw articles he had written. A man named Pisarevskii "spoke and wrote for Cherniaev"; others

53. TSGIAL, f. 776, ll. 30, 36, 140–142, 227–229.

54. *Russkii Mir*, 7 May 1874, p. 1, "Ob ekonomicheskom znachenii vsesoslovnoi voinskoi povinnosti," 8 May 1874, pp. 1–2.

55. Ibid., 10 June 1875, p. 1, "Podatnyi vopros i gosudarstvennye nalogi"; 5 July 1874, "Nemetskaia pechat o russkoi armii" (probably by Fadeev).

56. Gradovskii, "Arkhistratig," pp. 121–122.

57. L. Slonimskii, "Dva pisma," VE (Feb. 1909), p. 887.

exploited him to spread reaction and denounce Miliutin.[58] Actually, Cherniaev played a most active role in *Russkii Mir.*

Within the paper personal conflicts raged. Though founded by wealthy aristocrats such as Prince N. A. Lobanov-Rostovskii, financing became difficult.[59] Deploring inadequate aristocratic support, Cherniaev turned to his Moscow merchant friends for aid. "Taking upon myself at the end of last year publication . . . of *Russkii Mir*," he wrote F. V. Chizhov in September 1874, "I had in view a press organ in which all current questions about Russian reality would be discussed." Beginning with 734 subscribers, he had increased this to 2,800 readers, 500 of them in Moscow. Needing more money, he asked Moscow merchants "to make *Russkii Mir* an expression of the views of Russian commercial leaders." Chizhov helped the paper over its financial crisis.[60]

However, Fadeev wanted to rely wholly upon the aristocracy, "so far the only tool in the government's hands to help develop public life" and reform Russia.[61] Some members of the editorial board urged that Fadeev's "Russian society in the present and future" become *Russkii Mir*'s social program. Following their plea came the caustic comment: "'Russian society' of Fadeev in its backwardness, mediocrity and prejudice is a model of its kind. The time for gentry rule is past. This is the period of the zemstvo. The revival of the gentry as a cultural class is pointless. Russian society has always consisted of *raznochintsy* [men from various classes]." Cherniaev remarked scornfully: "This is the Russian intelligentsia formed by reading European books."[62]

During 1874–1875 *Russkii Mir*'s circulation and staff expanded. It would become, exulted Cherniaev, an organ to unite Russian conservatives and reform the existing order "combining conservative goals with a progressive party's methods."[63] He decided to assume the editorship openly and resign from service.[64] He had discovered

58. Gradovskii, pp. 122–123.

59. iisg, ed. khr. 20. See V. Ia. Laverychev, "Russkie kapitalisty . . . ," *Istoriia SSSR*, no. 1 (1972), pp. 36–37.

60. orbl, Chizhov, 59/8, Cherniaev to Chizhov, 15 September 1874 and 26 March 1875.

61. *Russkii Mir*, 11 May 1874; 4 October 1874; 1 May 1874, "Chto nam nuzhnee vsego?"

62. gim, ed. khr. 29, ll. 3–4, written on *Russkii Mir*'s stationery. Cherniaev's comment was dated Oct. 8, 1874.

63. Ibid., ll. 1–2, "Zapiska o napravlenii *Russkogo Mira*", n.d. Later, Cherniaev commented: "Our entire aristocracy gave *Russkii Mir* 34,000 rubles and refused to help any more when this sum had been expended."

64. tsgial, f. 776, l. 254.

that running a newspaper was incompatible with his military status; he begged the emperor's indulgence. On May 30, 1875, Alexander consented to his request.[65]

Cherniaev's first editorial lacked the clarity and forthrightness which he had advocated. Reaffirming the paper's antiwesternism and concern with the military, he denied any tendentious opposition to the war ministry. Censorship was but partly responsible for his vagueness: "We always believed that our literary opponents' efforts to place obstacles between us and the public would fail eventually and that our public would differentiate firmness and straightforwardness from indeterminate equivocation, active sobriety from empty chatter, conscious aspiration to serve the common good from liberalism's superficial empty phrases—in short a political from a commercial spirit."[66]

His signed editorial of July 20 was no more explicit. *Russkii Mir* would "pursue in the future the same direction we have followed hitherto." Russia faced a magnificent future if it honored its past. "The time for impulsiveness [the 1860s] has passed, irrevocably one hopes." Much space would be given to the zemstvos, army, finance and railroads (but not to Fadeev's gentry?). *Russkii Mir* would provide detailed information about the Slav peoples "whose lives and many of whose daily interests are, we feel, indissolubly connected with Russia's future." Its Panslav orientation was most cautiously stated. In foreign affairs the paper would be independent and concentrate on issues of direct concern to Russia.[67]

Such obscurity veiled the newspaper's ideological and personal differences. A reckless general had become a cautious editor. Eschewing further attacks on fon-Kaufman and Miliutin, *Russkii Mir* avoided the censor's ire until it asserted in December 1875 that Germans dominated Russia's higher civil and military administration.[68] Even this favorite theme of Cherniaev's was not elaborated. Only the revolt in Herzegovina, which revived the Slav question, rescued *Russkii Mir* and its editor from a dull obscurity.

65. GIM, ed. khr. 37, ll. 10–11, Cherniaev to A. L. Potapov, 22 May 1875, draft; ed. khr. 1, ll. 7, 15–18.

66. *Russkii Mir*, 6 June 1875, lead, "Posle priostanovki."

67. Ibid., July 20, "Ot redaktsii."

68. TSGIAL, f. 776, l. 275, 4 November 1875.

CHAPTER VIII

Launching the Slav Crusade

IN JULY 1875 Slav Christians in Herzegovina revolted against ty-
rannical Turkish officials; within a month the insurrection spread
to Bosnia. The local authorities could not quell uprisings which
attracted sympathy and aid from other Balkan Slavs and Russia.
While the European powers sought pacification and reform,
neighboring Serbia and Montenegro, linked to the rebels by
blood, religion, and language, became deeply involved. The crisis
threatened a general Balkan war and opened the way for
Cherniaev's Panslav crusade.[1]

Since the fifteenth century the Ottoman Turks had ruled most
of the Balkans. The north and west, inhabited largely by Catholic Croats and Slovenes, were slowly reconquered by Austria.
Until Napoleon the Turks retained a firm hold over the southern
and eastern Balkans containing Serbs, Bulgars, Rumanians, and
Greeks. Only tiny Montenegro, secure in its mountain strong-
holds, stood unsubdued. Serbia gradually freed itself and by 1875
both Serbia and Montenegro were independent in all but name.
To the west Bosnia and Herzegovina remained Turkish provinces
whose largely Serbian population yearned to join their neighbors.

1. MacKenzie, *The Serbs*, p. 31.

Serbs in all these regions had long looked to Russia, the only Slav great power, to free them.

The Balkan insurrections reawakened Cherniaev's hopes and pro-Slav sentiments. For a decade he had been closely associated with Panslavs in Moscow and St. Petersburg. His friend and ideological mentor, Ivan Aksakov, became president of the Moscow Slav Committee in 1875. They shared common sentiments of antiwesternism, antisemitism, intense Russian nationalism, and loyalty to traditional autocracy. Cherniaev's newspaper was the first in Russia to report the Herzegovina insurrection and to actively support the rebels. While Russian Panslavs arranged financial and military aid for the Slavs, *Russkii Mir* campaigned with apparent idealism and unselfishness in their behalf. "The Slav movement arising in 1875 was for him [Cherniaev] an affair not just of foreign but also of domestic politics," recalled Slonimskii, "He believed in Russian national enthusiasm and expected from it the most favorable effects upon the country."[2] War in behalf of the Slavs, Cherniaev hoped, would halt liberal reform in Russia and sweep men like himself into top governmental and military posts. His task was to transform vague pro-Slav feeling in Russia into a military crusade to emancipate the South Slavs.

Russkii Mir, absurdly optimistic about Slav prospects, urged little Serbia to unify the South Slavs as Piedmont had united Italy. "Serbia is destined to become the Piedmont of the Balkan Peninsula uniting the Turkish Slavs in new national and civilized life." Serbia's heroes would smash the Turkish hordes. Its army was large, well-equipped and organized. "Every [Serbian] soldier thirsts to gain revenge for ancient wrongs." However, events would soon refute these claims. Preventing Serbia's immediate entry into the fight to free its brethren, claimed *Russkii Mir*, were "the Arguslike glances of Austria-Hungary and England's hostility." Both powers favored the status quo in the Balkans. Therefore Serbia must establish complete domestic order and wait for events to divert Austria's attention.[3]

Confidence grew in Russia that the Slav Christians alone could throw off the Turkish yoke. The Turks, predicted *Russkii Mir*, could not crush the insurgents if assisted by Serbia, Montenegro, possibly Rumania, and a Bulgarian uprising. The Dreikaiserbund[4] could not

2. Slonimskii, "Dva pisma," ve (Feb. 1909), p. 887.
3. *Russkii Mir*, 15 July 1875, lead, "Volneniia v Gertsegovine."
4. The Three Emperors' League, a loose defensive arrangement formed in 1873 by the

forestall a general South Slav rising. Serbia was the logical nucleus of a Yugoslav state, but would timid Prince Milan lead a war of national liberation? Prince Nikola of Montenegro seemed a more likely choice. *Russkii Mir* denounced efforts of the powers to preserve the moribund Ottoman Empire and urged Russia to assist the Serbian states. "For us some success by Serbia and Montenegro and their extension would be desirable because it would shield us from Austria which once it enters Bosnia and Herzegovina would be in the center of the Eastern Question."[5]

The Bosnian revolt pushed Serbia to the brink of war. On August 19 Prince Milan, bowing to a bellicose minority, appointed an "action ministry." dominated by Jovan Ristić, the principal Liberal leader. The Serbian Assembly voted to assist the insurgents, but the Dreikaiserbund, fearing a European war, acted to restrain Serbia. With its encouragement Prince Milan on September 22 forced Ristić to resign and resumed a more peaceful course. Without Serbian initiative, Montenegro would not budge.[6]

Infuriated by the intervention of the Dreikaiserbund, Cherniaev denounced Russia for cooperating with Austria and deplored Prince Milan's subservience to Vienna. A firm pro-Slav statement by Russia would force the Turks to yield, declared *Russkii Mir*. "Our clear duty . . . is to seek without ulterior motives the liberation of the South Slav peoples from the Moslem yoke."[7] But most Russian newspapers still backed St. Petersburg's policy of a peaceful, European solution. Only *Russkii Mir,* scorning Turkish promises, urged Russians to send money and volunteers to the insurgents. It pressed the public to express its sympathies openly and criticized the passive attitude of the Slav committees.[8]

Mikhail Grigorevich sought to lead unofficial efforts to aid the insurgents. He was the first Russian editor to raise money for the South Slavs, and in the fall he tried to recruit a band of volunteers to join the rebels. Ivan Aksakov, believing dramatic events were at hand, supported him heartily. Through Chizhov they appealed to some Moscow merchants to finance an expedition, but Chizhov

rulers of Russia, Germany, and Austria-Hungary.

5. *Russkii Mir*, leads of 1, 8, 9, 23, and 29 August 1875.

6. MacKenzie, *The Serbs*, pp. 50 ff.

7. *Russkii Mir*, 2, 16, 24, and 30 September 1875.

8. Ibid., 26 August 1875; *Obshchestvenno-politicheskie i kulturnye sviazi narodov SSSR i Iugoslavii* (Moscow, 1957), p. 12.

doubted that the necessary seventy thousand rubles could be collected: "Cherniaev proposes to go to the scene of battle with ten officers
and they wish to take privately about fifty retired soldiers, to arm
volunteers there and enter the ranks of the Herzegovina insurgents.
The soldiers would be taken across [the frontier] disguised as their
servants or as private travelers." Irritated at the Moscow
committee's inaction, Cherniaev told Chizhov that it was like
jelly in which there was no point of support. He blamed this
partly on "the German family" (the Romanov dynasty) which
had "misbehaved" in Russia for over two centuries!

Skepticism and lack of funds doomed Cherniaev's scheme. Chizhov and the merchants concluded it was impractical and its author
a visionary. How would he organize a volunteer detachment in
Herzegovina? How would it affect the uprising?

> Perhaps Cherniaev believes in success, perhaps inside himself he
> nourishes the expectation that his name and recruiting a few Russian
> officers under his command will attract a native army. Perhaps
> he dreams . . . that they [Herzegovinians] will make him their
> leader. . . . All that may be . . . , but can we accept such a creed?
> You do when you talk with him and Komarov,[9] who is also very
> enthusiastic and a fanatical believer, but each of us when he is alone
> gives way to doubts. At least I cannot take such youthful enthusiasm
> seriously.

If the enterprise failed, noted Chizhov, Cherniaev and the Slav cause
would be discredited.[10] Sadly Cherniaev abandoned a scheme which
foreshadowed his larger venture of 1876.

Ristić's fall ended prospects that Serbia would fight in 1875. The
powers, concluded *Russkii Mir*, would achieve peace by surrendering
Bosnia and Herzegovina to Turkish vengeance. Cherniaev and the
Panslavs were dismayed. But the Serbs, noted *Russkii Mir*'s Belgrade
correspondent, were preparing for war in the spring. If Prince Milan
proved cowardly, Montenegro might become the South Slav Piedmont.[11]

9. V. V. Komarov, an intimate friend of Cherniaev and a journalist associated with *Russkii
Mir*.

10. ORBL, Chizhov, Dnevnik, VI: 115–117; S. Nikitin, *Slavianskie komitety v Rossii* (Moscow,
1960), pp. 273–275; IISG, "Avtobiografiia," p. 17.

11. *Russkii Mir*, 5 October 1875, lead; 15 October 1875, "Inostrannaia pochta" (Belgrade,
Oct. 5); 23 October 1875, "Inostrannaia pochta."

Foreign Minister Julius Andrássy of Austria-Hungary directed diplomatic efforts to work out reforms which Europe could impose on insurgents and Turks alike. The Andrássy Plan of December 1875 would grant autonomy to the insurgent provinces and introduce mild reforms while preserving the territorial status quo in the Balkans. *Russkii Mir*, supporting Ambassador Ignatiev's unilateral Panslav approach, commented, "Under existing conditions of Ottoman rule in the Balkans, the Andrássy Plan's bankruptcy is clear."[12] The Russian press generally agreed. *Golos*, which backed the official peaceful policy of Petersburg, was left isolated.

Russkii Mir reaffirmed the Panslav doctrine of Slav unification. Russia's mission, it proclaimed, was to liberate and unite the South Slav world as Prussia had for Germany. Austrian efforts to prevent the Serbs from fighting Turkey, it warned, would provoke a Russian-backed Slav insurrection. The Balkan Orthodox looked to Russia's might, and Europe could not preserve decaying Austria and Turkey. Allied with her twenty-five million fellow Orthodox, Russia would be irresistible.[13] Cherniaev shared this view, and he warned Slonimskii: "I felt somewhat uneasy when I read today in *Russkii Mir*'s lead article a proposal for a pacification commission for a people [in Herzegovina] which has lost patience . . . , when there is no longer any pity [by the Turks] for women and children. . . . Is it possible that such a vital question could be solved by a commission created in the foreign ministry?" Russia, he continued, must break with Austria and encourage the Slavs to fight the Porte.[14] Cherniaev believed that they could defeat the Turks unaided.

In February 1876 the Third Section, the political police established in 1826, suddenly called him in. General A. L. Potapov, its chief, repeated the emperor's words: "You know that he [Cherniaev] is traveling to the Herzegovinians. Summon him and obtain his promise not to join those robbers." Cherniaev replied: "Please repeat those words since I cannot believe that the emperor called the Herzegovinians robbers. But since the emperor requests it, naturally I will not travel to them."[15] Instead he would go to Serbia.

To ascertain Cherniaev's connections with the insurgents, Alexan-

12. Ibid., 10 January 1876.
13. Ibid., 23 December 1875, p. 1; 1 January 1876, "Inostrannaia pochta" (21 December 1875).
14. Slonimskii, pp. 888–889, Cherniaev to Slonimskii, n.d.
15. IISG, "Avtobiografiia," p. 17.

der had the Third Section place him under surveillance. Letters from his correspondent in Herzegovina were being published in *Russkii Mir* under the pseudonym, P. Petrov. Lieutenant Colonel Remer, assigned to watch Cherniaev, reported that "Petrov" was P. A. Monteverde, a Spaniard who contributed to several French newspapers. His articles for *Russkii Mir* were ardently pro-Slav; those for *Figaro* of Paris strongly Turcophile. Probably at his instigation, the insurgents had urged Cherniaev to command their forces. The general, noted Remer, was an influential member of the St. Petersburg Slav Committee and knew all its affairs and secrets. He maintained direct ties with Popović, editor of *Glas Crnogorca*, semiofficial Montenegrin paper influential with the insurgent leaders.[16] Curiously, Cherniaev's police file then remained blank until he reached Belgrade. Was this just inefficiency or a deliberate oversight by the authorities?

Despite clear official disapproval, Cherniaev was determined to reach Serbia. In Moscow he told Aksakov: the Serbs "must be given a shove or else they will just talk without taking action."[17] The Moscow Committee backed him, but to his chagrin Metropolitan Mihajlo wrote that Serbia would prefer General Fadeev, renowned for his bellicose pamphlet, *Opinion on the Eastern Question*. Learning that Fadeev was unavailable, Belgrade encouraged Cherniaev to come.

Financing his trip proved troublesome. "Here are 6,000 rubles which is all that I—that is the Slav Committee—has at present," declared Aksakov. He must leave money for his family and *Russkii Mir*, objected Cherniaev, and could not arrive in Serbia penniless.[18] Aksakov could give him no more, but he decided to go anyway. A foreign passport was obtained illegally in Moscow. A friend presented his police certificate and affadavit of retirement at the governor general's office. An old official, not realizing that Cherniaev was the conqueror of Tashkent, asked his destination. "The general is ill," explained his friend, "he is traveling to the Holy Places and will stop in Kiev on the way." The unsuspecting official ordered Cherniaev's name and rank inscribed in a passport already signed

---

16. TSGAOR, f. 109, Sekretnyi arkhiv, opis 4, d. 436, ll. 1–6.

17. IISG, "Avtobiografiia," p. 17.

18. Ibid., Aksakov, recalled Cherniaev, had offered him 5,000 rubles. "What can I do with those 5,000?" he objected. "But after thinking things over, I decided to go nonetheless."

by the governor general. Leaving immediately (April 7), the general announced that he was going to St. Petersburg.[19]

Bearing a letter from Aksakov, he traveled to Kishinev and met I. S. Ivanov, a Bulgarian in the Slav movement. Ivanov, giving him messages to deliver en route to Belgrade, advised Cherniaev to go to Bendery, which lacked a telegraph office, then hire horses to Kuvai, an obscure frontier station.[20] Cherniaev recalled:

> We arrived at the [Rumanian] frontier about 8:00 P.M. The frontier barrier was closed. Two merchants had arrived with me. We were supposed to spend the night there and cross the frontier the next day. The situation was critical. I began to urge the official to let us through. He said that if he opened the barrier, they would not let us through on the Rumanian side anyway. But I gave him my affadavit of retirement and asked him to deliver it to the station commander. A few minutes later the chief of customs came in bringing with him the head of the Rumanian customs. Both introduced themselves and let me pass through.[21]

The Third Section's agent in St. Petersburg apparently did not know until three weeks later that Cherniaev had left Russia. "There are rumors in town that Cherniaev . . . has gone to Serbia," reported Remer on April 28. *Russkii Mir* still appeared under his signature, and its employees assured Remer that he was in Moscow.[22] But on April 26 at Cherniaev's request the Main Press Administration transferred the paper's ownership to F. F. Berg. Slonimskii became editor.[23]

From Belgrade, Mikhail Grigorevich requested the Moscow Committee for funds to intensify the Bulgarian insurrection. From Kishinev to Bucharest he had talked with Slav Committee agents. He was struck by their optimism:

> I feared that this mood was not common to the entire population beyond the Danube and might be limited to a few individuals, but

19. N. Durnovo, "K istorii serbskoi-turetskoi voiny 1876 g.," IV, LXXV (Jan.–March 1899), 534–536. Miliutin (*Dnevnik*, II: 53) claims Cherniaev had promised Potapov not to travel to Serbia and confirms that the government disapproved of his trip. Nikitin, *Slavianskie*, pp. 291–292.

20. I. S. Ivanov, "Bolgarskoe opolchenie i ego sformirovanie," RS, LXII (1889), 136.

21. ORSS, f. 1009, f. N. M. Cherniaeva, ed. khr. 2; IISG, "Biografiia," p. 237.

22. TSGAOR, f. 109, ll. 9–12, reports of 28, 30 April 1876, 11 May 1876.

23. TSGIAL, f. 776, ll. 292, 301.

the Bulgarian revolt on this side of the Balkans confirmed everything
I heard on the way here. I was told everywhere that never before has
there been such unanimity among the Bulgarians, that even some
who had always been pro-Turkish had joined the general movement,
that all arms available in Rumania had been bought up and trans-
ported across the Danube, all property is buried and *the population
merely awaits a signal from Serbia to begin war.*[24]

Cherniaev traveled toward Belgrade, secure in the belief that destiny
had selected him to give that signal and emancipate the Balkan
Slavs.

His surreptitious departure from Russia marked escape from inglorious retirement, obscurity and bitterness. After ten years' search
he had discovered a cause to devote himself to. Believing in his and
Russia's mission to lead the Slavs from the wilderness of disunity, he
would now become to millions of Russians and Slavs a crusader in
a holy struggle to smash Turkish tyranny and unite the Slavs, an
heroic figure symbolizing mother Russia's aid to her helpless brethren. Would not such a noble enterprise bring acclaim to Cherniaev
and glory to Russia?

In Belgrade he enjoyed his greatest prominence since Tashkent.
Cherniaev's coming, noted the nephew of the Russian consul in
Belgrade, was wholly legal. As a retired officer he was a private
citizen, not a representative of Russia. But his arrival encouraged the
war hawks in Russia and Serbia. "Now a major public and military
figure had appeared on the scene. With the penetration characteristic of Balkan peoples, the Serbian ministers realized immediately
what a powerful trump M. G. Cherniaev's popular name represented. One must conclude that M. G. scarcely concealed from them
the important fact that he was corresponding with V. V. Zinoviev,
court marshal for the heir to the Russian throne."[25] Prince Milan,
having yielded to the war faction, realized Cherniaev's significance.
Taking the letter he brought from Aksakov, Milan declared: "I am
very happy that you have arrived. We are already prepared to
declare war, but if your government demands your return, we must
send you. My advice is to accept Serbian citizenship, then I can say
that I am a constitutional ruler and cannot send you out."[26]

24. orss, f. Aksakov, no. 387, Cherniaev to Aksakov, 29 April 1876 (my italics).
25. Iu. S. Kartsov, "Za kulisami diplomatii," rs, cxxxiii (Jan.–March 1908), 69–70.
26. orss, N. M. Cherniaeva, ed. khr. 2.

Why had Cherniaev traveled to Serbia? What did he expect to achieve? Did he truly believe his own subsequent explanation: "Having decided in 1876 to go to Serbia to fight for its political independence, I was convinced that the principality with its dynasty must become the Piedmont of the entire Serbian nation."[27] Cherniaev went, chorused his critics, to rehabilitate his career and find glory.[28] Not so, replied his defenders. For many years he had believed that Russia must lead the Slav cause. Perhaps an outburst of unreasoning optimism and enthusiasm contributed to his decision. Crusader, adventurer, and opportunist—Cherniaev in Serbia was all of these.[29]

Events now moved swiftly. The weak Kaljević government resigned. Prince Milan acquiesced reluctantly to the return of Ristić's "action ministry." Behind a smokescreen of peaceful declarations it hurried war preparations already underway for months. Moderate elements within the cabinet were overshadowed by Jevrem Grujić's militants. Since the prince now favored war, perceptive foreigners realized that only European intervention could now restrain Serbia.[30]

Its military leaders differed over strategy. During the winter Colonel Orešković of the General Staff had drawn up a cautious, realistic plan: Turkish strength must be ascertained before resorting to war. In April a large majority in a Military Council of army leaders and cabinet ministers, counting on a Bulgarian insurrection, decided upon a southeastward offensive against the main Turkish army at Niš.[31] Major Sava Grujić, who drafted this plan, attributed this decision not to Cherniaev, but to Serbian commanders who were confident that they could beat the Turks. Officially Russia strongly opposed war, but Serbian leaders ignored its warnings; Cherniaev adopted their war plan.[32]

27. GIM, Cherniaev, sv. 6, 67220/123, Cherniaev to [Catargi?].

28. *Golos*, 11 June 1876.

29. Antonina traces his deep involvement with the Slav cause to his appeal in 1862 to the Navaginsk regiment (see p. 28) and portrays him as an idealistic crusader against Moslem tyranny: "Pisma vlastitelei," p. 25; MacKenzie, "Panslavism in practice," JMH, XXXVI, no. 3 (Sept. 1964), 279 ff.

30. HHSA, Belgrad. Konsulate, XXXVIII, Wrede to Andrassy, 25 May 1876, no. 70. Prince Nicholas Wrede was Austrian consul in Belgrade.

31. DAS PO, 29, "Operacionji plan," 19 April 1876; "Nacrt ratne operacije protiv Turske," 10 May 1876, by S. Grujić and R. Alimpić; S. Grujić, Operacije Timočko-moravske vojske: beleške i uspomene (Belgrade 1901–1902, 3 vols. in one), I: 44 ff.

32. Ibid., p. 55. Some Russians in Serbia believed that Cherniaev had imposed the east-

Writing Aksakov, Cherniaev was less sanguine than the Serbs about a Bulgarian rising. "The Bulgarians lack what all other Slavs do—leadership. How they will develop this is hard to say, but until they do, many will die in vain." He added, "I was received everywhere very well here, but unfortunately they place excessive hopes in me." Could Aksakov arrange a large loan for Serbia to make it economically dependent upon Russia?

> Moscow would be giving great assistance to Serbia, aid which the country would never forget since with this loan she would acquire means to fight for her existence. For God's sake help this cause. If 1,500,000 rubles cannot be invested in it, then one-third that sum would help considerably. A flat refusal would greatly damage our influence which, because of our government's [pacific] policy, has already given the Austrian party of Karadjordjević[33] weapons against the Serbs devoted to Russia.

A change in the Serbian cabinet or dynasty, added Cherniaev, would not imperil repayment. He was about to leave, at Milan's request, to inspect fortifications near the frontier guarding the Morava valley.[34]

Still a private Russian citizen, Cherniaev accompanied General Zah, Serbian chief of staff, on a two week inspection trip. He recalled: "Upon my return to Belgrade I told the prince that I had been struck by the popular apathy to imminent war. I had not noticed even the slightest enthusiasm among the mustered militia. 'The question of war is decided by the intelligentsia,' the prince told me, 'while the people, especially the agrarian class, never speaks out for war.' I said that when war is decided upon in Russia, the popular mood always favors it."[35]

Why did Cherniaev not urge the prince to wait until Serbia was fully prepared? "He embodied the [Slav] movement," ex-

---

ward offensive on Serbian leaders. A. N. Khvostov, *Russkie i serby v voinu 1876 goda* (St. Petersburg, 1877), p. 24.

33. Petar Karadjordjević, pretender to the Serbian throne, was supported by Austrophile elements in Serbia.

34. ORSS, Aksakov, no. 387, Cherniaev to Aksakov, 29 April 1876. Metropolitan Mihajlo wrote that without a Russian loan Serbia would be doomed. TSGAOR, f. 1750, Moscow Slav Committee, op. 1, ed. khr. 83, ll. 12–13 reverse, Mihajlo to Aksakov, 1 June 1876.

35. GIM, ed. khr. 14, l. 84, draft of memorandum of Nov. 28, 1876; IISG, "Avtobiografiia," p. 18; S. Grujić, *Operacije*, I: 61.

plained Iurii Kartsov. "It raised him up and carried him on: to return [to Russia] for him was unthinkable." Since Serbian resources were inadequate, the only hope was help from Russia. Also Cherniaev was still a leader of the opposition at home. Kartsov observed, "War with the Turks became a type of decoy; the true struggle was conducted against official Russia or rather against the Winter Palace."[36] With rare insight Kartsov continued:

> Cherniaev was not a practical person—he lived in his imagination. He was always surrounded by a multitude of people who said yes to his fantasies and secured his trust. Like Don Quixote Cherniaev never recognized obstacles, he fought all his life against evil genii and giants. . . . As a commander his qualities of will unquestionably predominated over his critical faculties, his heart over his reason. This sympathetic responsiveness was the main element of his character and explains the secret of his colossal successes and later his equally unusual failures.[37]

He was the impractical adventurer posing as military genius.

Mikhail Grigorevich deceived Serbian leaders. Urging them into a hopeless war, he spoke as if the Russian public backed him solidly and would force the government to follow.[38] Returning to Belgrade, he accepted Serbian citizenship and command of the vital Morava army. As the Austrian consul noted, Cherniaev was no peacetime soldier and had only accepted this post because war was imminent.[39]

Cherniaev sent a misleading report to the Russian public about his entering Serbia's service and its military prospects. He had come to obtain the facts for his newspaper "since most news has been coming from the Austrian press, hostile to all Slavdom." The Serbs had welcomed him enthusiastically. In peasant homes and billeting stations portraits of Russian tsars stood next to the Obrenović. When they had asked him to join the Serbian army: "Any hesitation on my part would have been inappropriate: my refusal would have been equivalent to a desire to avoid obvious danger. . . . My departure

36. The imperial family's official residence in St. Petersburg.
37. Kartsov, "Za kulisami," rs, cxxxiv: 312–313.
38. orbl, f. Kireev, Dnevnik, VII, 20 December 1876 and 28 January 1877. Kosta Protić, commander of the Serbian Aleksinac corps, assured M. Dj. Milićević: "Cherniaev truly persuaded our leaders to enter the war." asanu, 9327/7, Dnevnik Milićevića, 26 December 1876, p. 183 reverse.
39. hhsa, Wrede to Andrassy, 25 May 1876, no. 70.

from Serbia, after examining the front lines, would be interpreted by Slavdom's enemies as showing my conviction that they [the Serbs] could not win the forthcoming struggle. Actually I saw the opposite. . . . One can say that Serbia has much basis for success against the Turks, but naturally victory is in God's hands." In Serbia the Karadjordjević party, he claimed, lacked support. Every Serb understood the need for war. "I hope that my countrymen will not blame me for deciding to join the Serbs' ranks in the coming struggle against the Turks."[40] His estimates of Serbian popular devotion to Prince Milan and the army's strength were grossly exaggerated.

Cherniaev's entry into Serbian service shocked A. N. Kartsov, the Russian consul in Belgrade. The general's action undermined those Serbs favoring peace by "establishing in the minds of the naive Serbian people the erroneous conviction that the moment for action has at last arrived since Russia herself has sent one of her generals to lead them on the battlefield."[41]

Late in May Kartsov was summoned to the north German spa of Ems where Alexander II and Gorchakov were enjoying a luxurious, carefree life. The emperor, angry at Cherniaev for accepting a Serbian command without permission, intended to strip him of his Tashkent decorations. "Try to persuade the emperor not to do that," Gorchakov told the consul. "We, his retinue, have lost our influence over him." Such severity, cautioned Kartsov, would merely enhance Cherniaev's popularity. "All right," replied Alexander, "but I forbid you to receive Cherniaev." Kartsov was not to permit Serbia to go to war. But Gorchakov, bidding him goodbye, declared: "Do not forget that although the emperor is against the war, his son, the heir to the throne, heads the [Slav] movement." Kartsov, left, bewildered by his government's dual policy. Nonetheless, he severed relations with the general and sought to restrain Serbia.[42]

Alexander left Cherniaev his decorations but ordered the Third Section to recall him to Russia.[43] When Kartsov showed him the

40. *Russkii Mir*, 25 May 1876, lead (Belgrade, May 16). In "Avtobiografiia," p. 18, Cherniaev stated more truthfully that although on paper there were 120,000 Serbian militia troops, they were badly armed and possessed antiquated artillery.

41. Kartsov to Alexander II, 14/26 May 1876, cited by D. Harris, *A Diplomatic History* . . . (Stanford, 1936), p. 394; HHSA, Wrede to Andrassy, 25 May 1876, no. 72.

42. Kartsov, RS, CXXXIV: 70–71; OSVOB, I: 241–242.

43. Ibid., p. 231, A. L. Potapov to A. E. Timashev, 24 May 1876. N. K. Girs told the German ambassador how displeased Gorchakov and the emperor were at Cherniaev's appearance in Belgrade. Earlier, Cherniaev had sought to convince Girs that the issue in the Serbo-Turkish quarrel was to end Turkish rule in the Balkans. L. von Schweinitz, *Denkwürdigkeiten* (Berlin, 1927), I: 332.

secret order, the Austrian consul, Prince Wrede, predicted that Cherniaev would disregard it but agreed it revealed "how strongly the tsar disapproves of Cherniaev's conduct."[44] On the other hand, Serbian militants such as Metropolitan Mihajlo welcomed Cherniaev's assumption of command of the Morava army. To the Serbs he was the conqueror of Tashkent. "We consider it good fortune to have such a hero in our midst," commented Mihajlo. Cherniaev's coming revealed his "brotherly Slav sympathy" and Russian public support for Serbia.[45]

After being sworn in, General Cherniaev left for Aleksinac near the Turkish frontier. Ristić, noted Kartsov, was glad to rid himself of a troublesome general who desired war "to cover himself with glory." In Belgrade Cherniaev and Colonel Valdemar Bekker (his first chief of staff in Serbia) had urged an immediate attack on Turkey. "From their viewpoint," continued Kartsov, "this is very natural since their position in case of a decisive shift to a peaceful policy would become most embarrassing and stupid." Could Ristić control the general? "Knowing the character of Cherniaev, I cannot guarantee that he won't attack without orders."[46] Kartsov's fears recall those of Kryzhanovskii in 1865.

In Russia, despite official disapproval, Cherniaev enjoyed considerable public support as the champion of South Slav liberation. He had a perfect right, commented *Novoe Vremia*, to assume a Serbian command and attract other Russians to his banner: "We express our sincere sympathy to all Russians not bound by duties of service who set forth to fight for the holy cause of Slavdom's liberation from the Turkish yoke. There in the common struggle with the Ottomans will be tied the firmest knots between Russian society and the self-liberating Slav world."[47] For the Moscow Committee Aksakov declared: "Only Cherniaev can save the honor of the Russian name."[48] Even semiofficial *Golos*, influenced by pro-Slav public feeling, wrote that Russian society wished Cherniaev greater success than Fadeev had scored in Egypt. But the Russian public would disapprove emphatically of *condottieri* "who are ready to change their homeland every day

44. HHSA, Wrede to Andrassy, 10 July 1876, no. 107.

45. TSGAOR, Moscow Slav Committee, op. 1, ed. khr. 83, ll. 8–9, Mihajlo to Aksakov, 19 May 1876.

46. OSVOB, I: 242–243, Kartsov to Ignatiev, 31 May 1876.

47. *Novoe Vremia*, 9 and 12 May 1876, cited in Nikitin, "Russkoe obshchestvo i voprosy balkanskoi politiki Rossii, 1853–1876 gg." (Moscow, 1946), pp. 972–973.

48. ORBL, Chizhov 15/10, Aksakov to Chizhov, 27 May/7 June 1876.

for even the shadow of authority, for the momentary satisfaction of ambition!"[49]

Russkii Mir exhorted Serbia to fight and assured its readers that the whole populace supported war preparations. Unless war should come, a popular upheaval in Belgrade was likely, reported its Belgrade correspondent, "If the war succeeds, [Serbia] will occupy first place in the Balkans. If there is no war, Serbia's role as an important force is ended forever." Unlike other papers it promised Serbia support even if she attacked Turkey: "As for Russia her role toward Serbia is no longer open to the doubts which still seemed possible a few months ago."[50]

Responding to such unofficial intimations of support, *Istok,* Ristić's organ declared: "Tsar Alexander need not call upon Serbia and Montenegro as Nicholas I did during the Crimean War. Serbia and Montenegro stand already like loaded cannon which will burst into flame if that is the request of Slav Russia. . . . War for Serbia is inevitable."[51]

In Aleksinac Cherniaev waited impatiently. He learned that he had been ordered back to Russia, but he paid this no heed. He reported that defensive fortifications had been completed. "Deligrad can no longer be taken. The same is true of Aleksinac." With the Morava valley secure, he persuaded War Minister Nikolić to proclaim full mobilization.[52] With some forty thousand men Cherniaev boasted that in three days he could reach Sofia, Bulgaria.[53]

Conclusion of a Serbo-Montenegrin alliance ended the suspense. When Prince Milan informed Cherniaev of the alliance he added that he needed only a decent pretext for war. Resolving to attack unless the powers intervened, the prince cautioned: "I hope, my general, that you will tell no one among your friends of our firm and definite intention, for I wish, if possible, that all be done secretly and that at the last moment Europe will be awakened by the news that Prince Nicholas and Prince Milan, joining hands, are marching to liberate their oppressed brethren." Money was pitifully short, but

49. *Golos*, 30 May 1876.

50. *Russkii Mir*, 23 May 1876, 12 and 17 June 1876.

51. *Istok* (Belgrade), 23 May 1876, no. 56.

52. S. Grujić, *Bugarski*, p. 10; *Operacije*, I: 61–62, 83. Grujić noted that the staff, selected by War Minister Nikolić, included Lt. Colonel Valdemar Bekker recently resigned from the Russian army; Major Pera Arandjelović, chief of engineers; Major Sava Grujić, chief of artillery; a priest and three orderlies.

53. Ivanov, "Bolgarskoe," RS, LXII: 139–140.

Milan counted on Serbian patriotism and the Slav world to support the war: "I . . . count on you, dear general, to act energetically, to prepare victory."[54]

The Serbo-Montenegrin accord doomed the Dreikaiserbund's eleventh hour diplomatic efforts. From Aleksinac, Cherniaev wrote Aksakov: "We are on the eve of momentous military events. I should like to write you of many things, but I don't trust paper [the mails]. Do not believe the newspapers' twaddle about the Bulgarian insurrection and use your influence so that the papers do not divide up the skin of a beast which has not yet been slain [Turkey]. Bulgaria without Serbia can do nothing."[55]

In mid-June Serbian troops and supplies moved in a steady stream to Cherniaev's army on the Bulgarian frontier. On the 17th Prince Milan went to army headquarters. At the border Colonel Horvatović's vanguard stood awaiting the signal to advance. A conflict fateful for Serbia and Cherniaev was about to begin.

THE SERBIAN WAR THEATER IN 1876

To Vienna

Sava River

AUSTRIA-HUNGARY

To Russia

Belgrade

Danube River

Drina River

RUMANIA

Veliki Izvor

SERBIA

BOSNIA

Paraćin

Zaječar

Timok River

Ražan

Knjaževac

Deligrad

Kruševac

Aleksinac

Djunis

Babina Glava

Niš

Pirot

Ibar River

Morava River

BULGARIA

Trn

TURKEY

Vranje

Sofia

To Constantinople

ADRIATIC SEA

0   25   50
MILES

▲   BATTLE SITES
—··—   SERBIAN FRONTIER
OF 1875

54. RA (1914), I: 34–38, Prince Milan to Cherniaev, 5/17 June 1876.
55. TSGAOR, f. 1750, op. 1, ed. khr. 83, l. 39, Cherniaev to [Aksakov], 12 June 1876.

We are fighting for the sacred idea of Slavdom. . . . We are fighting for freedom, the Orthodox cross, and civilization. Behind us stands Russia. If fickle fortune should desert us, this holy ground will be drenched with the costly blood of our Russian brothers, and these hills and ravines will resound for the last time with the clash of arms and the thunder of cannon. If we, wading in blood to our shoulders, are unable to open the doors to freedom and civilization, the iron hand of Russia will break them open. . . . Long live freedom, long live the Slavic idea! (Cherniaev[1])

CHAPTER IX

The War Begins

ON JUNE 18, 1876, Serbia declared war on Turkey and Montenegro followed promptly. The belligerent forces were about equal in size, but Turkish regulars faced Serbian militia taken right from the plow.[2] Yet the Serbian war plan called for Cherniaev to strike a devastating blow at Turkish forces at Niš and force the Ottoman Empire to conclude peace.[3]

As war broke out, Prince Milan greeted his principal commander at Aleksinac. The young, heavyset prince shook hands warmly with the lean, balding Russian. The two leaders of the Slav struggle conversed briefly in French. Dr. Vladan Djordjević, hearing extravagant praise of Cherniaev's prowess, was amazed at his unassuming dress: a blouse with a Serbian general's insignia, red trousers, and boots. Only his sabre, his sharply curled black moustache, and white Saint George's cross gave him a military look. Dr. Djordjević observed, "His expressive blue eyes betokened a good heart and an idealist believing in human uprightness."[4]

1. W. L. Langer, *European Alliances and Alignments* (New York, 1956), p. 90.
2. Against the Serbian states the Turks had about 126,000 men, mostly facing Serbia. When the war began Montenegro had 24,000 men and Serbia 98,000, but only a few thousand Serbs were regulars. Of the Serbian first line troops Alimpić on the Drina had 18,000; Zah on the Javor 12,000; Cherniaev on the Morava 48,000, including 18,000 under Horvatović; and Lešjanin on the Timok 15,000. S. Grujić, *Operacije*, I: 74.
3. DAS PO, 29/11, 12 June 1876.
4. V. Djordjević, *Srpsko-turski rat*, 2 vols. (Belgrade, 1907), I: 4 ff.

Cherniaev as commander in chief of Serbia's eastern armies in 1876

Cherniaev and his staff in Serbia in 1876

Counting upon assistance from other Balkan orthodox, Cherniaev exhorted them to fight the infidel Turks: "We are coming to your aid. Rise Slavs, the dawn of your freedom has come. You descendants of the glorious Greeks in Epirus and Thessaly. You fighting sons of Albania, you also suffer from the degenerate Ottomans. Join with us no matter what your faith and all together with common pressure we shall banish the strangers from the soil given by God to our ancestors. Forward against the common foe and let us shout unanimously: 'God is with us, let the heathens know it!' "[5] Could Russia fail to support this great crusade? Cherniaev's initial objective was Babina Glava, a fortified Turkish camp just inside Bulgaria. Horvatović's two assaults on the Turkish trenches were repulsed with considerable loss. Antonina described Cherniaev's timely arrival, "At the decisive moment, when Horvatović's reserves had been committed, an orderly galloped up to report that Cherniaev was coming. This news, affirmed Sava Grujić, gave the Serbs new strength. The commander in chief inspected all the batteries and "his personal courage had an especially favorable effect upon our young artillerymen." The third Serbian attack succeeded, and the Turks withdrew toward Pirot.[6]

This account of the battle at Babina Glava suggests how pro-Cherniaev newspapers in Russia covered the war and why he became the hero of the hour:

Shortly after 7 A.M. on June 20 the Serbian army under General Cherniaev's command carried fourteen cannon up the slopes of a steep mountain and prepared to storm the camp. General Cherniaev personally placed the guns and ordered fire opened on a blockhouse. . . . The Turks replied with heavy rifle and cannon fire. . . . Our general, the valiant Mikhail Grigorevich, stood on the mountain and scrutinized the action of our guns. To the remark of one of his entourage that as commander in chief he was exposing himself to excessive danger, Cherniaev replied: "I am in battle with the Serbian army for the first time. I must show myself." And truly he revealed himself as the valorous arch-strategist. . . . Serbian troops clearly saw his fearlessness and courage.[7]

5. ΙISG, ed. khr. 18.
6. Ibid., "Biografiia," pp. 252–253; S. Grujić, *Operacije*, I: 115–116.
7. *Sovremennye izvestiia*, no. 188, 1876, in VISB (1915), no. 2, p. 78.

Novoe Vremia's summary of the situation after the battle was rosy. The border population was rising. At Pirot, Cherniaev's army was distributing one hundred thousand rifles to the Bulgarians. A major battle was expected near Sofia, "unless the Turks retreat sensibly toward Adrianople."[8] Actually, Cherniaev never reached Pirot and the Bulgarians mostly refused weapons whose number was wildly inflated. On June 21 several Petersburg newspapers placed Cherniaev's army near Niš "on the road to Constantinople."[9] Such reports fed baseless beliefs in Russia that the Serbs, aided by the Russian public, could crush Turkey and solve the Eastern question.

In fact, after taking Babina Glava Cherniaev's troubles multiplied. The Serbian army was untrained, undisciplined and woefully short of officers. Prior to the war Cherniaev had neither learned its shortcomings nor carried out military exercises.[10] Now some subordinates refused to obey him. A Serbian colonel would not return to camp and had to be removed. General Djordje Stratimirović, a volunteer from the Austrian Vojvodina, abandoned his command and was expelled from the army. Mikhail Grigorevich wrote plaintively to Prince Milan: "I ask Your Highness to issue clear instructions to eliminate disobedience in the army." Other Serbian columns, supposed to advance with Horvatović, failed to capture their objectives. Toshev, the Bulgarian leader, when ordered across the Nišava River, declared, "I do not wish to go under a crossfire with my troops." Losing patience, Cherniaev petulantly handed over command to Horvatović. He threatened to resign his commission and go to Belgrade! His senior officers begged him to remain since his departure would doom the Serbian cause. He yielded and when reinforcements arrived, his spirits revived.[11]

After Babina Glava, A. L. Izmailov, an unsavory member of Cherniaev's staff, demanded money from the Moscow Committee for himself and his general: "Mikhail Grigorevich, because of his position . . . must expend much money. He is not receiving a salary. He has not been given money for receptions nor for secret expenses. . . . Besides there have come and are still coming Austrian officers and

8. *Novoe Vremia*, 27 June 1876.
9. *Golos*, 4 July 1876.
10. S. Grujić, *Bugarski*, pp. 10–11.
11. IISG, "Biografiia," pp. 252–255. Even Antonina's account reveals that Cherniaev acted emotionally, capriciously and without reflection.

penniless Serbs from the Military Frontier [a border region in Croatia between Austria-Hungary and Turkey]. They are worthy people and Mikhail Grigorevich gives each of them ten or fifteen ducats . . . out of his own pocket." Izmailov accompanied his demands for five thousand rubles with boasting reports of storming a Turkish blockhouse. He pleaded, "Please don't abandon me! Can't you assign me a grant of 800 rubles a month? We are dying here for the holy cause. Please don't abandon Mikhail Grigorevich. I have been recommended for a decoration for bravery."[12] During the first encounter he had fled the battlefield and had to be forcibly returned to his post. He soon joined the dregs of the volunteer movement in Belgrade's cafés.

Meanwhile Cherniaev remained in camp paralyzed by indecision. His fatal hesitation caused open dissatisfaction among his officers. Colonel Mileta Despotović, a Russian officer of Serbian origin, told him that his inactivity was ruining Serbia, that he could not handle such an important command and should return to Russia. Sava Grujić urged his reassignment to an inactive role as the prince's military adviser. Furious at such criticism, Cherniaev rushed to Aleksinac and complained to Milan. He would leave Serbia unless he was given command of all forces in the east. The prince, already under his spell, yielded; Cherniaev returned as de facto commander of the Timok-Morava armies.[13]

In Babina Glava Cherniaev learned that the Turks were concentrating at Veliki Izvor just inside Serbia. He gathered seven battalions and marched hastily to Zaječar where he called a council of war to be held at Vratarnica: "The enemy under Osman Pasha's command occupies on our territory a fortified position at Veliki Izvor from which he threatens Zaječar. Our task is to drive him from this position and occupy it ourselves." So confident was he that he made no plans for retreat. Applying his Central Asian tactics he sent one column around the Turkish right, then attacked the Turkish camp frontally. By noon the Serbs were prevailing in a stubborn battle; there was confusion in Osman's army. But at the decisive moment, inexperienced troops in Lešjanin's left column halted, refused to obey their officers, and retreated in disarray. Osman's cavalry attacked the Serbian right which fled in panic. The vanguard continued to fight bravely, but the battle was lost irrevocably. Profoundly

12. TSGAOR, f. 1750, op. 1, ed. khr. 83, ll. 18–19 reverse, Izmailov to Aksakov, 23 June 1876.
13. Grujić, *Bugarski*, pp. 10–14.

discouraged, Cherniaev spent the night with his staff at Vratarnica.[14] His dream of emancipating the South Slavs in one blow lay
shattered.

The defeat at Veliki Izvor was a turning point in the
war. Cherniaev's advance had ended. The small Bulgarian detachments sent across the frontier returned without distributing
many guns. Their leader, I. S. Ivanov, blamed the Serbs for not
providing adequate arms for his men, and left for Belgrade
in disgust.[15] The Serbian militia, unable to implement an offensive strategy, retreated into Serbia at all points. Cherniaev's Russian-
style frontal assaults undermined its morale. Whether the Serbs
could defend their own soil remained to be proven. Eastern Serbia
lay open to Turkish conquest.

Cherniaev, with Belgrade's consent, drew a veil over operations at
the front concealing reverses and dramatizing successes. To exploit
Russian gullibility he established a "Correspondence Bureau" at his
Deligrad headquarters under Colonel V. V. Komarov, his crony
from *Russkii Mir*. Komarov was intelligent and devoted to Cherniaev
but petty and absent-minded. He enforced such strict controls over
the press, that until late July only correspondents from pro-Cherniaev papers were permitted at headquarters. Only after repeated
protests to Prince Milan were foreign correspondents allowed even
in Aleksinac. The Bureau enabled Cherniaev to deceive the Serbian
and Russian public. Most approved newspapermen—Komarov,
Monteverde, and Lavrentiev—were members of Cherniaev's staff
anxious to "improve" the news, and when outside correspondents did
reach headquarters, they were treated as spies. "Jupiter" Komarov
ordered them to describe "heroic deeds" or face expulsion. When
journalists unearthed the truth, they had to cross the Danube to
Austria to report it to the world. The pro-Cherniaev press dismissed
articles criticizing the conduct of the war as Austrian or Turkish
fabrications. Cherniaev even concealed facts from the Serbian government and whenever he was opposed, threatened to leave Serbia
and cut off Russian aid.[16] The Deligrad "Correspondence

14. IISG, "Biografiia," pp. 255–261; Djordjević, I: 83–96.

15. Ivanov, "Bolgarskoe," RS, LXII: 141–143; Grujić, *Bugarski*, pp. 49–53.

16. After the war P. A. Viskovatov, *Golos*'s Belgrade correspondent, exposed the Bureau
concluding: "Not a single honest line could reach the Russian press from the battlefield."
Editor Kraevskii confirmed that Cherniaev's censors had cleared only one of Viskovatov's
many dispatches. *Golos*, 18 November 1876, "Deligradskoe korespondentsburo." See also nos.
308, 327, and 339.

Bureau" was the natural successor to *Russkii Mir*'s assaults on the war ministry and Turkestan regime.

Even then news of Cherniaev's reverses reached foreign newspapers. The perceptive Austrian consul reported: "Serbian troops realize the superiority of better armed Turkish infantry and have been demoralized by their fire at many points." From Belgrade Stratimirović condemned Cherniaev's plan of operations and predicted that it would lead to defeat.[17] "Cherniaev has already managed to quarrel with his subordinates," commented Miliutin. Stratimirović has "reproached Cherniaev for indecisiveness, hesitation, and muddleheadedness. What did they expect of him? What was his great fame based on? Probably we shall soon see the idol dethroned."[18] But the Serbs and the Russian public were deceived by Cherniaev's rhetoric and inflated reports of his achievements.

Official Russia reacted coolly to the outbreak of war. The Austro-Russian proclamation of nonintervention at Reichstadt allowed the conflict to be fought to a decision, though nationalists like Count Ignatiev pleaded for intervention in the Slavs' behalf. Russian Slavophiles, hailing the war as a crusade, responded warmly but ineffectively to Serbian appeals. "Everything depends now upon Cherniaev's successes. . . ." declared Ivan Aksakov. "Either he will defeat the Turks or lay down his life for the just Slav cause," predicted A. A. Kireev of the St. Petersburg Committee. Except for *Golos* and official newspapers, the Russian press defended the Serbian attack and urged benevolent neutrality. Prohibited from advocating Russia's open involvement, *Novoe Vremia* declared: "Upon Russian society there lies a sacred obligation to assist these heroic fighters with all its means, principally with money. The Serbian loan must be subscribed by our resources. . . . Nothing can prevent noble sacrifices by society itself."[19] Such appeals brought contributions and Russian volunteers.

Soon after Veliki Izvor the Turks penetrated eastern Serbia deeply. For six days Horvatović's corps defended Knjaževac against superior Turkish strength. On July 22 Horvatović received a telegram from Cherniaev: "With a large mass of infantry and many guns I will attack the Turks from the rear." Sagging Serbian morale revived. The next day Horvatović attacked and drove the Turks back

17. HHSA, Wrede to Andrassy, 10 July 1876, no. 106.

18. Miliutin, *Dnevnik*, II: 55, entry of 8 July.

19. *Novoe Vremia*, 27 June 1876, no. 117, in AII, Ristić, XVIII/634. Ristić underlined the significant passages in red pencil.

all along the line, but Cherniaev failed to appear and "our tired infantry felt itself betrayed." Without food or water for two days and suffering twenty percent casualties, they wavered and then broke. As Cherniaev and his staff at Sveti Arandjela finished their feast of roast pork, news came that Knjaževac had fallen. "We Serbs on the staff were terribly downcast," recalled Dr. Djordjević, "Cherniaev walked up and down for a long time hitting himself on the right thigh with his clenched fist, then ordered us to remain where we were."[20] Failure to reinforce Horvatović cost Serbia its frontier defense line.

This reverse left Mikhail Grigorevich deeply depressed. He returned to Deligrad, transferring command temporarily to Colonel Kosta Protić. He contemplated resigning but again contented himself with more power. At Deligrad, Prince Milan approved Cherniaev's dispositions and confirmed his control over the Timok corps; then at his request the prince dismantled his own headquarters, and returned to Belgrade leaving Cherniaev in full control.[21]

Serbian leaders were dismayed at the loss of the eastern frontier towns. In a gloomy letter to Foreign Minister Ristić, the prince depicted the army's low morale and material position and blamed his cabinet for involving Serbia in a hopeless war. However, the ministers and Cherniaev persuaded him to continue it in order to obtain Europe's sympathy and better peace terms.[22]

Fresh from his meeting with Milan, Cherniaev with typical grandiloquence exhorted his soldiers to fight on:

Warriors of the Morava-Timok army! Fighters for independence and the Orthodox faith! For more than a month you have been fighting heroically with an enemy superior in numbers and weapons. In battle you have died heroically and borne severe wounds courageously. Know that upon you lies not only the defense of your country, families and property, but you are now the main fighters for Christian peoples beneath the Moslem yoke. So far you have not been defeated. . . . Continue to fight bravely. Carry our your commanders' orders pre-

20. Djordjević, ı: 174–178.
21. ɪɪsɢ, "Biografiia," pp. 262–264; P. Todorović, *Odlomci iz dnevnika jednog dobrovoljca* (Belgrade, 1938), pp. 4–5.
22. J. Ristić, *Diplomatska istorija Srbije*, 2 vols. (Belgrade, 1896–1898), ı: 127–128; J. Grujić, *Zapisi*, ııı: 103–105.

cisely and without debate and the Lord God will give you victory.[23]

He appointed Colonel Komarov chief of staff and had a new defense line built before Aleksinac. The Turkish advance along the Morava's right bank was halted. Troops at Deligrad and Aleksinac were given daily bayonet and rifle drill. When Cherniaev inspected his men in early August, he was gratified by their progress.[24] The militia, now defending its homes, began to resemble an army.

Enthusiasm in Russia for the Slav struggle, fostered by dramatic reports from Cherniaev's headquarters, rose rapidly that summer. The nationalist press and the Slav committees collected money and clothing and sent medical aid to the Serbs. Thousands volunteered to fight with Cherniaev. Excitement, raging like a prairie fire throughout Russia, "seized hold of all layers of society and thrust all other interests into the background."[25] "Our public's entire attention has been attracted by the [South Slavs]," affirmed *Novoe Vremia*.[26] The chairman of the St. Petersburg Committee agreed that such a popular movement had rarely been seen before in Russian history. In Moscow "on every wall . . . hang portraits of Cherniaev and Serbian heroes. Through the commercial districts go collectors bearing the sign: for the Slavs. In the Slav Committee office surges a crowd of reserve officers, soldiers and intellectuals signing up as volunteers."[27] In the provinces, noted the police, pro-Slav sentiment was also widespread.[28]

Soon Cherniaev became the most celebrated name in Russia. Pamphlets protrayed him as a selfless hero of vast prowess, a military genius, a pure knight who epitomized all Russian virtues: "The famous name of M. G. Cherniaev is known to every Russian," proclaimed a Moscow pamphlet. "Not a day passes

23. IISG, "Biografiia," p. 266.

24. Ibid., pp. 266–268; V. P. Meshcherskii, *Pravda o Serbii* (St. Petersburg, 1877), pp. 260–261.

25. A. D. Gradovskii, *Sobranie sochinenii* (St. Petersburg, 1901), VI: 227.

26. P. Ia. Miroshnichenko, "Otnoshenie russkogo obshchestva k balkanskim sobytiiam, 1875–1878 gg.," 3 vols. (Stalino, 1946), II: 56–59.

27. *Pervye 15 let sushchestvovaniia S-Peterburgskago Slavianskogo Blagotvoritelnago Obshchestva* (St. Petersburg, 1893), pp. 379–380; A. Golubev, *Kniaz A. I. Vasilchikov* (St. Petersburg, 1882), pp. 115–116. The prince, a cautious man, was not prone to exaggeration.

28. OSVOB, I, nos. 185, 187, 242, and 243; MacKenzie, *The Serbs*, p. 116.

without his name being repeated in every corner of Russia and from everywhere come blessings and wishes that he may issue forth victorious and unharmed from the bloody struggle."[29] His popularity was not limited to Slavophiles. The uneducated, contributing their hard earned kopecks "consider Cherniaev sent by God to defend the cross and their belief is strong that he will drive the Turks from Europe and reestablish Orthodoxy over the entire Balkan peninsula."[30] Even *Golos* reported that children, playing a game called "the Eastern Question," all wished to be Cherniaev.[31] Russians glorified the Slav cause whose symbol he had become.

The Slav committees, borne along by this tide, attempted to lead the movement. Aksakov's Moscow organization succeeded better than his conservative Petersburg confreres. Organized recruitment of volunteers for Serbia began in July, reached a peak in August, then declined gradually. Slav societies in Odessa and Kiev assisted. "All Russia was ready to cover itself with branches of the Slav committee," noted Aksakov, but the government forbade it. Recruitment in the capitals was generally careful, but some drunkards and adventurers enlisted there and many more in provincial centers. Of the five thousand Russian volunteers dispatched to Serbia, about three thousand saw action.[32]

Their motives varied: a few officers were idealistic Panslavs anxious to liberate their brethren; most reserve officers went because war was their profession. These elements generally arrived early in the war and made a fine impression. Ordinary Russian soldiers went to "smite the Turks" or liberate the Slavs. Then later came adventurers, fortune hunters, and riffraff, eloquent testimony to serfdom's deplorable heritage.[33]

The official Russian attitude toward these activities was ill-defined. The government lacked a clear policy or the will to enforce one. Alexander II epitomized this indecisiveness. Though angry at Cherniaev, he did not insist that he return to Russia; barring official financial or military aid to the Serbs, he permitted considerable unofficial assistance. The Slav committees and pro-Slav press had

29. M. G. *Cherniaev, glavnokomanduiushchii serbskimi voiskami* (Moscow, 1877), pp. 3–4.

30. osvob, i: 464, no. 325, report of chief of gendarmes, St. Petersburg, 25 October 1876.

31. *Golos*, 11 July 1876.

32. I. S. Aksakov, *Sochineniia*, 6 vols. (Moscow, 1886), i: 224; Nikitin, *Slavianskie*, pp. 316 ff. On recruitment see osvob, i, nos. 211, 213, 218, 220, 226.

33. Nikitin, *Slavianskie*, p. 321; osvob, i: 429–431.

wide latitude. On August 8 Alexander legalized temporary retirement of army officers who went to Serbia as volunteers without losing seniority. The court cooperated so closely with the Petersburg Committee that its chairman concluded, "Here the popular agitation has taken on an official look."[34] Yet the tsar and his ministers firmly opposed war. The more bellicose heir was warned by his tutor, "All groups are playing with your name constantly. Without hesitation they place you at the head of the action party which would surely rush to the Slavs' aid if you were in power." He should avoid zealots and remain silent.[35] Official Russia's ambiguity encouraged Panslav agitation.

In Petersburg, Milosav Protić, the Serbian envoy sent to arrange a Russian loan, began to question Cherniaev's motives. Late in July he received a letter by a confidant of the general urging a coup d'état against the Serbian Assembly. Milan would become an autocrat under Russian guidance. The tsar, reported Protić, detested Foreign Minister Ristić and wanted him removed. "Poor Serbia, what awaits you?" the envoy wrote Ristić, "Burn this letter immediately after reading it or it will damage me much both here and there. In view of all this should I stop the dispatch of Russian officers?"[36] Cherniaev's telegram to Aksakov, describing the beneficent results of a coup against the Assembly and the constitution, confirmed Protić's suspicions: "Russia's influence upon Serbia would be real and would rest on firm foundations. The chief of state [Milan] and the entire people sympathize with Russia. The ministers gradually could be named from Russians. Hostile parties would disappear and one of the Slav states would become de facto a Russian province."[37] Ristić was too absorbed with urgent diplomatic and military developments to heed these warnings.

During August, while bitter battles raged in eastern Serbia, the Ristić government, Cherniaev and the powers debated a possible armistice. Ristić argued that the war must continue since the Turks would demand Milan's abdication otherwise. Ristić would accept an armistice only if Serbia retained her prewar status and territory.[38] But the prince and Cherniaev changed their minds with every turn of military events.

On August 7 a battle which was to last five days broke out on the

34. Golubev, pp. 116–117.
35. *Pisma Pobedonostseva k Aleksandru III* (Moscow, 1925), 25 June 1876, pp. 45–46.
36. AII, Ristić, xxvi/716, 717, Protić to Ristić, 25 and 26 July 1876.
37. TSGAOR, f. 1750, d. 90, l. 235, cited in Nikitin, "Russkoe obshchestvo," p. 1025.
38. AII, Ristić, xviii/46, Ristić to Protić, 30 July 1876.

Morava. The Turks sought to smash Serbian positions, capture Aleksinac, and open the way to Belgrade. Before it began Cherniaev
telegraphed Ristić: "In Belgrade they are talking of concluding
peace. . . . At present any talk of peace is inappropriate. Our position now is better than ever before. In any case I beg you to await
my letter explaining our entire situation in the war theater." Ristić replied that all the powers but Germany advised Serbia to seek
an armistice, but the government would question all commanders
first before committing itself.[39]

During the Aleksinac battle the fortunes of war careened crazily.
On August 7 the Turks threw themselves upon the Serbian vanguard. "Our men resisted," Cherniaev reported, "and near evening
the Turks retired to camp . . . [after] burning all frontier villages.
Frightful barbarism." On the ninth, Eyub-Pasha attacked Horvatović and compelled Cherniaev to commit his reserves. As the enemy
prepared a decisive assault, Cherniaev complained to the Serbian
war minister: "It is easy to sit in Belgrade and criticize actions at the
war front. Many troops lack overcoats. The nights are cold. Volunteers are barefoot. Half of each battalion is so poorly armed that
it can act only as reinforcements. . . . Serbian officers are so educated that they refuse to obey the commander in chief's orders. All of
them are out for themselves." While other Serbian troops relaxed,
he complained, "the entire Turkish army is concentrated against
me." Nonetheless, he would do his duty to the prince and to Serbia:
"Tomorrow the fate of Serbia may be decided."[40]

Prince Milan promised Cherniaev reinforcements and asked
whether he could repel the Turks. The general replied gloomily:
"The enemy has over fifty battalions against us. . . . I cannot forsee
the outcome of Aleksinac battle. I shall continue to fight to the end.
Only six battalions in reserve. We have 500 wounded. . . . You
know the state of the troops' morale. They won't hold up long and
must continually be replaced to be able to continue the fight. We
have held our positions on the fourth day of battle. Losses are
great. . . . Foe has much greater forces." At his recommendation,
the prince agreed to seek an armistice.[41]

39. Ibid., xviii/56, 58, Cherniaev to Ristić, 6 August 1876 and Ristić to Cherniaev, 7
August 1876, telegrams.

40. Ibid., xviii/63, Cherniaev to War Minister, 10 August 1876, telegram.

41. Ibid., Cherniaev to Milan, 11 August 1876; S. Grujić, *Operacije*, iii: 35. On August 12
Cherniaev telegraphed Ristić: "Try to conclude immediately not peace but an armistice." DAS

Then the military situation changed abruptly. After frontal assaults on Aleksinac failed, the Turks hurled themselves against Šumatovac heights guarding the Serbian right flank. On the previous
evening, Antonina wrote, Cherniaev had discovered that its defenses
were incomplete and ordered trees felled in front of the Serbian
trenches. The Turkish cavalry stumbled among the tangled vines
and stumps and was repelled. At dawn on August 12 dense masses
of enemy infantry moved against the Šumatovac garrison led by
Captain Živan Protić. Accurate Serbian artillery fire cut them down
by the hundred. Cherniaev, despite his staff's entreaties, personally
directed the guns in the forward trenches. Suddenly a shell struck
Captain Protić, standing close to the general, and tore his head off.
The torso fell onto Cherniaev bathing him in blood. Cherniaev
tearfully kissed the corpse saying: "Farewell Živan Protić, farewell
dear friend!"

Šumatovac was virtually surrounded, cartridges were running out.
Only along a narrow, tortuous path could the Serbs bring in grenades. Major Živković remonstrated: the commander in chief
should direct the army, not expose himself in the front lines. Cherniaev replied calmly: "Perhaps you are right, sir, but if at this
moment I left the trench, its garrison would flee drawing with it the
troops outside the trench who are now holding on bravely . . .
perhaps because they know that the army's entire general staff is here. If we
leave, it will undermine the troops' morale, the Turks will easily
capture Šumatovac, and by this success will become masters of Aleksinac. Therefore, gentlemen, we must stand firm at this spot no
matter what comes!" No one raised further objections. When the
Serbs repelled the fourth Turkish assault, Cherniaev concluded that
he could leave without discouraging the defenders.[42] That day the
Serbian troops and their Russian commander reached their apogee
of glory.

Šumatovac's resistance discouraged the Turks, but Cherniaev did
not know this. Expecting another assault, he ordered all available
troops concentrated in the area. Next morning occurred a tragic
incident. Worried about Šumatovac's defense, Cherniaev paced up
and down in great agitation. Major Stevan Velimirović, commanding thirteen battalions, was announced. "Where are your

---

PO, 29/98–vii.
   42. Djordjević, I: 242–252.

troops?" inquired Cherniaev tensely. "The artillery is in camp, but I do not know where the infantry is," responded Velimirović through S. Binički, a Russian-speaking Serbian officer. The general exploded: "You, a commander, dare to tell me that you do not know where your men are? That is impossible!" His detachment had had to retreat, explained the major, and while he extricated the artillery, the infantry had scattered. The general shouted: "There is no justification or excuse for this. You are a dastardly coward. You must have fled first since you do not know where your men are. I was counting on your detachment, and you have wrecked my entire plan. My positions stand bare and unoccupied before the Turks. I need troops, I need your detachment. Give me soldiers, you miserable wretch!"

Attracted by the commotion, officers and men crowded around. Cherniaev, his eyes bloodshot, paced up and down in uncontrollable fury. Then he turned to Binički: "Tell him that I shall courtmartial him, I'll shoot him,, I'll hang him, the useless woman!" He rushed up to the major who sat pale and dejected on his horse. With fists clenched he shouted hoarsely: "Give me troops, I must have troops, you miserable coward!" In a shaken voice Velimirović replied, "I have no troops." Cherniaev belabored him with curses. Then his target shifted abruptly: "I must escape from here, I shall leave this miserable country where nobody obeys me or carries out my orders and everyone argues with me. . . . Accursed be the hour when I entered this country. I'll lose my mind, I'll kill myself!" His chief of staff, Komarov, hovering solicitously, soothed his friend. More quietly Cherniaev ordered, "Take his sabre and write the second corps commander that I am putting this creature under arrest. Let him be taken to Belgrade under guard. . . . I don't need women in my army."

At Komarov's instruction, Binički took the major's sabre. Velimirović's expression was a mixture of pain, anger, and irony. While Komarov put away the sabre, Binički whispered, "The Russians aren't in Belgrade, you will go before a Serbian court." Velimirović replied: "It doesn't matter, nothing matters any more."

Dr. Djordjević told Cherniaev that the major was a highly respected staff officer, and that after every battle Serbian militiamen returned to camp on their own; they were probably there already. Cherniaev appeared oblivious but realized his incredible harshness. After a few minutes he turned to Velimirović: "I forgive you. Go collect your troops and if we hold our positions today . . . , I shall make you lieutenant colonel." The major replied curtly: "Forgiveness is unnecessary since I do not see my guilt, and a reward is superfluous since up to now I have fought without any." Reclaiming his sabre, he wheeled his horse around and disappeared into the woods.

This scene occurred at 9 A.M.; before noon the Morava's waters claimed Stevan Velimirović's body. Called a traitor and a coward before his comrades, this gentle, sensitive man left a letter for his younger brother and drowned himself. At first thunderstruck at the news, Cherniaev then declared: "An insulted soldier should not die like a girl who has sinned. In his place I would either have killed him who had shamed me without cause . . . , or still better taken a company of brave men to attack the enemy where he was strongest so that at least my death would be remembered as long as my people survived. To drown oneself? A terribly unmilitary death!" Only later did the staff and the Serbs learn of this tragedy. At the time they rejoiced that Cherniaev's warm heart had prevailed over his sudden and terrible anger.[43]

Šumatovac's defenders saw with joy that the Turks had withdrawn leaving fezzes scattered on the battlefield. Cherniaev now telegraphed Belgrade: "Yesterday we had a major victory. In two days the situation has changed drastically. Russian officers are arriving en masse. The troops' morale is rising. It is essential to draw out truce negotiations until the situation is clarified."[44] That same day, August 13, Prince Milan responded: "After the brilliant victory which you have won after six days of hardship, exhausting labors and struggle . . . , I am executing my duty by expressing to you my heartfelt congratulations. . . . A feeble sign of my gratitude, which pervades the entire Serbian army for its glorious commander, is the enclosed Order of Takovo."[45] The Turks had been prevented from breaking through to Belgrade, and the Serbs had fought valiantly, but to claim Šumatovac as a great victory was ridiculous. However, Cherniaev, exploiting his hold over the prince magnified this temporary success to prevent peace and enhance his influence.

43. S. Binički, *Odlomci iz ratnih beležaka 1876 g.* (Belgrade, 1891), pp. 14–20; Djordjević, I: 275–278.

44. AII, Ristić, XVIII/80, Cherniaev to Ristić, 13 August 1876.

45. IISG, "Biografiia," pp. 268 ff. Typically, Antonina called Šumatovac a glorious victory gained because of "the selfless dedication of the commander in chief."

CHAPTER X

The Kingmaker of Deligrad

SERBIA'S FORTUNES waned after Šumatovac, but Cherniaev sought ever greater military and political power. Arrogantly ignoring the Serbian ministers, he dealt directly with the prince. In an effort to force Russia into the war, he proclaimed Milan king of Serbia, but his attempt to play Warwick eroded his standing with Serbian and Russian leaders and could not forestall defeat.

The prince deplored Cherniaev's bad relations with the cabinet. Only the Ristić ministry, argued Milan, could combat a pacific public opinion. Congratulating Cherniaev over Šumatovac, he criticized his telegram to Ristić favoring an armistice: "Why didn't you send me that telegram? Did they tell you perhaps that I . . . [was] preoccupied with my wife's health? Perhaps you were offended that I failed to answer your two letters? . . . Knowing your sentiments for the Serbian and Slav cause, I prefer that you write me directly." Milan, still uncommitted to the powers, inquired: "Should we, in your opinion, work for peace or not? An armistice . . . would be difficult to obtain and could lead us to peace willy-nilly. Upon your reply will depend my subsequent conduct."[1] Again Milan left Serbia's fate up to Cherniaev.

1. "K M. G. Cherniaevu," RA (1914), I: 40–45, Milan to Cherniaev, 18 August 1876.

Šumatovac had changed the military situation very little. Cherniaev, his nerves stretched taut by battle, had but a few days respite before Abdul Kerim, seeking to bypass Aleksinac, attacked along the Morava's left bank. On August 21 the Serbs abandoned the key position of Adrovac. From his Deligrad headquarters Cherniaev telegraphed Milan: "Today the Turks attacked about 8 A.M. with formidable artillery support. We were crushed by the enemy's compact masses. We held our positions thirteen hours. Shattered by superior force, we must give way tomorrow. Despite our recent successes, despite the army's valor, I feel it is difficult to continue the struggle without reinforcements." He asked Milan to negotiate an armistice.[2] Replying that neither the Porte nor the powers had yet responded, Milan pressed him to request more officers and men from Russia. Cherniaev begged General V. V. Zinoviev, marshal of the heir's court, to arrange a truce: "An armistice is essential to make good losses already suffered. The army is completely exhausted and half naked. Winter weather is beginning. The soldiers have already begun to go home on their own. I have only 22,000 men under arms against 50,000 Turks. Turkish artillery surpasses ours in range. To continue the war with the army in its present state can jeopardize all the results won so far."[3] Only three days later another battle, though indecisive, restored Cherniaev's optimism. He sent P. A. Monteverde, his assistant chief of staff, to Belgrade to block an armistice.

Prince Milan asked Monteverde, "Thus the general feels that a truce would harm us?" The envoy nodded energetically, "Unfortunately steps have already been taken to obtain a truce, and I am only awaiting a reply from Petrograd," declared the prince. With present prospects of victory, warned Monteverde, an armistice could ruin the cause. The prince replied, "But yesterday I received a telegram from the [Russian] emperor stating: 'I sincerely desire the cessation of hostilities'—and it was an open telegram." With supreme effrontery Monteverde asserted: "The fact that the telegram is open proves that it is not really serious." If necessary, noted the prince, the Turkish proposals could be rejected. Monteverde then demanded that Cherniaev be given charge of the Javor army, the Kragujevac arsenal,

2. AII, Ristić, XVIII/108, Cherniaev to Milan, 21 August 1876; Ristić, I: 135; IISG, "Biografiia," pp. 277–279. Binički (pp. 23–33) blames the loss of Adrovac on faulty tactics by Cherniaev.

3. S. Grujić, *Operacije*, III: 36, Cherniaev to Zinoviev, 27 August 1876.

and parts of the war ministry. "We shall easily settle that," the prince temporized, "once the question of war and peace has been resolved."

The Turks and Ristić desired hostilities suspended, so from September 3 to 12 fighting virtually ceased. Most Serbian leaders believed, at least in retrospect, that peace should have been made then while they held the key Morava positions. But Cherniaev, overestimating his strength, insisted that the war be continued.[4]

The very day the truce took effect Cherniaev's army proclaimed Milan king of Serbia. Horvatović reported that his troops had acted "in a state of the greatest enthusiasm and unanimity." Lieutenant Colonel Bogičević telegraphed Cherniaev from Paraćin that the news "caused indescribable joy here. Officers and men are all shouting: Long live King Milan."[5] Mikhail Grigorevich telegraphed Milan that the kingship movement was irresistible.[6] The next day he explained: "The movement broke out yesterday towards evening in Horvatović's command. The people swore to defend the rights of the Crown to their last drop of blood. Entire battalions kissed the ground and swore loyalty. Frenetic enthusiasm. Commanders, officers, militiamen, clergy and volunteers shared the same sentiments. . . . To restrain the movement is no longer in my power. Any attempt to do so would destroy all authority in the army."[7] "I give you my word of honor as a soldier," pledged Cherniaev, "that this fervent proclamation is no act of indiscipline but a popular, spontaneous movement."[8]

He had sent Dr. Djordjević to persuade Milan to accept the royal title, but the prince wrote back: "I regret, my dear general, that I cannot grant you my permission for the important step you have planned. . . . I do not consider the moment favorable. Now . . . what is absolutely essential for us . . . is an armistice. The proclamation of Serbia's independence would surely alienate all the powers, and unfortunately we need them to achieve this desirable goal." Milan doubted that this would force Russia into war since the emperor himself decided such questions. The prince coveted the title,

4. Ibid., pp. 37–39.
5. GIM, ed. khr. 15, Horvatović to Komarov, 3 September 1876, telegram; Bogičević to Cherniaev, telegram.
6. AII, Ristić, XVIII/159, Cherniaev to Milan, 3 September 1876, telegram.
7. GIM, ed. khr. 15, 4 September 1876, telegram in French.
8. DAS PO, 29/100–vi, telegram.

"but my duty to my country compels me to refuse my consent. . . ."[9]
When Cherniaev went ahead anyway, Milan telegraphed him: "I
find that it would be very sad if movements in the army should
dictate my internal and foreign policy and it would be wholly contrary to all discipline. You will thus oblige me greatly by [repressing]
this movement you speak of which is wholly contrary to the
country's interests dictated by our domestic and foreign situation."[10]

Undeterred Mikhail Grigorevich held an elaborate ceremony in
Deligrad. After Horvatović's courier announced that his army had
proclaimed Milan king, the entire staff gathered. Cherniaev announced Serbia's transformation into an independent kingdom. The
camp, decorated with national flags, buzzed with excitement. The
general addressed the troops with a few words in Serbian; in reply
came "Živio!" ("Long live!") mixed with Russian hurrahs. The
army, declared Cherniaev, would fight to the end for Serbia's freedom.[11] A Slav committee agent, traveling from Deligrad, saw how
the people rejoiced. "As for sensible officers they just shake their
heads and add: 'How is it that we are proclaiming a king when the
Turks hold Serbian territory and we cannot expel them?' "[12]

Cherniaev had sworn that the kingship movement was spontaneous. His prior explanations to Dr. Djordjević reveal how worthless
his promises were. He was engineering a coup, he confided, to prevent a humiliating peace which would mean "political death" for
Serbia. Rather than yield to shameful Turkish terms, Serbia must
perish. Proclaiming a kingdom after recent defeats, objected Djordjević, would cause laughter in Europe. Carried away by his grandiose vision, Cherniaev argued:

This would not be just an army pronunciamento. Who is in our army?
The entire people from the highest official to the lowliest peasant.
There is no more legal representative of the people than a militia
army. . . . I know very well that Serbia lacks the strength to achieve
such a goal alone, and precisely therefore I must take this step. Does
that sound paradoxical? If you had read the mass of letters and
telegrams I receive daily from Russia, you would realize that I am not
so frivolous as I might seem. . . . Never before in Russian history has

9. "K M. G. Cherniaevu," pp. 44–46.
10. AII, Ristić, XVIII/159, Odgovor Knjažev," 3 September 1876.
11. *Vsemirnaia illustratsiia*, no. 406, 1876, cited in VISB (1915), no. 2, p. 74.
12. OSVOB, I: 384–385, Teplov to Aksakov, 6 September 1876.

there been such a popular movement as this. . . . Up to now no *ideal* has swayed such masses of people in Russia as that of a Russian war to liberate the Slavs. That movement is so powerful that no government in Russia can resist it.

The general's delusions built upon themselves. His prestige and popularity would bring victory. What did Kartsov's hostility matter now? He showed the doctor a telegram from one of Alexander II's confidants. Privately the tsar wished him success and drank his health: "As you see this is the first result of the powerful popular movement. The ice has been broken, now we need only persist and everything will be won. When Serbia proclaims its independence and itself a kingdom, it will compel official Russia either to recognize the Serbian kingdom and declare war on Turkey, or not recognize it and be forced to resign by the popular movement. In place of the present official Russia will arise another, popular government." The Bariatinskii aristocratic-military party would direct the regime and the docile Russian people would obey. "In one case or the other the Serbian and Slav cause will gain. A third course, because of the situation in Russia, cannot be envisioned. This is why I decided upon this step." His commanders had assured him that the army would respond enthusiastically. "Surely the prince has approved your intentions?" interjected Djordjević. "Oh no, His Majesty does not know about it yet. I wanted to make sure the army would approve my idea before submitting the matter to his decision." Djordjević objected that the Serbian army would be overwhelmed before Russia could help her. But Cherniaev insisted that it could hold on near Aleksinac: the winter would be worse for the Turks than the Serbs. His proclamation would bring great benefits. Djordjević should inform Prince Milan: "Tell him not to judge Russia by Kartsov who is only the puny representative of one official clique in Russia which the national movement will crush easily. . . . Official Russia will have to enter the war against Turkey . . . and proclaiming a Serbian kingdom will only hasten its decision. . . . Ah, if I had only *one* Russian division, the Turkish army would not have invaded Serbian soil. . . . Our position, thanks to Turkish stupidity, is such that I hope to finish the Turks even before the Russian division reaches me."

When the good doctor had explained all this, the prince objected that the kingship proclamation would make his position impossible:

"The whole edifice constructed by Cherniaev from logical deductions has a single flaw: it is built on the false supposition that public opinion in Russia is so powerful that the tsar himself must yield to it. The popular response to Slavophile aspirations to aid our cause so surprised and blinded them [Panslavs] by its grandiose nature that they now think that they can compel the tsar himself to do their bidding." Russia would repudiate the title and leave Serbia in Austria's grasp. Removing the unwarranted assumption about Russian public opinion, "the entire palace of Cherniaev's fantastic kingdom immediately goes up in smoke." With Turks on Serbian soil, such a proclamation would be madness.

Even then Milan discerned that Cherniaev had staged the affair. Reading one of his telegrams, the prince remarked: "They say the soldiers are so enthusiastic that no force can restrain them. You, doctor, have been behind the scenes enough to know how one 'directs' popular enthusiasm. Isn't there any cure for it?" Djordjević doubted that Deligrad's rejoicing was genuine, but when he brought the prince's veto, Cherniaev merely declared: "We cannot reverse it now. The thing is done!"[13]

Later, Mikhail Grigorevich admitted to Aksakov that he had instigated the movement partly because of political conditions in Serbia: "In Belgrade, under the consuls' influence, . . . the view prevailed that the war should not be continued. The ministers were disturbed that power had passed out of their hands and into Cherniaev's and they joined the general chorus for peace. The growing pressure on Milan for peace made him hesitate. The army saw no point in continuing the struggle. . . . It was essential to indicate a goal which would flatter everyone, unite all parties and force them to desire a continuation of the struggle."[14] Cherniaev, a Russian, insisted that Serbia fight on.

To compel Milan to accept the title, Cherniaev urged that a four battalion "delegation" be sent to Belgrade "to lay at Your Majesty's feet the feelings of fidelity and devotion of their constituents." This force, claimed Ristić, was to overthrow the government and the constitution. Ristić convinced that Cherniaev was becoming Serbia's dictator, told the Austrian consul that his cabinet was being by-passed.[15] Contrary to Cherniaev's expectations, Milan supported the

13. Djordjević, I: 408–432.
14. GIM, ed. khr. 43, Cherniaev to Aksakov, 2 October 1876.
15. DAS PO, 29/100–xi, Cherniaev to Milan, 5 September 1876, tgr.; HHSA, Wrede to Andras-

cabinet, disavowed the proclamation and forbade the army "delegation" to depart. War Minister Nikolić went to Deligrad to explain
the powers' opposition and Milan's refusal of the title.[16] Unless the
general obeyed the prince, warned Ristić, he would be removed from
command. He told the Austrian consul that the cabinet would ignore
Cherniaev's foolish act, and the movement's spread to other Serbian
armies would be prevented.[17] Over this united opposition Cherniaev
could only prevail by force.

His mild reaction to Belgrade's veto revealed that he lacked the
decisiveness to become a dictator. He had the force to overwhelm the
regime but using it would cost him most of his support and bring on
defeat. Thus he temporized: refusing to withdraw his proclamation,
he withheld his "delegation" and, outwardly confident, awaited
Russian reactions. On September 8 he telegraphed Milan: "I am
beginning to receive telegrams from Russia which prove that the
proclamation . . . has been received in Russia with joy and enthusiasm." He enclosed a typical example.[18]

Milan remained in an embarrassing dilemma. To remove or disa-
vow Cherniaev would alienate Russian Panslavs and weaken army
morale. For the moment Cherniaev was indispensable. However,
inaction would provoke the powers. The Austrian consul warned
that unless the prince repudiated the pronunciamento, Cherniaev
would not obey when Milan wished to make peace. The anomaly of
being king on the Morava's right bank and prince on the left must
be quickly resolved.[19]

The prince pursued a middle course by refusing the title without
disavowing Cherniaev. The general's mild telegram of September 13
opened this path by requesting merely that the proclamation remain

sy, (7)/19 September 1876, no. 151. Earlier the Serbian writer, Miličević, declared: "Serbia
is now open field for all Russian scoundrels and adventurers. It is no longer a country which
determines what it wants, but a province ceded to Cherniaev for his glory or burial . . . O
Liberals! O patriots! To serve your country thus!" ASANU, 9327/7, Dnevnik Miličevića, 16
August 1876, l. 166.

    16. "K. M. G. Cherniaevu," pp. 44–46, Milan to Cherniaev, 6 September 1876.

    17. HHSA, Wrede to Andrassy, (7)/19 September 1876, no. 151; (17)/29 September 1876,
no. 157. Even before the coup, Ristić and his colleagues had intimated that "General Cher-
nyaeff had acted throughout more like a Russian general working for Imperial or even
Panslavic objects than as one in command of the Serbian forces . . . ," FO, 78/2487, White
to Derby, (2)/14 September 1876, no. 133.

    18. DAS PO, 29/100–xx, Milan to Cherniaev, 8 September 1876. The mayor of Kazanchov
in Orel province had telegraphed congratulations to King Milan.

    19. HHSA, Wrede to Andrassy, (11)/23 September 1876, no. 154.

in effect two weeks so Russian public reactions could be ascertained. Otherwise, threatened Cherniaev, he would launch a desperate attack on the Turks and perish, or return to Russia with his volunteers.[20] Russia would repudiate the proclamation, predicted Milan, and it could only bring Serbia a humiliating peace. Why was Cherniaev opposing him? "If this situation persists," warned Milan, "European envoys will withdraw and perhaps empower Austria to occupy Serbia." Unable to execute the army's manifesto for political reasons, the prince called upon the Morava army "to continue its valiant struggle for the defense of the fatherland under its heroic leader."[21] He wrote the tsar that he had not framed the royal proclamation nor would he implement it.[22]

Oblivious to Russia's difficult international position, Cherniaev anticipated massive public and press support. The tsar was weak and would accept a *fait accompli*; the heir and Prince Bariatinskii were with him.[23] But Zinoviev wrote that the heir could not supply the weapons he desired nor even guarantee Cherniaev's return to Russia after the war. "Wishing you, with all Russia, the fullest success in your holy cause . . . , I remain at your service."[24] This was hardly the dramatic backing Cherniaev needed.

Official Russia repudiated Cherniaev's move decisively. Foreign Minister Gorchakov promptly wrote his ambassador in London: "We have emphatically condemned Cherniaev's crazy escapade."[25] The war minister commented acidly: "This stupid undertaking . . . greatly complicates our diplomacy," undermining the efforts of the powers to arrange peace for Serbia.[26]

Unofficial responses were more favorable but left Petersburg unshaken. Slav committee leaders pledged continued support, but even Aksakov disapproved of the proclamation. Most congratulatory tele-

20. J. Grujić, *Zapisi*, iii: 224.

21. das po, 29/143, n.d.; 29/43, 14 September 1876.

22. aii, Ristić, xxvi/10, Milan to Alexander ii, draft copy by Ristić. To calm Austrian fears Ristić assured Wrede that the title would not be accepted. hhsa, Wrede to Andrassy, (23 September)/5 October 1876, no. 158.

23. Zisserman, ra (1891), iii: 371–372, Cherniaev to Bariatinskii, 29 August 1876.

24. osvob, i: 395–396, Zinoviev to Cherniaev, 13 September 1876.

25. R. W. Seton-Watson, "Russo-British Relations," *Slavonic Review* (June 1925), p. 185, Gorchakov to Shuvalov, 5/17 September 1876.

26. "The new madcap adventure of Cherniaev disturbed him [Alexander ii]. Nonetheless, I feel that the tsar attributes too much significance to Cherniaev's senseless joke. . . . He forsees Cherniaev's intention to overthrow Prince Milan and proclaim a republic reserving the presidency for himself." Miliutin, *Dnevnik*, ii: 79, 6 September 1876.

grams which Cherniaev received were for the victory at Šumatovac, not for his kingmaking.[27] Pro-Cherniaev newspapers were enthusiastic (Katkov's *Moskovskie Vedomosti* called the proclamation "the chivalric outburst of the Serbian army"),[28] but they did not reflect public opinion meaningfully.

Other papers denounced the move. Encouraged by the foreign ministry, *Golos* considered it ridiculous and desperate; it praised Prince Milan for blocking a step reminiscent of the Roman Praetorian Guard.[29] The proclamation was a callous violation of the Serbian Constitution, declared the radical émigré organ, *Vpered!* If Cherniaev triumphed, Bariatinskii's reactionaries might oust the Miliutin liberals. Russia's leaders would be Cherniaev, Fadeev, Monteverde, and Komarov! How could a conservative general liberate the Slavs?[30] From such negative Russian reactions it became clear that Cherniaev's grandstand bid to buttress his position had failed.

The kingship wrangle did not disturb Milan's close personal relations with Cherniaev. "You have demonstrated toward me personally since the beginning of our relationship so much devotion and interest," wrote Milan September 12, "that I believe I can address myself to you now about certain personal affairs convinced that you would keep them absolutely secret." Could Cherniaev get him a loan of two to three hundred thousand rubles? The general offered forty thousand. Milan accepted eagerly and requested more. But on the title the prince, not daring to defy the powers, remained adamant. He merely consented to let the proclamation remain in effect in Deligrad if Cherniaev pledged not to expand the movement.[31]

Cherniaev's kingmaking might have succeeded only had the prince been equally irrational. Instead, Milan displayed unusual tact and subtlety. Caught between a rebellious commander and the angry insistence of the powers, he had arranged a compromise which mollified both sides. He was the only superior Cherniaev never quarreled with seriously. Though overestimating Cherniaev's military ability and standing in Russia, the prince refused to become a puppet of the "Deligrad kingmaker." However, Cherniaev retained

27. Meshcherskii, *Odin iz nashikh Moltke* (St. Petersburg, 1890), p. 293; Aп, Ristić, xviii/118 and 146.

28. мv, 14 September 1876, no. 234; Nikitin, "Russkoe obshchestvo," p. 1026; *Russkii Mir*, 22 September 1876, "Za tridtsat dnei."

29. *Golos*, 7 September 1876, no. 247; 9 September 1876, no. 249.

30. *Vpered!*, 15 September 1876, cited in osvoв, i: 399 ff.

31. "K M. G. Cherniaevu," pp. 50–52, 12 September 1876; p. 56, 15 September 1876.

enough influence to persuade Belgrade to resume a hopeless war.
Arguing that peace on the prewar basis would doom Serbia, he was
ready to fight to the last militiaman and volunteer. Thus he was
largely responsible for Serbia's crushing defeat at Djunis.

Mikhail Grigorevich pondered whether to extend the armistice or
resume fighting. He accused the Turks of violating the truce, and he
refused to discuss a regular armistice with the enemy's envoys. A
brief truce, he asserted, would let the Turks bring up reinforcements.
On September 8 he wrote to Milan: "Sire! I am more and more
convinced that the enemy is evacuating his positions between Aleksinac and Deligrad to concentrate them at an unknown point. . . .
I can do nothing while my arms are bound by the truce . . .
which . . . is only a respite for the Turks. My position as commander in chief is becoming more and more difficult. Unable to
act freely I bear only the responsibility."[32] A lengthier armistice
would permit reorganization of the tired army while he obtained
large-scale aid in Russia. Unless a regular, demarcated truce were
concluded before September 13, he would attack. But on that day
he telegraphed: "Our position is better than that of the Turks. I
doubt that the Turks have been able during these weeks to attack
us. . . . Our army's morale is excellent. I have not decided yet
whether to attack the Turks . . . because I do not wish to risk a
repulse."[33]

The perplexed Serbian ministers asked Russia's advice but no
clear answer came. Kartsov and the other envoys urged Serbia to
observe the truce, but St. Petersburg did not press her to extend it.
Privately Kartsov intimated that Russian armed aid was imminent.
From Russia's embassy in Constantinople came exhortations
to the Serbs to hold on one more month and victory would
be theirs.[34] The Russians with greatest influence over Milan—
Cherniaev, Kartsov, and Ignatiev—all advised him to continue the war.

The issue split the Serbian cabinet. Its leaders—Ristić, J. Grujić,
and R. Milojković—favored extending the truce. Cherniaev, they

32. DAS PO, 29/100–xv, Cherniaev to Milan, 6 September 1876, telegram; xix, 8 September
1876.

33. Ibid., 10 and 13 September 1876, telegrams.

34. AII, Ristić, xviii/346; HHSA, Wrede to Andrassy, (7)/19 September 1876, no. 148. From
Constantinople Zelenyi wrote to A. N. Kartsov on September (3)/15 : "Determination to
resist to the utmost until the rains come, even just a month, will decide victory in favor of the
Serbs." GIM, ed. khr. 14, ll. 68–69.

believed, was too optimistic about military prospects; peace should be made on the prewar frontiers. Since Cherniaev could not take the offensive, why struggle on? Šumatovac provided a favorable basis for a settlement. But Cherniaev, sanguine and persuasive, drew along Milan and the other ministers. They believed his boast that he was closer to the Balkans than the Turks were to the Morava, though the foe was watering his horses in that river! On September 14 Milan backed the war faction and broke the cabinet deadlock.[35]

Cherniaev now planned a powerful assault to end the Morava fighting at one blow and make himself the Slav Garibaldi. "We must attack tomorrow at dawn," he exhorted his men. "The purpose is . . . to strike the enemy flank and rear, throw him back to the Morava and drive him from our land. Tomorrow shall be glorious for Serbia and worthy of your brave ancestors." The Serbo-Russian brigade, swelled by newly arrived volunteers, left Deligrad for the front singing and its band playing. In bitter fighting, September 16–18, both sides suffered heavy losses. Cherniaev committed his last reserves. "The Battle of Krevet," recalled Sava Grujić, "redounded to the honor and glory of our arms," but it strained Serbian endurance to the utmost. After that the Serbs weakened whereas the Turks were constantly reinforced.[36]

Serious friction persisted between Cherniaev and the Ristić government, which he still sought to overturn. He accused the war ministry, as he had done in Russia, of inefficiency and incompetence:

> In all my previous demands I have taken into account our country's economic resources which I know well [in reality, Cherniaev knew next to nothing about Serbia's economic resources]. Failure to fulfill these requests resulted solely from petty personal intrigues fostered to a significant degree by the war minister. During his stay here [Deligrad] in my army he sought to reduce my authority in every way, became intimate with dissatisfied elements . . . , and aided officials accused of abuses or inactivity. Because of the ministry's ignorance and incapacity, the army here . . . has not received coats, the soldiers are ragged and barefoot, and soon we will be threatened by an insufficiency of bread and meat.

He attacked War Minister Tihomir Nikolić, an honest patriot who

35. Ristić, i: 144–145, 152–153; S. Jovanović, *Vlada Milana*, i: 342–344.
36. IISG, "Biografiia," pp. 326–330; Djordjević, i: 486 ff.

had sought to prepare Serbia for war, and announced that he would ignore him: "Over such an individual who in any other country would not rise by ability above the rank of battalion commander, strict supervision is needed. Consequently, I shall turn with my requests directly to the ruler, who, I am convinced, has Serbia's interests too much at heart to be put aside in such an improper way."[37] To mollify Cherniaev the prince promised to remedy the supposed disorder and bureaucracy in the Serbian war office.[38] From the start Nikolić and Cherniaev had clashed. The war minister dealt continuously with the general and blocked his road to power. Nikolić had criticized him sharply for tight military censorship, abandoning the eastern frontier, and making frontal assaults which undermined the army's morale. Cherniaev retaliated by usurping war ministry functions. He issued promotions at will and meted out punishments prohibited by Serbian law. Milan, rejecting Nikolić's offers to resign, allowed Cherniaev to bypass his war minister.[39]

Their feud reached a showdown when Cherniaev received a tactlessly worded letter signed by the war minister:

> From all sides both from Belgrade and the provinces complaints reach me against Russian volunteers who overindulge in liquor and in this [drunken] state commit scandalous acts in hotels, cafés and the streets, who insult honest women, do not pay their bills, and who refuse to obey the police and even use arms against them. I possess the coercive power to compel all of them to respect our laws and citizens, but the profound thanks which the country, its government and I personally owe Russia . . . make it extremely painful to use such means.

Unless Cherniaev prevented such incidents, it continued, the guilty would be expelled and the Slav committees would be asked to stop sending volunteers.[40]

Reading this accurate description of the disreputable Russian element in Belgrade's cafes, Cherniaev grew purple with rage.

---

37. AII, Ristić, xviii/165, Cherniaev to Lj. Ivanović, 8 September 1876, tgr. But during Nikolić's visit to Deligrad about 10 September, Cherniaev had declared that without his capable administration, the army would have been helpless! Djordjević, i: 468.

38. "K M. G. Cherniaevu," p. 54, 18 September 1876.

39. *Golos*, 16 November 1876, report from Belgrade of 9 November; Khvostov, pp. 54 ff.

40. AII, Ristić, xviii/363b, War Minister to Cherniaev, 1 October 1876.

Until calmed by Milan's uncle, Colonel Catargi,[41] he threatened to leave Serbia immediately with his Russians. He demanded a prompt apology from Ristić:

> You will understand, Mr. Minister, that I am not replying to the signatory of that letter, insulting to me and to the Russian soldiers and officers who have come to defend this country. In any army incidents mentioned in the minister's letter occur frequently. Besides it would be pointless to rely upon Colonel Nikolić's assertions and especially his deductions. . . . Striking satisfaction is due me and the Russians serving under my orders for the injury which the war minister has done us. Take well into consideration, Mr. Minister, that once I and the Russian officers have left and this letter has been communicated to the Slav committees, you cannot expect any moral or material assistance from the Russian people.

He asked that Nikolić's letter and his own reply be read aloud to the Serbian council of ministers.

Catargi informed Milan that the letter, though signed by Nikolić, had been written by a subordinate, "Insulting in form and content, [it] could produce misfortune for the country. . . . The general is outraged." The Serbian ministers empowered Ristić to express their regret. Nikolić had signed it unwittingly, Ristić wrote Cherniaev; the government would support the general as before. "Incidents such as these . . . cannot affect in any way the thankfulness of the Serbian people for the eminent services you are rendering the country."[42] To avoid a damaging ministerial crisis, Milan let Nikolić remain briefly in office.[43] The Ristić government survived this confrontation with Cherniaev because the prince considered it indispensable.

Serbia was now so poor that Milan feared he might have to seek an armistice. He explained to Cherniaev that lack of money was felt everywhere and "results in delays in executing your requests from Deligrad, delays which you often wrongly attribute to bad will." Unless Russia joined the war or provided funds, Serbia could not

---

41. Djordjević, ı: 465. "Just think, doctor," Cherniaev declared, "he is minister of war, . . . he has everything needed to maintain order among those unfortunate drunkards . . . , yet he demands that I from Deligrad, besides my huge task, carry out the duties of the Belgrade police! . . . Today I'll send him my resignation, then let them [the Serbs] stew."

42. AII, Ristić, xvıı/363, Cherniaev to Ristić, 6 October 1876; Ristić to Cherniaev, 11 October 1876; J. Grujić, ııı: 232–233; das po, 29/101–v, Catargi to Milan, 6 October 1876, telegram.

43. "K M. G. Cherniaevu," pp. 184–188, Milan to Cherniaev, 12 October 1876.

fight on through the winter. The powers were pressing for an armistice. If Russia supported them, Belgrade could not refuse peace on the prewar basis which, Milan believed, would do Serbia great injustice. Someone must be sent to see the emperor and the heir, inform them of Serbia's plight and seek their advice. "This person," wrote Milan, ". . . could in my opinion only be you, my dear general, who alone by your presence in Russia could exert an immense influence upon the government's decisions."[44]

In response Cherniaev described armistice terms which the Turks could never accept and opposed a truce imposed by the powers. A Turkish attack, he argued, would surely be repelled and the enemy would be in a bad position: "In two weeks at the most the rains will come. . . . On the other hand, the Cossacks are arriving from Russia. We are on the verge of cutting the enemy's communications. In that condition he would have to abandon his positions without fighting and his retreat this time would become a disastrous rout."[45] Within three weeks his optimistic predictions would all be disproved.

Relying upon the Slav committees for money and troops to prosecute the war, Cherniaev continually demanded funds, volunteers, clothing and medicines. Aksakov, doing his utmost to oblige, chided the general for not thanking the Russian public for its generosity:

> Do not forget that yours is now the most popular name in Russia. . . . Do not forget that you stand before the Russian people and public opinion which bestows so much love upon you. The Slav Committee seeks by every means to support this feeling among the people. It would not hurt you sometimes, especially after a success, to send the Committee an informative telegram. I publish almost all your telegrams and all bring instant response. Yesterday I printed one about boots and coats, and today several thousand of these have already been brought in. . . . I am besieged with requests: . . . isn't there any news from Cherniaev? Does he make only demands? Doesn't he report anything else? The Slav Committee's strength and importance is tied to your significance and strength.

Cherniaev's direction of Serbia's struggle, confirmed Aksakov, had made him a major historical figure.

The Moscow chairman noted that Bulgaria was dividing the Panslavs. Agreeing that Serbia must remain the focus of the Committee's

44. Ibid., pp. 58–64, 22 and 26 September 1876.
45. DAS PO, 29/45, "Conditions d'une armistice . . . ," 28 September 1876.

efforts, he backed Cherniaev against General Fadeev, who wished to liberate Bulgaria. But Aksakov was disturbed by reports that Cherniaev was anti-Bulgarian: "I fear that you because of your passionate and nervous temperament may unwittingly have yielded to the Serbian viewpoint. One must not *get angry* with the Bulgars. One must consider how they can be utilized." "Russia," he warned, "sees in you not a narrowminded Serb, but a *Russian* to whom Bulgars and Serbs are equally close."[46]

Mikhail Grigorevich responded on September 24: "I could write you every day and inform you of everything being done here and what I intend to do. But I cannot forget that you sent me here at your own risk. Who then understood the significance of my arrival in Serbia besides you? But I cannot write you frankly, hampered by a twofold censorship. To explain the situation means explaining it not to you but to those who would use that information to oppose me." Cherniaev rejected Fadeev's ideas as impractical, and saw two possible solutions for Bulgaria: a Russian occupation or a Serbian advance to the Balkan Mountains. Until the Turks were driven out, Bulgarian volunteers would be ineffective. If he reached Sofia, Cherniaev had told Bulgarian exiles, he would leave the Serbs and join them. Fadeev's idea of a separate Bulgarian movement was "fantasy."

Cherniaev demanded redoubled efforts from the Slav committees to achieve victory. Diverting funds to Bulgarian schemes might doom the Serbian cause: "The Serbs have already gained a three-quarters victory over Turkey, but in this struggle they have exhausted their last penny and put forth their last man. Now has come the decisive time to help them *fundamentally*, all at once, not in driblets." Russia must subscribe the Serbian loan promptly; the Serbs could not even pay their officers' salaries. Within a month he must have a million rubles. The General complained, "My position here is difficult because I must do everything myself. . . ." The Serbian government was incompetent; Consul Kartsov was even worse "and does not know how to behave." Completely controlled by the Austrian and British consuls, he "rejoices along with them at Turkish victories" and should be removed immediately. Once Serbia's forces were reorganized, he would launch a mighty offensive. With ten thousand volunteers and fifteen hundred Cossacks, "I

46. GIM, ed. khr. 14, Aksakov to Cherniaev, 7 September 1876.

guarantee that few from the army of Abdul Kerim will return home, I will be in Sofia this winter, and consequently Bulgaria will be free." For Aksakov's benefit Cherniaev was as confident and boastful as ever.

He still dreamed of solving the Eastern question with his forces. Russia's official participation, he felt, was now unnecessary and would merely cause diplomatic complications: "Against whom would vast Russia fight when the entire Turkish strength has been broken against little Serbia?" Miliutin must not garner easy but expensive laurels as Kaufman had done in Khiva. He, Cherniaev, had done the difficult work in both areas. A full-scale Russian campaign against Turkey would cost six hundred million rubles. Give him unofficially ten million, a few long-range batteries and some rifles, and he would finish the job. "Turkey is at her last gasp!" he proclaimed.[47] But the committees, as Aksakov had warned, could not satisfy such demands.

From St. Petersburg, Serbia's special envoy Milosav Protić reported strange actions by Cherniaev's subordinates. Lavrentiev and Count Keller from his staff were spreading vile rumors about Serbian cowardice. Unless Russian aid came promptly, all would be lost. Money and volunteers should be sent directly to Cherniaev, not to the unreliable Serbian government. When he learned that Keller was Cherniaev's envoy, the heir refused to see him. Meanwhile Cherniaev's brother-in-law Colonel Vulfert boasted that Belgrade would long since have fallen but for the general's ability and courage. He sent volunteers recruited in Petersburg directly to Cherniaev. Though disgusted by all this, Protić concluded: "Cherniaev himself . . . is completely honorable."[48]

At Cherniaev's Deligrad headquarters life followed a regular pattern. In the morning, recalled Djordjević, they were awakened by cannonfire. The officers, shivering in the morning chill, would gather round the huge samovar outside the kitchen for tea with rum. Partly to impress visiting correspondents and dignitaries, the old school building had been painted and refurnished. Cherniaev's guard of Serb militiamen in tattered uniforms had yielded to a "Slav guard" drawn from every South Slav region, attired in expensive national costumes. Over the kitchen, stocked from a special shop in

47. ORSS, Aksakov, no. 387, Cherniaev to Aksakov, 24 September–2 October 1876.

48. AII, Ristić, XXVI/728, 729, 731, Protić to Ristić, 5, 15 and 23 September 1876. Aksakov had admitted, however, that Cherniaev had paid personal debts with Slav Committee money.

Belgrade, presided a Russian cook, invariably drunk but dressed immaculately in white with a chef's hat. In his larder were Swiss cheeses, sausages, sardines, and imported hams. To ease the campaign's rigors were Russian vodka, French Bordeaux and champagne, and Serbian plum brandy. Daily at 12:30 the staff gathered in the dining room and stood behind their chairs in animated conversation. When Cherniaev entered they took their seats. Father Gavrilo, the Russian priest, would say a prayer. At Cherniaev's right usually sat Colonel Catargi, Milan's uncle; at his left the chief of staff, Colonel Komarov.

After dinner Cherniaev with an imposing entourage sometimes went to visit the front. A single cavalryman galloped ahead bearing the general's personal flag. Of white silk with a blue cross in the middle, it was inscribed: "For the freedom of the Slavs," a gift from his Moscow admirers. Next came the general's troika surrounded by staff officers resplendent in Russian uniforms covered with decorations. Some paces back the "convoy" commander followed with a platoon of cavalry.

The staff personnel was not so impressive. Colonel Komarov was fussy, absentminded, and inefficient. Vital telegrams remained forgotten in his pockets or under a chaotic mass of papers in his quarters. His assistant, P. A. Monteverde, was an arrogant, inconsequential adventurer. The largest apartment in the staff building was occupied by his "wife," a Paris import. Apparently, Monteverde hoped that Mistress Masha would charm Cherniaev into making him chief of staff, but handsome young staff officers like Lieutenant I. P. Alabin attracted him more. Their liaison would last almost a decade. The ablest staff officer was Colonel Dokhturov who succeeded Komarov late in the campaign.

At Deligrad Cherniaev had little time to ponder strategy. Every volunteer believed he must see the commander in chief on even trivial matters, so he was constantly besieged with callers. Rarely did he have two hours a day to himself.[49]

In September General S. K. Novoselov, a quiet, elderly Russian officer, assumed command of the Ibar army. Establishing friendly relations with Consul Kartsov and Belgrade, he attracted Russian volunteers and aroused Cherniaev's jealous rage. Cherniaev wrote the prince: "I have just learned that 250 volunteers were sent to the

49. Djordjević, ı: 434 ff.

Ibar army. This war has revealed that my opinion of the Morava valley's capital importance . . . was correct. . . . Here the country's fate will be decided. . . . Every man sent from Russia augments here an already formed nucleus. . . . It is here that they must come, all without exception. . . . Also please order that all volunteers from Russia . . . be sent here. . . . This will be a guarantee for me which may discourage those who wish to work against me in the future."[50] Obscured by these military arguments was his fear that Novoselov might become a dangerous rival.[51]

Soon Cherniaev had graver worries. Early in October the Turks probed Serbian positions on the Morava. Heavy Krupp guns bombarded Aleksinac. With heavy numerical superiority the Turks attacked Horvatović at Veliki Šiljegovac and on October 9 broke the fortified line guarding the Morava valley. When a counterattack failed, Cherniaev ordered a withdrawal to the high left bank. By this time, confirmed N. V. Maksimov, a Russian staff officer, the exhausted Serbian militia often refused to fight. Serbian officers favored immediate peace on Turkish terms. Many Russian officers had lost confidence in their chief. Rarely at the front, Cherniaev remained ignorant of his army's plight.

In mid-October Maksimov accompanied a delegation of Russian officers to see Cherniaev in Deligrad. Monteverde received them with arrogant suspicion, informing them that the general was too ill to see them. Staff officers confirmed that Cherniaev was badly upset, cried and threatened to shoot himself. Probably because the officers were asking probing questions, Monteverde threatened them with deportation to Russia. Dokhturov, the new chief of staff, told Maksimov categorically that the war would end within a week, that even Cherniaev favored an armistice. The officers, accusing Cherniaev of sending false reports to Russia, left very disgruntled.[52]

But Mikhail Grigorevich did nothing to obtain an armistice. On October 11, after repelling an enemy attack before Djunis, Horvatović reported that his men were exhausted and discouraged. Foreign Minister Ristić requested Ambassador Ignatiev to arrange an armistice. Otherwise, he warned, "our situation may be compromised

50. DAS PO, 29/101–iii, Cherniaev to Milan, 4 October 1876, telegram.

51. Consul Kartsov advised his nephew, Iurii, to serve under Novoselov who "is occupied with military affairs, not politics. As to Cherniaev . . . , he is surrounded by all kinds of filth and busies himself with manifestoes." Kartsov, RS, CXXXIV: 311.

52. N. V. Maksimov, *Dve voiny, 1876–1878 gg.* (St. Petersburg, 1879), pp. 211 ff.

irretrievably."[53] On the 15th the ministers forwarded a similar message to Protić in Russia. Nikolić summoned all available Russian volunteers: "Gentlemen, I have received a telegram from General Cherniaev. He informs me that in recent battles, the army has suffered heavy losses and requests me to send all volunteers in Belgrade as reinforcements. I hope that everything is not yet lost, but nonetheless I decided to beg you to hurry to his aid without delay." Shouting, "Long live Milan and Serbia!" they departed for the front.[54] Nikolić's fears were well founded. On October 17 the Djunis disaster decided the campaign. From it came recriminations and conflicting accounts.

Antonina depicted Cherniaev, the wise and watchful generalissimo. Supposedly he told his assembled commanders at Deligrad on October 16: "Gentlemen! Tomorrow will come a decisive battle. I have received news that the enemy has decided to attack us all along the front. Let us remember that we were sent here by our mother, Russia. Let us not cast shame upon her and let every man do his duty to the end! May God be with us and realize we are fighting for a holy, just cause. Return now to your units and at 2 P.M. open fire simultaneously on all enemy positions. Let us and not the Turks strike first. I shall be at Djunis."[55] When the enemy attacked the next day, she continued, the Russians fought and died heroically while the Serbian militia fled abandoning its artillery. At 3 P.M., seeing that his army could no longer resist huge enemy forces drawn from the "entire Ottoman empire" Cherniaev telegraphed Belgrade: "The Serbs have conducted themselves in cowardly fashion. They have fled, led by the artillery, all along the line. Half the Russians have been massacred. The only hope is . . . an immediate armistice. Telegraph the emperor urgently to request an armistice within twenty-four hours; otherwise the Turks will be in Belgrade in ten days."[56] As Serbian troops and civilians fled westward, Cherniaev shepherded them across the Morava, then ordered the bridges blown up. "This was the exciting and crucial moment," wrote Antonina. "The entire Cherniaev staff led by Dokhturov participated in directing this crossing. About 5 P.M. when Cherniaev issued final orders in the little schoolhouse to defend the Deligrad positions, enemy shells

53. AII, Ristić, XVIII/174, 12 October 1876, draft by Ristić; Ristić, I: 147–150.
54. V. Iasherov, "V Serbii 1876–77," RV, CXXXIII: 214.
55. IISG, ed. khr. 18, copied by Antonina.
56. AII, Ristić, XVIII/179, Cherniaev to Milan, 17 October 1876, telegram.

began to fall and burst over Cherniaev's building." Despite the tragic situation at the front, he calmly prepared a final defense of Serbia. Then came the Russian ultimatum halting the Turkish advance.[57]

Other accounts describe in quite a different manner his generalship and the roles of Serbs and Russians.[58] Sveti Nestor hill, the key to Djunis, had been well fortified. Even Dokhturov, the professional, declared that properly defended, it was impregnable. The enemy was clearly preparing an assault, but Cherniaev did not reinforce the Sveti Nestor garrison though the Timok army lay idle. A Serbian brigade and Russian Colonel Mezheninov's mixed Serbo-Russian unit comprised its five thousand defenders. For ten days they had sat in trenches in the chill fall rain. Even Russian volunteers in greatcoats and boots found the damp trenches virtually unbearable. The Serbian militiamen, often barefoot, wore only thin summer uniforms. The day before the attack the first snow of the season began to fall. Djordjević recalled that Cherniaev's staff shivered constantly even when warmly dressed and fortified with hot tea and rum, and he wondered how the defenders could remain on the cold hilltop. Their numbed fingers could scarcely hold a rifle.

On October 17, thirty-five battalions of Turkish regulars moved against them. After Horvatović, at Cherniaev's hasty order, had retreated toward Kruševac, the Turks assaulted Sveti Nestor in overwhelming force. The hill did not fall to the frontal attack but to a smaller force which surprised the defenders from the flank. The "heroic" Mezheninov, without awaiting final returns, rushed off to Deligrad. About 4 P.M. he burst into Cherniaev's office crying, "The Serbs all fled, the Russians all perished!" The generalissimo succumbed to a frenzied but impotent rage. Cornering every Serbian officer in sight, he shouted hoarsely, "Your Serbs all fled, and my Russians all perished!" He repeated this over and over and telegraphed it to Belgrade and Russia. But more than four hundred Serbs died that day and eight hundred were wounded. Mezheninov's brigade, where most of the Russians served, lost fewer men than the Serbian Rudnička and Valjevo brigades!

57. IISG, "Biografiia," pp. 332–339.

58. See Djordjević, I: 568–590; S. Grujić, *Operacije*, III: 227–245; S. Jovanović, *Vlada Milana*, I: 347–350; NFP, no. 4396, 19 November 1876, "Die Schlacht bei Trubarevo am 29. [17] Oktober." Contemporary accounts, both Serbian and Russian, were mostly very critical of Cherniaev's generalship and behavior at Djunis.

Where was the generalissimo during the crucial battle? Encouraging Sveti Nestor's defenders? Not at all. Though alarming reports reached Deligrad that morning, Cherniaev and his staff dined as usual at 1 P.M. By the time he reached the front, the Serbs were crossing the Morava bridge and the Turkish crescent flag flew over Sveti Nestor. He and his staff did help at the Morava crossing, but his subsequent actions scarcely suggest the cool, resourceful commander. With an armistice imminent, he ordered vital Aleksinac evacuated and all Russian officers to abandon their still resisting Serbian troops. On the 18th, after a final Deligrad dinner, Cherniaev turned over command there to Serbian Colonel Jovan Djordjević. His staff was to wait there until dark, then proceed westward to Ražan. Cherniaev preceded them. So his sudden departure would not alarm the Serbs, relates Dr. Vladan Djordjević, he sent his "convoy" ahead. Ostensibly to "inspect Deligrad's defenses," he hastily entered his troika and rushed westward to Paraćin. Of the entire staff only Miliutin's envoy Dokhturov kept his head. It was he who issued the orders which prevented a complete Turkish breakthrough while Cherniaev tore his hair.

Official Russia, despised by Cherniaev, saved Serbia from destruction. Within hours of receiving Kartsov's dispatches about its plight, Russian leaders conferred anxiously. They could not permit the Turks to conquer the unfortunate country. On October 18, St. Petersburg issued an ultimatum to the Ottoman government: halt or face war with Russia. The Turks promptly accepted a two month armistice with the Serbian states. Cherniaev's crusade was over.

CHAPTER XI

Aftermath of Defeat

SERBIA LAY prostrate before the Turks when the Russian ultimatum arrived. The Russians expected to fight while the Serbs rejoiced. But Turkish acceptance of the ultimatum delayed war and dashed Cherniaev's hopes that Russia's entry might salvage his shaken position. Djunis had undermined his prestige seriously. Could he maintain himself somehow in Serbia until Russia fought? Could he still utilize his sword or must he take up his pen in self-justification? Might he pose as a Slav hero abandoned by Russia and overwhelmed by Ottoman might?

Pro-Cherniaev newspapers sought to rescue something from the wreckage. Russia, asserted *Russkii Mir*, would now assume the Slavs' grievous burden: "Serbia would have been crushed had not Russia's saving voice boomed forth. . . . The active role of little Serbia is ending. It is high time to transfer this role to more powerful hands." Despite Djunis, Serbia had survived and achieved its orignial aims. Before leaving Russia, affirmed the paper, Cherniaev had considered a Serbo-Turkish war merely a prelude to the solution of the Eastern question by Europe: "To suppose that Serbia could decide the entire Eastern question by itself was believed only by a few Serbian dreamers unacquainted

with the European and Balkan situation."¹ Had not Cherniaev
been such a "dreamer"?

From Paraćin Mikhail Grigorevich put the best face on defeat.
He wrote Prince Milan: "Sire! The first phase of this war has just
ended. Despite the fact that the results obtained have not been
decisive for the cause, it is indisputable that this struggle of a country
of 1,300,000 inhabitants against the entire Moslem world has raised
Serbia morally and changed completely her relationship to the powers of the entire world." He requested that Horvatorić replace him
during his absence.²

Cherniaev was received coolly in Paraćin. At first the Serbs there
refused to supply a sentry. Some of the Russian officers accompany-
ing him balked at forming an honor guard until warned that the
Serbs of Paraćin might trample him in the mud unless the Russians
showed him due respect. Initially, Cherniaev had yielded to despair.
G. A. Devollan, a liberal Russian Slavophile, found him in a small
room choked with agitation. "All is lost now," he groaned, "the Serbs
have no love of country. I held out against the Turks for four months,
but finally the Serbs lost patience. This is understandable. They were
overcome with desperation when help failed to arrive. Now everything is over here." Then the weeping general noticed Colonel
Lishin outside. Had he brought Cossack reinforcements? "God, how
late this all is! Everything is too late, nothing is needed any
more." Recovering some composure, he added, "But we shall
find work for them even now. Send them to the villages to protect
the population against Cherkess raids."

Cherniaev emerged after conferring with Serbian commanders
who were impressed by the Russians' continued loyalty to him. He
told the cheering volunteers: "I hope, gentlemen, that none of you
will leave Serbia unless absolutely necessary. If you must go on leave,
I want you to pledge to return when the armistice ends." "We shall
stay, we shall return!" they shouted. Cherniaev exhorted them:

> I am certain that we shall meet here once again. Remember that you
> are pioneers in the Slav cause. Serbia raised Slavdom's banner believ-
> ing in the rightness of the cause and hoping for support from powerful
> Russia. When I arrived the Serbian army consisted mostly of peasants
> without arms, organization or clothing. But it fought wholly indepen-

1. *Russkii Mir*, 20, 23, and 26 October 1876.
2. DAS PO, 29/101–xxi, Cherniaev to Milan, 23 October 1876.

dently against the entire Moslem world. . . . Serbia placed its hopes in Russia. Aid came in the form of you, gentlemen, but few came. . . . You helped prolong the struggle two months, but one cannot fight against the impossible. . . . Many of you blame the Serbs for lack of martial qualities, but do not forget that the Slav question's entire weight fell upon the Serbian people. . . . Do not forget that one third of the country was devastated. . . . I hope that none of you will speak badly of the Serbs.

He concluded bravely, "They [Russian leaders] will receive me in Livadia, and then. . . ." To the Serbs those words, implying Russia's full support, resembled a sign from heaven.[3]

Cherniaev proceeded to Belgrade as if in triumph, revealing once more his ability to profit from circumstances. The Serbs seemed to attribute the Russian ultimatum to him. Prince Milan sent two official carriages and a detachment of horse guards to the pier. A crowd, including government leaders and intellectuals, cheered him when he arrived on the "Merkury."[4] Retaining Milan's support, he reserved an impressive hotel suite. In Belgrade Russian influence still prevailed and a Russo-Turkish war was anticipated momentarily.[5]

Mikhail Grigorevich was guest of honor at banquets and received many congratulatory messages. A Belgrade delegation led by the mayor thanked him for his heroic efforts. Matija Ban, chief of the Serbian press bureau, drew up a laudatory petition from the intelligentsia. The prince and the cabinet gave him a state dinner. "Cherniaev is as popular in Serbia as he is in Russia," concluded a correspondent for *Russkii Mir*.[6] Actually, the Serbs deeply resented Russian influence in Belgrade and felt humiliated by it.[7]

During the armistice Cherniaev planned to obtain military aid in Russia; Colonel Catargi and Dr. Djordjević were to accompany him. Then came the shattering news that the emperor had prohibited Cherniaev from coming.[8] Metropolitan Mihajlo complained to Nil

3. G. Devollan, "Nedavniaia starina," RA (1879), no. 7, pp. 374–376; *Grazhdanin*, nos. 36–37, 1 November 1876, p. 897. The Serbian minister of interior reacted warmly to Cherniaev's defense of the Serbs. DAS PO, 29/52, R. Milojković to Milan, 24 October 1876.

4. *Russkii Mir*, Nov. 5, p. 2, "Vesti iz Serbii," 28 October 1876.

5. *Golos*, 2 November 1876, report from Čačak of Oct. 22; Nov. 17, "Zagranichnye izvestiia," Belgrade, 8 November 1876.

6. *Russkii Mir*, Nov. 5, "Vesti iz Serbii," 28 October 1876.

7. Devollan, p. 376.

8. TSGAOR, f. 109, op. 4, d. 436, l. 151, order of Oct. 21. The instructions to the frontier

Popov, a prominent St. Petersburg Panslav, that this was a grievous mistake which would "kindle the hatred of his foreign enemies and the café party here who are ready to throw themselves at him like keen dogs" and denounce him as a fool and an adventurer. "Why strike at a man who brought all Russia into the good common cause . . . ? It is a pity that we always hurt ourselves more than our enemies do."[9] Through his brother-in-law Vulfert, Cherniaev angrily informed the Moscow Committee that he had been denied reentry into Russia: "Things are in a muddle. This prohibition has further complicated relations between Serbs and Russians. Not for me personally but for the [Slav] cause my immediate arrival is essential. *I shall* write to Alexander [II], but the matter is urgent. . . . The English and the Austrians are losing no time sowing discord and disorder in this country. I have done all that I could. More is impossible without large-scale assistance." He was being treated like a traitor, he complained to his wife. Could she and the two eldest children join him?[10]

Vulfert urged Mrs. Cherniaev to seek imperial permission to go. More than six months had passed, she wrote Alexander, since unforseen circumstances had separated her from her husband. It had been a period of anguish for her. When she heard from him, "Finally a ray of sunshine appeared on the horizon causing me and my husband to hope to see each other again. . . ." Then she had heard no more and concluded that Cherniaev had abandoned his plans to return to his family. She appealed to the tsar: "If so nothing remains for me but to rejoin him confiding my six small children to the protection of God—the eldest is only eight and the youngest [Aleksandr] but seven weeks. . . . [I] hope, Sire, that you will not refuse me this final consolation." The emperor authorized this reply: "I shall not hinder her from traveling to her husband, but I definitely will not consent to *his* return to Russia now."

Rumors spread in Gatchina where the Cherniaevs lived that the

---

authorities are in ll. 18–27; ннѕа, Wrede to Andrassy, [Oct. 31]/12 November 1876, no. 174. Miliutin explained Cherniaev's exclusion from Livadia: "in the tsar's eyes Cherniaev acted both dishonorably and illegally: dishonorably because he had promised General Potapov to carry out the emperor's will forbidding him to go to the war theater; illegally because without permission he gave up his Russian citizenship and entered the service of a foreign state. Under Russian law, Cherniaev should be tried and punished for criminal actions." *Dnevnik*, ii: 105.

9. ORBL, f. Nil Popov, 13/48, Mihajlo to Popov, 12 November 1876.

10. ORSS, Aksakov, no. 103, Cherniaev to Vulfert, 1 November 1876, enclosed in Vulfert to Aksakov; 4 November 1876, enclosed in Cherniaev to Vulfert.

general would arrive on the Warsaw train. Local merchants opened a subscription and planned to present him with a silver dish. The collection proceeded smoothly until the town commandant intimated that it contradicted official views. Many civil servants then withdrew support. The rumors proved false: a General Chertkov was on the train.[11]

Even Russian Panslavs now criticized Cherniaev. Ivan Aksakov deplored his fantastic dreams of liberating the Slavs alone. Serbia and the Russian public, he warned, could not possibly solve the Eastern question: "In no case can *Serbia* lead Russian society nor can Russian society follow behind Serbia's tail. As it turned out, even *together* they cannot stand. . . . Only Russia can solve the Slav question, not even Russian society . . . , but Russia as a whole, as a *state* organism *headed by the government*." Russia must liberate the Slavs, curb their tribal egoisms and foster their unity. For Cherniaev or Prince Milan to enter Constantinople would have been ridiculous. Russia's mission and ideals were much broader and higher "because in short we are older, more numerous, stronger, and more capable of ruling." Cherniaev's mission, affirmed Aksakov, had been to conquer Old Serbia or Bosnia, or defeat the Turks in a few battles, but he had forgotten this. Even with ten thousand volunteers he could not have defeated the Ottoman Empire.

Aksakov urged him to beg the tsar's forgiveness. With war imminent, the union between tsar and people had grown closer making public opposition to the government intolerable. The emperor had left open a route of reconciliation, but the general had not written him. "That was not even courteous, it was more than a mistake," Aksakov argued. For the emperor he was a subject who had illegally accepted foreign citizenship. For himself and the Slav cause he must submit. Aksakov advised Cherniaev, "Write the emperor throwing off any Garibaldinism. . . . But it must be sincere, heartfelt and honorable. . . . Do not sacrifice the cause to your pride, anger and nervous irritation." He added: "If you have already written the emperor, write him again, but hurry!"[12]

Perhaps in response to this plea, Cherniaev wrote the tsar from Belgrade. But was this the humble letter Aksakov had advised?

11. TSGAOR, f. 109, op. 4, d. 436, ll. 29–30, A. A. Cherniaeva to Alexander II, 3 November 1876; ll. 33–34, report of 5 November 1876.

12. GIM, ed. khr. 42, Aksakov to Cherniaev, 1–2 November 1876.

When Serbia, reaching the limit beyond which her continuance under Moslem rule would bring complete moral disintegration, raised the banner of independence of the South Slavs, I decided to dedicate myself completely to that Christian and humanitarian cause. I firmly believed that after the great work of liberating millions of your subjects [emancipating the serfs], You, my Sovereign, had been destined . . . to emancipate peoples related to your people by faith and blood. But I understood that your imperial decision could not follow immediately and that my modest task consisted merely of restraining Moslem pressure against a country which had entrusted its defense to me until your majestic word was spoken. Not victories or glory did I seek leading peaceful peasants who had taken up arms against an enemy thirty times stronger.

Serbia had fought bravely until overwhelmed. "Completing my modest task, I venture to submit to your gracious opinion, Sire, this country's present situation . . . , receiving from you its salvation from external enemies and domestic disorder." Serbia's eastern provinces had been devastated and it was exhausted physically and financially, but "I am convinced that at your first word, Sire, the Serbian people would make a final exertion . . . to achieve the goal Providence has destined for you." He signed this letter: "Your faithful subject, Mikhail Cherniaev, retired major general."[13] The emperor commented: "Whose faithful subject? The king of Serbia's?" Miliutin queried: "What right does Cherniaev have to speak in the name of the Serbian people?"[14]

Cherniaev's role in Serbia was played out. He sought once again to get Milan to conduct a coup d'état against the ministry and constitution, but in vain. Then he left with his staff for Vienna to meet his family.[15] He arrived by train and took up quarters in the Grand Hotel, where two servants stood watch before his door. At the Russian embassy he talked with Ambassador Novikov, next he visited the Serbian envoy, Kosta Ćukić. Then in full uniform the wandering generalissimo sat for a formal portrait.[16]

In Vienna Cherniaev drew up a memorandum justifying the war

13. ORSS, Aksakov, no. 613, Cherniaev to Alexander II, 17 November 1876, draft.
14. OSOB PRIB, no. 1, p. 72.
15. FO, 78/2488, White to Derby, (12)/24 November 1876, no. 209; *Russkii Mir*, Nov. 20, telegram of 19 November 1876. Miličević ascribed the crowd's happiness to Cherniaev's departure! ASANU, 9327/7, 18 November 1876, p. 178.
16. NFP, (20–24 November)/2–6 December 1876, nos. 4409–4413. "He is a stately man with a sympathetic appearance." 2 December 1876, no. 4409, p. 6.

and criticizing Serbian institutions. The war, he claimed, had prevented disorder or revolution in a country demoralized by the Turkish yoke and corrupting European influences. The Serbian Assembly, imported from the decadent West and unresponsive to popular desires, was "a miserable comedy, . . . the plaything and blind tool of a few ambitious intriguers . . . in Belgrade." Ignoring Assembly decisions, the Serbian people "wallow in narrow egotistical home-centeredness" and lack true patriotism or religious feeling. The Serbs disliked the war. They were deficient in leadership, training, and discipline, but buoyed by Cherniaev's arrival and expecting decisive aid from Russia, they had struggled as long as they could against great odds. After Šumatovac he had vainly sought to arrange an armistice, then had held on hoping for Russia's aid. The Russian embassy in Constantinople urged him to resist one more month; they had fought for two months. A few days before Djunis came the message: "Hold out another month and victory is certain." But the Serbs could fight no longer. Two million rubles and 2,640 volunteers could not tip the scales. Cherniaev denied responsibility for the defeat. Serbia had strained its resources to the utmost, but neither Belgrade nor Russian society had supported him adequately. The Serbs had entrusted most of their forces to him only when the enemy had become too powerful to resist.

At present, continued the memorandum, "Serbia may be considered crushed. Without the *most potent* aid from Russia, both moral and material, she cannot cooperate or resist." The country was defenseless with the armistice due to end in three weeks. Russian aid, even if it were sent, would arrive too late. To defeat Turkey now, Russia would have to raise an army of three hundred thousand men.[17] But only two months earlier Cherniaev had asserted that ten thousand volunteers could do the job!

Soon he was summoned to the Kishinev headquarters of Grand Duke Nikolai Nikolaevich, newly appointed commander in chief of Russia's Balkan army. The Third Section permitted him to cross the Russian frontier.[18] From Kishinev, without official authorization, he urged the Slav committees to recall Russian volunteers from Serbia immediately. "Your telegram . . . amazed and angered me," re-

17. GIM, ed. khr. 14, ll. 82–94, Cherniaev's draft memorandum, 27 (?) November 1876, Vienna.

18. TSGAOR, f. 109, op. 4, d. 436, ll. 51–56; GIM, ed. khr. 14, l. 115, Vasilchikov (Russian Embassy, Vienna) to Cherniaev, 29 November 1876 (the summons).

sponded Aksakov indignantly. "It is up to the Russian government to determine matters in Serbia . . . and the Committee wishes to cooperate with it. In this . . . now lies our salvation. We are not . . . recalling anyone." It would be contemptible, he added, "to invite the Russians to run away from danger."[19]

Serbia was defenseless, explained Cherniaev. If the Turks advanced into the country, its populace would submit tamely. The volunteers alone could not resist until the Russian army arrived. Only a separate peace or an extension of the armistice could spare Serbia destruction and humiliation. In addition, ten thousand volunteers and five million rubles must be given to "the person entrusted with organizing the Serbian forces." Cherniaev still hoped to be that person. Given timely aid Serbia would regard the emperor's slighting words[20] as "fatherly anger followed immediately by forgiveness."[21]

But Petersburg refused to reassign him to Serbia. When this was discussed, noted Miliutin, "the tsar, forgetting all his tricks, was prepared to . . . entrust him with a command in the active army." Foreign Minister Gorchakov, anticipating Austrian objections, protested and the idea was dropped. "His popularity has evaporated," concluded Miliutin. "In Serbia they won't even hear of his return."[22] The Russian authorities permitted him to settle with his family in Odessa or Kiev or go abroad.[23]

Faced with inglorious retirement in Russia, Cherniaev chose exile. From December 1876 to April 1877 he wandered around Europe gaining notoriety. Sometimes hailed, sometimes hooted, he carried his crusade from railroad platforms to banquet tables. From the Kishinev headquarters he returned to his family in Vienna, where Bulgarian students celebrated his sacrifices for South Slav liberation. Then the Czechs invited him to Prague, and his family returned to Russia.

The majestic city on the Moldau was the seat of Austrian authority in Bohemia and the center of Czech nationalism. To young

19. Ibid., ll. 97–98, Cherniaev to Vorontsov-Dashkov and Aksakov, 7 or 9 December 1876; l. 99, Aksakov to Cherniaev, 9 December 1876.

20. In the tsar's Kremlin speech of 29 October, he referred negatively to the military showing of the Serbs against Turkey.

21. TSGAOR, f. 109, ll. 101–104, Cherniaev to A. I. Vasilchikov and Vorontsov-Dashkov, 14 December 1876 (Kishinev).

22. Miliutin, *Dnevnik*, II: 120–121, entry of 11 December 1876.

23. ORSS, Aksakov, no. 387, Cherniaev to Aksakov, 22 December 1876.

Czechs, seeking independence from the Habsburgs, Cherniaev symbolized the Slav struggle against foreign oppression. Czech newspapers urged the populace to welcome him warmly to Prague. Several Czech leaders, including J. S. Škrejšovský, had boarded his train near the frontier. A large vociferous crowd, mostly students and artisans, jammed the Franz Josef station. When Cherniaev, attired in a new suit, dark overcoat, and a cylindrical black hat, emerged with his Czech hosts, there were deafening cries of "Slava!," "Živio!" and "Ura!"

The mob pressed around him shouting: "Long live Cherniaev!" With great difficulty his entourage carved a pathway through the crowd. On the Wenzelsplatz, Prague's principal square, the entire first floor of the hotel, "Zum Erzherzog Stephan" had been reserved for Cherniaev. A huge crowd gathered on the square shouting: "Down with the Magyars! Down with the Turks! Long live the Russians!" Slav songs were sung lustily. When Cherniaev showed himself, the multitude broke into a stormy "Živio Cherniaev." After conferring with Škrejšovský, he declared in Czech: "I thank you for your sympathy and ask you to disperse quietly." After more shouts the crowd melted away. Commented one reporter: "This is quite an uproar for a general who was continually defeated. The Russians and Serbs let Cherniaev fall; the Czechs are lionizing him."[24] In reality they were demonstrating for Slav solidarity and against Austrian rule.

Next day Czech leaders greeted the Slav champion. Mayor Skramlik appeared with a delegation from the city council, then the general toured the city with Dr. Rieger, a prominent nationalist. A banquet was planned for Sunday, January 2/14 at which an honorary sword was to be presented. Numerous church services and a special National Theater performance were dedicated to Cherniaev. "All this," sputtered Vienna's *Neue Freie Presse* indignantly, "is occurring in an Austrian provincial capital under the eyes of the Austrian authorities." Despite Austro-Turkish friendship, "an agitator hostile to our country's peaceful attitude is being celebrated in a way damaging to our state policy." The Czechs, desperate for a hero, did not realize the absurdity of enthroning a fallen idol. "In the Czech pantheon even a Cherniaev finds a place as a demigod."[25]

24. NFP, no. 4446, (31 December 1876)/12 January 1877, p. 6, Prague, 11 January 1877, telegram; no. 4447, (1)/13 January 1877, p. 4, "Tschernajeff in Prag."
25. Ibid., no. 4448, (2)/14 January 1877, lead.

Fearing that demonstrations might unleash a Slav revolution, Vienna ordered the Prague authorities to expel Cherniaev. Shortly after noon on January 1/13, the police knocked. Cherniaev greeted them warmly, believing they had come to wish him a happy New Year. But Officer Kreuter, forbidding him to receive anyone or leave the hotel, ordered him to depart by evening. Expectant Czech delegates were turned away. "I am a prisoner!" shouted the general turning crimson, "I will not go voluntarily, but only by force!" Fat Khludov, gourmet son of a Moscow merchant, soothed him: why not use influence to get the order revoked? They telegraphed Ambassador Novikov and Foreign Minister Andrássy in Vienna but in vain. Insisting he would yield only to force, Cherniaev declared dramatically: "I would rather be shot than leave Prague!" In a dinner jacket and white necktie, he showed himself demonstratively at the window.

By late afternoon another mob gathered on the Wenzelsplatz shouting: "Long live Cherniaev!" and "Hej Slovene!" When the general came to the window, the Czechs cheered, waved their hats and sang national songs. By 6 P.M. the police could not control the crowd; the army was called in and artillery rolled into position. When soldiers arrested their cheerleaders, the crowd retreated still singing into a side street.

Cherniaev packed his bags with utmost deliberation. Again he addressed the crowd, but the troops prevented further demonstrations. Finally, the police commissar came to hurry him along. As they emerged from the building, Cherniaev tried to approach the crowd but his escort forced him into a carriage on a dark street behind the hotel. Hemmed in by three policemen, he was driven quickly by a devious route to the station. There too disorders had occurred. Troops had had to clear the square by force. Now all was quiet. Waiting for the train, the general walked up and down smoking cigarettes. Jokingly he offered to pay the police commissar's fare to the frontier! On the platform some students shouted: "Long live Cherniaev!" A hotel employee brought a huge bouquet and laurel wreaths to "the conqueror of Prague." At midnight his train reached the German border.[26]

---

26. IISG, "Biografiia," pp. 367–368; NFP, no. 4448, p. 7, telegram, Prague, 13 January 1877; no. 4449, (3)/15 January 1877, p. 2, "Der Tschernajeff Scandal in Prag." Cherniaev's parting shot was a message published in the Czech paper, *Narodny Listy*: "I express my sincere thanks

Vienna was greatly relieved, but *Neue Freie Presse* castigated the government for handling the affair clumsily. Why had it not barred Cherniaev from Prague or removed him without such a commotion? While the Czechs required "instruction in the firm rule of law," Cherniaev had defied the law and revealed blatant discourtesy and lack of breeding. No wonder the Serbs had disobeyed him! How could one give orders when one could not obey them?[27] Perhaps so, but Cherniaev had revealed how fragile was Austria's hold over the Czechs and that the polyglot Habsburg monarchy was a powder keg. He was being scolded for this, not for bad manners.

The European press continued to follow his movements. At Aussig he entered the station restaurant where "Mr. Cousal's famous delicacies held an irresistible charm for him." "The heroic gourmet" left so reluctantly that the stationmaster had to remind him repeatedly to board the train. On January 5/17 he arrived in Dresden, but no one met him. After two dismal days there, he moved on to Paris. Queried the *Journal des Débats*: "Is this odyssey of the general who played such a disastrous role in Serbia, ruining for a long time the country he had come to save, despite which deplorable people can still be found to cheer him—is not this odyssey a sign of the times and a symptom of the confusion prevailing in Europe? Need one really only make noise to become a great man?"[28]

In England, Gladstone's Liberals, accusing the Disraeli government of having driven Serbia into war and of condoning Turkish massacres of Bulgarians, considered Cherniaev a hero. They surrounded him with flattering attention. He stayed at Symond's Hotel in Brook Street which, recalled Olga Novikova, "became the headquarters of unofficial Russia, regarded with but scant sympathy by the official Russia in Chesham Place. General Tchernaieff saw a good many anti-Turks." The caricaturist of *Vanity Fair*, struck by his appearance, even asked him for a sitting. Cherniaev refused indignantly.[29] His European peregrinations brought him ridicule as well as applause.

---

to the Czecho-Slavs for their greetings of Dec. 30/Jan. 11 and sincerely regret that for reasons beyond my control, I was unable to deliver my thanks in person to the representatives of the Czecho-Slav nation." Prague, 1/13 January 1877, the Slav-Russian, M. Cherniaev, ibid., no. 4451, (5)/17 January 1877, p. 5.

27. Ibid., no. 4450, (4)/16 January 1877, lead.

28. Ibid., no. 4454, (8)/20 January 1877, p. 5, "Tschernajeff."

29. O. K. [Olga Novikova, A. A. Kireev's sister], *The M. P. for Russia* (London, 1909), I: 309.

Meanwhile Monteverde, his disreputable colleague in war and journalism, reputedly offered his services to the Russian heir. Russia, he asserted, had no active general who could beat the Turks. Either they were too old to mount their horses or lacked battle experience. "Your Mr. Cherniaev did not win any battles," replied the heir. "He increased his fame as a champagne connoisseur, *voilà tout*. Others will handle the Turks better." Cherniaev should reside quietly in Kiev.[30]

Monteverde wrote Cherniaev that his relations with the government "stand *badly* (which in my view . . . is excellent)." During the Prague events, Monteverde had found Petersburg officials and Slav committee members fearful. They had severed connections with Cherniaev, believing that he was defying his government. Even the heir had been intimidated, and former Slav enthusiasts, including Vorontsov and Aksakov, had attacked Cherniaev in order to display their "patriotism." But the general's position was excellent, concluded Monteverde; his opponents were losing influence and strength.[31]

Cherniaev remained in touch with Serbian leaders. He wrote Prince Milan denying that he had refused to reenter the Serbian army, "I would be happy to continue the struggle against the common enemy with my comrades of last year if His Majesty, the emperor, authorizes me to do so and if you consider my presence . . . useful."[32] Milan replied warmly but did not urge him to come.[33]

Cherniaev's former chief of commissariat Kosta Ristić handled his remaining affairs in Serbia, selling the general's carriages, horses, and other effects. Ristić claimed that he had saved him much money and refuted many press lies. The general's travail in Serbia, declared this servile flatterer, had resembled the sufferings of Christ. Remembering him as a benefactor, the Serbs stood ready to fight beneath his banner until Slav liberation was complete. He should continue his holy work disregarding slander and intrigues. "All Slavdom appreciates your efforts. Had it not been for you, the Turks would long ago have been in Belgrade."[34]

30. NFP, no. 4461, (15)/27 January 1877, pp. 1–2, "Petersburger Stimmungen," from (11)/23 January 1877. The reliability of this article is uncertain.

31. GIM, ed. khr. 48, ll. 48 reverse–53, Monteverde to Cherniaev, 29 January 1877.

32. Ibid., ed. khr. 14 [Cherniaev to Milan], draft n.d.

33. "K M. G. Cherniaevu," pp. 192–194, February 1877.

34. GIM, ed. khr. 15, ll. 20–26, Konstantin Ristić to Cherniaev, 13 February 1877 and "na Sretnje."

Another admirer, Colonel Catargi, wrote that he rejoiced to be counted among Cherniaev's devoted friends: "The cause you defend is just. You are, flattery aside, so noble and great that all my sympathy is forever yours. May you ultimately bring about the triumph of justice and reassume sooner or later in your country the place due you by right of which a petty and tortuous policy deprives you at the moment."[35] Such letters fed Mikhail Grigorevich's delusions of grandeur and his belief that an evil conspiracy was robbing him of deserved prominence.

He continued to correspond with Ivan Aksakov and tolerated the latter's frank criticism. "Every defeat leads to misunderstandings," he wrote Aksakov from Vienna, "but I hope that when everything has been explained and we meet again, you will extend a friendly hand as you did when we parted." Cherniaev criticized sharply the Nikitin mission to Serbia.[36] Inadequate funds (one million rubles) had placed it in a false position: "Had I had that money at the start of the war, I could have made out of Serbia an extremely useful tool of the Russian government." Unofficial aid had not brought victory. Now Petersburg should promise Serbia aggrandizement and independence if she joined Russia in war.[37]

Though dismayed at the results of their efforts in 1876, Aksakov denied that he was angry with Cherniaev. During the campaign he had refused to judge military operations or believe hostile newspaper reports. Turkish victory had been inevitable. He wrote to Cherniaev, "Out of all the filth which clouded last year's episode, *one* name came out *entirely clean*—that is yours." Aksakov deplored Serbia's ruin and bitter recriminations between Serbs and Russians: "The Russian name's fascination has been lost in Serbia and among the Slavs generally. . . . Russian society is losing faith in its enthusiasm . . . and its independent activity. This is what causes despondency. Naturally, defeat is to blame." Why, queried Aksakov, had everybody lost his head after Djunis? Why had the entire staff departed without insuring or-

---

35. Ibid., ed. khr. 46, Georges Catargi to Cherniaev, 22 February 1877.

36. In December 1876 Miliutin sent General A. P. Nikitin to Belgrade to ascertain the status of the Serbian army and the Russian volunteers.

37. ORSS, Aksakov, no. 387, Cherniaev to Aksakov, 22 December 1876.

derly retreat? Doubtless Cherniaev had suffered greatly and been exhausted. "Your nerves must have been terribly upset. . . . A cooler headed individual should have been on the scene." But would another have risked what Cherniaev had undertaken?

"You are hampered by excessive personal pride and irritability," continued Aksakov. The worst blunder was to alienate the emperor, a potential ally "for the *cause*, not just for yourself." His letter to the tsar had been pompous and rhetorical, a manifesto from the Serbian people, and his behavior after Djunis had been deplorable. Humility and modesty were qualities of a true hero. More damaging than Djunis itself were the elaborately uniformed Cherniaev squadron and its silken banner. "All that scarcely accords with Suvorov . . . or your style at the start of the war." A return to Kiev in degradation was preferable to grabbing empty applause in Europe and "alienating yourself from Russia." Cherniaev could no longer defy the government; he should return and write his memoirs. "The more one seeks to exalt one's services, the more he loses in general esteem. . . ." He hoped Cherniaev would accept this criticism in a friendly spirit.[38]

Cherniaev's lengthy response, defending his actions in Serbia and denouncing official Russia, was never sent: "Russia has not yet drained the cup of humiliation. The Petersburg government . . . must renounce its German traditions and become national, but for that the first step is to gather up its things and move to Moscow." Aksakov must continue to promote war. The Panslavs and public must apply relentless pressure on the government so it could not retreat into helpless passivity. Even an unsuccessful struggle with Turkey would benefit Russia by discrediting Miliutin and restoring him (Cherniaev) to rightful honor. "Instead of bureaucratic reforms, we could stand on free national ground. German commands would be replaced by Russian administration. Then we would know what we need and what is superfluous." As for humility, "meekness on my part would be pretense and no one would believe it."[39] Cherniaev, though still angry with the government and his

38. GIM, ed. khr. 14, Aksakov to Cherniaev, 4 January 1877.
39. Ibid., Cherniaev to Aksakov, 17 March 1877. This original letter is torn and incomplete and was supplemented with the complete copy in IISG, ed. khr. 10.

critics, remained friends with Aksakov.[40] Very soon he would follow his advice, swallow his false pride, and return home.

40. Ibid., "Biografiia," pp. 366–367. Aksakov, asserted Antonina, was competing with Cherniaev for leadership of the Slav movement and thus sought to "teach" him to correct his mistakes in Serbia.

CHAPTER XII

"The Cherniaev Question" and the Russo-Turkish War

IN RUSSIA the Serbian campaign and Cherniaev's role in it became important issues. Russians in and out of public life discussed "the Cherniaev question" which went beyond his generalship or Panslav activities. Cherniaev symbolized contention between two important groups. Conservative nationalists, seeking a military hero in Cherniaev, wished to recover influence lost in the era of reforms. To liberals he epitomized Panslav bellicosity threatening to plunge Russia into needless war and Nicholaevian darkness. It was a press debate, muffled by censorship. Should foreign glory or domestic change have priority in Russia? If Cherniaev were discredited, would not Miliutin triumph over the reactionaries?

Russians disputed Cherniaev's character and actions. Early in the war Miliutin had commented: "What filth are these ambitious little men [Cherniaev and Fadeev] and their entourage—they intrigue and quarrel among themselves." After Djunis how could the tsar "spare and spoil a man who in another country would have been condemned to perpetual banishment?"[1] Consul Kartsov's reports

1. Miliutin, *Dnevnik*, II: 97–98, 112. Grand Duke Nikolai Nikolaevich, influenced by Kartsov's reports, now considered Cherniaev an egotistical maniac prepared to sacrifice others to his own glory. ORBL, Kireev, Dnevnik, VI: 130–131, 20 August and 21 September 1876.

from Serbia provided Cherniaev's opponents with copious material.[2]

Russian volunteer officers in Serbia criticized Cherniaev freely. Back in Russia, they transmitted their negative views to the public and government. He had not led or coordinated his army properly, argued Maksimov, and should have remained on the defensive. His staff had been "a rabble of petty little men," mostly young low-ranking officers, some "almost literally expelled from the Russian army." Cherniaev did not use the competent ones on his staff.[3]

Major A. N. Khvostov, before arriving in Serbia, had admired Cherniaev and grew angry when anyone criticized him: "For reasons of national pride it was pleasant to see a Russian leading a worldwide Christian protest against Moslem barbarism. Any Russian general, to say nothing of Cherniaev, would have been placed on a pedestal as a Slav Garibaldi. His fame was produced by our own enthusiastic, electrified condition. We needed an idol." Three months in Serbia turned him into a bitter critic. Now he could not bear to read *Russkii Mir*. "*Golos* has become my voice of truth." Cherniaev had purposely misled the Serbs about Turkish strength. For personal reasons he had risked Serbia's existence. He had visions of crushing enemies with one blow. "The affair will succeed and I will go down in history as a Slav Washington." Cherniaev had assured the Serbs: "All Russia is with you! The Cossacks will trample all Turkey with their horses." Isn't sarcasm in order? asked Khvostov.

Cherniaev's generalship, he asserted, was disastrous. Risky offensives and frontal assaults had ruined morale. His dispositions were foolish and for weeks he avoided the front. Cherniaev utilized the volunteers to build his prestige and support in Russia. His victories were imaginary: at Babina Glava the Turks retired with little resistance; Šumatovac was a clever Turkish maneuver.[4] Deceiving the Serbs and Russian society, Cherniaev succumbed to the sordid intrigues of his entourage. "Cherniaev is brave, honorable and good (in a private sense)," concluded Khvostov, "but is an administrator

2. osvob, i: 241–243, Kartsov to Ignatiev, 31 May 1876.

3. Maksimov, pp. 46–50, 65–68.

4. A Serbian officer, Jovan Stefanović, echoed these criticisms and assessed Cherniaev's strategy and tactics like his Russian volunteer critics. "Černajev u Srbiji kao vojskovodja i političar," *Otadžbina*, viii: 513 ff.

good without strong willpower and intelligence especially when this is accompanied by boundless ambition and vanity?"[5]

Many Slav committee members agreed. A. A. Kireev of Petersburg, who had predicted that Cherniaev would triumph or die, wrote sadly: "I cannot forgive him for not finding death at Djunis." A general who cried and tore his hair was finished.[6] Devollan, another Petersburg Slavophile, concluded that Cherniaev had erred badly in undertaking the unequal fight. But history would describe him as having inspired the Russian volunteers and the South Slavs: he succumbed to grandiose illusions, but his sincere, direct approach had won them.[7]

Two leading Panslav officials now repudiated him. During the campaign, declared Count Ignatiev, he acted stupidly and kept bad company.[8] Russia's volunteers, agreed Prince V. A. Cherkasskii, were led by "a man politically foolish, yes, and in general rather limited . . . , continually spoiled by excessive egoism, self-importance and the crudest vainglory."[9]

The greatest contemporary writers joined the debate. To Fyodor Dostoevsky, apostle of Orthodoxy, Cherniaev was a great Slav champion. "His military talent is unquestioned," he wrote during the campaign, "while his character and the lofty impulse of his soul, no doubt, stand on the level of Russian aspirations and aims. . . . Russia understands that he has initiated, and is pursuing, a cause coinciding with her best and most heartfelt aspirations. . . ." Later he defended the defeated general as having embodied Russia's unique historical mission: "The Slavic cause, of necessity, had . . . to embark upon its active phase—and without Cherniaev it would not have reached such development. . . . Once the Slavic cause started, who, if not Russia should have headed it? Herein is Russia's mission, and Cherniaev grasped it and hoisted the banner of Russia. . . . This decision . . . could not have been [made] by a man devoid of a special power." Russia's ultimatum had vindicated him. Had it come sooner, Cherniaev would stand blameless. Would a careerist or adventurer persist so long or suffer so much? Serving a great cause, he preferred to sacrifice his name, career, and even his

5. Khvostov, *Russkie i serby*, pp. 24 ff.
6. ORBL, Kireev, *Dnevnik*, VI–VII.
7. Devollan, "Nedavniaia," RA (1879), no. 7, pp. 355–356.
8. Kartsov, RS, CXXXIV: 311–312.
9. ORBL, f. Cherkasskii, cited in Nikitin, "Russkoe obshchestvo," p. 1033.

life. "He was laboring consciously for Russia's honor and benefit."[10] Now this noble man was the victim of a dastardly conspiracy.

Very different was the devastating assessment of Cherniaev, the
man and commander, by the novelist, Ivan Turgenev, who
did not know him:

> I consider Cherniaev a vulgar person. . . . Everyone here [Paris],
> naturally, is convinced of his extreme military *incompetence* . . . : his
> whole command was a series of the most blatant mistakes, and old
> Abdul Kerim Pasha twirled him around like a stick, but in the West
> they see in him a clever intriguer, a Warwick, a faiseur des rois, and
> actually he is just—I repeat—a vulgar person, Khlestakov, a cheap
> copy of Garibaldi (There is a *real* hero!). "Upon what do you base
> your opinion?" you may ask me. On everything. On his frightfully
> false telegrams . . . , on the fact that he could surround himself with
> such known thugs as Komarov, Monteverde (I know that sly dodger
> personally!!!) and the like—upon all his words and actions. He is one
> of the most worthless Russian types. And that in Russia they would
> receive him with enthusiasm, bow down to him, give dinners in his
> honor etc. proves nothing at all. Russians would worship a blank wall
> taking it for a wonder-working icon. Give it time and the present
> intoxication will pass and Cherniaev will sit in the English Club
> playing whist and only the barkeepers will know that it is the former
> Serbian generalissimo who is trumping. I do not reproach him be-
> cause he was beaten. It seems to me that he would be even more
> repulsive had he triumphed.[11]

Underestimating Cherniaev's symbolic significance, Turgenev was
appalled that Russians could worship one so unworthy. His prediction that public admiration would yield to forgetfulness was only
partially realized.

Nearly every literate Russian had strong views about Cherniaev
which fed newspaper polemics. *Birzhevye Vedomosti*, a liberal bourgeois organ, began the press attack. By convincing the Serbs that
Russia backed Cherniaev, the Panslavs had triggered a disastrous
war: "The entire result for us consists of a mass of Russian corpses
at the feet of Cherniaev's glory. The reason for Serbia's suffering lies

10. F. Dostoevsky, *The Diary of a Writer (1876)* (New York, 1954), pp. 426–427, 476–477.
Cherniaev's critics, he added, could never have accomplished what he had militarily. The
intrigue against him, Dostoevsky concluded, had been fostered by the English and by highly
placed Russian bureaucrats (pp. 477–478).

11. I. S. Turgenev, *Polnoe sobranie sochinenii i pisem. Pisma*, xi: 351, Turgenev to Ia. P.
Polonskii, 11 November 1876.

in its leaders' extreme political immaturity in imagining that Serbia could play Piedmont and General Cherniaev become a Slav Garibaldi. . . . It was criminal to suggest to [Russian] volunteers that they could decide a political question without mobilizing the Russian army." It deplored Cherniaev's glorification by newspapers which defamed the Serbian army. The general, it concluded, had proven unequal to his task.[12]

Golos, Russia's chief liberal daily, accused Cherniaev of seeking personal glory at the expense of the Slav cause. Its correspondent, Viskovatov, exposed the infamous "Correspondence Bureau." "The Bureau was really a weapon of political blackmail of the most criminal kind," commented editor Kraevskii. "By lies and deception it hoped to involve Russia in war with Turkey. Returning volunteers will reveal the Bureau's falsehoods and expose the adventurers who tried through this lie to build themselves monuments of military and political glory." Deligrad headquarters had been full of vodka and playing cards. Its drunken cook received the same decoration for bravery as men at the front. Cherniaev bestowed orders of Takovo so liberally that they lost meaning—Horvatović returned his in disgust. Cherniaev impressed the Serbs with theatrical gestures, his large staff and troika with a white flag. Now his "luxury procession" of Serbs, Bulgars, and Albanians was continuing through Austria. Kraevskii endorsed these accusations and denied that Cherniaev epitomized the Slav cause or had attracted volunteers to Serbia. Higher motives had inspired those Russians. Why conceal the sordid truth and blame Cherniaev's misdeeds on others? asked Kraevskii, "History punishes those who place their personal interests above their people, utilize others' blood, and worry more about externals than the heart of the matter even facing the enemy."[13]

Most non-official papers defended Cherniaev and the volunteers. In a major article, "Cherniaev before the court of the Rus-

12. bv, 28 October 1876, "Serbiia i vostochnyi vopros"; 2 November 1876, p. 1; 4 December 1876, p. 2.

13. *Golos,* 7, 11, 18, 26 November 1876, 16 January 1877. Their authors' personal interest to discredit Cherniaev reduces somewhat the credibility of *Golos*'s defamatory articles from Belgrade. "P," was a Serb, Nikola Petrović, whose brothers were chief of staff at Krevet and secretary to the minister of interior. Another, Mirković, who praised General Novoselov and disparaged Cherniaev, had been the former's adjutant. Nikitin, "Russkoe obshchestvo," pp. 1030–1032. *Golos* glorified Novoselov and War Minister Nikolić unduly, but its charges against Cherniaev were never refuted satisfactorily.

sian press," liberal *Nedelia* called *Birzhevye Vedomosti*'s accusations indecent, insulting, and uncorroborated. The lower key, more factual approach of *Golos*, it suggested, aimed to destroy public enthusiasm for the Serbs and dissuade Russia from Balkan intervention. To assert that the Russian public had been tricked into aiding the Slavs insulted Cherniaev and Russia. *Golos*'s notion that the Serbian war was a charade by political adventurers came straight from the Austrian press. "We find an analogy between him and Washington who had to create an army from untrained peasants," continued *Nedelia*. "That an army was created from nothing cannot be denied." Had not Serbian intellectuals in a letter to Cherniaev called him their country's savior and deliverer? Cherniaev's name, it concluded, had attracted most Russian volunteers to Serbia.[14]

Russkii Mir's defense of Cherniaev was lukewarm. After Djunis, Major Sava Grujić, his chief of artillery, hotly denied Austrian assertions that his men had mutinied and he reaffirmed the Serbs' loyalty and devotion to Cherniaev. The Serbs, asserted its Belgrade correspondent, had not disobeyed but had been overwhelmed. A letter signed by ninety-two volunteers in Belgrade expressed faith in Cherniaev and determination to fight on. "They [the Russians] demanded victory when all we could do was hold back temporarily the pressure of Moslem forces," Cherniaev had replied. "We must hope the time will come when they will not refuse us our due." The Balkan peoples' failure to rise had caused defeat, but the "heroic war" had not been in vain.[15]

His warmest defender was Prince V. P. Meshcherskii, editor of reactionary *Grazhdanin*. After visiting Deligrad, he composed *The Truth about Serbia* (*Pravda o Serbii*). Plunging into the newspaper fray, he bellowed: "You accusers are always at home or at the card table when danger threatens Russia or an ideal seizes hold of Russian society." Cherniaev, an honorable, brave Russian general, had been the Slavs' valiant standard bearer. "His honor is even dearer to us in defeat than in victory. He is a sufferer for the ideal of Slav freedom. . . ." The volunteers had sacrificed unselfishly for Russia and Slavdom. Cherniaev had blundered "in administration, politics and diplomacy . . . where he possessed neither innate nor inborn ability . . ." and had selected incompetent subordinates, Meshcher-

14. *Nedelia*, 14 November 1876, no. 42, pp. 1360–1363, "General Cherniaev pered sudom russkoi pechati."

15. *Russkii Mir*, 2, 4, 11 November 1876, 1 January 1877.

skii admitted. But remaining honorable and pure, he had been true
to his mission: "to suffer where one had to suffer and be a hero when
needed . . . , to be cool and cheerful, tireless and attach people to
himself." Inspiring love and respect, he had moved the masses and
prolonged Serbian resistance "by putting his whole soul into it . . .
with the boundless self-sacrifice which Russia expected." He had
been indispensable to the development of the Slav cause.[16]

In this morass of accusations Professor A. D. Gradovskii's article,
"The Cherniaev Question," deplored the violent polemics and
probed larger issues: "On the eve of the [Constantinople]
Conference[17] a vast question has been narrowed, shortened and
reduced in our press to the Cherniaev question. What will a future
historian of our times think of this? What will he say about journalism which at a most critical time for Russia chose as its subject for
debate *one* man . . . , petty biographical details about *one* person
even discussing which beer and wine he drank?" Here were symp-
toms of a grave national illness: a discussion of principles in the form
of persons. During the Balkan crisis, some papers had urged unilateral action by Russia and the Slavs; others recommended great
power diplomacy. As the Slav question became identified with Cherniaev it was argued: "If I prove that Cherniaev is extremely intelligent, honest and energetic, I will arouse public sympathy and support for the Slav cause and prove the need for a bellicose
policy." Others said: "If I can prove that Cherniaev is incapable,
dissipated, lazy and administratively incompetent, I will show the
need for peaceful waiting and diplomacy's superiority over military
means." The Serbs' desire to throw off the Turkish yoke had brought
war. England's rejection of the Berlin Memorandum was its immediate occasion. Had Cherniaev caused the war, enthusiasm for him
would not have engulfed Russia. He had gained popularity *because*
he participated in the war, but his failures in Serbia could not ruin
the Slav movement for genuine sympathizers. "If we must fight
[Turkey], it will not be Cherniaev who is responsible but Russian
interests which the government cannot renounce."[18]

The Russian public, reported the Third Section, deplored this
press polemic. Most educated persons believed both sides were partly

16. *Grazhdanin*, 25 October 1876, pp. 851–854.
17. Abortive meetings between the powers and Turkey (December 1876–January 1877)
to arrange a compromise solution of the Balkan crisis.
18. *S-Peterburgskie Vedomosti*, Nov. 30, A. D. Gradovskii, "Cherniaevskii vopros."

correct, but that their inopportune squabble discouraged gifts to the Slavs and stimulated foreign criticisms of Russia.[19] Soon the affair degenerated into a personal feud between Cherniaev and Kraevskii.[20]

From the debate both sides emerged badly scarred. *Golos* and its editor attracted popular hostility for questioning the motives of those who assisted the South Slavs. These accusations further clouded Cherniaev's dubious reputation, but many Russians considered him a martyr to the Slav cause.[21] Such sentiment, while not resurrecting Cherniaev, damaged the liberals and helped push the hesitant emperor into war with Turkey.

In April 1877 the Russian government reluctantly declared war on Turkey. For almost two years Russia had cooperated in diplomatic efforts to assist the Balkan Christians, but now Alexander II agreed sadly that war seemed the only honorable means to achieve Russia's aims. Cherniaev's actions had contributed importantly to the emperor's decision. The ultimatum of October 1876, the Kremlin speech and partial mobilization in November, provoked by Serbia's defeat, had committed Russia to win concessions for the Christians. Yet the Turks, buttressed secretly by England, refused to yield. Nor would the tsar accept peace at any price as some ministers advised. Unwilling to risk isolation and another Crimean fiasco, he sought support from the German powers. Berlin encouraged him to fight, but the tsar realized that this would be perilous without Austrian consent. In March 1877 Austria promised to remain neutral in a Russo-Turkish conflict unless Russia erected a great South Slav state. Russia pushed war preparations while Gorchakov continued to seek peace. Turkey's

19. osvob, i: 505–506, memorandum of 10 November 1876.

20. In *Sovremennye Izvestiia*, no. 353 (1877) Cherniaev defended the volunteers unconditionally and listed his expenditures. Kraevskii retorted in *Otechestvennye zapiski*, ccxxxiv (Jan. 1878), pp. 75–92. Cherniaev finally threatened Kraevskii personally unless *Golos* halted its attacks on his public activity. gim, ed. khr. 36, l. 50, Cherniaev to Kraevskii, 25 March 1878.

21. Professor S. A. Nikitin, a leading Soviet historian, makes this perceptive assessment: "Russian society judged not Cherniaev and the volunteers but Kraevskii and *Golos*. It did not make its judgment on the basis of the results, and its attitude toward the participants did not depend upon their successes. No matter how many drunkards and troublemakers there were among the volunteers, no matter how incompetent was Cherniaev, society saw in him and his fellow fighters the expression of their empathy, their aspirations to emancipate the Slavs. . . . By reflecting the official relationship toward Cherniaev, *Golos* created around itself an atmosphere of indignation and protest." "Russkoe obshchestvo," pp. 1034-1035.

rejection of the London Protocol, a last diplomatic device to avert war, aided Petersburg to justify a war which its blunders had helped to provoke.

Alexander II hastened to army headquarters in Kishinev with the heir, the grand dukes and a huge suite. To spare Russian blood he had avoided war as long as possible. "Once Russia's honor was affected," he told his officers, "I was convinced that all of us would stand by our country. God be with you!" On April 12, 1877, he signed the declaration of war.[22] Many foreign observers doubted official claims of Russian public enthusiasm for the struggle.[23] But months of frustration and uncertainty were over. Unity prevailed. The Panslavs, although disappointed by Alexander's failure to refer specifically to the Slav cause, mostly rallied behind the government; the Slav committees abandoned their independent activity.[24]

As Panslavs and officialdom were reconciled, Cherniaev's return became possible. In March his wife had implored the emperor: "Sire! Allow him to return to his homeland! He is neither a traitor nor a conspirator, but a loyal man devoted heart and soul to throne and country. . . . Besides, why prohibit his entry into his country? The query is bold since it is made to Your Majesty, but when the heart bleeds, it no longer uses words prescribed by etiquette and custom. It turns with courage and abandon to a great and illustrious Sovereign . . . [in behalf of] a family consistently slandered by implacable enemies and liars!" With his tiny pension her husband could not support his numerous family. A move to Kiev would ruin them. If the emperor spurned her request, she must rejoin her husband abroad. She pleaded, "Have pity, Sire! A trip in the midst of winter is a death sentence for the frail young beings and virtually so for me, pregnant and sick in body and soul." She enclosed Cherniaev's recent statement: "I know that I am not a conspirator, . . . and have always favored the monarchy."[25]

Cherniaev was authorized to proceed to Kishinev and left Paris just before war broke out. In Kishinev he stayed with a friend,

22. Tatishchev, II: 372–373.

23. See *Journal du Vicomte E. M. de Vögué* (Paris, 1932), pp. 37–39. Concluded the Austrian ambassador in Petersburg: "Genuine enthusiasm for this war does *not* exist in Russia." HHSA, Langenau to Andrassy, 27 April/9 May 1877, no. 24 A–D.

24. Aksakov, *Sochineniia*, I: 251 ff; Nikitin, *Slavianskie*, p. 342.

25. TSGAOR, f. 109, op. 4, d. 436, ll. 74–75, A. A. Cherniaeva to Alexander II, 10 March 1877. Mezentsov replied that the emperor still considered Cherniaev's return to Russia inopportune (l. 76).

Stolypin. At 5 A.M. Cherniaev was suddenly awakened: a colonel of gendarmes had come for him: "The thought flashed through my mind: they intend to arrest me and exile me somewhere. On the little table next to me lay my papers. Hastily gathering them up and awakening Stolypin, I asked him that in case I was arrested, to inform my family. He did not wish to believe that such a foul trick would be played on me here." The colonel asked him to come to the gendarmerie at nine. Why had he been awakened so early? asked Cherniaev. "To be sure to find you at home." At the gendarmerie General Mezentsov, telling him that the tsar would see him, warned him against being obstinate. "Has it gone so far," retorted Cherniaev, "that you even doubt my ability to speak with the Sovereign?"[26]

Still in retirement, he went in civilian clothes. Alexander received him coolly. He looked changed and sickly. "You promised me not to travel to Serbia," he began reproachfully, "but you did not keep your word." "That is not so, Sire," Cherniaev replied, "I promised Your Majesty not to join the Herzegovinians. . . ." "Why did you proclaim Milan king?" persisted the tsar. "That caused me much anxiety and alarm." Cherniaev answered, "I saw no other way to compel the Serbs to fight. I had to indicate a goal they would fight for. By proclaiming Milan king, I revealed such a goal to them: Serbia's complete independence." "But afterwards you were in Prague. You almost involved me in a quarrel with my friend and neighbor, the Austrian emperor," said Alexander sternly. Cherniaev explained, "Truly I was in Prague, Your Majesty, but since I was then the standard bearer of the Slav idea, I had to appear among the Austrian Slavs to ascertain their way of thinking and attitude toward the ideal I had fought for. But now when you, Sire, have taken the cause into your powerful hands, I have retired from this affair." The tsar replied more warmly: "All right, let us forget all that. We shall not talk any more about the past. . . . I forgive you. A decree will be issued tomorrow assigning you to service." Graciously he extended his hand to Cherniaev.

The next day Cherniaev presented himself in a borrowed uniform whose sleeves were too short. Alexander joked: "You resemble a police chief rather than a fighting general." Seemingly embarrassed, he said kindly: "I am sending you to the Caucasus. You have served

---

26. DAS PO, 26/229; IISG, "Biografiia," pp. 384–386; "Avtobiografiia," p. 19.

there and know the region well." At this clear sign of disfavor Cherniaev grew pale. As he began to protest, Alexander said: "Go see the war minister." Then recalling their bitter feud, he added hastily: "No don't go! He will write to you."

To be sent to the Caucasus, away from the Slav lands where he had support and knew the enemy, recalled Cherniaev, would amount to exile. His Russian and Austrian enemies must have been intriguing. Later he wrote: "Austria urged that I be sent a maximum distance from the Slavs for whose liberation Russia had resolved to continue the struggle begun by Serbia under my leadership."

Grand Duke Nikolai Nikolaevich, commander in chief of the Balkan theater, received Chernaiev heartily: "Well we declared war, are you satisfied?" "How many troops does Your Highness have?" asked Cherniaev bluntly. "200,000," responded the grand duke. "That is too few. You should have at least 500,000 or you will be beaten." The tsar's brother blanched. "How then did you hold out with a handful of Serbs?" "That was another time and under different conditions. With those forces you won't even reach the Balkan Mountains," warned Cherniaev. "I intend to reach Constantinople!" announced the grand duke. Cherniaev reiterated: "In view of the numerous Turkish army and the war theater's size, you will be beaten." Nikolai Nikolaevich denied this indignantly but twice requested the emperor to make Cherniaev his chief of staff. When Alexander refused, the grand duke gave Chernaiev a letter to his brother, Mikhail Nikolaevich, commander in the Caucasus.[27]

Forgiven and restored to his former rank, Cherniaev could travel freely until definitely assigned. Aksakov rejoiced at his return to Russia and urged him to accept any assignment. "I am still ignorant of the circumstances of this return, but even the most unfavorable, even apparently humiliating conditions are preferable and more worthy of you than remaining outside Russia in wartime. . . ." Aksakov asked his help in the struggle "with homegrown foreigners, petty intrigue, envy, triviality and stupidity." Cherniaev had a moral duty to participate in the war; "behind you will be the sympathies of all Russia."[28] Still under police surveillance, Cherniaev went to Moscow. Some two hundred persons, mostly merchants, accompa-

27. GIM, "Avtobiografiia Cherniaeva," pp. 9–10. Amazed at the tsar's unusual deference to Cherniaev, Miliutin helped persuade Alexander to assign him to the Caucasus. *Dnevnik*, II: 160, 16 and 17 April 1877.

28. GIM, ed. khr. 49, Aksakov to Cherniaev, 12 April 1877 (Moscow).

nied him through the streets shouting hurrahs.[29]

Aksakov deplored official Russia's refusal to use Cherniaev in the Balkans, but Prince Cherkasskii, a Panslav in charge of occupied Bulgaria, disagreed emphatically: "I saw him a few times and frankly he produced the most distressing impression. This is a man forever ruined by excessive false pride, conceit and the grossest vanity. I persuaded him to submit [to the emperor] unconditionally and accept whatever is offered him. I did this most cautiously (since he is obviously mentally ill) and told him with friendly but merciless frankness." No longer could Cherniaev help Russia in the Balkans, warned Cherkasskii, because of his tactlessness. Perhaps he could command a division in Asia Minor. The prince scoffed at Cherniaev's belief that he was indispensable. Army friends considered him incapable of holding a high military post.[30]

For two months Cherniaev awaited a worthy assignment. Writing Aksakov he blamed this delay on the war minister: "I am still in the same indefinite position. I was told that M. N. [Grand Duke Mikhail Nikolaevich] requested that I not be sent to the Caucasus for which imperial consent had been received. They are keeping me in uniform and give me nothing for my support. Miliutin remains true to his character to the end."[31] At Slav Committee functions in St. Petersburg he was greeted by applause but felt insulted at not being given an independent command. "He would have preferred most of all to obtain a 20,000 man corps for an attack on India!!" noted Kireev. Cherniaev believed that Russia would be defeated without his leadership. After a few military disasters, fate would thrust him forward. "I was sorry to hear him talk," wrote Kireev. "He seemed very petty to me. I advised him not to delay his departure."[32]

Rejecting this sound advice, Cherniaev still awaited that elusive summons to greatness. His prediction of Russian defeats came true. During July and August Nikolai Nikolaevich's army thrice assaulted the Turkish fortress of Plevna only to be hurled back with frightful losses. The grand duke's prestige was undermined, but few demanded that Cherniaev replace him!

Early July found him still in Moscow's Hotel Diuso. Everyone

---

29. TSGAOR, f. 109, op. 4, d. 436, l. 81, 25 April 1877 (Moscow).

30. "Perepiska Aksakova s Cherkasskim," *Slavianskii sbornik* (Moscow, 1948), pp. 167-171, Aksakov to Cherkasskii, 25 April 1877; Cherkasskii to Aksakov, 2 May 1877.

31. ORSS, Aksakov, no. 387, Cherniaev to Aksakov, 5 May 1877.

32. ORBL, Kireev, Dnevnik, VII: 51-52, 14 May 1877.

recognized him on the street and removed their hats. "Cherniaev does not seem to consider going to the Caucasus army and regards his assignment as insulting," reported the Third Section's agent. He pleaded illness "though he appears completely well." Even in Moscow the public deemed his feud with the war minister and his entire conduct most inappropriate. In a letter intercepted by the political police, a former *Russkii Mir* colleague, noting Cherniaev's continuing influence with the newspaper, questioned his opposition to the government. Would not the purity of *Russkii Mir*'s motives be suspect if it attacked Petersburg now? No opposition in wartime was justifiable. "If last year *Golos* paid heavily for its sallies against the Serbs and volunteers, how would it be with a paper attacking the actions of our own army and its leaders in the present excited condition of the entire society?" Continued his correspondent: "Complete restraint and caution are now required by censorship conditions, common sense and true Russian interests." "Very sensible ideas," commented the tsar, "but it also reveals what type of man Cherniaev is!"[33]

To Slonimskii, the editor of *Russkii Mir*, Cherniaev reiterated that the Turks should be driven from Europe. In the past Russia had fought unselfishly for its neighbors, but now the Eastern question could be solved. Cherniaev wrote, "We must not retreat before diplomatic threats but only before actual force, and then after crossing swords with it." If one powerful army remained at Kiev to watch Austria and another supported the Danubian forces, Russia could capture Constantinople and defy Europe. He continued: "A bitter struggle is occurring on the Danube between the diplomats and the military men. Upon who pulls harder will depend the [Russian] government's great popularity or the decline of its prestige among the people. *The latter is even more desirable for me.*"[34] Cherniaev still hoped that an unsuccessful war would discredit his opponents.

Cherniaev received his orders and on July 20 he finally departed for the Caucasus. In Aleksandropol, Grand Duke Mikhail Nikolaevich assured him coldly that everything was going well at the front. ("The true state of affairs was known to me," commented Cherniaev.) "At present I have no post for you, but when there is a

33. TSGAOR, op. 4, d. 436, l. 85, 9 July 1877; ll. 82–84, 25 June 1877, [Slonimskii] to Cherniaev.

34. "Dva pisma," VE (Feb. 1909), pp. 889–890, Cherniaev to Slonimskii, 11 July 1877. Cherniaev praised highly Slonimskii's lead of July 10 advocating destruction of Turkish rule in the Balkans.

vacancy, I shall assign you a command according to your rank." This would entitle him only to a brigade. The grand duke and his staff departed for the front leaving Cherniaev with the stores and hospital personnel.[35]

Dissatisfied with quiet Aleksandropol, he went to Piatigorsk "to take a cure" and sat out the war at this spa fuming and intriguing. The grand duke refused to remove an experienced general to give him a prominent command. Surrounding himself with young colonels, Cherniaev denounced the conduct of the war in Asia Minor and predicted that nothing could be achieved in 1877. Then Mukhtar Pasha's army was completely defeated on the heights which Cherniaev had pronounced impregnable.[36]

Meanwhile Monteverde encouraged him to oppose the government. Calling Plevna Russia's Sedan,[37] he urged Cherniaev to lead a nationalist party to unseat the liberals after defeat. The "entire existing order of things" would fall. At Plevna, claimed Monteverde, the tsar had been pitiful and the grand duke stupid. After repeated setbacks, "their situation is comical." Rejoicing at official discomfiture, he sought to make Cherniaev openly disloyal: "Your situation is magnificent and favorable since you have taken no part in this war. . . ." Afterward, he could lead the disaffected, but now he should prepare the way with a press campaign in *Russkii Mir*. He suggested, "It would be so easy for it to crack the whip a little without compromising itself particularly."[38]

Instead Mikhail Grigorevich limited himself to criticisms and complaints. He was no revolutionary. In mid-October he wrote Count Vorontsov-Dashkov:

> I turn to you when all others in power or near it have turned from me, and no wonder. I not merely began this war, but even before it began campaigned against all [the evils] which it has revealed. Official persons and their few adherents accuse me of causing national ruin and revealing Russia's insolvency in a strug-

35. TSGAOR, op. 4, d. 436, ll. 86–89; IISG, "Avtobiografiia," pp. 20–21; GIM, ed. khr. 14, l. 120, Cherniaev to Vorontsov-Dashkov, undated draft.

36. Gradovskii, "Arkhistratig," p. 124. At the time Gradovskii was serving in the Caucasus.

37. At Sedan in 1870 Napoleon III's French army was defeated ignominiously by Prussia. Shortly afterward his Second Empire collapsed.

38. GIM, ed. khr. 48, ll. 58–59, Monteverde to Cherniaev, 8 October 1877 (Paris).

gle with a weaker opponent. Meanwhile the entire people express-
es signs of sympathy and thankfulness towards me which they have
never before shown towards a private person.

In this war the government found that it had to restrain "the people's
aspiration to sacrifice to realize their historic destiny."[39] He alone
symbolized the true national Russia. Cherniaev's capacity for self-
delusion seemed endless.

His attempts to win an undeserved post contrasted unfavorably
with General M. D. Skobelev's behavior. Arriving in the Balkans
after the war began, Skobelev served first as an orderly, then commanded a secondary detachment. His willingness to accept what
was offered in order to see action won him deserved, though exaggerated, acclaim. Had Cherniaev participated as brigade commander
in a few battles, he could have shared in the glory of victory.[40]

Henceforth he would be overshadowed by Skobelev who emerged
from the war as the redoubtable "White General," renowned for his
courage. The capture of Plevna, advance to Constantinople and
victories in the Caucasus made nonsense of Cherniaev's dire prophe-
cies. Skobelev became the darling of conservative nationalists while
Cherniaev seemed slated for oblivion.

39. Ibid., ed. khr. 35, l. 37, Cherniaev to Vorontsov-Dashkov, 16 October 1877.
40. Gradovskii, *M. D. Skobelev* (St. Petersburg, 1884), pp. 17–20.

CHAPTER XIII

The Serbian Railway

AFTER THE Russo-Turkish War Cherniaev launched a new campaign: to build Serbia's railroads, prevent Austria from dominating
Serbia and open the way to Russian economic and political influence
there. Like many of his undertakings, this too proved to be unrealistic.

At the war's end Cherniaev was permitted to leave the Caucasus,
but his conduct there had made a new military assignment unthinkable. When he arrived in St. Petersburg, the railway station was
crowded with people of all ages and positions. As he descended from
the platform, heads were bared, and Orthodox Russia's favorite
song, "Spasi Gospodi liudi Tvoi," was sung. All national hopes and
aspirations, wrote Antonina with typical exaggeration, were cen-
tered behind General Cherniaev, bearer of the Slav idea. To the
disgraced general this was some consolation. "Out of favor with the
emperor and the omnipotent Miliutin, he could expect nothing in
the service." In semiretirement he busied himself with Slav affairs
and commercial ventures.[1]

Russia had been victorious in war. When the Russians reached
Constantinople, the Turks had agreed to an armistice embodying all

1. IISG, "Biografiia," pp. 422–430.

their demands. The resulting Treaty of San Stefano in March 1878 reflected the apparent triumph of the Panslavs, and its architect, Count Ignatiev, became the man of the hour. But the treaty caused dissension among the South Slavs and antagonized the powers. Ignatiev's Big Bulgaria alienated Serbia and helped drive her into the arms of Austria. Even *Russkii Mir* supported Belgrade's protests against San Stefano;[2] England and Austria insisted that it be revised. To avert war with a European coalition, Alexander II submitted the treaty reluctantly to the powers.

Even before the Berlin Congress convened in June 1878, Russian Panslavs predicted disaster and humiliation. If necessary, they declared, Russia should fight Europe singlehanded to preserve its honor and conquests. The tsar and Miliutin, his chief adviser, were more realistic. Russia's Balkan army, exhausted and weakened by disease, could scarcely handle the Turks, much less the powers. At Berlin, Russia yielded. The Panslavs' program was repudiated: Bulgaria was reduced and divided; other wartime gains were whittled down. Serbia, to gain territory from Bulgaria, concluded agreements which would make her an Austrian satellite.[3]

Russian nationalists were infuriated and dismayed. The war had been won, but the cowardly diplomats had lost the peace. Russia's position in the Balkans had been surrendered to Austria, thundered Aksakov in a great speech to the Moscow Slav Society. The Berlin Treaty signified her abdication as defender of the Slavs and Orthodox. Fighting on any terms was preferable to such a shameful settlement.[4] The government promptly closed the society and exiled Aksakov. To keep peace with the powers official Russia repudiated the Panslavs. Cherniaev, disgusted with government policy, found St. Petersburg intolerable and moved his family to a modest apartment in Moscow. Slavophiles there greeted them warmly, and he spent hours with intimate friends reflecting upon Russia's past. Russia had had five capitals: Novgorod, Kiev, Vladimir, Moscow, and St. Petersburg. "This wandering retarded our development but preserved our energy as a youthful people able to work out its own culture and fulfill its historical tasks," wrote Cherniaev. The St. Petersburg period had involved academic, unrealistic dependence upon Europe. Now the capital should return to Kiev: "The Baltic and Polish

2. *Russkii Mir*, 11, 19 February 1878.
3. MacKenzie, *The Serbs*, p. 311.
4. Aksakov, *Sochineniia*, I: 297–308, speech of June 22.

questions would solve themselves, our influence upon events in Turkey and Persia would increase tenfold, the Caucasus would become truly Russian, and our Central Asian possessions would be properly developed and consolidated. . . . But our principal benefit would be moral since new forces would emerge which outworn Petersburg, always alien to Russia, could not inspire."[5]

Russian prestige in the western Balkans declined sharply. Baron Jomini of the foreign ministry predicted accurately that the Serbian states would succumb to western influence because of Austria's industrial and commercial superiority over Russia. Material interests drew the South Slavs toward Vienna. "They have nothing to sell to us or buy from us, nor we to them," he lamented. "With the aid of railroads, their ties with Austria and the West will soon become indissoluble."[6]

Cherniaev sought to prevent this by winning the concession to build Serbia's railroads. After the Congress he wrote Prince Milan: "Sire, please accept my devoted congratulations on occasion of Europe's recognition of your people's independence, won with such effort and sacrifice. The Balkan Christians will always remember that it was to your initiative and that of your people that they owe the improvement of their condition." The prince thanked him warmly, recalling that in 1876 "you nobly and bravely fulfilled your duty and as commander in chief of the Serbian army helped Serbia greatly to reveal its vital strength and obtain the right to become an independent country."[7] Such assurances cost nothing. Could Cherniaev translate them into economic commitments?

Since the 1860s Serbian leaders had considered railway construction. In the mid-1870s Ponson, a French engineer, had made surveys but the war halted progress. At the Berlin Congress, Serbia promised to conclude a railway convention with Austria but theoretically could grant anyone the concession to construct its lines. The Serbian railways, some publicists believed, had dazzling commercial possibilities: linked with the Austrian and Turkish networks, they could stimulate Balkan trade with Europe and Asia Minor and bring their builder large profits.

Soon after the Congress Cherniaev and his former chief of staff

5. IISG, "Biografiia," pp. 425–426.
6. C. and B. Jelavich, *Russia in the East, 1876–1880* (Leiden, 1959), pp. 86–87, Jomini to Girs, 9 October 1878.
7. "K. M. G. Cherniaevu," RA (1914), I: 194, July 1878.

Colonel Komarov induced S. S. Poliakov, a wealthy Russian banker, to propose building the Belgrade-Niš railroad to bring "activity, money and progress to the Serbian people." Komarov's talks with the Serbs convinced him they wanted a Russian company to construct the line. If Baron Hirsch of Austria, controlling neighboring Austrian and Turkish railways, built it, Vienna's stranglehold over Serbia would be complete. Foreign firms, noted Komarov, had already made offers; the prince must decide.[8] When Poliakov put up capital, Cherniaev informed Prince Milan that his company could construct the Belgrade-Niš railroad after issuing stock in Serbia. All construction personnel must be Russian except for a few Serbian engineers. His plan would prevent the line from "passing into enemy [Austrian] hands."

Without the prince's encouragement, Cherniaev traveled to Paris to make arrangements with bankers. In January 1879 he went to Serbia to negotiate an agreement. His telegram to Milan was answered coolly by the minister of communications: "The railroad question is not yet ripe for negotiation." Cherniaev pressed for an interview, but Milan refused to see him.

Not to be put off, Mikhail Grigorevich urged Milan's uncle to assist him in assuring Serbia's emancipation: "Having decided in 1876 to go to Serbia to fight for its political independence, I was convinced that the principality with its dynasty must become the Piedmont for the entire Serbian nation. Thanks to the prince's energy and the people's sacrifices, Serbia has attained political independence, but to serve as the nucleus for Serbian unification, she has as yet done nothing to acquire economic independence." As the prince refused to see him, "I now find myself in an embarrassing position and ask you to sound out the terrain and tell me categorically whether the matter will be decided in my favor."[9] He moved on into Bulgaria, ostensibly to visit battlefields. As he approached Niš, Milan reluctantly agreed to talk but made no commitment on the railroad question.[10]

A few partisans greeted Cherniaev's reappearance in Serbia. "Your renewed presence in Serbia has excited lively enthusiasm among the population," wrote Kosta Ristić, his sly former

8. GIM, ed. khr. 24, ll. 1–6, V. V. Komarov to S. S. Poliakov, 3–4 October 1878.

9. Ibid., ll. 24–28, Cherniaev to Milan, 15 November 1878 and 17 January 1879; ll. 19–21, Cherniaev to "Mon Colonel" [probably Catargi], undated.

10. HHSA, Herbert to Andrassy, (21 January)/2 February 1879, no. 27.

treasurer. Cherniaev's "bold initiative, constant energy and sustained courage" had enabled the South Slavs to free themselves from the Turkish yoke. Such flattery aimed to extort new money although Cherniaev still sought to settle his staff's debts from 1876.[11] Russia's pro-Slav press expressed outrage at Milan's coolness toward Cherniaev, but N. K. Girs of the foreign office emphasized that his government had not authorized his trip. The Russian commander in the Balkans was instructed: "observe that agitator and send him home if he makes trouble in Bulgaria."[12] However, Cherniaev soon returned to Russia voluntarily. "As to the Serbian railway," he wrote Nikolai, "there is still nothing definite. . . . So far I have only succeeded in persuading the Serbian smart alecks not to hand over the railroad's construction to the Austrians despite their tempting promises."[13]

The Cherniaev-Poliakov offer was one factor in a complex struggle of Russophile and Austrophile factions in Serbia. Powerful pressure from Vienna was undermining Russian influence. When the Serbian minister of education advocated making Russian a compulsory subject in Serbian schools, he was dropped from the Ristić cabinet. Finance Minister Vladimir Jovanović had encouraged Cherniaev to create Russian steamship service between Odessa and Belgrade, but that scheme also had to be abandoned.[14]

Trying to balance Serbia between its two great neighbors, Ristić welcomed connections with Russia but could not secure favorable terms for railroad construction through open competition. Serbia's credit was poor and Austria's pressure too great. St. Petersburg urged Belgrade to let a Russian company construct Serbian railroads, but the Cherniaev-Poliakov firm insisted on Serbia's entire state revenue as security. Baranov's powerful Russo-Belgian company found Serbia's inability to meet old foreign debts an insuperable obstacle.[15] The railway issue remained unresolved.

Early in 1880 Cherniaev went to Belgrade empowered by Polia-

11. GIM, ed. khr. 15, ll. 28–29, K. Ristić to Cherniaev, 6 February 1879.

12. HHSA, Langenau to Andrassy, 15/27 February 1879, telegram no. 32; Miliutin, *Dnevnik*, III: 119, 10 February 1879.

13. GIM, ed. khr. 39, ll. 30–31, 16 April 1879.

14. HHSA, Langenau to Andrassy, (30 Nov.)/12 December 1878, no. 53E; Herbert to Andrassy, (12)/24 December 1878, no. 175; GIM, ed. khr. 15, Jovanović to Cherniaev, 15 November 1878.

15. ASANU, 9914/5, "Izveštaj odbora železničkog," 4 March 1881; 9327/9, Dnevnik Miličevića, 11 December 1878, p. 92; 11 March 1879, p. 109 reverse.

kov to negotiate a railroad agreement; he also carried Moscow Slav Society funds to commission a monument near Aleksinac to dead volunteers. Professor P. A. Kulakovskii, a Russian Slavophile in Belgrade, warned Aksakov that the volunteers and Cherniaev had become unpopular there: "I didn't wish to tell Cherniaev this in Moscow, but it is my duty to inform you." Now the generalissimo was a railroad entrepreneur! Non-Russians should construct Serbia's railroads, argued Kulakovskii. "We will scarcely build them well, and the Serbs will blame us for the financial difficulties." Austrian pressure was increasing Serbian sympathy for Russia. Why not let Vienna further oppress the Serbs?

Impecunious and naive as ever, Cherniaev took up residence at an expensive Belgrade hotel only to be fleeced by the Serbs. Wrote Kulakovskii: "He is an amazing individual! One can love and respect him, but one must always marvel at him. No sooner had he arrived than he was surrounded by all sorts of riffraff who swindled money from him. He just threw rubles in all directions giving them to anyone who asked. Sometimes gifts were as large as 250 rubles." Publicly Cherniaev denounced whatever he disliked in Russia, but he reacted angrily to similar criticisms in the Serbian press. At first he dealt with the Ristić government, but when it deceived him, he turned to the opposition. Soon he was completely alone.[16] Blocked on the railroad, his funds exhausted, he left Belgrade in disgust.

In May he returned for a longer stay. He told Milan Milićević that Ristić's recent railway convention with Austria[17] was treason. Praising the Bulgarians, he predicted that within fifteen years they would all speak Russian. "I am convinced that eventually the Serbs too will speak either Russian or German." To Milićević he sounded like "a true Muscovite beast. . . . My hair stands on end when I think how crazy are some of those damned brothers of ours."[18] Cherniaev's Panslavism had become Great Russian imperialism. The "Slav brothers" were to be subjugated, Russified and exploited.

Finding Belgrade Serbs cool to his schemes, he concluded that they were Russophobic and corrupted. The few Russians still living

---

16. "Pisma M. G. Cherniaeva i P. A. Kulakovskogo k I. S. Aksakovu," *Golos Minuvshego* (1915), IX: 241–243, Kulakovskii to Aksakov, 15 January and January 1880.

17. By the treaty of March 28, 1880, Serbia pledged to construct a Belgrade-Vranje railway within three years of ratification.

18. ASANU, 9327/10, Dnevnik Milićevića, 12 and 14 May 1880, pp. 56–57.

there, he claimed, yearned to leave as soon as possible: "In a few days I shall travel into Serbia's interior ostensibly to consecrate the foundations of the monument to the Russian volunteers who fell on the ungrateful Serbian plains, but actually to size up the mood of this lazy, cowardly people which nonetheless still places all its hopes in Russia." The Serbs had approved his sketch of the monument but would not help build it. Prospects for the railway were dark. The Serbs' footdragging was due to the "bribery of the prince and Ristić by Frémy and Fillèle Company." That was Serbia's seamy side. Behind Frémy and Fillèle lurked the Austrian Staatsbahn. Each had been promised two million francs. Cherniaev observed, "The minority [of Serbs] gnashes its teeth at this sellout of the country, but as you know the masses are sheep."

In Serbia's interior his mood was transformed. Aleksinac's populace greeted him and helped construct the monument. "Everywhere there are portraits of the tsar and pictures of the Battle of Plevna. . . . Everywhere they praise the volunteers' bravery and reproach their own officers." He sought funds to pay his Serbian workers,[19] but Aksakov warned that Russians would no longer sacrifice for the Slavs. On November 2, 1880, flanked by Russians and Serbian representatives, Cherniaev proudly dedicated the monument.[20]

On his return to Belgrade, Cherniaev denounced the Serbian intelligentsia's Russophobia and pro-westernism, which he ascribed to feelings of inferiority: "Undeveloped, semi-educated, irreligious, lacking moral standards or feelings of duty, the Serbian intelligentsia hates and fears Frenchmen, Englishmen, Germans and Russians, and even its brother Serbs beyond the Sava, realizing that they are all superior. . . . This feeling of hatred for Russia is one of self-preservation." Intellectuals, lacking roots in the Serbian people, saw their position crumbling. Serbia was too undeveloped to lead South Slav unification. Within five years Bulgaria would surpass it.[21] "Your letter is worth an entire article," replied Aksakov. "I agree completely with your views about the Serbian intelligentsia except that I do not believe in Austrian medicine." Serbian leaders, he

19. "Pisma . . . k Aksakovu," pp. 235–238, Cherniaev to Aksakov, 25 July 1880 (Belgrade), 8 August 1880 (Aleksinac).

20. GIM, ed. khr. 15, Aksakov to Cherniaev, 4 and 27 August, 16 September 1880; ASANU, 9327/10, Dnevnik Miličevića, 5 November 1880, p. 75.

21. "Pisma . . . k Aksakovu," pp. 238–240, Cherniaev to Aksakov, 14 September 1880.

cautioned, apparently had promised the railroad concession to Austria.[22]

His warning was well founded. The fall of the Ristić government before Austrian pressure in October 1880 dashed Cherniaev's hopes. Convinced that Serbia must cooperate with Vienna, Prince Milan brought Milan Piročanac's Austrophile Progressive cabinet into power. In a secret scramble for the railroad concession, E. Bontoux's Parisian firm l'Union Générale had decisive advantages: it was expert, amply financed, and Austrian-backed. Vienna put pressure on the prince and bribed leading Progressive and Radicals generously. Milan insisted that Bontoux's terms be accepted, and on January 22, 1881, the Progressive cabinet consented.[23]

Disregarding the signs, Cherniaev fought for his lost cause to the end. Taking undeserved credit for the fall of Ristić, he wrote that the new ministry was negotiating with his company. Defiantly he wrote Komarov who was working with Baranov's firm: "When Ristić, contrary to the prince, reacted hostilely to our proposal and compelled me to work against him here, you not only did not print any of my messages in your newspaper bu continually played up to him. This did very little damage to our affairs but greatly damaged your paper with Serbian public opinion. My efforts were crowned with success and Ristić's fall was received with enthusiasm by the entire country."[24] But it insured Serbia's complete subservience to Austria.

Not until mid-December, when Bontoux's victory was nigh, did Poliakov send Cherniaev a formal proposal for the railroad. Even then his terms were less generous than Bontoux's. If Belgrade accepted them, Poliakov would dispatch engineers and perhaps come himself. "I wish you success with all my heart," he telegraphed Cherniaev, "and greatly regret all your tireless efforts which the Serbian government, seeking to fall into Austria-Hungary's net, does not wish to utilize." If Bontoux won, Milan would fall and Serbia would be ruined. "At least you have done your work before God, your conscience, the Serbs, the whole world and Russia."[25]

22. GIM, ed. khr. 15, Aksakov to Cherniaev, 5 October 1880.

23. V. Vučković, "Pad generalne unije i proglas Kraljevine," *Glas Srpske Akademije Nauke i Umetnosti,* CCXVII, odeljenje društvenih nauka, n.s., knj. 4, pp. 49-51; E. Bontoux, *L'Union Générale* (Paris, 1888), pp. 38-56; S. Jovanović, *Vlada Milana,* II: 93-95.

24. TSGALI, f. 1643, Komarov, op. 1, no. 22, Cherniaev to Komarov, 4 December [1880].

25. GIM, ed. khr. 24, ll. 35–41, S. S. Poliakov to Cherniaev, 12 and 17 December 1880. Their telegraphic exchange is in ll. 41–67.

In January 1881 Mikhail Grigorevich, abandoning his defiant optimism, expressed to Aksakov his despair over the situation in Serbia: "Amazing things are happening in little Serbia with her strawlike independence. She has turned literally into an Austrian province and Milan into an Austrian official straining to display devotion to the House of Habsburg. . . . The swineherds [Serbs] are still dazed at this, but they probably won't make any major trouble." Except for Montenegro, Serbian unification under the Habsburgs seemed virtually complete. Cherniaev complained: "You cannot imagine what humiliation has been inflicted on me in nasty little Serbia. . . . It is truly indecent to keep an entire mission waiting here for nothing. . . . Milan has given the Serbian railroad to the Hungarians. . . . Needless to say Petersburg is taking bitter revenge on [national] Russia for daring to have its own view in 1876 . . . , 400,000 lives and 1,300,000,000 rubles [Cherniaev's exaggerated estimate of the cost of the Russo-Turkish War] for Austrian enslavement of the western half of the Balkan peninsula. It is sad, a thousand times sad." Unable to dominate or exploit Serbia, Cherniaev gave up on the country.

Bontoux's proposal still required Assembly sanction. The Radicals, some favoring Baranov or Poliakov, denounced the secrecy and high cost of the concession and the danger of economic subservience to Austria. But the prince was already committed to Vienna. During the debate he warned that if Cherniaev obtained the concession, four thousand Russian railway workers would invade Serbia! Kulakovskii found Serbian opinion deeply disturbed: some hoped official Russia would intervene in Cherniaev's behalf. But St. Petersburg had no such intention. Cherniaev was "a sick man with irritated nerves and thoughts," wrote Kulakovskii. "In Belgrade he often saw things wholly inside out, accepting as pure truth the . . . wildest inventions."[26]

On March 10, 1881, the Serbian Assembly voted ninety-seven to fifty-seven to ratify the arrangement with Bontoux. Cherniaev's work in Serbia was over. Though the monument to the volunteers and to his proudest hour in Serbia stood above Aleksinac, his other efforts had failed. He was completely disillusioned. Undeceived by the general, Prince Milan had yielded to European capital and

26. "Pisma . . . Aksakovu," pp. 240–241, Cherniaev to Aksakov, 19 January 1881; Kulakovskii to Aksakov, 4 March 1881.

Austrian power. Though many Serbs still looked to Russia for salvation, Serbia would remain firmly in the Austrian camp until the end of the Obrenović dynasty in 1903.

CHAPTER XIV

The Governor General

ON MARCH 1, 1881, Cherniaev's dreams were revived by an event which profoundly affected Russian history. A terrorist from the conspiratorial group, Narodnaia Volia, threw a bomb at Alexander II on the banks of the Ekaterinskii Canal in St. Petersburg. The mortally wounded tsar died an hour later in the Winter Palace attended by the shocked imperial family.[1] This bloody deed delivered Russia to the heavyhanded reaction of Alexander III and brought the country to a turning point. The dead tsar had just approved Count Loris-Melikov's "constitution" granting selected representatives a consultative voice in legislation. The assassination produced confusion and panic. But soon a new regime emerged directed by K. P. Pobedonostsev, procurator of the Holy Synod.

This grey eminence of moribund tsarism became the most powerful man in Russia. Tutor to the new emperor, distinguished jurist and author, Pobedonostsev wholly dominated Alexander III during that first crucial year and framed most public pronouncements. His stern presence returned Russia politically to the times of Nicholas I. Enthroned were the sacred principles of the 1830s: Autocracy, Orthodoxy and Nationalism. Pobedonostsev wrote his former pupil:

1. Tatishchev, II: 655–657; Schweinitz, II: 151–152.

"The people believes in the will of God and at His order places its hopes in you and in the powerful authority God has entrusted to you. May . . . the people's faith give you strength and intelligence to rule, a strong hand and a powerful will." There must be no compromise with revolution or the siren songs of liberalism. "The insane villains who killed your father will not be satisfied by concessions. . . . They can be stilled, the evil seed can be torn out only by . . . blood and iron." Remove liberal ministers, he suggested, and rely on that true Russian, Count Ignatiev. A new policy should be proclaimed immediately. Talk about freedom of the press, free meetings and a representative assembly must cease. Pobedonostsev advised, "They are the lies of empty, flabby people and must be discarded for national truth and well-being."

Alexander III, a heavy, powerful, stubborn man of limited intelligence, readily obeyed his mentor. He disliked ceremony, was straightforward and fervently religious. Pobedonostsev fostered his ardent nationalism, his suspicion of the intelligentsia and of the evil West. At his tutor's advice, he had renounced old dreams of Slav emancipation as unrealistic. In Moscow, he declared early in his reign, "Russians have never ceased to feel that whoever is the enemy of the Russian tsar and legal authority is an enemy of his fatherland. . . . May God help me introduce order and truth and teach all honest Russians to serve the faith, truth and the state."[2]

He and Pobedonostsev despised liberalism. In the Committee of Ministers the constitutional project was defended by Loris-Melikov, Miliutin, Abaza and Count Valuev. Pobedonostsev declared that it and all of the late emperor's reforms were misguided. The project was dropped.[3] The procurator's own program was largely negative. European ideas of change, he believed, had destroyed tradition and brought mental, moral, and material decline and disorder. Lack of a directing will had caused bewilderment and public distrust of the government. Thus the entire liberal program must go. The police and central authority would be strengthened. A regenerated Russian aristocracy must lead a society joined organically to the government. Here was a platform for Cherniaev.

Two hostile groups emerged. After the tsar removed Grand Duke Konstantin Nikolaevich from all his posts, Miliutin directed the

---

2. *Pisma Pobedonostseva k Aleksandru III* (Moscow, 1925), pp. 314–318, 65.

3. P. A. Zaionchkovskii, *Krizis samoderzhaviia* (Moscow, 1965), pp. 325–332; Miliutin, *Dnevnik*, IV: 35 ff.

remaining liberals. Pobedonostsev and Ignatiev headed the reactionaries. When the liberal ministers opposed Pobedonostsev *en bloc* on April 21, Alexander backed his tutor fully. "I cannot expect any good from these ministers," wrote the tsar. "Their words carry neither sincerity nor truth."[4]

To end the uncertainty Pobedonostsev drafted a carefully worded manifesto for Alexander's approval. Making no concessions to the people, the autocracy would "govern boldly relying upon God's work, believing in the strength and truth of autocratic authority which we are called upon to affirm and protect for the public good from all feeble impulses." The liberal ministers promptly resigned; Count Ignatiev became interior minister.[5]

Ignatiev's "dictatorship of smiles" replaced Loris-Melikov's "dictatorship of the heart." The count sought power, fame, and fortune with little regard for the well-being of others, reported the German ambassador. He was clever if unveracious, inventive, and active.[6] His simplistic views on domestic policy resembled Pobedonostsev's. He demanded extreme economy, he fought "sedition" with an army of spies, and he made the Polish and Jewish minorities his scapegoats. The chauvinism of this patriarchal aristocrat so impressed Alexander and Pobedonostsev that he soon became first minister.[7]

The mood in Russia was far from joyous. The liberal historian K. D. Kavelin described "the chaos, complete disorder, complete lack of energy, intelligence, knowledge and talent in higher government circles." Near the throne stood "weakminded fanatics and intriguers" such as Katkov, Aksakov, Pobedonostsev, and Ignatiev, the guardians of the Russian national spirit.[8] Their bombast about unity and strength camouflaged terrible insecurity. The public, asserted G. K. Gradovskii, distrusted a government whose autocracy concealed bureaucratic chaos and intrigue. No one respected Ignatiev, "the plaything of parties and intrigue."[9]

4. *K. P. Pobedonostsev i ego korespondenty: pisma i zapiski*, I: 104–120, "Zadachi novogo tsarstvovaniia," 10 March 1881; p. 49, Alexander III to Pobedonostsev, 21 April 1881.

5. Zaionchkovskii, *Krizis*, pp. 371–378; *Pisma Pobedonostseva*, pp. 329–335.

6. Schweinitz, II: 178.

7. Zaionchkovskii, *Krizis*, pp. 336–338, 380–382.

8. "Iz pisem K. D. Kavelina k grafu D. A. Miliutinu, 1882–84 gg." VE (Jan. 1909), p. 9, Kavelin to Miliutin, 15 January 1882.

9. Gradovskii, *Itogi*, pp. 95–96, letter of 10 April 1882. Count Kalnoky, Austrian ambassador in St. Petersburg, fully confirmed this pessimistic assessment: HHSA, Kalnoky to Haymerle, no. 22 A and B, 9/21 April; no. 25 A–D, 22 April/4 May 1881.

While liberals despaired, Cherniaev and his friends rejoiced and prospered. Count Vorontsov-Dashkov became chief of the Imperial Guard, then minister of court. M. N. Katkov, whose *Moskovskie Vedomosti* was read regularly by the tsar, became a semiofficial organ and its editor a spokesman for the regime.[10]

With his patrons in power and conservatism in vogue, Mikhail Grigorevich emerged from obscurity. Since March 1881, when fon-Kaufman suffered a paralyzing stroke, his old Turkestan post had beckoned. Later that year Vorontsov arranged his nomination. "My appointment to Turkestan has already been decided," he informed Aksakov. "Office formalities still prevent publication of the order."[11] Fon-Kaufman, moribund and speechless, was the principal "formality."

As Cherniaev waited, General M. D. Skobelev, who had decimated the Turkomans at Geok-Tepe, grabbed the headlines. Sharing much of Cherniaev's ideology, the "white general" was popular, forceful and successful. As reckless in speech as in battle, he castigated the intelligentsia and resolutely supported the Herzegovina insurgents against Austria. With no war to fight, he rushed to Paris. "Aliens" were to blame for Russia's recent departures from its Slav mission and her subservience to foreign powers, he told some Serbian students. Russia could free itself "only with arms in hand." Germany was the mortal foe of Russia and Slavdom. In a coming and inevitable struggle, the Slavs would triumph over the Teutons. If the South Slavs' existence were threatened, Russia and probably France would fight by their side.[12]

Skobelev's unauthorized, bellicose speech shocked European diplomats and presaged the subsequent Franco-Russian alliance. Official St. Petersburg, desiring friendship with Berlin, was much embarrassed. "Skobelev is becoming more the hero of the hour with his speeches," commented the friendly Prince Meshcherskii, "than he was by his battlefield exploits."[13]

Mr. Charles Marvin, a British correspondent, rushed to St. Petersburg to interview Skobelev and other prominent Russians. Asked about a possible invasion of India, Skobelev replied: "I would not like to command such an expedition. The difficulties would be

10. Florinsky, *Russia*, II: 1089–1090.
11. IISG, ed. khr. 10, Cherniaev to Aksakov, 25 January 1882.
12. E. Tarlé, "Rech generala Skobeleva v Parizhe v 1882 g.," KA, XXVII (1928), 215–221.
13. *Golos*, Feb. 12, 1882, p. 1, "Interesy dnia."

enormous." General L. N. Sobolev, chief of the Asian section of the general staff stated: "We could invade India, but we do not wish to." The key to this problem, he hinted, lay with Cherniaev, soon to replace fon-Kaufman.

Marvin expected a man of gay and sparkling temperament but found a Cherniaev marked by illness and misfortune. He retained vigor and charming simplicity, but next to Skobelev, "worth a whole army to Russia," he was disappointing:

> Skobeleff is intoxicatingly young; Tchernaieff is in sere and yellow leaf. Skobeleff is a man of great promise, great things are expected of him; he has such uncommon and brilliant parts that it is difficult to assign any limits to his career. With Tchernaieff the case is different—his career lies behind him. Skobeleff may be a Suvaroff, a Wellington, a Napoleon; but Tchernaieff can only be an administrator of the ordinary type. . . . Skobeleff's past career stamps him as a born hero; Tchernaieff's as a casual one.[14]

Cherniaev assured Marvin that as Turkestan governor general he would adhere strictly to instructions. The British had objected to fon-Kaufman because he kept advancing in Central Asia. Marvin noted, "We are convinced that you would advance even faster." Cherniaev was silent. "Do you intend to annex Bukhara?" queried the Englishman. Cherniaev was evasive: that would depend on his instructions. "Bukhara," he added, "lies on the direct and only route of our communications with the Caspian Sea, and most of that khanate's inhabitants themselves desire annexation to Russia purely for commercial reasons."[15] However, London need fear no fresh annexations. He opposed an Anglo-Russian demarcation line in Central Asia: "If we continue to be friends, it is useless to lay down a frontier; if we quarrel no frontier will restrain us."[16]

British diplomats worried over Cherniaev's reemergence. London's remonstrances, speculated a memorandum, had perhaps delayed his appointment. Real grounds existed for fearing "a display of misdirected energy" by him against Bukhara. Unre-

14. Charles Marvin, *The Russian Advance Towards India* (London, 1882), pp. 5 ff.
15. *Novoe Vremia*, Feb. 28, 1882, no. 2156, p. 2, by V. Krestovskii.
16. Marvin, pp. 128–134.

markable as an administrator, he would likely "pursue a policy in Central Asia of a decidedly militant character."

Foreign Minister Girs denied that Cherniaev would be appointed. To Ambassador Thornton he dismissed him as an impetuous man with character defects like Skobelev. Later Girs admitted that Cherniaev was being considered, but added that he was convinced that he would not secure the post.[17] Was Girs deliberately kept in the dark?

On May 25, 1882, the government named Cherniaev Turkestan governor general and promoted him to lieutenant general. His reception by the imperial family confirmed his return to favor. Rejoiced Prince Meshcherskii: "Cherniaev is far from being a genius either as general or statesman. But he is an unusually bright, deeply sympathetic, gifted and highly cultured Russian. Everywhere he operates he illuminates and glorifies the Russian name. He was named to Tashkent, his Tashkent which he acquired for Russia. God grant him a happy choice of subordinates . . . since bad choices can hinder him in everything."[18] His personal staff was headed by V. V. Krestovskii and included the strange (apparently homosexual) Captain Alabin. Many old comrades sought to attach themselves to a rising star; his secretaries answered over two thousand letters.[19]

On June 25 Skobelev died suddenly after an all night orgy. Nationalists were plunged into gloom. "There was in Russia in our time no person more national, a closer neighbor to the Russian than Skobelev," wrote Meshcherskii, "a legendary figure, a live but ancient hero." His way of life had been most irregular, but even official Petersburg must honor him: "A monument to Skobelev? That is too little. One must erect a live memorial to him. The military youth by the hundreds and thousands, from the very school bench should fall in love with the military ideal in Skobelev's form and work to make itself like Skobelev . . . [who] represents the genius of the Russian spirit and creativity."[20] Here was the reactionary ideal: a nation of militarists too absorbed in conquest to demand domestic change, worshipping aggressive generals like Skobelev and Cherniaev. Re-

17. fo, 65/1151, J. Michell to [Thornton], 10/22 April 1881; Thornton to Granville, 12/24 and 17/29 April 1881.

18. Meshcherskii, *Dnevnik*, 20 May 1881, p. 186; 28 May 1881, pp. 196–197.

19. gim, ed. khr. 56, ll. 49–50, "M. G. Cherniaev v Turkestanskom krae," by S. A. Bronskii, who became Cherniaev's adjutant in January 1882.

20. Meshcherskii, *Dnevnik*, pp. 249–251, 262–263.

gretting the passing of a military genius, Miliutin commented: "In him ambition predominated over all qualities of mind and heart. To the degree they served his ambitious goals, he considered all means and paths allowable."[21] This applied equally to the greyhaired Cherniaev who was applauded at Skobelev's funeral.

After bidding farewell to the imperial family, Cherniaev received a triumphal send-off at Nikolaevsk station in Petersburg. A priest recounted his services to Russia. Former volunteers presented him with an icon in a silver chasuble, representing the Kazan Mother of God. A Slav Society member lauded his "wonderful participation." He hoped, replied Cherniaev, that he would justify their trust and aid Russia. Bells rang, the icon was borne to the railroad car and "Spasi Gospodi liudi Tvoi" was sung. Colonel Komarov staged this ridiculous performance and added an immodest speech.[22]

En route to Turkestan Cherniaev paused in Samara on the Volga to address a banquet in his honor given by local merchants. Why had he beome a shining symbol to millions of Russians? "People greet, honor and caress me. But for what? If for Tashkent, then Tashkent has not yet brought Russia either political or economic benefits. If for the Serbian campaign . . ., that was settled by the Berlin Congress. Then why do they caress me? I believe it is because I think, feel and act in the Russian manner."[23]

This was basically correct. He was applauded less for what he had done than for what he represented. Ordinary Russians were attracted by his apparent audacity, simplicity, and openness, his defiance of obstacles and odds. He won acclaim by taking on a military bureaucracy supposedly honeycombed with corruption and foreigners. Cherniaev was a superb propagandist. His public statements and military reports magnified his achievements and screened him with false humility. He posed as a man of principle with ideals which many Russians admired. So anxious were they to believe in him that contrary evidence could not undermine their faith: hypnotized by mystic ideals of Russian patriotism and Slav liberation, they remained blind to his fanatical, self-seeking ambition. Full of renewed hope and confidence, the merchants' plaudits ringing in his ears, Cherniaev traveled toward Tashkent to slay the dragons spawned by fon-Kaufman.

Cherniaev now had a final chance to salvage his career. His principal

21. ORBL, Miliutin, k. 6, no. 5, "Dnevnik 1882–1888," ll. 25–26.
22. MV, 1 September 1882, p. 3; Meshcherskii, *Dnevnik*, p. 371.
23. IISG, ed. khr. 6, l. 43.

rivals were gone: Skobelev and fon-Kaufman dead and Miliutin retired. Believing that fon-Kaufman's rule had been one long operetta, Mikhail Grigorevich sought to uncover chaos and malfeasance. In St. Petersburg he had promised the emperor to reduce expenditures, eliminate useless institutions and make Turkestan profitable for Russia. Despite assurances to Marvin, he had also resolved to expand Russian Central Asia.

He lacked fon-Kaufman's financial resources and vast powers. A new steppe governor generalship had absorbed eastern Turkestan, and as Transcaspia's importance grew, Turkestan's strategic significance waned.[24] Had Cherniaev returned too late? He must make up lost time. Bukhara was to be his first victim followed by Khiva and Afghanistan.[25]

He took the arduous Orenburg-Kazalinsk route, then went along the Syr-Daria. In Tashkent friends prepared an ecstatic official welcome for his second coming. The local population, proclaimed *Moskovskie Vedomosti*'s friendly correspondent, "recalls him fondly and awaits him like the rising sun. There is not a sart, a kirgiz or a Tatar who would not know General Cherniaev, and [they] recall his bravery and justice with benedictions."[26] En route he began dismantling fon-Kaufman's work. At Kazalinsk he ordered the Aral Flotilla's steamer and barge service discontinued; later he abolished the flotilla itself. The ensuing Afghan Crisis of 1885 revealed how impulsive and foolish this was.[27]

The Uzbeks welcomed him warmly back to Turkestan. At Kazalinsk local merchants brought bread and salt on an inscribed silver platter; crowds gathered at his residence. At Chimkent, greeted by the merchants, he entered a magnificent tent to "The March of the Russian Volunteers." Near Tashkent a native cavalcade of twenty thousand horsemen met his party. They rode into the city through a triumphal arch inscribed "M. G.," "April 8, 1866" (the day he left Tashkent), and "October 5, 1882." Near the arch Russians gave him bread and salt, and Bukharan Jews a carpet richly woven of silks. A solid wall of Uzbeks enclosed the route to his palace. Receiving the father superior's blessing in the cathedral, Cherniaev, showered with silver coins, proceeded to the governor general's residence.[28]

24. FO, 65/1151, Michell to Thornton, 22 April 1882, in Thornton to Granville, 12/24 April 1882.

25. Terentiev, III: 329–330.

26. MV, 7 September 1882, p. 3, "Iz Tashkenta," by S. Pereletnyi.

27. FO, 65/1153, Thornton to Granville; Terentiev, III: 356.

28. MV, 13 December 1882, "Iz Tashkenta," 6 October 1882 by "Ch——n."

He arrived exhausted, somewhat ill and barely able to walk on his injured leg. "We all saw a bent, wrinkled general who made a bow," recalled G. P. Fedorov, "then without a word of greeting, entered his quarters." The initial impression boded ill.[29] Speaking briefly to his assembled commanders, he cautioned that everything would remain as before until the Girs inspection commission had finished its work. It soon became evident that he would not abide by this policy.

On October 30, Senator F. K. Girs arrived with a team of government inspectors. In St. Petersburg the foreign minister's brother—a verbose, humorless and pompous bureaucrat—had decided that fon-Kaufman had committed gross malfeasance in office. To discredit fon-Kaufman, he and Cherniaev blamed him for even minute departures from the Temporary Statute of 1867. Only strict adherence to legality, he told Cherniaev's commanders, could promote public well-being: "Your supreme commander [Cherniaev] provides an example rare in our administrative history: he begins his rule not with requests to strengthen his personal powers as governor general, but to grant the region legality. The glorious conqueror of Tashkent has the worthy task of bringing final administrative order to the region."[30] But the investigation produced little evidence of malfeasance.

Cherniaev and his staff settled down in fon-Kaufman's magnificent, labyrinthine palace. Though segregated from Russian Tashkent, they had lively dinners. Krestovskii told fascinating stories. When military affairs were discussed, Cherniaev would converse animatedly, sometimes jumping up and pacing nervously. Visitors were entertained hospitably without distinction of rank. The staff's isolation produced extravagant rumors in town, embroidered by fon-Kaufman's former adherents. At the palace drunkenness and debauchery supposedly prevailed with Cherniaev setting the pace. Actually, nervousness and previous overindulgence in alcohol had so undermined his health that now he was abstemious. Apparently the company was exclusively male.[31]

At first Cherniaev intended to bring his family to Tashkent. "I am inhabiting a magnificent house where there will be plenty of room

29. G. P. Fedorov, "Moia sluzhba v Turkestanskom krai (1870–1910)," IV (Nov. 1913), p. 438.

30. MV, 26 October 1882, p. 2; 21 December 1882, p. 5, "Iz Tashkenta," 17 November 1882.

31. GIM, ed. khr. 56, ll. 55 ff., Bronskii; Fedorov, p. 439.

for all of you," he wrote Antonina. "Inside are two winter gardens with fountains and tropical plants, and behind it is a large park with a waterfall and an orangery. . . . I embrace you and everyone a thousand times." Did he now regret his criticism of fon-Kaufman's luxury? Later, during an inspection trip of Turkestan, he wrote her:

> In Tashkent I began to prepare the house for your arrival. Mamasha's part consists of rooms with an upright piano, a large red drawing room, a small rose drawing room, and a large corner bedroom. . . . There are eight rooms for you in the large house and five in the wing. I had a large pond dug near the house . . . and am bringing from the dacha a menagerie of two sea lions, a family of wild caribou and two wild horses. . . . I am awaiting your arrival here impatiently and am very, very lonely without you.[32]

For unexplained reasons the family never went to Turkestan.

Tashkent shook off the sadness and apathy evident during fon-Kaufman's terminal illness. Old Tashkent was a typical Asian city, but beside it had arisen since the conquest a Russian town of six thousand persons with broad streets and fine squares bordered with poplars. New Tashkent resembled a European provincial city and boasted a public library, museum, city assembly, and two newspapers. "It has become," affirmed the priest, Neofit, with exaggeration, "one of the Russian empire's first cities."[33] From barren wastes and native sakli fon-Kaufman had built a European island in the heart of Asia.

To reciprocate their warm welcome, Cherniaev gave an elaborate dinner for the Tashkenters. A large riding field beyond the Salar was jammed with people. Uzbek dishes were served to the accompaniment of Russian and native music. Like an Asian potentate Cherniaev surveyed the scene from a huge tent and distributed awards to deserving Uzbeks.[34]

Concentrating first on domestic affairs, he described to Aksakov the mess which fon-Kaufman had supposedly left behind: "It is very difficult to clean up after fifteen years of confusion. Besides

---

32. IISG, ed. khr. 17, "Lettres du général Michel Tchernaieff à sa fille ainée" [Oct. 1882], 11 November and 14 December 1882.

33. MV, 9 January 1884, p. 3, Neofit; 5 October 1882, p. 4, Pereletnyi; Henri Moser, *À Travers de l'Asie centrale* (Paris, 1885), pp. 82–83.

34. MV, 25 November 1882, p. 3.

officials' knavery at the treasury's expense . . . , so much invented nonsense has piled up here that those responsible throw up their hands before the inspectors while the populace openly deplores the "khanly ways" [of fon-Kaufman] which I learned about en route to Tashkent. Imagine a machinist whose machine does not operate. That is my position now." He was not yet ready for external adventures: "I do not foresee a war and do not want one until we are linked with the Caspian Sea and have reordered Turkestan's internal affairs."[35]

In an attack on "unnecessary" institutions, Cherniaev moved against Tashkent's Public Library. The Library, which had over thirteen thousand volumes and was warmly praised by visiting scholars, was one of fon-Kaufman's proudest achievements.[36] Cherniaev ordered his senior official, Krestovskii, to investigate it. Few persons use the library, reported this fortune hunter. It was subscribing mostly to humorous journals and popular newspapers. Patrons were reading trash and radical writers such as Saltykov-Shchedrin, Pisarev, and Nekrasov. The library had become "a public reading room with a rather low and partly tendentious character."

Cherniaev welcomed this palpably false report, tailored to his own conservative convictions. Besides, he had heard that the library director was circulating forbidden literature and letting the reading room become a lovers' rendezvous. Without verifying these rumors or correcting minor shortcomings, he ordered the library closed immediately: "Finding that the library's policies . . . do not at all correspond to the serious purpose which the Turkestan administration had in view in establishing this book collection, especially since the Treasury expends considerable annual sums to maintain it, I consider it best to discontinue the Tashkent Public Library as an independent institution on January 1, 1883." Worthwhile books would go to various Tashkent institutions; "worthless" ones would be auctioned off. Journal subscriptions were suspended, and thousands of volumes were removed (some reached the city bazaar). Cherniaev believed that he had shown restraint in not ordering the entire library burned!

35. IISG, ed. khr. 10, Cherniaev to Aksakov, 23 December 1882.

36. Academician Middendorf praised fon-Kaufman's foresight in creating a library with adequate materials to study Central Asia. A. Middendorf, *Ferganskaia dolina* (St. Petersburg, 1882), pp. iii–iv.

This amazing act of official vandalism left Tashkent temporarily without a library. Protests poured in. The local *duma* proposed that the city take over the library, but Cherniaev flatly refused. As the uproar continued, he relented: boxed volumes were placed in the Tashkent Museum. In December 1883 he formally opened the museum and book collection. *Moskovskie Vedomosti* ascribed its resurrection exclusively to him![37] General fon-Rosenbakh, his successor, restored the library and recovered volumes from all over Tashkent. Goaded by press criticism, Mikhail Grigorevich asserted that he had merely shifted the library to larger quarters, but he could not explain away his decree abolishing the library.[38]

Next he eliminated the chemical laboratory established by fon-Kaufman and distributed its assets. This caused many objections and its utility was so evident that in November 1883 Cherniaev restored it. Not until 1888 was all its equipment recovered—much of it broken. The laboratory's fate revealed "the hastiness of destroying everything built under Kaufman."[39] The bold governor even abolished fon-Kaufman's school for silkworm breeding and cotton farm, intended to help develop Turkestan's economy.[40]

Claiming that they conflicted with native custom and burdened the population, Cherniaev abrogated fon-Kaufman's "Temporary Rules for the Irrigation of Turkestan Region." He created a new administration "conforming to local conditions and customs," and Uzbeks took charge of the irrigation works. In Tashkent this provoked serious criticism; in Samarkand they had to be replaced with Russians. As he destroyed fon-Kaufman's work Cherniaev commented: "It is time to stop this Offenbach affair."[41]

The governor general, testified Fedorov, adopted none of the constructive measures which Turkestan urgently required. Bored by routine administration, he listened wearily to daily reports. After four months he had not even met the section chiefs of his chancellery.

---

37. A. I. Dobrosmyslov, "Turkestanskaia publichnaia biblioteka i muzei," *Sredniaia Aziia* (Feb. 1910), kn. 2, pp. 106 ff.; мv, 24 January 1884, p. 3, "Iz Tashkenta," 24 November 1883, by "Turist." This dishonest article failed to mention that Cherniaev had abolished the old Public Library.

38. *Novoe Vremia*, 14 November 1885, no. 3490, p. 3, "Pismo v redaktsiiu," by Cherniaev.

39. N. B. Teikh, "Istoricheskii ocherk . . . ," *Sbornik materialov dlia statistiki Syr-Darinskoi oblasti*, vi: 50 ff.; Terentiev, iii: 333.

40. Dobrosmyslov, "Uchebnye zavedeniia . . . ," *Sredniaia Aziia* (April 1910), p. 117; N. Maev, *Turkestanskaia vystavka*, pp. 112–113.

41. Dobrosmyslov, *Tashkent*, pp. 163–165; Terentiev, iii: 333.

"I know them well enough from their activity under Kaufman," he declared. Finally, at Director Nestorovskii's urging, Cherniaev invited the three officials to dinner. He greeted them hospitably, the ice melted and good relations were established.[42] Though blinded by hatred of fon-Kaufman, Mikhail Grigorevich retained his charm.

Running out of institutions to destroy, Cherniaev was seized by wanderlust. In March 1883 he and his staff inspected Fort Petro-Aleksandrovsk on the Khivan frontier. No directive announced his departure. Assuming that he could issue orders wherever he happened to be, he left no replacement.[43] The attentive Captain Alabin, winning his complete trust, persuaded him that unless he (Cherniaev) were present at the coronation of Alexander III in Moscow, something terrible would happen. Cherniaev promptly requested permission to attend.

He did not await War Minister Vannovskii's reply (which forbade his departure). Dreaming of discovering a new route between Central Asia and Russia, he, Alabin and another aide crossed the bleak Ust-Urt plateau from Kungrad by wheeled carriage. The steamer, "Volodei," was to meet them on the Caspian Sea, but shallow water forced it to anchor far offshore. Cherniaev and his companions boarded a small fishing boat. A powerful current carried them off irresistibly. A storm burst and the mast toppled onto them narrowly missing the general. Shaken and discouraged, they were about to make for shore when they spied the steamer's smoke. This "voyage of discovery" caused untold merriment in Tashkent.[44]

From Astrakhan, congratulating the emperor on his imminent coronation, Cherniaev telegraphed proudly that he had inaugurated a new, convenient route from Central Asia. "I thank you for your congratulations," replied Alexander, "and sincerely rejoice at the news that Russia has come closer to Central Asia. I hope that the new shorter route will enliven commerce and bind the region to the center with common interests."[45] Actually, this route was too arduous to be very useful.

Cherniaev then sought official approval for his new route in Moscow and Petersburg. Attending summer maneuvers in Krasnoe Selo

42. Fedorov, pp. 441–442.

43. Ibid., p. 442; Terentiev, III: 338.

44. GIM, ed. khr. 56, ll. 58–64, Bronskii; FO, 65/1173, Kennedy to Granville, 29 August 1883, no. 196, enclosing Michell's memoranda of 6 and 15 July.

45. GIM, ed. khr. 2, l. 4, Alexander III to Cherniaev, May 1883, telegram.

near the capital, he told the British military attaché that he had proposed immediate construction of a light railway from Mertvyi Kultuk to Kungrad. But would the impoverished imperial government spend money on a railroad whose terminus would abut for six months a year on a frozen sea? "All Russians," reported a British envoy, "recognized the ability and energy of General Tchernaieff, but even his friends admit that he is a visionary."[46]

In late August Cherniaev left for Orenburg accompanied by Henri Moser, a Swiss traveler who had succumbed to his spell.

> His face is wholly military with pronounced features and lively, dominating eyes. He speaks little, but each word is measured. Great goodness combined with remarkable energy form the basis of his character. He has time for every petitioner, an ear for every request. This ready accessibility, this great natural affability have contributed greatly to his popularity . . . , and his career has confirmed his bravery, energy, coolness and military skills. He owes his reputation and advancement solely to himself.[47]

Moser traveled to Tashkent with Cherniaev's cavalcade. En route they were welcomed by local Russian authorities and besieged by tattered exiles begging Cherniaev for pardon.[48]

Tashkent received them with oriental pomp. To the beat of drums Cherniaev descended from his carriage and saluted his commanders. Moser spent two weeks at his palace "where the luxury of the West joins harmoniously with that of the Orient." Despite the splendor, Cherniaev remained "as simple and kind as during our trip." Dinner at six was formal with all the officers and high officials, but luncheon was intimate. "It is then that the general talks and . . . shows us the sabres given to him by the rulers of Khiva and Bukhara." The French military attaché attended an audience for the Bukharan ambassador: "At precisely three P.M. Cherniaev entered in formal uniform. Everyone stands. The general advances. On one side are the two ambassadors; on the other we form a semi-circle around the general. . . . He, as is his custom, speaks slowly and in a low voice stressing almost every word."

46. FO, 65/1174, Kennedy to Granville, 31 August/12 September 1883, enclosing Colonel F. Trench's memorandum to Kennedy, no. 22; 65/1175, Russian Abstract, no. 37; 65/1203, Thornton to Granville, 9 February 1884.

47. Moser, p. 5.

48. MV, 6 August 1883, p. 2, telegram from Astrakhan.

The visitors attended a review of the Turkestan troops. Cherniaev addressed the soldiers "with that military eloquence which electrifies." His soldiers bore him triumphantly to his troika, and he returned to the palace amidst cheers from an Uzbek crowd. Cherniaev, concluded Moser, was a worthy successor to the great fon-Kaufman, "a humane and energetic administrator."[49] He could still deceive and captivate men.

A few days of intensive labor bored the "humane administrator." He inspected provinces, met visiting delegations and dedicated monuments. Inaugurating a reign of Christian virtue, he forbade the transportation and sale of opium, hashish, and other drugs.[50] He listened apathetically to administrative reports and played cards with his entourage while Turkestan's urgent needs went unmet.

Cherniaev became deeply involved in Russo-British contention over the approaches to India. After the Berlin Congress, Russia had penetrated the region bounded by Khiva, Bukhara, Persia, and Afghanistan. The conquest of Turkmenia increased the ascendancy of the Caucasus over Turkestan. Cherniaev hoped to reverse that trend. The British, controlling teeming India with modest forces, wondered where the Russians would finally halt. The imperially minded Conservatives anxiously watched Merv oasis, Herat, and Afghanistan. Associating Cherniaev with plans to invade India and with disregard for instructions, they were worried by his appointment to Turkestan. Gladstone's Liberal cabinet dismissed such alarmism, but even Conservative fears, admitted *Golos*, were based on a laudable concern for British interests.[51]

The London press speculated about new exploits by Cherniaev. Undersecretary Sir Charles Dilke had replied to anxious queries in Commons: "The Government do not know the exact point the Russians have reached, but there is no reason to suppose that they have arrived at Merv." Britain, objected *The Standard*, had permitted Russia to absorb the khanates (actually, only Kokand had been annexed

49. Moser, pp. 84–108. Shocked at Cherniaev's recall, Moser wrote: "For anyone who knew of the vast and useful plans he had conceived for Turkestan's future must have felt profound regret at his sudden removal. . . . I have remained one of the general's sincere admirers . . ." (p. 107); MV, 28 September 1883, p. 2, telegram from Tashkent of 27 September.

50. Ibid., 3 October 1883, p. 4 (Tashkent, 11 Oct.); 31 October 1883, p. 1 (Tashkent, 30 Oct.); 7 November 1883 (Tashkent, 6 Nov.); 18 November 1883 (Tashkent, 16 Nov.).

51. *Golos*, 7 November 1882, p. 2, "Opasenie angliiskikh konservatorov nashchet Srednei Azii."

by Russia) and approach India. "A single generation has sufficed to behold the march of Russian troops from the Orenburg frontier to the borders of Khorasan and the banks of the Heri Rud." Prohibitive Russian tariffs injured Indian foreign trade and British prestige. In Asia, England stood isolated before the insatiable Russian bear. Unless the Indian government acted promptly, Russia might conquer Afghanistan. "Both Russia and the races of Asia [must] know what we shall and what we shall not tolerate. . . . The policy of letting things alone has been pursued long enough."[52]

Despite some bellicose statements, neither Petersburg nor London desired a confrontation. *Golos* repeated foreign assertions that an Anglo-Russian conflict in Asia was imminent and inevitable. However, Ambassador Thornton noted that the Turkestan army could not conduct offensive operations, and the Russian foreign ministry suggested a compromise to prevent strife.[53] General Cherniaev's appearance at Petro-Aleksandrovsk in March 1883 revived British fears that Russia would occupy Merv oasis, the only important unconquered Turkoman territory. Earlier, the khan of Khiva, without consulting Cherniaev, had named a new governor in Merv and had forbidden him to deal with England, Afghanistan, or Persia. This intensified Turkoman strife and Russian efforts to exploit it. In April Cherniaev, with St. Petersburg's support, compelled the khan to install another governor.[54]

Tashkent's triumph was shortlived. Late in 1883 Caucasus troops advanced eastward and brought a Mervite faction to power which requested Russian rule. In January 1884 Merv was annexed to the Transcaspia. "In occupying Merv," commented Cherniaev, "the Russians will have as many advantages over the Afghans as the English at Quetta."[55] Merv's annexation, subjecting the Turkomans wholly to Russian authority, was another step along the road to India.

The British feared such encroachments. Persia and Afghanistan, warned their minister to Teheran, must block Russian expansion. One Russian told Kennedy frankly: "Russia is perfectly justified in

52. *The Standard*, (16)/28 November 1882 in fo, 65/1153.

53. fo, 65/1173, Thornton to Granville, 20 December 1882; 12 March 1883, no. 65, enclosing Kennedy's memorandum of 23 February/7 March 1883; 65/1171, 7 February 1883.

54. M. Alikhanov-Avarskii, "Zakaspiiskiia vospominaniia 1881–1885," ve (Sept. 1904), pp. 106–109; V. Bartold, *Istoriia kulturnoi zhizni Turkestana* (Leningrad, 1927), p. 237; Becker, pp. 101–102.

55. gim, ed. khr. 8, ll. 18–19, "Occupation de Merve," n.d.

advancing as near to the frontiers of British India as possible in order to be able to harass the British Government in case of necessity." Russian influence on the borders of Afghanistan was rising. Bukharan troops, reported Robert Michell, would be drilled to Russian words of command. The emir of Bukhara and khan of Khiva did nothing without Cherniaev's consent.[56]

Trouble flared in Shugnan, a Bukharan dependency on Afghanistan's eastern frontier. After its ruler received a visiting Russian explorer, the khan of Badakhshan, an Afghan vassal, occupied Shugnan in August 1883. St. Petersburg ordered Cherniaev to ascertain the facts. Confirming the invasion, he urged that the khan of Badakhshan be induced to withdraw. St. Petersburg concurred, but to avert trouble with Britain, Foreign Minister Girs warned Cherniaev not to exert pressure on Afghanistan.

Cherniaev's lengthy absence from his post had complicated matters. Agitation in Afghanistan, warned a St. Petersburg newspaper on August 25, had restored Tashkent to prominence, but it was confused and drifting. "Measures should be adopted immediately to stop this."[57] Cherniaev was being warned to restore order forthwith.

Back in Tashkent he supported the emir in order to prepare Bukhara's annexation to Russia. Earlier, prominent Russians had favored this, but confronted by implacable foreign office opposition, fon-Kaufman had tolerated Bukhara's autonomy certain that it and Khiva would fall eventually into Russia's lap.[58] In June 1882, before assuming his post in Tashkent, Cherniaev at a special conference in St. Petersburg had urged the khanates' immediate annexation. Russia's existing frontiers were unfavorable, he argued; the khanates virtually cut Tashkent off from Orenburg, its principal supply base. Their incorporation would strengthen Russia strategically and economically. The "Russian party" of Bukharan peasants and merchants would welcome annexation which would bring Russia "a thickly populated region more fertile and wealthy than all our ac-

---

56. FO, 65/1172, A. Condee Stephen, 11 May 1883. He wrote: "Perhaps the most noticeable and interesting feature of the policy of Russia in Central Asia has been that she has valued each fresh annexation of territory not so much for its intrinsic worth as for the advantages it possessed as a stepping stone to further and more important conquests." Thornton to Currie, 31 March 1883; 65/1173, Michell memorandum of 11 July 1883.

57. Ibid., 65/1175, Vlangali memoire [late 1883] in Thornton to Granville, 31 December 1883; 65/1174, Kennedy to Granville, 3 October 1883; *St. Petersburg Gazette*, 25 August 1883.

58. K. P. fon-Kaufman, *Proekt vsepoddanneishago otcheta* . . . (St. Petersburg, 1885), pp. 9, 133–134, 349, 352.

quisitions in Central Asia." Under Russian rule Bukharan revenues would eliminate Turkestan's deficit.[59]

Cherniaev had cavalierly overlooked economic and diplomatic realities and his program to annex, exploit, and Russify the khanates was rejected. The existing protectorates, argued his opponents, guaranteed Russian security cheaply; annexation would require an expensive Russian administration, needless extension of the empire and would provoke British hostility. The foreign minister admonished Cherniaev to uphold the status quo.[60] St. Petersburg would not tolerate infringement of Bukhara's independence or trouble with England.

In Bukhara popular dismay at high taxes and corruption reinforced by clerical opposition to his pro-Russian policy shook the emir's position. Muzaffar left his capital for long periods. The disaffected turned to his eldest son, Abd al-Malik, living in India on a British pension. On December 12 Cherniaev informed the war minister of rumors that a former bek backed by the Afghans had seized two Bukharan districts. He ordered General Ivanov, commander of Zeravshan district, to prepare to move troops to support the emir.[61]

These rumors caused the December alarm in Tashkent. There was a sudden burst of activity; commanders conferred. If Petersburg consented, a campaign would be launched. But Cherniaev's chief commissary asserted that the troops would be short of supplies. Until transports arrived from Russia, warned the artillery commander, shells and powder would be insufficient. Captain Alabin composed grandiose orders of the day: "The powerful eagle has spread his mighty wings," began one. Presumably they would fight the Afghans. Then came a telegram from St. Petersburg summoning Cherniaev to Russia.[62]

The emir, affirmed Antonina, had sought Cherniaev's assistance against the Afghans. Avoiding direct intervention but trying to utilize this quarrel in Russia's interests, he requested permission to distribute rifles to the emir's troops and move a Russian detachment

59. TSGVIA, f. Voennyi Uchenyi Arkhiv, op. 1, d. 73, ll. 20–23, cited in Khalfin, *Prisoedinenie*, pp. 408–410.

60. Ibid., ll. 24–39, cited in Khalfin, pp. 410–413.

61. F. K. Girs, *Otchet revizuiushchago . . . Tainogo Sovetnika Girsa* (St. Petersburg, 1883), pp. 459–460; B. I. Iskandarov, *Iz istorii Bukharskogo emirata* (Moscow, 1958), pp. 87–89.

62. GIM, ed. khr. 56, ll. 70–71, Bronskii.

(Ivanov's?) to the Bukharan border. Cherniaev explained these measures in a long telegram to War Minister Vannovskii.[63] Two weeks passed without a reply. Cherniaev telegraphed General O. V. Rikhter regretting that no response had come. Cherniaev described what followed in his autobiography:

> Next day the war minister replied that the emperor had approved all my proposals, that he would permit me to distribute a few hundred rifles to the Bukharans and move up an observational detachment. With such a reply I considered myself fully authorized to act when suddenly only a few days later I received an invitation from the same war minister to come to St. Petersburg to participate in the work of a commission to reform the Turkestan administration. . . . The idea that with this telegram they were recalling me from my post never entered my head. I quickly gathered my things together and without saying farewell properly to anyone took only the most essential things. Only in Petersburg, on the way from the railroad station, did one of those who met me give me the news that I was being removed.[64]

Hadn't he omitted something? Receiving the summons to St. Petersburg, noted S. A. Bronskii, a member of his staff, Cherniaev telegraphed Prince Vitgenshtein in code to discover why and whether he really must go. The prince went to the General Staff which graciously decoded it and sent a copy to the war minister who reported to the emperor. That telegram, recalled Bronskii, sealed Cherniaev's fate. At a formal breakfast before he left the general feeling was that for Cherniaev the last trumpet had sounded.[65]

Why had he been removed so abruptly? His friends blamed domestic intrigue and British machinations. The emperor had appointed him, asserted Prince Meshcherskii, over powerful opposition from selfish military bureaucrats. Everyone in Turkestan had loved him for erring in its interests "against the laws and holies of centrali-

63. The author could not obtain this telegram in TSGAOR and no draft of it could be found in Cherniaev's archive. Cherniaev, notes Count Adlerberg's "Iz zapisnoi knizhki," RA (1909), II: 296, sent telegrams to War Minister Vannovskii and Foreign Minister Girs, each costing 400 rubles, asking permission to move up troops to help Bukhara. When no answer came, he telegraphed Rikhter to inform the tsar, threatening otherwise to act without permission. Ten days later Cherniaev's proposal was approved but his troops were to advance only as a last resort and he was ordered to proceed promptly to St. Petersburg.

64. A. Cherniaeva, "Aleksandr III i Cherniaev," IV (Oct. 1909), 154–155; IISG, "Avtobiografiia," p. 21.

65. GIM, ed. khr. 56, l. 71, Bronskii.

zation and the bureaucratic catechism. He permitted himself to be too independent of Petersburg."[66] Ivan Aksakov attributed the government's "deplorable action" to "the strength of envy and intrigue," and "the mass of scum" Cherniaev had expelled from Turkestan.[67]

Other accounts suggest more cogent reasons. The annexation of Merv, affirmed Terentiev, had roused Cherniaev's aggressive designs; his telegrams urged an attack upon Afghanistan and he had bypassed the war minister.[68] Ambassador Thornton, at first referring to his "intemperate habits," later transmitted the foreign minister's comments. Because Cherniaev was "a very imaginative person," declared Girs, in Tashkent he might have "provoked unnecessary conflicts." Cherniaev had sent extraordinary suggestions to the war minister. When Vannovskii refused to submit them to the emperor, Cherniaev sought unsuccessfully to reach him through Vorontsov-Dashkov, then had written the tsar directly. Thornton heard that Cherniaev had submitted a plan to invade India if Anglo-Russian relations were ruptured.[69] He was removed apparently for disregarding the chain of command and advocating war with Britain over Afghanistan. Cherniaev's successor, added Girs, would avoid conflicts with neighboring states and execute his government's orders conscientiously.

The announcement on February 21 of Cherniaev's removal provoked comment from the heavily censored press. The moderate *Novosti* speculated that he had "placed himself in the region in an uncomfortable position vis-à-vis our Central Asian neighbors, toward higher administrative authorities and even toward the native population in whose eyes he had supposedly lost his former prestige." Denying the claims of Aksakov's *Rus* that Cherniaev knew Turkestan better than anyone, *Novosti* noted that he had not been there since 1866: "Turkestan is now wholly different from the province he left then."[70] The press was not encouraged to probe deeper.

Replacing him was Lieutenant General M. O. fon-Rozenbakh, an

66. IISG, Cherniaev, ed. khr. 20, citing Meshcherskii, *Moi vospominaniia*, III: 157.

67. *Rus* (Moscow), 15 February 1884, no. 4, pp. 6–7.

68. Terentiev, III: 340.

69. FO, 65/1203, Thornton to Granville, no. 43, 24 February 1884; 65/1204, 17 March 1884.

70. *Novosti i Birzhevaia Gazeta*, 23 February 1884, p. 3.

unspectacular career officer. He "knew as little about Turkestan as about Zululand," but he speedily restored the Public Library, Aral Flotilla, and the cotton and silkworm farms. Despite the Afghan crisis, he reduced Turkestan's alleged deficit by twenty-eight percent.[71] Cherniaev was not indispensable.

In St. Petersburg Cherniaev saw the war minister and the tsar. Vannovskii informed him that he had been appointed to the Military Council. Warned in advance, Cherniaev replied calmly: "If that is the emperor's will, I shall obey without complaint." As he went to see the emperor, Vannovskii and Rozenbakh had just emerged. "You quarreled with everyone," Alexander told Cherniaev. "You could not remain there."[72] According to Antonina, he talked with the emperor an hour and a half. The finance ministry was not solving Russia's economic difficulties, he asserted; productive resources lay unexploited. The army was dissatisfied with its pay, especially the officers. Alexander retorted that at his coronation he had increased officers' salaries. That raise, claimed Cherniaev, was wholly inadequate. He told the tsar that he was not a true autocrat. Authority had devolved upon his ministers or their bureau chiefs. The tsar was burdened with trifles: approving double travel allowances or equalizing the pay of officials. Vannovskii had objected to Cherniaev: "Is it possible that the emperor can decide such matters himself?" To Alexander Cherniaev cited this as evidence that bureaucracy had undermined the autocracy. The tsar blanched: "You received that reply because before they are reported to me, matters of this type are discussed in commissions and committees." Cherniaev was indeed *plus royaliste que le roi.*

As their interview ended, Alexander told Cherniaev: "Your relations with the war minister and general staff are bad. Wait awhile and I will give you an assignment, but for now stay in the Military Council." Alexander II had offered similar advice in 1866. To quiet Cherniaev's concern lest the public misinterpret his sudden removal, the tsar declared, "You have nothing to fear. All Russia knows you." Unwilling to sit in a Military Council under Vannovskii, Cherniaev asked to live in Moscow or retire. "No, why retire," objected Alexander, "live wherever it is most convenient for you."[73]

71. Fedorov, p. 444; Terentiev, III: 340–342.
72. Adlerberg, "Iz zapisnoi knizhki," pp. 296–297.
73. A. Cherniaeva, "Aleksandr III," pp. 155–157.

The second recall from Turkestan ended his active career. Even his imperial patron found his insubordination, recklessness, and administrative incompetence intolerable in a region requiring constructive leadership. Could a firebrand remain in Tashkent while tensions boiled with England over Afghanistan? The cautious emperor agreed with Girs and Vannovskii that Russia could not risk a war in Central Asia provoked by Cherniaev's dreams of conquest.

CHAPTER XV

Retirement and Death

MIKHAIL GRIGOREVICH lived his last fourteen years in relative obscurity in St. Petersburg and at his estate, Tubyshki. Though still tortured by frustration and self-doubt, he gradually grew more resigned. He continued to seek recognition and recompense for past services and write on current issues. Despite his interest in his family, as his health deteriorated he often retreated into a brooding isolation.

In 1884 Cherniaev traveled to the Orient. From Paris he wrote Nina that he was sailing from Marseilles. After stops at Naples, Suez, Aden, Colombo, Saigon, Hong Kong, and Shanghai, he would board a Japanese ship for Nagasaki and Tokyo. "I shall reply to your telegrams from all these points," he promised. On board ship he complained nervously: "The discipline is too severe. One can smoke only on one small portion of the deck."

During a stopover in Naples where Mrs. Cherniaev joined him briefly, Cherniaev ardently defended classical education: "Only superficial and ignorant people . . . question the need for classical education or the use of Latin and Greek in life. Upon leaving school they are quickly forgotten . . . , but the development of the mind, heart, will and taste . . . remain with an individual and direct his life. . . . For those who wish to stand out above the rest, it is just as essential as a deep foundation for a tall building."

Along the route Cherniaev described to Nina his experiences and state of health. At Kobe, Japan, he was received by an official of the war ministry. Exhausted by the heat and constant travel, he was glad to rest in Tokyo. There Russian ambassador, A. P. Davydov, introduced him to high Japanese officials. "All the ministers speak English and conduct all their dealings with Europeans in that language," he wrote Nina. "Unlike our ministers they all know their country and people very well. The day after my arrival I was presented to the emperor." While in Japan, he was decorated by the Mikado. He returned home via Siberia.[1]

He resided for a time in a St. Petersburg apartment, feeling keenly his isolation from the family. "I have been here now for over two months and except for Vera, none of you has written me a line," he complained to Nina. "It is hard for me with such a large family as ours to experience such loneliness. My health is improving, but slowly. . . . I live alone in my room and read from morning to night." He hadn't yet written up the Japanese trip: "I have a natural antipathy to written work which I overcome with difficulty."[2]

As the Afghan crisis heated up, he wrote Aksakov predicting war. Anglo-Russian negotiations would fail; both Ignatiev and the visiting Ristić assured him that Germany wanted Russia to fight England. He could not participate because of the war ministry's animosity.[3] To his surprise the Afghan affair blew over: Tashkent had seconded the conciliatory policy of Girs.

In St. Petersburg, Cherniaev occasionally attended the Slav Society where he had many friends. On April 10, 1885, he went to a banquet honoring foreign Slavs attending the Methodius celebration. Present were members of the State Council, two marshals of nobility and several generals. The magnificent hall was decorated with the Slav peoples' coats-of-arms. Slav liberation, proclaimed one speaker, already begun morally and politically, should be capped by unification of the entire Slav world. Amidst loud applause came a toast to Cherniaev, fighter for Slav liberation. Declared O. Naumovich: "We have drunk to the health of the hero, Mikhail Grigorevich, whose valor amazed not just the Slavs whom he served with his

1. IISG, ed. khr. 17, Cherniaev to A. M. Cherniaeva, 7 April and 1 July 1884.
2. Ibid., 8 March 1885.
3. Ibid., ed. khr. 10, Cherniaev to Aksakov, 2 May 1885.

genius and his life, but the whole world. We venerate such heroes who with their swords intervene on behalf of the rights of enslaved peoples, covering their names with deathless glory."[4] The pageantry and praise were balm to Cherniaev's wounded spirit.

Count Vorontsov-Dashkov obtained money for the education of Cherniaev's children. On November 30 Alexander III, though refusing to receive Cherniaev, granted him three thousand rubles annually until his youngest should attain majority.[5] Mikhail Grigorevich thanked him in unique fashion. In March 1886 in *Novoe Vremia* he published a savage attack on the Transcaspian Railroad being built by the war ministry. His "letter" provoked a fatal breach with Alexander, ending his career beyond redemption and revealing how little he had mellowed. The railroad, begun to aid Skobelev's Geok-Tepe campaign, completed its first section in 1881. The unknown wastes beyond Kyzyl-Arvat were then explored, but Governor General Cherniaev's vehement opposition delayed further construction. Fearing that it might further undermine Turkestan's importance, he proposed his own line across the Ust-Urt Plateau. However, the skirmish at Kushka in March 1885, bringing England and Russia close to war, induced the government to resume building the Transcaspian Railroad. When Cherniaev's blast appeared, it was approaching the Merv oasis. By 1888 the railroad reached Samarkand and Tashkent a decade later. Two army battalions aided by unskilled native labor constructed a line which Lord Curzon affirmed was one of the cheapest ever built.[6]

Cherniaev's letter expressed his accumulated bitterness against the war ministry: "The public . . . believes that soon it will travel to Tashkent not on camels across shifting sands but comfortably in first class carriages." It surmised that when the railway was complete, "we will become formidable in Central Asia and the English will be transformed from perfidious foes into obedient allies." The railroad had not helped Skobelev subdue the Turkomans, but the war ministry continued it despite periodic sandstorms. "We consider the railroad's continuation through Merv to Bukhara practically impossible . . . ," announced Cherniaev. Hundreds of thousands of *pud*s

---

4. V. Aristov, *Poslednie desiat let* . . . (St. Petersburg, 1893), pp. 101–112.

5. The emperor, noted the count, would find Cherniaev's thanks "disagreeable." "Do not conclude that his refusal to see you stems from any other reason." GIM, ed. khr. 1, ll. 26–28, Minister of Court to Cherniaev, 6 and 10 December 1885.

6. George Curzon, *Russia in Central Asia* (London, 1889), pp. 35–54; Becker, pp. 126–127.

(a pud is thirty-six pounds) of rails and ties would be buried in the sands. Even if completed, it would be militarily useless and economically unprofitable. Why was it being built? "Only to prove academically that a railroad can be constructed through waterless shifting sands," he concluded. In the Afghan crisis—whose peaceful solution he deplored—Russia had needlessly yielded to England, lowered its prestige and shut herself up in the desert.[7]

The editors of *Novoe Vremia* sharply but respectfully disagreed. The Afghan emir had provided no pretext for war. Russia's position in Turkestan and Bukhara was solid and strong. Cherniaev had purposely underestimated the new railway's carrying capacity and military value.[8] His tirade proved expensive. For publishing an unauthorized article on a military issue, he was dropped from the Military Council, placed in the reserves, and lost half his salary. Again he had been found guilty of a breach of discipline.[9]

Soon regretting his outburst, Cherniaev sought to restore himself to favor through Vorontsov. "I have violated proper form," he admitted, "and submit to his [the emperor's] will unconditionally." Only duty had impelled him to speak so frankly. He hoped Alexander would "not deprive me wholly of his favor which he has shown me for twenty years." But his attitude toward official foreign policy remained hostile:

> We have been placed [in Central Asia] in the same false position as in Sofia and Belgrade. To extricate ourselves, one could drive the English back from the Amu-Daria to the mountains and from Herat, but without war this cannot be achieved now. One cannot regard our position just from Turkestan's standpoint. In Asia we have 11,000 versts of frontier. The entire billion population of the continent follows our rivalry with England. The slightest English advantage over us and the entire billion will be against us and with them. Why should we voluntarily give this advantage to our rivals? The emperor inherited the Berlin Congress, insulting to Russian national feeling. Despite his determination to remove Russia from this false position which reflects upon all our domestic affairs, the [foreign] ministry has placed it in even greater humiliation.

7. M. Cherniaev, "Akademicheskaia zheleznaia doroga. Pismo v redaktsiiu," *Novoe Vremia*, 31 March 1886, no. 3623.

8. Ibid., 1 April 1886, no. 3624, p. 1.

9. IISG, ed. khr. 20, "Vypiski i zametki"; Gradovskii, "Arkhistratig," p. 124; Terentiev, III: 229–230.

To him war remained the best solution to Russia's problems. Weakness abroad would produce disorganization at home. "It is high time to do something drastic," he urged. Russia's prestige fell daily; popular agitation grew; the masses distrusted the government. There was great danger of a popular revolt.[10] But Alexander did not alter Russian foreign policy or restore Cherniaev to favor. Cassandra went unheeded.

Again he explained his plight to the emperor. His troubles had begun with Tashkent's capture. Would the emperor condemn him to misery during his few remaining years? Alexander's acceptance of the title, ruler of Turkestan, and that region's brilliant gains suggested the contrary. "My case merely awaits an impartial advocate," he wrote.[11] When no answer came, he implored forgiveness: "I stand guilty before you, Sire, but having had the good fortune to enjoy your merciful favor for twenty years, I venture to hope [for pardon] from you, Sire, after you listen to the sincere confession of your faithful servant."

Cherniaev stressed his sincere repentance for the diatribe against the railroad. "There was no ulterior motive, merely the wish to benefit my country." In 1865 his defiance of Miliutin's order had added a vast region to the empire, and Alexander II had forgiven him.

> I dare hope, Sire, that you likewise will forgive my transgression, taking into account that during my lengthy service there is not a spot of self-interest nor a single reproach for wavering convictions. At the end of life, with advancing decrepitude, I have arrived at a desperate position where I cannot support my family decently, treat my ailments or pay my debts. . . . I do not even have the consolation of leaving an honorable memory. I place all my hopes in my monarch's generosity and justice.

He repeated his tale of woe to Count Vorontsov, urging him in vain to arrange an audience for him with Alexander III.[12]

So great was his need that when this failed, he begged

---

10. IISG, ed. khr. 10, Cherniaev to Count Ilarion Ivanovich [Vorontsov-Dashkov], 4 May 1886, draft.

11. Ibid., Cherniaev to P. A., 1 February 1889, draft.

12. Ibid., Cherniaev to Alexander III, March 25, copy; Cherniaev to Vorontsov-Dashkov, draft, n.d.

forgiveness again "not for myself who am close to the grave, but for my family." He had erred grievously, lost the emperor's trust, and everything he had begun in Turkestan had been abandoned. Would not the tsar forgive his temporary departure from discipline? Never would he repeat his verbal foray. Three months later Alexander commented tersely: "Ask him what he wants,"[13] but he neither forgave Cherniaev nor assisted him further. Appeals to other prominent figures brought no response. Even Vorontsov wrote: "Reply that I can do nothing more."[14]

Cherniaev spent much time now at his quiet Tubyshki estate which he had repurchased in 1887. He lived in one wing alone with the servants while workmen dismantled or rebuilt decrepit buildings. Pondering his past career and present misfortunes, real or imagined, he wrote Nina: "Leading my life in an unequal struggle, rarely winning, mostly defeated, I must finish out my days insulted and unfairly treated. . . . Fortunately, I am not at all irritated and regard the entire past—good and bad—as if from another world. Only mental anguish for your future and my physical sufferings remind me that I still inhabit this world." There he would await the outcome of his pleas for aid. The estate had a calming effect though his letter of November 18 was scarcely resigned: "I am busy now expelling two unbearable yids [Jews]: the miller and the innkeeper. But this operation is not as easy as it seems at first glance. The [imperial] court and the administration are on their side, and consequently they are complete masters in the area." To intimate that the regime of Alexander III was protecting Jews was lunacy.

A recent trip to Mogilev over bad roads, he wrote Nina, had left him ill and exhausted, "The slightest exertion increases the nerve pain in my legs." Officialdom would surely ignore the twenty-fifth anniversary of the capture of Tashkent: "Had I been supervisor of latrines in some palace or other, then surely on the day of the jubilee I would have received some order of the white sparrow or a rescript praising my useful service to the country. That is the way the world is and one cannot change it. Since the subjugation of Mexico by Cortes and Pizarro, there has been no episode equivalent to the conquest of Tashkent." Eventually history would acclaim his exploits. Meanwhile he must suffer poverty and humiliation. The

13. Ibid., Cherniaev to Alexander III, 27 February 1890.
14. ORBL, Vorontsov-Dashkov, 82/23, Cherniaev to Vorontsov-Dashkov, 12 June 1889 and comment of June 15.

The main house at Tubyshki (Cherniaev's estate)

The priest and villagers of Tubyshki

masses had worshipped him, "but those in power never forgave me for Tashkent." His persecution complex remained strong: "They say that I am unfriendly and stubborn, but if a man is persecuted and beaten by two sticks, can one expect him to be calm and considerate? Is it any wonder that after such an uneasy life I long for solitude and that Tubyshki is dear to me as the place where I passed a carefree childhood experiencing my father's attachment and my mother's affection?"[15]

Late in 1890 he wrote Nina from St. Petersburg asking her to sort through items he had selected for the village church. "Brilliant surroundings in a church," he remarked, "have a beneficent effect on the crowd, especially upon the wild, semianimal types who live in Tubyshki." Russian rural life could only be improved by altering the environment. Cleaning up village taverns would reduce excessive drunkenness. In Tubyshki he would build a fine school to improve the next peasant generation: "We place too much stress on literacy and mental development whereas upon the half-wild masses, the force of example has a much stronger and more positive effect."[16] For an impoverished and restless peasantry his recipe was gentry paternalism.

Passionately interested in everything which transpired at Tubyshki during his absence, he queried Nina in May 1891: "How is the kitchen garden and the flower beds? Is construction of the threshing machine completed and on the bakery at the bridge and the school?" Nina and the others were to draw up a complete report. He sent detailed instructions for the gardener on watering newly planted trees. His preoccupation with his estate bordered on obsession.

His relationship with Nina, who resembled him in many ways, deepened with the years. In December 1891, seeking to bring her out of a deep fit of depression, he reminded her that she had experienced none of life's cares or sorrows. Instead of blaming the world for disappointed dreams, she must labor earnestly to achieve her goals: "Dear Nina, you are dearer to me than the others because you consider yourself doomed to misfortune whereas actually your happiness resides inside you and no one can give it to you except yourself. My dear one, take yourself in hand. . . . Compel yourself to do not

15. IISG, ed. khr. 17, Cherniaev to Antonina, 20 October, 18 November, and 22 December 1889.

16. Ibid., 7 and 28 November 1890.

merely what is desirable but what is necessary even if unpleasant."[17]
He should have followed his paternal advice.

In 1892 he remained in Petersburg until late summer seeking to
solve his financial problems. How expensive it was to restore
a ruined estate! His money was gone and the weather was foul:
"I cannot say definitely when I will be delivered from this Petersburg, so hateful to me, where I am living literally a hermit's life.
Business is proceeding slowly . . . and I am beginning to grumble
at my fate."[18] Then on July 24 he announced that the heir, the future
Nicholas II, had granted him thirty-nine thousand rubles for
Tashkent's capture. With that sum he could pay all his creditors
except Vorontsov, spend more time with the family and perhaps buy
additional land.[19]

Less burdened financially, he rented an apartment in St. Petersburg for the family, and in the summer of 1893 vacationed with Nina
in a cottage near Odessa. Taking the cure prescribed by his doctor,
he reported regularly to his wife, and predicted optimistically that
his health would soon be fully restored. Even there he worried about
Tubyshki's mismanagement under the incompetent caretaker he
had rescued from a St. Petersburg gutter. He wrote his wife July 28:
"We must immediately throw that imbecile off the estate and his
wife from the dairy."[20]

In 1895, after accumulating new debts, he approached the imperial family explaining he needed a lump sum to pay his creditors.
Nicholas II's own chancellery granted him fifty thousand rubles as
a "completely private subsidy."[21] In his final letter to Vorontsov he
thanked him for interceding with the tsar and for his "chivalrous
delicacy." Now he could pay his debts and redeem Tubyshki. "Convinced that I cannot restore my chances of securing my family after
my death, I have left Petersburg forever to live out my days at my
home in the most isolated corner of Mogilev province."[22]

Instead, Cherniaev spent considerable time in the capital in 1896
and 1897. In the latter year limping and leaning heavily on his cane,
the old general, in the emperor's presence, delivered his valedictory
address to the assembled cadets of the former Noble Regiment:

17. Ibid., May (?) and Dec. 5, 1891.
18. Ibid., 30 May and 15 June 1892, from St. Petersburg.
19. Cherniaev to "Fanny" [A. A. Cherniaeva], 1, 24, and 29 July 1892.
20. Ibid., 16, 28, and 31 July 1893, from near Odessa.
21. Ibid., ed. khr. 10, n.d.; GIM, ed. khr. 1, l. 30.
22. ORBL, Vorontsov-Dashkov, 82/23, 4 May 1895.

Cherniaev in old age (1897)

Cherniaev's wife and daughters at his grave

More than half a century ago I entered the Noble Regiment. . . . Let me turn to you, young friends, with some parting words. Considering you my great-grandchildren by education and hoping that the forefather's voice will find a place in your hearts. . . . Much has changed during this half century and I have felt and experienced much since the day I left the place where I was educated. In my time they taught us far less than they teach you today. . . . But the pre-reform institutions . . . , despite their obvious backwardness, provided men for military careers and all other spheres of human activity who made names for themselves and of whom this institution is terribly proud.

In our remote times the main, almost exclusive attention was paid to those moral qualities without which there can be no soldier in the full sense no matter how much knowledge he may have amassed. Self-sacrifice, realization of one's duty, an aspiration to be good and just were demanded in our time before knowledge because only these qualities inspire all knowledge and lead to creative work (and to fame). . . .

Hold firmly in your hands then, young friends, the banner of your fathers and grandfathers by education . . . upon which is inscribed only this motto: "All to tsar and country save honor."[23]

To the end he adhered to this romantic view of the Nicholaevian era.

On his fiftieth anniversary as an officer, the St. Petersburg Slav Society opened a subscription for a Cherniaev prize for the best history of the Herzegovina insurrection or the Serbo-Turkish War. On Cherniaev's saint's day, November 8, five members came to congratulate him: "By your selfless and inspiring courage, you presented Tashkent to Russia with your fiery summons, and by your selfless example brought our holy Russia to the aid of the Serbian people. Eternal glory for the sufferings you have borne, for your burdens and Herculean exploits. And now receive the plaudits of those who admire your heart and spirit. . . . May a merciful God let triumph the cause you served so gloriously—the cause of Slav liberation and brotherhood." Deeply touched, the general replied that he would have this statement placed above his grave already prepared at Tubyshki.[24]

Heartened by this praise, Cherniaev traveled to Tubyshki for the

23. iisg, ed. khr. 10.
24. Ibid., ed. khr. 6, ll. 44 and reverse; *Russkii Trud*, 15 August 1898, no. 33, "Chem pochtit pamiat M. G. Cherniaeva?"

last time. He found the house shaded by tall growths. "The balcony is impenetrable right up to the sunroof, the path from the gate to the bridge has become an arched alleyway." Reading through his sizable archive, he was seized by melancholy. "How many struggles and adversity have I endured," he wrote Nina on July 8, 1898, "enough for twenty lives and yet near the end, I have not achieved the calm I have sought so long." He tried to remain active despite failing, painful legs. "I walk twice to the church and back, resting half way on benches. . . . After dinner I go riding in a chariot along the border of our estate. I embrace all of you with all my heart."[25]

That was the last letter to his daughter. On August 3, Mikhail Grigorevich pruned bushes in the garden, took a ride into the forest and measured several acres of land. After dining as usual, he complained of a pain in his left side. He worried because the mail had not come. He refused to call a doctor; he dismissed the servant and retired. The next morning he failed to ring at ten as was his custom. At noon the servant, entering his room in the wing, found him. Death had come from a heart stoppage during the night. The calm expression on his face confirmed that the restless general had found peace.[26] He was laid to rest in his Tubyshki churchyard. At the graveside a local seminary graduate, paying homage to his military glory, added: "As a man he was truly good, responsive, deeply humane, a sympathetic individual to the highest degree. He was simple, readily accessible and always kind."[27] Thus would he be remembered by conservatives and romantics.

25. IISG, ed. khr. 17, Cherniaev to Antonina, 8 July 1898.
26. *Russkii Trud*, 15 August 1898, pp. 7–8, "O poslednikh minutakh zhizni i pogrebeniia M. G. Cherniaeva."
27. GIM, ed. khr. 1, ll. 113–116, 8 August 1898.

Time will pass and unquestionably Cherniaev's name will shine as brightly as the great Suvorov's and above that of Skobelev. (Antonina to Stepanović, May 30, 1923)

Rededia's [Cherniaev's] military reputation was much exaggerated. His comrades from the Noble Regiment asserted, to be sure, that he claimed credit for several valorous encounters in Tashkent, but . . . it was never made wholly clear whether these battles took place in geographic Tashkent, or in the tavern, 'Tashkent.' . . . (M. E. Saltykov, *Sovremennaia idilliia*, p. 164)

CHAPTER XVI

His Place in History

DOES CHERNIAEV belong, despite obvious failures, in Russia's pantheon of great men for his aspirations and conquests? What contributions did he make to Russian expansion, Panslavism, and South Slav emancipation? Was his a legacy of constructive achievement for Russia and mankind? His defenders led by the faithful Antonina affirm this categorically. Her capacity to extol her father's work was equalled only by her anticipation of endless compensation for it from every domestic and foreign source. Of his Serbian campaign she wrote:

> Having transformed by the exceptional efforts of his moral force a vassal principality into an independent kingdom, he lived on for twenty-three years, but neither he nor his widow ever received a [Serbian] pension. . . . Cherniaev attracted to Serbia volunteers who comprised the cadre of its army, . . . contributions from Russia and all Europe's attention. He finally dragged Russia into a war [Russo-Turkish] which changed the map of the Balkans. And he did all this despite the existing Russian government's anti-Slav policy and Alexander II's blatant Germanophile sympathies.

Then came this preposterous claim: "Just as he initiated the Serbo-Turkish War, so would he also have taken Constantinople, and we would now [1923] not be experiencing the ruin of Russia."[1] Had official Russia taken Cherniaev's advice, suggests Nina, tsarism would not have yielded to Soviet communism.

D. N. Logofet, an enthusiastic tsarist imperialist, lauded Cherniaev's role in Central Asia as a major contribution to Russia's greatness: "Modest, conscious of his own worth, extremely independent, with unbreakable will power, M. G. Cherniaev is particularly close to the hearts of the Russian people as a full-blooded Russian . . . [who] conquered much of Central Asia within a few years with few troops and extremely small expenditures and resources." He overcame great obstacles with courage and determination, "bringing huge results, creating respect for the Russian name and facilitating the region's conquest by subsequent commanders."[2]

Aside from General Skobelev, commented *Novoe Vremia* after his death, "in the past thirty years no name has been so famous to the Russian soldier, so popular in the best sense as Cherniaev's." As commander and statesman Skobelev outshone him, but they shared and promoted two great causes: the Slav idea and the need to conquer Central Asia so Russia could threaten England in India. "The spirit of both was Russian and national." Skobelev's career was an uninterrupted success story; Cherniaev had enjoyed only isolated historical moments: taking Tashkent, saving Serbia from Turkish destruction and bringing on the war for Bulgaria's liberation. In between there had been long years of inactivity. "He possessed all the qualities distinguishing an outstanding commander. All his military undertakings were marked by speed and risk, to a slow attack he preferred an assault. . . . There was something Suvorovesque about . . . [this] truly Russian commander." All Slavs, especially those abroad, had mourned Cherniaev's passing.[3]

---

1. IISG, ed. khr. 12, Antonina to Smirnov, 12 July 1923.

2. *Istoriia russkoi armii i flota* (Moscow, 1911–1913), XII: 107–108.

3. *Novoe Vremia*, 5 and 15 August 1898, nos. 8060 and 8069. The necrologs in *Moskovskie Vedomosti* and *Svet* were also laudatory. The war ministry's organ published this generous tribute: "In M. G. Cherniaev the Russian army has lost a brave, fighting general decisive and unhesitating, who aspired undeviatingly to a set goal. . . . His unshakable energy inspired subordinates and troops who were ready to follow him on the boldest undertakings. A man of pure heart, direct, and alert to the needs of the masses, he produced a fascination on all who knew him. Soldiers knew and admired him and the Russian people gave him in its songs the form of a legendary hero." *Russkii Invalid*, 8 August 1898, no. 171, "General-leitenant Cherniaev."

To *Birzhevye Vedomosti* Cherniaev stood as a much maligned knight who had exemplified the Russian spirit at its noblest:

> Mikhail Grigorevich belonged to those Herculean Russian figures capable of great deeds and who accomplish them under favorable circumstances at one stroke, but for this inspire against themselves dissatisfaction and envy which deflect them from their historic tasks and bring down upon them . . . a hail of slander. Imagine a man with ebullient spirit, iron energy and deathless service to his country nonetheless compelled to remain inactive right to his death. The psychology of Cherniaev is a tragic one.[4]

On the other hand, Grigorii Gradovskii, the general's most vehement critic, condemned in a distorted and inaccurate manner his activities on the Danube, in Central Asia, and in Serbia. Instead of assessing his historical significance, he merely compared him unfavorably to Skobelev.[5] Such liberal contemporaries, anxious to discredit him and Panslavism, could not put his career in perspective.

Despite Nina's claims, Cherniaev was no ideologist. Uncreative intellectually, he made few contributions to conservatism or Panslav theory. These were developed by more abstract, philosophical minds: Pogodin, Danilevskii, and Fadeev—to mention some Russian contemporaries. Cherniaev's ideology epitomized an aristocracy declining in wealth and political influence, guarding its prerogatives against an upsurging bourgeoisie. Raised in a frontier region, the general shared the antisemitism and animus toward Polish and German elements common to the Slavophiles and many of his class. Cherniaev, conspicuously Russian himself, detested St. Petersburg's modern European spirit. He deplored liberal reform and clung desperately to "the good old days" of Nicholas I, though he did not oppose all change.

After 1866 he became a destructive critic of the era of reforms. He diagnosed some of Russia's ills but prescribed no practical remedies for a country in flux. His perpetual denunciations of the military bureaucracy, prompted mostly by personal jealousy, blinded him to Miliutin's essential reconstruction of the Russian army. Despite Russia's poor top leadership, the Russo-Turkish War vindicated Miliutin, not his critics. And Cherniaev's attacks and intrigues against his successors in Turkestan exposed surface abuses but contributed little to their elimination.

4. IV, LXXIV (1898), 406–407, citing *Birzhevye Vedomosti*, 8 August 1898.

5. Gradovskii, "Arkhistratig," pp. 115–125.

As an imperial administrator Cherniaev was not very successful. Like many generals of his time, but unlike fon-Kaufman, he was incapable of sustained, effective administrative work. After his brief term as Turkestan governor (1865–1866), it took years to unravel the political and financial chaos he left behind. However, he won the respect and support of much of the Uzbek population. His rule as governor general (1882–1884) was so destructive that even an emperor-patron who shared his views soon realized that his appointment had been a mistake. It is difficult to understand how Russian emperors, aware of his unbalanced mind, could forgive his repeated violations of discipline and common sense and entrust him with responsible positions.

As a general in Central Asia Cherniaev did not fully deserve the praise which even the war ministry heaped upon him. His forte was commanding small forces in brief, audacious campaigns. Sharing hardships with his men, he won their loyalty and devotion. His victories were over numerous but undisciplined and inadequately armed hordes. The tremendous disparity between Russian and native casualties in Central Asian warfare tells an eloquent story. Cherniaev's reputation rested partly upon his pen: dramatic military reports magnified minor successes into major victories. He was unable to obey orders, an adventurer thrust forward by the age of imperialism, gaining glory by conquering the weak and the backward. Afterward he lived upon a military fame gained more by boldness and bravado than by solid, consistent labor.

What about Cherniaev's military role in the Serbo-Turkish War? His incompetent strategy revealed the hero's shaky underpinnings. He encouraged the Serbs to launch a war for which they were manifestly unprepared. He could not organize, discipline or lead a large militia army, nor could he adapt his tactics to the different conditions there. He persisted in frontal assaults which undermined morale and contributed to defeat. Toward a Serbian government which tried hard to accommodate him, he was unreasonable and demanding. In any case the Serbs would have been vanquished, but Cherniaev did little to delay their defeat. Coming ostensibly as Serbia's rescuer, he contributed to its near ruin. Nonetheless, he secured the devoted and enthusiastic support of most Serbs and Russian volunteers.

Was Cherniaev truly motivated in his Central Asian and Serbian campaigns by selfless patriotism and love of the Slavs? Were their

results as far-reaching as his admirers asserted? Both were undertaken largely to enhance his personal prestige and satisfy his endless
ambition. However, because of his initiative and daring, the heavily
populated oases of Turkestan were conquered and annexed by Russia. The finance and foreign ministries, on the other hand, wished
to avoid needless frontier wars during a period of domestic change.
Eventually Tashkent would probably have been seized. For political,
economic, and military reasons Russia was drawn on inexorably, as
Gorchakov explained, to fill a Central Asian power vacuum and
establish defensible frontiers on the rim of British power. To be sure,
Cherniaev's quarrel with his superiors was partially over how rapidly
to advance, but it was he who committed Russia to absorb Turkestan
and make war against Bukhara.

Cherniaev's Serbian campaign led to a costly war with Turkey
which proved largely barren for Russia, but it liberated Bulgaria and
aggrandized the Serbian states. The Serbian war, however, had
revealed Panslavism as a sad failure, Slav brotherhood as hollow,
and had accelerated Serbia's turn toward the west. Cherniaev's
notion of seizing Constantinople in a Russian solution of the Eastern
question disregarded European power realities which Alexander II
and Gorchakov assessed more correctly. The collapse of tsarism was
actually hastened by reckless adventures abroad. The autocracy
might have been preserved longer by timely domestic reforms which
Cherniaev opposed.

Cherniaev's historical significance lies neither in ideological innovation nor exceptional military skill but in embodying ideals prized
by Russians and Slavs abroad and in seeking to implement them.
Though actually favoring Russian rule over the Slavs and opposing
genuine Slav liberation and unification, he epitomized for them
Panslav fervor, sacrifice, and activism in a manner unequalled by his
contemporaries. While not the first volunteer, he symbolized
Russia's support to Turkish and Austrian Slavs in their painful
struggle for emancipation and independence. The delusion that he
was the oppressed Slavs' white knight induced him to lead Serbia
into war. The Serbian campaign was his greatest adventure making
him even in defeat a unique historical figure. In his century there
were greater generals and administrators, but none equalled Cherniaev in his fanatical pursuit of a romantic ideal. He became the
latter day Don Quixote. His fame and reputation were enhanced
beyond measure by Russia's psychological need for heroes, by its

striving for equality with a West more advanced economically and technologically, by its efforts to achieve an exalted historic mission. For self-respect in an age of expansion Russia required the equivalent of a Rhodes, a Kitchener, or a Lord Cromer. Unfortunately, Russian conservative nationalists glorified unworthy men. They created giants out of Cherniaev and Skobelev, restless and ambitious spirits who craved conquest and fame for their own sake.

Epilogue

MIKHAIL GRIGOREVICH enjoyed the loyalty and devotion of his family as well as his soldiers. His wife, son, and four daughters forgave him his faults and fostered his fame. His favorite, Antonina, dedicated her life to glorifying and perpetuating his memory in Russia and abroad. In her writings she defended him fervently against aspersions, real or imagined, and continued his old feuds with the fon-Kaufmans and the war ministry. She presented Cherniaev as he viewed himself: a pure, noble, misunderstood hero rebelling against bureaucracy and academic generals.

They were similar in character and outlook. Tall, intense, and serious, Nina was subject to moodiness and depression. But her stubbornness and determination were unredeemed by her father's geniality and magnetism. Unattractive and withdrawn, she avoided male company and had few friends. Nina, who shared his deep religious convictions and reactionary politics, so adored her father that no mortal man could replace him in her affections.[1]

After Cherniaev's death, his wife handled the funds and the family managed better financially. Not wishing to be involved with running the Tubyshki estate, Mrs. Cherniaev turned it over to Antonina who

1. Some of these impressions were gained from two interviews with Baron Boris N. fon-Grevenitz, executor of her estate, in Jan–Feb. 1966.

maintained it in loving memory of her father until the Bolshevik Revolution. Money often provoked bitter dissension among the four daughters, but during the Balkan war of 1912, they raised forty thousand rubles for the Serbs by selling postcards with Cherniaev's picture.[2]

The Russian Revolutions of 1917 engulfed the family and scattered its members. Mrs. Cherniaev, aged, hungry, and appalled by a cruel age she could not comprehend, died in Moscow early in 1919. The death in 1917 of her only son Aleksandr extinguished the Cherniaevs' direct male line. Of the daughters, only Vera married and she, after divorcing her husband, returned with her son and daughter to live with the others. After the Bolsheviks confiscated Tubyshki, the family lived in wartorn Soviet Russia by selling their remaining possessions and performing hard physical labor. Their apparently hopeless position induced the sisters to seek a way out. In February 1922 Nina, the eldest and boldest, paying a guide, fled by night across the frozen Gulf of Finland pursued by fears of a grim Bolshevik prison. Reaching newly independent Finland, she sought aid for herself and her family, appealing to Aleksandar Karadjordjević, king of Yugoslavia, and to his premier, Nikola Pašić. Neither responded.

Then Nina approached S. N. Smirnov, architect at the Yugoslav court, who was handling the affairs of a Russian emigré princess. After prolonged negotiations with the Yugoslav State Commission for Russian Refugees, Smirnov secured three thousand dinars for each sister (about 270 Swiss francs apiece). One of them, Tania, had succumbed to typhus and imprisonment in Siberia. The others received the money as they were about to abandon hope, but they could not leave Russia. In 1923 Nina traveled to Belgrade in response to Smirnov's assurances that Yugoslavia would probably support the Cherniaevs if she appeared there.[3]

She spent twenty years in Belgrade maintained by a Russian refugee organization but never received the grateful recognition which she believed was due her as Cherniaev's daughter.[4] When Yugoslavia fell apart during World War II, her cousin, Marshal

2. IISG, Cherniaev, ed. khr. 9, "Lettres de ma mère, Antonina A. Tchernaieff, née Wulfert"; ed. khr. 20, "Serbiia."

3. Ibid., ed. khr. 12, correspondence between Antonina and Smirnov; ed. khr. 13, "Pismo o Tane."

4. Ibid., ed. khr. 20, "Serbiia."

Mannerheim, arranged her return to Finland.[5] At the war's end she and Nadia were the sole survivors of a once numerous family. Vera and her children, though nursed faithfully by Nadia, had died of starvation during the German siege of Leningrad. Nina's subsequent efforts through the international Red Cross to arrange Nadia's emigration to Finland proved unavailing;[6] she died in Leningrad in the 1950s.

At eighty-five Nina fought her last campaign against the emigré Russian military establishment. In 1948, to perpetuate Cherniaev's memory, she had bequeathed his precious icon, the Kazan Mother of God, to the Russian cathedral in Paris. But the generals of the Russian Military Alliance, associated with the former imperial war ministry, having provided funds to house the icon, insisted on placing their own inscription on the icon case. Angrily Nina accused them of self-glorification and disrespect for Cherniaev and the Slav cause.[7] To the end the fiery spinster fought what she believed was the evil conspiracy of Miliutin's heirs against her father.

For forty years Nina had labored on her father's biography—first in imperial Russia, then in libraries in Belgrade and Helsinki. She sent the manuscript to several émigré publishers; none would issue it in a form she considered appropriate. Finally, she willed it and her papers to the Society for the Preservation of Cultural Valuables in Paris. On August 24, 1955, she died at eighty-seven in an old people's home in Helsinki. Thus perished the Cherniaev family which flourished in the soil of bygone aristocratic Russia.

5. Ibid., ed. khr. 21, "Pisma kuzena."

6. Ibid., ed. khr. 13, Antonina to "Chère Madame," 18 January 1947.

7. Ibid., ed. khr. 4 and 19. She wrote Grigori Lomako on February 18, 1952 insisting that the inscription be removed since it revealed "the sick and distorted vanity of its creators. Who puts up a monument to himself, to twenty-five years as refugees, to a humdrum existence outside the fatherland!!!"

248

BIBLIOGRAPHY

BIBLIOGRAPHICAL NOTE

The bibliography includes all material utilized or consulted for this study. Vitally important was General Cherniaev's extensive personal archive in the Historical Museum in Moscow. Cherniaev, who was profoundly interested in history and sensitive to its verdict, preserved official papers, memoranda, essays, correspondence, and drafts of his letters to others. With his usual pessimism, he doubted that the war ministry would permit this collection to survive, but the entire archive has been preserved. Shortly before the revolutions of 1917, Antonina Cherniaev entrusted it to the Museum retaining possession of a smaller assortment of personal materials which she took with her to Finland in 1922. After her death in 1955, the latter were sent to Paris and thence to the Institute of Social History in Amsterdam for safekeeping. Her archive, containing drafts of the biography of her father and all of Cherniaev's letters to her, helped to reveal his character and personality.

Other valuable unpublished materials from the U.S.S.R. are the papers of D. A. Miliutin, Cherniaev's nemesis, and those of I. I. Vorontsov-Dashkov, the family's principal benefactor. In the Central State Archive of the October Revolution (Moscow), I read the police dossier compiled during the Third Sections's surveillance of Cherniaev. Documents relating to Cherniaev's newspaper, *Russkii Mir*, were utilized in the Central State Historical Archive in Leningrad. Unfortunately, his original military reports from Central Asia were unavailable, and Cherniaev's letters to his wife, mentioned by Antonina, could not be located in the U.S.S.R.

These rich Russian materials were supplemented with documents from foreign archives. Especially valuable was the Ristić collection (Serbian Academy of Sciences) for Cherniaev's role in the Serbo-Turkish War. This was complemented by papers from the State Archives of Serbia and the Austrian State Archives. British Foreign Office reports provided interesting data and reactions about Cherniaev's activities in Central Asia. Original newspapers were utilized in Moscow, Leningrad, Belgrade, Helsinki, and Vienna.

Among the published sources the most valuable was *Turkestanskii krai*, a multivolume collection of documents which Colonel A. G. Serebrennikov culled from numerous archives of Imperial Russia to provide a detailed picture of Russian expansion in Central Asia while Cherniaev was active there. Brief comments have been made on books or articles of particular interest.

I. *Unpublished Documents*

AUSTRIA-HUNGARY

Haus-, Hof-, and Staatsarchiv, Vienna. Politisches Archiv, x, Russland, 66–73, 76. Berichte, Weisungen, und Varia 1875–1878, 1881; xxxviii Konsulate. Belgrad, 1875–1878.

GREAT BRITAIN

Public Record Office, London. Foreign Office papers, 65/867–869, 1151–1153, 1171–1175, 1203, 1204; 539/9, 11, Correspondence respecting Central Asia (1869–1873); 78/2487, 2488.

THE NETHERLANDS

Internationaal Instituut voor sociale Geschiedenes, Amsterdam. Arkhiv Cherniaeva. The most important folders (ed. khr.) utilized were: 2–3: Notebooks containing "Biografiia generala M. G. Cherniaeva"; 5: "Avtobiografiia"; 8: Correspondence between Cherniaev and Aksakov; 9: Letters of A. A. Cherniaeva; 10: copies of Aksakov's letters and other documents; 12: Correspondence with S. N. Smirnov; 17: Cherniaev's letters to Antonina; 18: family photographs; 19: Correspondence about Cherniaev's icon; 20: notebooks concerning the biography of Cherniaev; 21: Mannerheim's correspondence with Antonina.

U.S.S.R.

1. Gosudarstvennyi Istoricheskii Muzei, Moscow. Otdel pismennykh istochnikov, fond 208 (M. G. Cherniaev). These ed. khr. were utilized: 1–2: Personal documents of Cherniaev; 3: Official documents of Cherniaev: the Moldavian campaign; 4: Service in Central Asia (1858–1859); 5: Correspondence with A. L. Danzas; 6: Second period of service in Central Asia (1863–1866); 7: Memoranda on Central Asia (1864–1867); 8: Turkestan governor generalship (1882–1884) and "Turkestanskie pisma" (1872); 11: Memoranda on Turkestan governor generalship; 13: Service in the Caucasus (1860–1862); 14: Participation in the Serbo-Turkish War (1876); 15: Materials on Serbia (1867, 1876–1877); 17: Materials on a possible Bulgarian insurrection; 19: Materials on Russian army administration; 21: The Iaroslavl-Rybinsk railway; 22: The Central Asian Society of Navigation and Trade (1870–1872); 24: The Serbian railway (1878–1881); 28: *Russkii Invalid*'s proposed suspension (1868); 29: Materials on *Russkii Mir*; 30: Activities of the Slav Benevolent Society (1861–1880s); 31: Articles by M. G. Cherniaev; 34: Correspondence with I. S. Aksakov; 35–38: Drafts of letters by Cherniaev; 39: Cherniaev's letters to his brother, Nikolai (1868–1879); 42: Aksakov's letters to Cherniaev (1876–1885); 43–51: Letters to Cherniaev (in alphabetical order); 53: Letters and telegrams to Cherniaev from relatives; 56: Reminiscences about Cherniaev (especially by S. A. Bronskii); 57: Letters of I. P. Alabin to A. A. Cherniaeva; 58: Letters of Aksakov to A. A. Cherniaeva; 59–65: Materials of A. M. Cherniaeva; 68–73: Materials on the Tubyshki estate; 91: Photographs and portraits.

2. Otdel rukopisei biblioteki imeni V. I. Lenina, Moscow.
   a. Fond F. V. Chizhova, especially Dnevnik Chizhova.
   b. Fond A. A. Kireeva, especially Dnevnik Kireeva.
   c. Fond D. A. Miliutina, especially "Moi starcheskie vospominaniia" (1862–1873).
   d. Fond Nil Popova.
   e. Fond Vorontsov-Dashkovykh.

3. Otdel rukopisei publichnoi biblioteki imeni M. E. Saltykov-Shchedrina, Leningrad.
   a. Fond I. S. Aksakova.
   b. Fond N. M. Cherniaevoi.
   c. Fond A. A. Kireeva.
   d. Fond A. A. Kraevskogo.

4. Tsentralnyi Gosudarstvennyi Arkhiv Literatury i Iskusstva, Moscow. Fond V. V. Komarova.

5. Tsentralnyi Gosudarstvennyi Arkhiv Oktiabrskoi Revoliutsii, Moscow.
   a. Fond 109, Sekretnyi arkhiv, opis 4, delo 436.
   b. Fond 1750, Moscow Slav Committee, opis 1, ed. khr. 83.

6. Tsentralnyi Gosudarstvennyi Istoricheskii Arkhiv Leningrada.
   a. Fond 1100; Fadeevykh.
   b. Fond 776: Glavnoe Upravlenie po delam pechati, delo 2, chast 2.

YUGOSLAVIA

1. Arhiv Srpske Arkademije Nauke i Umetnosti, Belgrade. No. 9327: "Dnevnik M. Dj. Miličevića"; No. 9914: "Dokumenti o železničkoj konvenćiji sa Bontom,"; No. 10101, "Biografija M. G. Černjajev i Srpsko–turski rat 1876 g."

2. Arhiv Istoriskog Instituta, Belgrade. Zbirka Jovana Ristića.

3. Državni Arhiv Srbije, Belgrade. Fond Poklon i otkupa.

II. *Newspapers* (principal ones utilized)

Golos (St. Petersburg)
Russkii Mir (St. Petersburg)
Moskovskie Vedomosti (Moscow)
Novoe Vremia (St. Petersburg)
Birzhevye Vedomosti (St. Petersburg)
Grazhdanin (St. Petersburg)
Istok (Belgrade)
Neue Freie Presse (Vienna)

III. *Published documentary collections*

Jelavich, Charles and Barbara. *Russia in the East 1876–1880*. Leiden, 1959.

Osvobozhdenie Bolgarii ot turetskogo iga. 3 vols. Akademiia Nauk sssr. Institut Slaviano-vedeniia. Moscow, 1961–1967.

Osobye pribavleniia k opisaniiu russko-turetskoi voiny, 1877–78 gg. na Balkanskom poluostrove. St. Petersburg, 1899–1903. Voennoe Ministerstvo. Izdanie Voennoi-istoricheskoi Kommissii Glavnogo Shtaba. No. 1.

Russkii Turkestan, Vypusk iii (Moscow, 1872).

Seton-Watson, R. W. "Russo-British Relations during the Eastern Crisis." *Slavonic Review*, iii–vi (1924–1928).

Slavianskii sbornik: Slavianskii vopros i russkoe obshchestvo v. 1867–1878 godakh. Ed. I. Kozmenko. Moscow, 1948.

Srpska Akademija Nauke. "Zapisi Jevrema Grujića," knj. iii. Belgrade, 1923.

Turkestanskii krai. Sbornik materialov dlia istorii ego zavoevaniia. 10 vols. published. Ed. A. G. Serebrennikov. Tashkent, 1908–1915.

IV. *Writings of the Cherniaevs*

Cherniaev, M. G. "Akademicheskaia zheleznaia doroga. Pismo v redaktsiiu." *Novoe Vremia*, no. 3623, March 31, 1886.

————. "Akademicheskii vzgliad na vooruzhenie." *Russkii Trud*, no. 33 (1898), pp. 11–13. (Posthumous.)

————. "Dnevnik M. G. Cherniaeva (1858)." *Russkii Arkhiv* (1906), i: 459–486.

————. "Malenkaia zapiska o velikom dele." *Novoe Vremia*, no. 7070 (1895).

————. "Nashe voennoe vospitanie." *Russkii Vestnik*, April 1889, pp. 244–263; January 1890, pp. 35–54.

————. "O pisme Admirala Butakova k Kniaziu Bariatinskomu." *Russkii Arkhiv* (1889), iii: 272.

————. "Pismo v redaktsiiu o Tashkentskoi biblioteke." *Novoe Vremia*, no. 3490, November 14, 1885.

————. "Sultany Kenisary i Sadyk." *Russkii Vestnik*, cciii (August 1889), 27–39.

Cherniaeva, A. M. "Gosudar Imperator Aleksandr iii i M. G. Cherniaev." *Istoricheskii Vestnik*, October 1909, pp. 152–157.

————. "Iz proshedshikh sudeb Turkestana. Pravda o nachete na M. G. Cherniaeva." *Russkii Arkhiv,* XLIX (1911), I: 443–462.

————. "K perepiske M. G. Cherniaeva." *Russkii Arkhiv,* LII (1914), I: 25–33.

————. "Letopis semi Cherniaevykh." *Russkii Arkhiv* (1909), I: 175–208.

————. "M. G. Cherniaev i serbskii mitropolit Mikhail." *Ruskii Arkhiv* (1907), I: 305–316.

————. "M. G. Cherniaev v Kishineve." *Istoricheskii Vestnik,* CXXXII (June 1913), 910–917.

————. "M. G. Cherniaev v Moskve 1878." *Russkii Arkhiv* (1906), I: 486–487.

————. "M. G. Cherniaev v Srednei Azii (1857–59)." *Istoricheskii Vestnik* (1915), no. 6, pp. 840–872.

————. "M. G. Cherniaev vo vremia russko-turetskoi voiny, 1853–56 gg." *Russkii Arkhiv* (1906), I: 449–458.

————. "O M. G. Cherniaev—iz pisma ego docheri k izdateliu 'Russkago Arkhiva.'" *Russkii Arkhiv* (1909), III: 525–528.

V. *Books*

Abaza, K. K. *Zavoevanie Turkestana. Rasskazy iz voennoi istorii: ocherki prirody, byta i nravov tuzemtsev.* St. Petersburg, 1902.

Aksakov, I. S. *Polnoe sobranie sochineniia I. S. Aksakova.* 6 vols. Moscow, 1886–1887. I: "Slavianskii vopros."

Alabin, P. V. *Pokhodnye zapiski v voinu 1853, 1854, 1855 i 1856 godov.* 2 vols. Viatka, 1861. (Interesting and valuable.)

Allworth, Edward, ed. *Central Asia: A Century of Russian Rule.* New York, 1967.

Alston, Patrick. *Education and the State in Tsarist Russia.* Stanford, Calif., 1969.

Aristov, V. I. *Poslednie desiat let pervago dvadtsatpiatiletiia sushchestvovaniia S-Peterburgskago Blagotvoritelnago Obshchestva.* St. Petersburg, 1893.

Bartold, V. V. *Istoriia kulturnoi zhizni Turkestana.* Leningrad, 1927.

Becker, Seymour. *Russia's Protectorates in Central Asia: Bukhara and Khiva, 1865–1924.* Cambridge, Mass., 1968.

Binički, S. *Odlomći iz ratnih beležaka 1876 g.* Belgrade, 1891.

Bogdanovich, M. I. *Vostochnaia voina, 1853–1856 gg.* 2 vols. St. Petersburg, 1876.

Borodkin, M. *Graf D. A. Miliutin v otzyvakh ego sovremennikov.* St. Petersburg, 1912. (Valuable.)

Curtiss, John S. *The Russian Army under Nicholas I, 1825–1855.* Durham, N.C., 1965.

Curzon, George N. *Russia in Central Asia and the Anglo-Russian Question.* London, 1889.

Djordjević, Vladan. *Srpsko-turski rat, uspomene i beleške na 1876, 1877 i 1878 godine.* 2 vols. Belgrade, 1907. (Very useful, sometimes unreliable.)

Dobrosmyslov, A. I. *Tashkent v proshlom i nastoiashchem. Istoricheskii ocherk.* Tashkent, 1911–1912.

Dostoievsky, Fedor. *The Diary of a Writer.* New York, 1954.

Fedorov, A. V. *Russkaia armiia v 50–70 gg. XIX veka.* Moscow, 1959. (Unreliable, excessively ideological.)

Florinsky, Michael T. *Russia: A History and an Interpretation.* 2 vols. New York, 1953.

fon-Kaufman, K. P. *Proekt vsepoddanneishago otcheta Gen. Adiutanta K. P. fon-Kaufman*

I po grazhdanskomu upravleniiu i ustroistvu v obliastiakh Turkestanskogo General Guberna-torstva. 7 noiabria 1867–25 marta 1881. St. Petersburg, 1885.

Girs, F. K. *Otchet revizuiushchago, po Vysochaishemu poveleniiu Turkestanskii krai, Tainogo Sovetnika Girsa.* St. Petersburg, 1883.

Glinoetskii, N. P. *Istoricheskii ocherk Nikolaevskoi Akademii Generalnogo Shtaba.* St. Petersburg, 1882.

Glinskii, B. B. *Revoliutsionnyi period russkoi istorii.* 2 vols. St. Petersburg, 1913.

Golubev, A. *Kniaz A. I. Vasilchikov.* St. Petersburg, 1882.

Govori Radikalaca protiv železničkog ugovora u Skuptini za 1880/1 god. Belgrade, 1881.

Gradovskii, A. D. *Sobranie sochinenii.* 6 vols. St. Petersburg, 1901.

Gradovskii, G. K. *Itogi. 1862–1897.* Kiev, 1908.

—————. *M. D. Skobelev: etiud po kharakteristike nashego vremeni i ego geroev.* St. Petersburg, 1884.

Grekov, F. V. *Kratkii ocherk voenno-uchebnykh zavedenii.* Moscow, 1910.

Grujić, Sava. *Bugarski dobrovoljci u srpsko-turskom ratu 1876 godine.* Belgrade, 1892.

—————. *Operacije Timočko-moravske vojske: beleške i uspomene.* 3 vols. Belgrade, 1901–1902. (Excellent for Serbo-Turkish War.)

Harris, David. *A Diplomatic History of the Balkan Crisis: The First Year.* Stanford, 1936.

Ignatiev, N. P. *Missiia v Khivu i Bukharu v 1858 godu Fligel-Adiutanta Polkovnika N. Ignatieva.* St. Petersburg, 1897.

Iskandarov, B. I. *Iz istorii Bukharskogo emirata.* Moscow, 1958.

Istoriia Russkoi armii i flota. 15 vols. Moscow, 1911–1913: vol. 12: D. N. Logofet, "Zavoevanie Srednei Azii," pp. 72–84.

Iuzhakov, S. N. *Shestnadtsataia godovshchina.* St. Petersburg, 1882.

—————. *Itogi dvadtsatisemiletnago upravleniia Turkestanskim kraem.* St. Petersburg, 1895.

Jovanović, Slobodan. *Vlada Milana Obrenovića.* 2 vols. Belgrade, 1926–1927. (Still the standard work.)

Khalfin, N. A. *Politika Rossii v Srednei Azii v 1857–1868 gg.* Moscow, 1960.

—————. *Prisoedinenie Srednei Azii k Rossii (60–90–e gody XIX v.).* Moscow, 1965. (Very valuable.)

Khan, M. A. *England, Russia and Central Asia, 1859–1878.* Peshawar, 1963. (Shoddy and inaccurate.)

Khvostov, A. N. *Russkie i serby v voinu 1876 goda.* St. Petersburg, 1877.

Komitet Ministrov. *Nasha zheleznodorozhnaia politika.* Ed. Kulomzin. 4 vols. St. Petersburg, 1902.

Koshelev, A. I. *Zapiski.* Berlin, 1884.

Kostenko, L. F. *Sredniaia Aziia i vodvorenie v nei russkoi grazhdanstvennosti.* St. Petersburg, 1871.

Kropotkin, P. A. *Zapiski revoliutsionera.* Moscow, 1966.

Lobysevich, F. I. *Postupatelnoe dvizhenie v Sredniuiu Aziiu v torgovom i diplomatichesko-voennom otnosheniiakh.* St. Petersburg, 1900.

Logofet, D. N. *Bukharskoe khanstvo pod russkim protektoratom.* 2 vols. St. Petersburg, 1911.

MacKenzie, David. *The Serbs and Russian Pan-Slavism, 1875–1878.* Ithaca, N.Y., 1967.

Maksheev, A. I. *Istoricheskii obzor Turkestana.* St. Petersburg, 1890.

Maksimov, N. V. *Dve voiny, 1876–1878 gg.* St. Petersburg, 1879.

Markov, Evgenii. *Rossiia v Srednei Azii.* St. Petersburg, 1901.

Marvin, Charles. *The Russian Advance toward India.* London, 1882.

Meshcherskii, Prince V. P. *Dnevnik za 1882 god.* St. Petersburg, 1883.

—————. *Moi vospominaniia.* 3 vols. St. Petersburg, 1898.

—————. *Odin iz nashikh Moltke.* St. Petersburg, 1890.

—————. *Pravda o Serbii.* St. Petersburg, 1877. (Very polemical and tendentious.)

Middendorf, A. von. *Ocherki Ferganskoi doliny.* St. Petersburg, 1882.

Mikhail Grigorevich Cherniaev, glavnokomanduiushchii serbskimi voiskami. Moscow, 1877. (Worshipful pamphlet.)

Mikhailova, A. [A. M. Cherniaeva]. *M. G. Cherniaev: Biograficheskii ocherk.* St. Petersburg, 1906. (Panegyric.)

Miliutin, D. A. *Dnevnik D. A. Miliutina.* Ed. P. A. Zaionchkovskii. 4 vols. Moscow, 1947–1950. (Indispensable.)

Miller, Forrestt. *Dmitrii Miliutin and the Reform Era in Russia.* Nashville, Tenn.: Vanderbilt University Press, 1968. (Useful.)

Moser, Henri. *À travers de l'Asie Centrale.* Paris, 1885. (Strongly pro-Cherniaev.)

Nevedenskii, S. *Katkov i ego vremia.* St. Petersburg, 1888.

Nikitenko, A. V. *Zapiski i dnevnik.* 3 vols. St. Petersburg, 1893.

Nikitin, S. A. "Russkoe obshchestvo i voprosy balkanskoi politiki Rossii, 1853–1876 gg." Unpublished doctoral dissertation, Moscow State University, 1946.

—————. *Slavianskie komitety v Rossii.* Moscow, 1960. (Very valuable and accurate.)

O. K. [Olga Novikova]. *The M. P. for Russia.* 2 vols. London, 1909.

Obshchestvenno-politicheskie i kulturnye sviazi narodov SSSR i Iugoslavii. Moscow, 1957.

Ostroumov, N. P. *Sarty.* Tashkent, 1896.

Pashino, P. I. *Turkestanskii krai v 1866 godu, puteviye zapiski.* St. Petersburg, 1866.

Pemberton, W. G. *Battles of the Crimean War.* New York, 1962.

Pervye piatnadtsat let sushchestvovaniia S-Peterburgskago Slavianskago Blagotvoritelnago Obshchestva, po protokolam obshchikh sobranii. St. Petersburg, 1893.

Pierce, Richard A. *Russian Central Asia, 1867–1917.* Berkeley, Calif., 1960.

—————. *Soviet Central Asia: A Bibliography.* 3 vols. Berkeley, Calif., 1966.

Pobedonostsev, K. P. *Pisma Pobedonostseva k Aleksandru III.* Moscow, 1925.

—————. *Pobedonostsev i ego korespondenty.* Moscow, 1923.

Ristić, Jovan. *Diplomatska istorija Srbije za vreme srpskih ratova za oslobodjenje i nezavisnost, 1875–1878.* 2 vols. Belgrade, 1896–1898.

Romanovskii, D. I. *Zametki po sredne-aziatskomu voprosu.* St. Petersburg, 1868.

Rozhkova, M. K. *Ekonomicheskie sviazi Rossii so Srednei Aziei 40–60–e gody XIX veka.* Moscow, 1963.

Rupp, G. H. *A Wavering Friendship: Russia and Austria, 1876–1878.* Cambridge, Mass., 1941.

Saltykov, M. E. *Sovremennaia idilliia.* Moscow, 1959. Originally published in *Otechestvennye Zapiski* (1877–1883), this satire of contemporary Russian life contains the character, General Rededia, "the travelling general," a composite of Cherniaev and Fadeev which exposes them to ridicule (pp. 157–177).

Salusbury, Philip H. B. *Two Months with Tchernaieff in Servia.* London, 1877.

Schuyler, Eugene. *Turkistan: Notes of a Journey in Russian Turkistan, Khokand, Bukhara, and Kuldja.* 2 vols. New York, 1876.

Schweinitz, Lothar von. *Denkwürdigkeiten.* 3 vols. Berlin, 1927.

Severtsov, N. A. *Puteshestviia po Turkestanskomu kraiu.* St. Petersburg, 1873 (republished Moscow, 1947).

Shilder, N. K. *Graf Eduard Ivanovich Totleben.* 2 vols. St. Petersburg, 1885–1886.

Shubinskii, P. O. *Ocherki Bukhary.* St. Petersburg, 1892.

Skalon, D. A. *Moi vospominaniia 1877–78 gg.* 2 vols. St. Petersburg, 1913.

Smirnov, E. T. *Sultany Kenisary i Sadyk.* Tashkent, 1889.

Stoletiia Voennago Ministerstva 1802–1902. 13 vols. St. Petersburg, 1902–1914.

Tarlé, E. V. *Krymskaia voina.* 2d edition. 2 vols. Moscow-Leningrad, 1950.

Tatarinov, A. *Semimesiachnyi plen v Bukhare.* St. Petersburg, 1867.

Tatishchev, S. S. *Imperator Aleksandr II: ego zhizn i tsarstvovanie.* 2 vols. St. Petersburg, 1903.

Terentiev, M. A. *Istoriia zavoevaniia Srednei Azii.* 3 vols. St. Petersburg, 1906. (Indispensable.)

——————. *Rossiia i Angliia v Srednei Azii.* St. Petersburg, 1875.

——————. *Statisticheskie ocherki Sredne-aziatskoi Rossii.* St. Petersburg, 1874.

Todorović, Pera. *Odlomci iz dnevnika jednog dobrovoljca.* Belgrade, 1938.

Totleben, E. I. *Opisanie oborony Sevastopolia.* St. Petersburg, 1863.

Tukhtametov, M. G. "Rossiia i Bukharskii Emirat vo vtoroi polovine XIX-nachale XX v.v." Unpublished doctoral dissertation, Karshi, 1967.

Turgenev, I. S. *Polnoe sobranie sochinenii i pisem: Pisma,* XI. Moscow, 1960–.

Valuev, P. A. *Dnevnik 1877–1884.* 2 vols. Moscow, 1961.

Veselovskii, N. I. *Kirgizskii rasskaz o russkikh zavoevaniiakh v Turkestanskom krae.* St. Petersburg, 1894.

Vögué, E. M. de. *Journal du Vicomte E. M. de Vögué: Paris-St. Pétersbourg, 1877–1883.* Paris, 1932.

Zaionchkovskii, A. M. *Vostochnaia voina 1853–1856 v sviazi s sovremennoi ei politicheskoi obstanovkoi.* 2 vols. St. Petersburg, 1908–1912.

Zaionchkovskii, P. A. *Krizis samoderzhavii.* Moscow, 1965.

——————. *Voennye reformy 1860–70 gg. v Rossii.* Moscow, 1952. (Very valuable.)

Zhukovskii, S. V. *Snoshenii Rossii s Bukharoi i Khivoi za poslednee trekhsotletie.* Petrograd, 1915. (Superficial.)

VI. Articles.

A. P. "Neskolko slov po povodu iuzhno-slavianskogo voprosa." *Vestnik Evropy* (1876), no. 10, pp. 876–898.

A. Sh-skii. "Cherniaev." *Voenno-istoricheskii sbornik* (1915), no. 2, pp. 63–70; no. 3, pp. 109–118.

A. T. "Cherniaevskii muzei." *Voenno-istoricheskii sbornik* (1915), no. 3, pp. 93–108.

Adlerberg, A. V. "Iz zapisnoi knizhki." *Russkii Arkhiv* (1909), no. 2, pp. 296–297.

Alikhanov-Avarskii, M. "Zakaspiiskiia vospominaniia." *Vestnik Evropy* (Sept. 1904), pp. 73–125.

Arandarenko, G. "Pamiati Dmitriia Ilicha Romanovskogo." *Russkaia Starina* (May 1905), pp. 464–468.

Bilderling, A. "Graf Dmitrii Alekseevich Miliutin." *Voennyi sbornik* (Feb. 1912), pp. 3–16.

Devollan, G. A. "Nedavniaia starina. Poezdka v Serbiiu v 1876 godu." *Russkii Arkhiv* (1879), no. 7, pp. 339–376.

Dobrosmyslov, A. A. "Turkestanskaia publichnaia biblioteka i muzei." *Sredniaia Aziia* (April 1910), pp. 113–148.

————. "Uchebnye zavedeniia v g. Tashkenta." *Sredniaia Aziia* (Feb. 1910), pp. 106–126.

Drozdov, I. "Posledniaia borba s gortsami na zapadnom Kavkaze." *Kavkazskii sbornik*, II: 388–391.

Dukhonin, L. G. "Pod Sevastopolia v 1853–56 gg." *Russkaia Starina*, XLVII (July 1885), 87–124; 255–288; 445–460.

Durnovo, N. "K istorii serbskoi-turetskoi voiny 1876 g." *Istoricheskii Vestnik*, LXXV (Jan.–March 1899), 534–538.

"Dvadtsatipiatiletie vziatiia Tashkenta, 1865–1890." *Russkii Vestnik*, CCVIII (June 1890), pp. 211–232. (Pro-Cherniaev, inaccurate on dates.)

Eroshkin, N. P. "Voennyi apparat tsarskoi Rossii v period Krymskoi voiny, 1853–1856 gg." *Moskovskii istoriko-arkhivny institut. Trudy*, IX (1957), 138–176. (Valuable.)

Evdokhimov, L. V. "Belyi General M. D. Skobelev v narodnykh skazaniiakh." *Voenno-istoricheskii sbornik* (1911), no. 2, pp. 33–60.

Fadeev, R. A. "Vooruzhennye sily Rossii." *Russkii Vestnik* (1868), nos. 2–7 (published in book form, Moscow, 1868).

Fedorov, G. P. "Moia sluzhba v Turkestanskom krae (1870–1906)." *Istoricheskii vestnik*, CXXXIII (1913), no. 11, 437–467.

fon-Kaufman, P. "K. P. fon-Kaufman i M. G. Cherniaev." *Russkii Arkhiv* (1910), no. 3, pp. 468–473.

Gradovskii, G. K. "Arkhistratig slavianskoi rati. Iz vospominaniia literatora." *Obrazovanie* (Jan. 1909), pp. 115–125. (Exaggeratedly anti-Cherniaev.)

Grigoriev, V. V. "Russkaia politika v otnoshenii k Srednei Azii. Istoricheskii ocherk." *Sbornik gosudarstvennykh znanii*, I (1874), 233–261.

Iasherov, V. "V Serbii 1876–77." *Russkii Vestnik*, CXXIII (Jan. 1878), 187–225.

Iudin, M. L. "Prenebrezhenie k pamiati geroia." *Voenno-istoricheskii sbornik* (1914), no. 4, pp. 101–108.

Ivanov, D. "Turkestanskie pokhody." *Voennyi sbornik* (1873), nos. 3–4, pp. 165–184 and 381–411; no. 6, pp. 379–392; XCII, no. 7: 189–202; XCIII, no. 9: 183–207; no. 10: 373–391.

Ivanov, I. S. "Bolgarskoe opolchenie i ego sformirovaniia v 1875–1879 gg." *Russkaia Starina*, LXII (April 1889), 135–159; LXVI (April 1890), 413–437.

"Iz arkhiva feldmarshala kniazia A. I. Bariatinskogo." *Russkii Arkhiv* (1889), no. 3, pp. 135–143.

"Iz zapisnoi knizhki Russkogo Arkhiva." *Russkii Arkhiv* (1909), no. 2, pp. 296–297.

"Iz dalekogo proshlago." *Russkii Arkhiv*, XIII (1875), no. 1, 219–221.

K. "Delo uraltsev pod Turkestanom v dekabre 1864 g." *Voennyi sbornik*, XLIII (May 1865), 115–124.

K[aufman], P. M. "Russkoe znamia v Srednei Azii." *Istoricheskii vestnik*, LXXVI (1899), 96–122, 895–924; LXXVII, 81–99, 477–493.

Kartsov, Iu. S. "Za kulisami diplomatii." *Russkaia starina* (1908), cxxxiii: 87–96, 341–349, 563–571; cxxxiv: 67–76, 303–315, 471–484; cxxxv: 3–12.

Khristiani. G. "Graf D. A. Miliutin i voennaia statistika." *Izvestiia Imperatorskoi Nikolaevskoi Voennoi Akademii*, xxviii (April 1912), 563–564.

"Kniaz M. D. Gorchakov v 1855–61 gg." *Russkaia starina*, xxix (Sept. 1880), 109–124.

Konstantinov, "Shturm Malakhova kurgana 27–go i 28–go avgusta 1855 g." *Russkaia starina*, xiv (Sept. 1875), 568–586.

Krenke, V. D. "Pervye gody intendantstvo v Peterburgskom voennom okruge 1865–1866." *Russkaia starina*, xxv (July, 1882), 113–140.

Kryzhanovskii, N. A. "Sevastopol i ego zashchitniki v 1855 g." *Russkaia starina*, l (1886), 401–435.

Laverychev, V. Ia. "Russkie kapitalisty i periodicheskaia pechat vtoroi poloviny xix v." *Istoriia SSSR*, no. 1 (1972), pp. 36–37.

Lobysevich, F. "Syr-Darinskaia liniia." *Voennyi sbornik*, xxxviii (Aug. 1864), 396 ff.

Lvov, I. "Zavoevanie Turkestana." *Russkii vestnik*, lxxvi (July 1868), 152–174.

MacKenzie, David. "Kaufman of Turkestan: An Assessment of His Administration, 1867–1881." *Slavic Review*, xxvi, no. 2 (June 1967), 265–285.

————. "Panslavism in Practice: Cherniaev in Serbia (1876)." *Journal of Modern History*, xxvi, no. 3 (Sept. 1964), 279–297.

————. "Schuyler: Honorable but Misled." *Slavic Review*, xxvii, no. 1 (March 1968), 124–130.

Meier, L. "Aralskaia flotiliia v otnoshenii k Sredne-aziatskoi torgovle." *Morskoi sbornik*, xl (1862), no. 7: 110–129.

Miliutin, D. A. "Starcheskie razmyshleniia o sovremennom voennom dele v Rossii." *Izvestiia Imperatorskoi Nikolaevskoi Voennoi Akademii* (1912), no. 30.

"O N. I. Grodekove." *Russkii Arkhiv* (1910), iii: 474–475.

Ovsianyi, N. "Nakanune Osvoboditelnoi voiny." *Voenno-istoricheskii sbornik* (1912), no. 4, pp. 59–72.

"Pisma M. D. Skobeleva K. P. fon-Kaufmanu." *Voenno-istoricheskii sbornik* (1914), no. 1, pp. 189–200; no. 2, pp. 135–152; no. 3, pp. 129–144; no. 4, pp. 167–180.

"Pisma M. G. Cherniaeva i P. A. Kulakovskogo k I. S. Aksakovu." *Golos Minuvshego* (1915), no. 9, pp. 232–249.

"Pisma vlastitelei Serbii k M. G. Cherniaevu." *Russkii Arkhiv* (1914), i: 34–65, 181–198.

Polferov, Ia. "Pozornoe delo." *Istoricheskii vestnik*, xcvii (Dec. 1904), 1011–1016.

Popov, A. L. "Iz istorii zavoevanii Srednei Azii." *Istoricheskie zapiski*, ix (1940), 198–240.

"The Russian Capture of Tashkent." *Central Asian Review*, xiii (1954), no. 2: 104–120 (semipopular account).

"Serbskaia voina i posrednichestvo." *Vestnik Evropy* (Sept. 1876), pp. 360–368.

Severtsov, N. A. "Pismo N. A. Severtsova iz Orenburga ot 1. Oktiabria 1858 g." *Russkii Vestnik*, xviii, 122–124.

Shemanskii, A. "Chto nam stoilo zavoevanie Srednei Azii–III." *Intendantskii zhurnal* (1910), no. 9, pp. 1–14; no. 10, pp. 65–78; (1911), no. 1, pp. 18–38; no. 2, pp. 67–82.

————. "General M. G. Cherniaev s intendantskoi tochki zreniia." *Intendantskii zhurnal* (April 1911), pp. 59–79.

————. "Skobelev i ego mysli, 1879–1881." *Voenno-istoricheskii vestnik* (Kiev, 1912), no. 1, pp. 21–30; no. 2, pp. 5–18; 1913, no. 2, pp. 79–87. (Valuable.)

Shkapskii, O. A. "Proshloe i nastoiashchee Turkestana." *Vestnik Evropy* (1915), no. 6, pp. 131–156.

Slonimskii, L. "Dva pisma M. G. Cherniaeva o vostochnom voprose." *Vestnik Evropy* (Feb. 1909), pp. 887, 889.

Stefanović, Jovan. ["Jedan stari vojnik."] "Černjajev u Srbiji kao vojskovodja i političar." *Otadžbina*, VIII (1931), 513–542.

Tarlé, E. V. "Iz zapisnoi knizhki arkhivista: Rech generala Skobeleva v Parizhe v 1882 g." *Krasnyi Arkhiv*, XXVII (1928), 215–225.

Teikh, N. B. "Istoricheskii ocherk ustroistva Tashkentskoi khimicheskoi laboratorii i 25-letnoi ee deiatelnosti." *Sbornik materialov dlia statistiki Syr-Darinskoi oblasti*, VI, 41–295.

Terentiev, M. A. "Turkestan i Turkestantsy." *Vestnik Evropy* (1875), no. 5, pp. 65–112, 499–529; no. 6, pp. 142–172.

[Trubachev, S.] "R. A. Fadeev i ego sochineniia." *Russkii Vestnik*, CCXVI (Sept. 1891), 117–141; (Oct. 1891), 320–335; CCXVII (Nov. 1891), 281–299.

————. "R. A. Fadeev kak voennyi deiatel i pisatel." *Russkii Vestnik*, CCXIX (April 1892), 90–122; CCXX (May 1892), 124–165.

Ushakov, N. I. "Zapiski ochevidtsa o voine Rossii protiv Turtsii i zapadnykh derzhav (1853-55 gg.)." *Deviatnadtsatyi vek* (Moscow, 1872), II: 193–197.

Vasilchikov, V. I. "Sevastopol. Zapiski nachalnika shtaba Sevastopolskago garnisona kniazia Viktora Ilarionovicha Vasilchikova." *Russkii Arkhiv* (1891), no. 8, pp. 167–256.

Vistengof, P. F. "Andrei Nikolaevich Karamzin." *Russkaia Starina*, XXXII (1878), no. 2, 197–207.

"Vodvorenie russkoi vlasti v Srednei Azii." *Voennyi sbornik* (1868), no. 8, pp. 245–276; no. 9, pp. 109–150.

Vučetić, N. G. "Vospominanie o M. G. Cherniaeve." RA (1880), pp. 214–221.

Vučković, V. J. "Pad Generalne Unije i proglas Kraljevine." *Glas Srpske Akademije Nauke i Umetnosti*, CCXVIII, odeljenje društvenih nauka, n.s., knjiga 4.

Zalesov, N. G. "Zapiski." *Russkaia starina*, CXIV (June 1903), 527–542; CXV (July 1903), 21–37; (Aug. 1903), 321–340.

Zisserman, A. L. "Kniaz general-feldmarshal A. I. Bariatinskii, 1815–1879." *Russkii Arkhiv* (1890), I: 448–453, 460–467; II: 256–258; III: 267–328, 385–424; (1891), I: 77–128, 161–300.

Index